Listening with Purpose

LISTENING WITH PURPOSE
Entry Points into Shame and Narcissistic Vulnerability

JACK DANIELIAN **and**
PATRICIA GIANOTTI

JASON ARONSON
Lanham • Boulder • New York • Toronto • Plymouth, UK

Published by Jason Aronson
A wholly owned subsidiary of Rowman & Littlefield
4501 Forbes Boulevard, Suite 200, Lanham, Maryland 20706
www.rowman.com

10 Thornbury Road, Plymouth PL6 7PP, United Kingdom

British Library Cataloguing in Publication Information Available

Library of Congress Cataloging-in-Publication Data

The hardback edition of this book was previously cataloged by the Library of Congress as
follows:

Danielian, Jack, 1934-
  Listening with purpose : entry points into shame and narcissistic vulnerability / Jack
Danielian and Patricia Gianotti
     p. cm.
  Includes bibliographical references.
  1. Narcissistic injuries. 2. Psychotherapist and patient. 3. Psychotherapy. 4. Shame. I.
Gianotti, Patricia, 1949- II. Title.
  RC455.4.N3D36 2012
  616.89'14—dc23
  2011052478

ISBN 978-0-7657-0878-6 (cloth : alk. paper)
ISBN 978-0-7657-1021-5 (pbk. : alk. paper)
ISBN 978-0-7657-0879-3 (electronic)

Printed in the United States of America

Contents

List of Figures

Preface

WHY ANOTHER book on psychotherapy? Our guiding objective has been to provide a useful, phenomenologically oriented training manual for practitioners in the field. There has been a void in the professional literature addressing ongoing training to improve what we refer to as listening to process. The implication is that it cannot be done without promoting rigidity and undermining the spontaneity of the practitioner. However, we believe that while it is not a substitute for supervision, instructive material can address the timing, the pace, and the integration of effective interventions in treatment. Our goal in this manual is to create a text about process that does not defeat process.

This is a text written with the practitioner, candidate, intern, resident, and graduate student in mind. It is dedicated to tracking the moment-to-moment nuances of patient and therapist exchanges, thereby highlighting "experience-near" intervention strategies for creating optimal opportunities for change. Theoretical contributions from various disciplines within the psychodynamic field are included throughout this text, beginning with Sandor Ferenczi and the strategically important work of Karen Horney and followed by recent advances from the interpersonal, intersubjective, and relational schools of psychotherapy.

The structure and organization of this book combine theory with application. Each chapter contains detailed case examples and verbatim exchanges between ourselves and our trainees. These questions and dialogues are meant to highlight typical questions that practitioners often have when faced with critical "choice-points" in treatment situations. We have included excerpts from these trainee sessions to illustrate how, as practitioners, we can become subjectively better attuned at sorting our way through the assumptions that inform our decision-making processes. The current therapeutic landscape offers multiple theoretical frameworks allowing practitioners more choices. Accordingly, a wide variety of treatment styles exist, often with no unifying principle to guide the treatment process. Our book, therefore, is an attempt to provide consistent touchstones anchoring clinical practice in a field rife with choice and inconsistencies.

What are the fundamental touchstones that ground solid clinical work? Can we come to agreement on what those elements might be? When we address the dynamics of character and history, therapists frequently feel "stuck," especially with the sometimes difficult transferential dilemmas that occur during the course of treatment. We have found few available texts that ask critical questions to illustrate the multiple decision-points within any given therapeutic encounter. Noted theorists in the field often gear their writings to the audience of each other, rather than to the practitioner in the field, and much of what is written on a theoretical level is not translated into application in a way that improves proficiency. Moreover, in recent years graduate training programs have geared themselves toward the short-term, "evidence-based" therapies covered by insurance company benefits. These limitations place the beginning and even the seasoned therapist in an unenviable position when complicated clients present with issues that require a more comprehensive understanding of the complexity of the human psyche.

How are we to fill this gap, both theoretically and practically? Our questions around these issues surfaced most clearly within our supervisory experience. We witnessed a wide discrepancy between levels of technical competence in licensed practitioners. In our experience, training programs across the country did not seem to be producing a uniform level of competence in training professionals. What constitutes adequate training? With the gap between theoretical understanding and practical application widening, many practitioners have unfortunately adopted the position that they don't need to concern themselves with "theoretical research," saying, "I don't want to get involved in metapsychology. I just want to get down to the business of doing psychotherapy." At the same time, many practitioners feel that the work of doing psychotherapy feels solitary, lonely, often frustrating, overwhelming, and even shaming. The consequences of leaving this much of a gap between theory and practice can be dire. Recent grievous evidence of how inadequate training/supervision, and the blatant objectification of clients, can lead to malignant and destructive outcomes is chilling (Dimen, 2003, 2011; Starr and Aron, 2011). These clinical attitudes need to be considered or we run the risk of breeding therapeutic pessimism, compassion fatigue, and burn-out.

Ours is a profession with a long learning curve, one that is often misunderstood and undervalued. Yet we glimpse an exciting evolution on the horizon. Many advanced practitioners have been engaged in online dialogues addressing practitioners' questions about ongoing training and education. Out of these dialogues emerges a paradigm shift in psychotherapy, new attitudes regarding how we can make practice more deeply engaging. The most fruitful questions seem to be: "How do we experience our clients?" and "How do we experience ourselves in the treatment process?" These questions, consistently posed side by side, demand a new way of thinking about psychotherapy—more experience-near and more intersubjective in their metatheoretical approach.

We have drawn on experience-near theorists in this text because they have come closest to bridging the gap between theory and practice. When we use the phrase experience-near, we are describing a process-orientation that requires close listening to each patient's subjective narrative as it unfolds in the present. Our subsequent theoretical constructs flow out of these empathic, introspective, and subjective attunements and processes. This text therefore originates from our desire to capture in words a methodology that clinicians can use to track the unfolding process of psychotherapy in an experience-near manner. Accordingly, we both operationalized and systematized key components of the listening process to provide the therapist with improved tools to engage with the patient in the immediate moment.

Ours is an innovative model that creates a dynamic picture of the psyche, addressing the intrapsychic, interpersonal/relational and systemic aspects of the self in a theoretically integrated whole. We tested the versatility of our model by getting experiential feedback from a wide variety of practitioners, and this proved to be invaluable.

We have presented the material in a way that can be of value to both beginning and experienced therapists. To guide us in this, we asked of our group of colleagues and supervisees several very specific questions regarding the model:

- How understandable and useful is the model in terms of practical application?
- How does it expand your powers of listening and observation?
- How did this book change the nature of how you practice?
- In what ways have you improved your effectiveness as a practitioner?

The feedback on the model was clearly positive in all these areas. The strategic use of self from a subjective/interactive viewpoint allowed trainees to stay in an experience-near position and thereby gain more confidence in the therapeutic process itself. They were able to hold the complexity of the material more tightly as it unfolded in the moment, differentiate more clearly between the therapeutic alliance and transference dynamics, and better connect various parts into a unified whole.

We should state that as we supervised our group of trainees through the development of this model, we found that we were also supervised by them. Our lively exchange of ideas and their questions around unclear material helped us to further anchor our experience-near model into the day-to-day, and sometimes moment-to-moment, practical application of case material. Through the question-and-answer sessions captured at the end of each chapter, we hope that you will witness the unfolding learning process that these trainees experienced and be able to apply your own questions and case material to the frameworks and concepts presented in this text.

The case material presented throughout this manual is excerpted directly from patients and therapists representing towns and cities all over the East Coast. With the exception of those cases where we received written permission from patients to use partial verbatim material, all other case material has been disguised to protect anonymity. In several instances clinical vignette examples reflect a combination of two or three client excerpts whose presenting issues reflect similar themes or concerns. Of course, all identities have been disguised.

Several of our training consultations, particularly in more distant geographic locations, were done through Skype and conference calls. Although these technologies as well as the printed page are no substitute for face-to-face supervision, their burgeoning capacities for growth may hold promising and still untapped potential. Manuals such as ours in combination with newer technologies may help to address training gaps and cut through the isolation often experienced in the field.

The title of this book, *Listening with Purpose: Entry Points into Shame and Narcissistic Vulnerability*, highlights our training goals and draws the reader's attention to how shame is a compelling component in defending against narcissistic injuries. We present a comprehensive and fluid description of narcissism as a *relative* term yet one entirely distinguishable from the development of an authentically integrated self. The model presents narcissism on a continuum, where injuries to the developing sense of self can be understood as an experience from which none of us is immune. The scope of narcissistic injury includes a full range of relational disappointments or failures, from minor ruptures of attunement to more severe experiences of trauma, abuse, and flagrant neglect. Listening with purpose involves improving our subjective ability to hear how disappointments and ruptures are defended against through levels of dissociation that have resulted from compensations against unacceptable feelings of shame and vulnerability. Shame, in our view, is the critical missing piece to the emerging puzzle of our subjective and more humane understanding of the challenges facing today's professional.

Acknowledgments

THIS IS an intensive training manual integrating many modern in-depth approaches to the dynamic treatment of narcissistic vulnerability. Our goal is very clear: to renew and reestablish attention to narcissism as a critical issue in contemporary psychopathology. In writing this book, we have come to rediscover for ourselves the power of Karen Horney's contributions to the field. Perhaps, it is only now that the field is catching up to what Horney offered over sixty years ago. The full relevance of her work becomes clearer as we integrate evolving iterations of intrapsychic, interpersonal, and systemic theories. We arrive thereby at a modern working application that facilitates the treatment of individuals who fall within an expanded spectrum of narcissistic injury.

Although Horney's contributions to the understanding of character formation as a defense against shame, self-hate, and vulnerability were not labeled as narcissistic injury per se, her descriptions of narcissistically driven overcompensation are as powerful today as they were sixty years ago. In that regard, we begin our acknowledgments with thanks and appreciation to Karen Horney, a brilliantly intuitive mind whose contributions were overlooked, misinterpreted, black-balled, and even appropriated with little credit given. Proper credit is overdue, and perhaps now the timing is such that her vision can be acknowledged.

Of necessity, this type of treatment manual must involve the willing participation of many contributors. Some we are able to identify by name; others we cannot. Numerous patients have shared their private lives with the hope that their experiences can benefit others. We thank them for their generosity and courage. The openness with which they have been willing to expose their process has left a powerful imprint on this manual. In reading their words, we hope that the reader will be struck by the palpable integrity of the therapeutic journey. As authors trying to capture the nuance of therapeutic process, we are struck once again by one of psychotherapy's most profound discoveries: how healing and recovery from past wounds invariably produces the wish to bring encouragement and hope to others.

Trainees, supervisees, and candidates have offered unstinting time and keen insight to the development of our manual. In particular we wish to thank G. Robert Taseff, Christyn Sieve, William Lusenhop, Catherine Lamond, and Jennifer Kinsey, all of whom participated in our trainee groups and whose incisive questions have helped shape and refine the text. As clinicians representing a wide range of experience and training, your ongoing feedback helped us employ language and concepts to create a manual which is more "hands-on" and understandable to a larger range of practitioners. Your enthusiastic participation is woven into the fabric of this endeavor.

Our friends and colleagues were steadfast. Their ongoing encouragement as well as personal and scholarly contributions were invaluable. Kenneth Cohen never flagged in his passion for the project from its earliest stages. L. R. Berger and Donna Giovaniello Knudsen offered their wisdom as consultants to the entire manual, helping us shape our thoughts as we were developing the language and tone of the manuscript. In particular we are grateful for their expertise and feedback on the chapters on shame and trauma. A special thanks goes to Annemarie Slobig for her encouragement that opened initial doorways to this project. Constance Johannessen, Shelley Cushner Gardner, and Patricia Kincare, senior clinicians representing various therapeutic disciplines, combined their knowledge to offer feedback around the evolution of the book. Throughout the process they offered their patient support as colleagues and friends. And we owe an existential debt to Louis DeRosis, the training analyst of Jack Danielian, for his deeply human approach to psychoanalysis. His early treatment impact never wavered nor diminished over time.

Our publisher Jason Aronson exhibited confidence in our views from the very beginning and actually solicited our interest in converting our material into a book. We are grateful to the entire staff, and wish to give a special thanks to Julie Kirsch for her steady support throughout this process. Without her early encouragement, this manual would not have been written. Such training manuals are rare in the literature these days and we appreciate Julie's vision in recognizing this in advance.

Finally, we happily acknowledge the support, trust, and tangible contributions of our families. Special thanks are given to Stephen Gianotti for his help in contract negotiations, technical support, indexing, and the initial design of many of the manual's graphs, tables, and figures. Ani Danielian Huang did critical work in communicating with Jason Aronson staff and in reading, reviewing, editing, and formatting the document. Emiko Danielian applied her creative talents to the many visualizations so integral to the text. In addition we give her thanks and credit for her time and assistance in the cover design of this book. Our spouses, Hasmig and Stephen, hovered over us like protective birth-attendants to allow us the time and energy to complete our task. All of you have sustained us at every step of the way.

CHAPTER 1

Fundamental Principles of Therapeutic Listening

The deeper one probes into the person's history, experience, and unconscious wishes, fears, and fantasies, the more it becomes evident how powerfully they are all linked to the *ongoing* patterns between people in the patient's life today.

—PAUL L. WACHTEL (2008, P. 121)

By Way of Introducing This Manual

This manual has been written for a wide range of dynamic practitioners involved in treating patients with narcissistically infused issues. The treatment model and case material presented cover the spectrum of narcissistic vulnerability and may be applied to the relatively intact patient as well as to the more severely impaired patient. We refer to issues of narcissistic vulnerability throughout this manual, although our references do not necessarily conform to historical DSM diagnostic categorizations. Our assumption throughout is that narcissistic mechanisms are implicated in all levels of personality functioning and in all people. They exist both in therapists and clients, differing only in the level of prominence and degree of disturbance in the personality. This view differs from early classical thinking which consigned narcissistic issues and the accompanying "splits" to a more primitive state than the role accorded to repression. More recent thinking, in our view correctly, has placed dissociation at least on a par with repression as a widespread human mechanism to which we are all prone.

When we place narcissistic defenses on a continuum, it forces us to address the scope of these issues in all patients and in ourselves. It also compels us to become more familiar to thinking in the *characterological present* rather than the *instinctual past*. The reader will note that we have used a process approach to understanding character structure and character change, focusing as closely as we can on the experiential present to palpate and address the narcissistic issues. This again is different from classical approaches because narcissistic issues were not in the forefront of classical theory. Clearly, we now see huge numbers of narcissistically disturbed patients in our practices; thus the evolution in our field has been timely, fortuitous, and enormously helpful.

Addressing splits involves a somewhat more forward-leaning therapeutic posture. The posture is more interactive and interpersonal, but the process still always involves careful titration of material in accordance with what the patient can tolerate. Empathic failures come and go, and countertransferential reactions are inevitable. Yet, the clinical reward of addressing psychic splits results in a deeper engagement with the patient and more intimate contact with both the patient's vulnerabilities and the patient's strengths.

In reading this manual, a note of philosophical caution may be in order. The closer one gets to describing "pure process," the more a paradoxical effect enters into the use of language. Language is linear, yet we are attempting to describe non-linear process. Systemic thinking, which we hope to demonstrate as crucial to understanding seemingly disconnected splits in the cognitive and emotional lives of our patients, cannot be reduced to a list of rules, procedures, or techniques. Rather, the reverse is true. Systemic thinking is itself the very process which allows us to identify non-linear splits in narcissistic mechanisms.

At some point language will fail us. When "process" is committed to paper, something will always be lost. Words will fail the experience. Yet, the perspective of this manual is optimistic. Each iteration of meaning comes closer to the subjective reality of our patients, and with that meaning, we are more able to engage the inner dynamics of psychic change.

In this text, as much as humanly possible on the written page, we have tried to sustain the subjective aliveness of the therapeutic enterprise. The quality of *presentness* has been our epistemological guide and *experience-near* our theoretical commitment. To preserve its aliveness, dynamic psychotherapy cannot be diced and examined from a distance. Its aliveness for both patient and therapist rests on levels of empathic immersion where passion and enlightenment, heat and light, cannot be separated from each other. Anything less reduces the enormous potential of the process.

CREATING THE CONTEXT

Major changes in the understanding of the process of psychodynamic therapy have taken place in recent years and continue to take place to this day. These changes alter in profound ways how we see the meta-connection between the psychological past and the psychological present. As such, the process of how we listen to the unfolding narrative of our patients' lives and how we engage in the dynamic relationship of psychotherapy is intrinsically linked to our metatheoretical orientation.

As the field has grown, the theoretical landscape has changed, resulting in an ever-widening variety of approaches to treatment. They range from a classical, archeological orientation which assumes a linear, cause-and-effect connection between the past and the present, to a current solution-focused orientation on the alleviation of symptoms in the present, and finally to a dynamic orientation that is more systemic and non-linear, one that embraces the reciprocal connection between all elements of the psyche: past and present, cognitive and affective, and interpersonal and intrapsychic.

With such a range it is easy to see how we have lost a unifying principle that firmly grounds us, one that not only embraces the familiar psycho-dynamic basics but incorporates more recent contributions that are comprehensive, cohesive, efficient, and clearly more *experience-near* in their approach. Wachtel (2008) maintains that a reappraisal of conscious experience is not at all "a retreat from the 'hard-won' insights Freud achieved [but that it is] the archeological mode of thought and the associated rush to *dig under* conscious experience that is the retreat—a retreat from what is perhaps the chief virtue of the psychoanalytic method, its intense attention to and immersion in the subjective world of the other" (p. 150).

Developing a better understanding of how to listen directly to the subjective world of our patients, to know what to listen for (listening for what is *not* being said as much as to what is being said) requires a therapeutic posture that allows us to identify a range of contingencies in the emerging dynamic present. These are aspects of therapeutic listening that allow us to link the psychological past in ways that help our patients to uncover deep emotional wounds which are continuously defended against in the present by split-off parts of the self. This manual probes into how clients may both know and not know how such splits operate as part of a larger whole.

Knowing and not knowing one's history as well as one's contemporary self requires a "holding" that utilizes a non-linear approach to therapy, one in which deeper therapeutic listening is the beneficiary. Our manual builds on the premise that such listening leads to deeper change and psychological integration. These are aspects of the therapeutic process that can be taught. However, developing a proficiency in our craft is also a long learning curve, one that requires patience, ongoing supervision, and an ability to hold the dialectical tension between multiple viewpoints in an integrated and cohesive way. The approach that will be described utilizes an experience-near metapsychological framework that values the intersubjective dynamic between the patient and therapist, one that requires letting go of the stance of "therapist as expert," and adopting a position of intense immersion in the subjective world of our patients. Such a posture allows for increased curiosity on both sides of the therapeutic relationship, or, in Schwaber's words (1983), "The world we perceive must include ourselves as perceiver" (p. 274).

Recent observers (Watkins, 2011) have noted the marked discrepancy between the number of studies of the effectiveness of psychodynamic therapy vs. the number of studies of the effectiveness of psychodynamic training. A cursory examination of the literature bears this out. Certainly there are political issues involved in institutions publicly evaluating the scope and method of their training, but we would like to stress a blindness more or less common to all institutions of training, an inattention to the (often unconscious) metatheory guiding their training.

When metatheoretical assumptions are unclear, both the metatheory and the training techniques following it become progressively more rigidified and reified. Thus, beyond issues of politics, the lack of study and improvement in training can be seen to account for a lack of fluidity between theory and practice, or in this case, between metatheory and techniques of training.

Although our commitment is clearly to training, our orientation is based on a distinct paradigm shift away from archeological uncovering of unconscious drive derivatives, away from linear connections especially deriving the present from the linear past, and away from objectifying postures. As a metatheory, we have emphasized moment-to-moment immersion into the subjective life of the patient, systemic attention to dissociated states operating in the dynamic present, and more intense focus on the permeable state of "knowing and not knowing" at any given point of time. Inevitably we are focusing less on the historical past and more on the phenomenological present.

As will be seen, this metatheoretical shift casts a long shadow: shame becomes more relevant than guilt, dissociation more relevant than repression, and the characterological present more relevant than the instinctual past. Our manual elaborates extensively on all these issues deriving from the paradigm shift, and in particular, how each affects how we process and understand the treatment as it unfolds.

It has become common in the field to understand character structure as something more or less fixed and therefore to understand character issues as more or less immutable and beyond the reach of the psychotherapist. Except for some noted theorists such as Ferenczi, Horney, and Reich, character has been seen as a pesky sidebar to dynamic therapy. Along with the above theorists and with our own explicit focus on metatheory, we have reversed the traditional therapeutic priorities.

Language plays a role in this reversal. If we describe character less in terms of *structure* or *disorder* and more in terms of the Horneyan framework of character *solutions*, we can hear how the framing of character affects our perceptions. Rather than viewing character as something that is a fixed entity, we can see it as a moving, evolving dynamic. In essence it enables us to see our clients as making very *live* attempts to clinically dissociate from pain, self-loathing, and toxic shame. As well, we can quickly see how the disconnected parts of the psyche, the magical idealized expectations of the self and of others, both fuel and are fueled by the individual's specific character solution. Thus, the traditional therapeutic pessimism attached to "character" gives way to an active and more optimistic engagement with all such overdetermined belief systems. A character solution is not to be seen as static. If we are not getting better, we are getting worse. If we are not getting worse, we are getting better. In other words there is no stasis when it comes to the dynamic construction and maintenance of character solutions.

There is yet a further very significant optimistic outcome of moment-to-moment involvement in the patient's struggle. This involves the increased capacity to identify the latent strength that is capable of emerging from the struggle. Systems theorists speak of a *process of emergence*. From a psychological framework emergence can be described as an attempt through subjective immersion to account for unexpected and seemingly disconnected outcomes, many of which hold the potential of accessing one's creativity, growth, and personal authenticity. Among other things, the term highlights the distinctly non-linear course of self-realization—we might say, the process of the self making room for itself. As we increase our therapeutic capacity to identify and support moment-to-moment signs of authentic self-realizing, we imbue the therapeutic process for both patient and therapist with a hopeful and active aliveness. As we will see, monitoring and supporting evidence of the realizing self is a very significant component of consolidating gains throughout the treatment process.

The purpose of this book, therefore, is two-fold. It is first a training manual for therapists to help facilitate a clearer understanding and proficiency in the use of skills sets that have been practiced for decades. It is also a theoretical contribution that attempts to identify and bring into alignment a paradigm shift that has slowly been occurring in our field over the last century, a shift that moves psychotherapy away from its roots in *objective* science where the therapist is the neutral, objective expert, to an approach to psychotherapy that is both experience-near in its metapsychological roots and intersubjective in its dynamic stance between the patient and the therapist.

Background: Addressing the Current Gaps in Post-Graduate Training

Like many other psychoanalytically trained practitioners, we have faced the challenge of how to systematically incorporate advances in theory over the past decades into our dual roles of clinicians and supervisors. Our own theoretical discussions began as an attempt to articulate how we might incorporate systemic, intersubjective, and relational approaches into our specific prior training.

In our supervision of post-graduate clinicians over the last fifteen years, we observed that many beginning therapists had little in the way of organizing principles to help guide them in their decision-making processes regarding treatment interventions. Once they got past the diagnostic and dynamic formulation phase, there was little uniformity in terms of knowing what the unfolding process of treatment was supposed to look like. Supervisees frequently asked basic questions such as, "How can I *know* whether I'm making a supportive comment to help build the therapeutic alliance as opposed to making a statement that colludes with the patient's dependency issues or entitlement?" Or, "I'm 'feeling stuck' in the treatment and don't know how to help the patient consolidate gains or move more deeply into transferential work."

Much of the time their questions reflected a lack of understanding of how to conduct a phenomenological inquiry process that addresses the complexity of listening. That is, they didn't know how to listen for "vertical" splits within the psyche. It was out of their questions that we began to notice a pattern of where and how clinicians typically stumble. When we thought about these stumbling points and put them into the larger context of the changing landscape of the field, we realized that a unifying paradigm or model would be helpful to make sense out of the multiple theoretical approaches that were available to present-day practitioners.

The four quadrant visual model (that will be introduced in greater detail in chapter 2) is meant to illustrate the various parts of the three-dimensional landscape of a patient's psyche. This multi-layered description is meant to capture a metatheoretical viewpoint that takes multiple aspects of the psyche into consideration simultaneously. We believe that the organizing principles that comprise the complexity of the human psyche must be collectively taken into account if therapy is to be most effective. Each of these influences constitutes part of a dialectical whole and can be conceptualized as follows:

- The intrapsychic aspects (the conscious and unconscious factors that comprise an individual's sense of self)
- The interpersonal aspects (how the individual relates to and treats others)
- The systemic aspects (how environment, cohort groups, resources, and cultural advantages or disadvantages impact the individual's sense of self in relationship)
- The intersubjective clinical aspects (how the therapeutic relationship is structured and evolves over time)

In addition to these aspects the model also differentiates the parts of the self into conscious awareness and the non-conscious (or dissociated) aspects of one's self and history. The framework that we have created allows for a clearer understanding of how these various split "parts" connect into a constructed "whole," one in which the individual can flow in and out of conscious states of awareness, both knowing and not knowing simultaneously.

Whether one uses a cognitive-behavioral approach, a dynamic approach, a neuro-biological approach, or a systemic approach, this model can help organize our conceptualization of the ever-increasing complexity of the whole human being. We believe that every approach to treatment can have specialized value *if* used within the framework of an understanding of the larger whole. Therefore, this is a model that can have universal applicability if one's treatment approach is not static or linear.

The overarching value of our model is that it is less "theory bound" yet offers a complex picture of how the parts of the psyche (moment to moment) relate to the larger whole in a non-linear way. This in turn allows the therapist to see how split-off parts of the self can affect individuals not only on a symptomatic level but on a characterological level as well. Regardless of your training and your approach, *not taking all of these aspects of the psyche into consideration* does not mean that all aspects of the individual's psyche aren't operating and influencing the treatment. Underattention to the whole runs the risk of reductionistic thinking, incomplete treatment, a shifting of symptoms, or a revolving-door approach to therapy.

This Four Quadrant Training Model is used as a teaching tool, a means of helping clinicians become more proficient at phenomenological tracking, listening for and facilitating the integration of split-off material in the psyche. It is also our hope that the utility of the model will advance clinical understanding across the spectrum of expertise and experience by providing a unifying organizing schematic for listening and interacting with our clients.

To test the robustness of our model we selected two different groups of clinicians, a beginner group, as defined by less than five years of experience, and an intermediate/advanced group, as defined by seven to twenty years of experience. In addition we received feedback from senior colleagues throughout the country and abroad to give us input on both the model and the chapters of this book. The two groups of clinicians will be referred to as "trainees" throughout the remainder of this book. Since this is partially a manual meant to help clinicians in graduate schools, residencies, and practitioners in the field, many of our trainees' questions and their dialogues are recorded in the remainder of this book. Their questions, feedback, and case reviews have been invaluable in helping us shape and refine the concepts of this book.

Another reason for this book is that after years of providing supervision, we began to witness trainees' approaches to therapy shifting in order to adapt to the demands of insurance companies' dictates. One of our concerns is that the actual practice of doing long-term dynamic work has been on the verge of becoming a dying art. A paradoxical effect seems to be occurring. Just as integrative breakthroughs were taking hold, and we began to expand our metatheoretical orientation to include both systemic and intersubjective approaches, training programs seemed to be going in the direction of "the short-term fix."

Buffeted by political and cultural forces, neither lay nor professional people have been able to resist the lure of short-term solutions to long-term problems. The field of mental health has been no exception. The principal casualty has been long-term dynamic psychotherapy. Even analytic institutes have been shrinking in numbers and influence. In these times, defending dynamic psychotherapy is no easy task. And yet the excellent progress being made in modern *experience-near* care cannot be allowed to wither in our quixotic search for the quickest solution.

None of us needs to be reminded that this problem is institutionalized in all levels of our society but, if change is to occur, a focus on mental health care can be crucial. A glaring example is our frantic pursuit of a short-term solution to trauma with first one "pie-in-the-sky" solution, then another, then another.

Our manual has taken a different approach. We have tried to resist the lure of "instant change" and to focus on the psychopathology both fueling and being fueled by such societal myopia. Inevitably this has taken us into the dynamics of dissociation and its complex relationship to shame and the narcissistic character structure. Our solution is not short-term but, especially with recent advances, we contend that dynamic therapy offers the real possibility of authentic, enduring, and substantive healing on many levels crucial to our common humanity.

UNDERPINNINGS OF OUR APPROACH AS VIEWED WITHIN A HISTORICAL CONTEXT

As stated, this manual will describe an integrated view of process, allowing us to present a more fine-grained, hands-on approach to therapeutic listening and technique. Offering a systematic way of tracking the therapeutic process was a task that Freud was never able to accomplish. Therefore, it is our hope that we might offer "a missing piece" in terms of operationalizing and unifying various therapeutic paradigms that have evolved since Freud's landmark contributions to our field over a century ago.

A bit of history concerning Freud may help to establish a perspective. Nearly a century ago, Freud wrote that he could train psychoanalysts how to begin an analysis and how to end it but could not train them on the practice of it, that is, what to do for the duration of the treatment. Ferenczi, in particular, implored him to write a prospectus on techniques, to focus on the "details regarding technique" (Phillips, 2002). We are told that in 1908 Freud was contemplating writing "A General Account of Psychoanalytic Technique." In 1909, Freud told Ernest Jones that he wanted to write "a little memorandum of maxims and rules of technique." In 1910, Freud himself wrote that he planned "A General Methodology of Psychoanalysis." But in reality, Freud was never able to meet any of his or anyone else's expectations in this area.

We are of the opinion that Freud's commitment to a nineteenth century philosophy of knowledge blocked him from seeing major psychic events as anything other than instinct-driven where behavior is essentially attributed to the discharge of psychic energy. Focus on instincts and their derivatives kept Freud within a closed-system of thinking of therapeutic change, heavily theory-driven and unable to accommodate a non-linear model of the mind. Within this closed-system Freud had little confidence in his ability or the ability of any of his peers to write about the training of analysts in any way that would not be misappropriated or misused by later analysts. But of course training that cannot be written down is training that cannot improve itself. This theoretical and clinical impasse began to be overcome in the early 1960s as dynamic psychotherapy began to rid itself of outmoded self-imposed strictures to its practice and to its science.

The Western scientific heritage has always felt more comfortable with observing and studying phenomena from an "objectified distance" (Danielian, 2010a). Subjective study of self or other through introspection, empathy, consciousness, or wholeheartedness has been traditionally denigrated as "non-scientific." As some have noted there seems to be an unconscious culturally rooted almost phobic-like fear of not being an outward bound results-oriented problem-solver.

Over the past few decades, a momentous change has begun to sweep through the mental health field, as systemic and phenomenological thinking allowed the incorporation of both intrapsychic and interpersonal thinking into a single unified clinical model, a model which opened up exciting new possibilities for therapeutic listening and therapeutic change. More and more clearly, classical theory began to be seen as a product of its culture and time, culture-bound as it were both in its content and in its process. Over-polemical and doctrinal rigidities began to dissolve. The pseudo-objectification of the mind, the hierarchical top-to-bottom thinking, the linear logic, and the dualistic Cartesian split between subjective and objective realities all gave way.

In their place developed a "meaning-making" metapsychology involving more intense receptivity to the characterological "present," which Karen Horney had already anticipated in 1950 when she described such metapsychology as being aware of not just individual factors but of their "connections and interactions . . . [e]very single factor must be seen in the context of the whole structure" (p. 341). By forgoing archaic metapsychology, Horney built upon the valiant but largely unsuccessful critique of Freud by his peers and ushered in a major move toward understanding psychotherapy as process-driven. Her emancipated metapsychology allowed her to develop a consistently experience-near receptivity to human functioning which , since her time, has also been followed by experience-near and helpful formulations by self-psychologists and the intersubjectivists. Because of the phenomenological richness of Horney's descriptions and the remarkably gender-free clarity of her self-systems analysis, the reader will notice that we have followed her clinical lead in many areas.

Like her, we process the interpersonal and the intrapsychic as an integrated system. Like her, we treat the characterological present as taking precedence over the instinctual past. Thus, the past systemically flows from the present, rather than the classical position of the present flowing in a linear fashion from the past. Put differently, the patient's character structure, as it appears in the here-and-now, becomes the focus of our clinical attention, not the historic binary focus on interpretations to make the past the present.

Horney's sub-systems, incorporating the reintegration of additional splits perpetuated in classical theory, will become clearer as we proceed. A systemic process by definition does not involve static moments nor does it allow any period of stasis. Listening to process therefore involves monitoring multiple macro- and micro-levels, which can best be viewed as an interacting matrix of concentric circles. We visualize all parts moving simultaneously and all parts connected reciprocally, with feedback loops to intrapsychic, interpersonal, transferential, family, and the larger society. However, lest this seem forbidding, the learning of a process is itself a process and a therapist who is constantly wondering, and constantly confronting "not knowing," is a therapist who is empathically immersed. Again, quoting Wachtel (2008), the "day we think we know all we need to know in order to help people is probably the day we cease to be able to help at all" (p. 303).

We have selected Sandor Ferenczi and especially Karen Horney as active instructional agents in our training manual. In addition we incorporated valued contributors whom we believe built upon Horney and Ferenczi's early metatheoretical views, theorists such as Kohut, Stolorow, Atwood, Orange, Brandchaft, Mitchell, Aron, Benjamin, Bowlby, Stern, and Wachtel. These relationally based theorists have broadened our understanding of utilizing an "experience-near, subjective approach to treatment. Though Horney and Ferenczi were not credited for beginning the shift in the theoretical landscape, we have found upon review that they had an uncanny ability to value the power of phenomenological attention to the raw subjectivity of psychic disturbances, the tumult, tyranny, terror, humiliation, and self-hate, which, in varying degrees, exist in all of us. Thus, they were able to communicate the aliveness of the treatment process on a printed page. As we have noted in the preface, words will fail experience. On this critical point of grounding themselves in the moment-to-moment, Horney and Ferenczi failed the least.

Bypassing the medical protocol of the times, these theorists placed narcissism on a continuum and refused to accept a qualitative difference between "normal" and "abnormal" narcissism, thereby placing patients, practitioners, and human-kind on the same map. People in the field, past and present, have appreciated the unwillingness of these theorists to allow the therapist to bask in a caste-like scientific aura above the patient. Ours is a learned craft, they maintained, but we are all made of the same stuff. In this they were in thorough agreement with Harry Stack Sullivan's adage, "All of us are much more human than otherwise."

Time has borne out the wisdom of their insistent focus on the narcissistic characterological underlay of emotional disturbances and clinical symptoms, even if we now know that some of these symptoms have a neuro-chemical component. Increasingly, patients seeking help are suffering from narcissistic vulnerability, dissociative splitting, and neurotically driven unattainable ideas of perfection. The phenomenological recognition and deeper understanding of the often hidden mechanisms involved in these disturbances facilitate a more effective treatment, leading to the goal of greater self-integration and more productive living. We might say that Ferenczi's and Horney's grounded work allowed for the much needed integration of science and humanism in the mental health field.

Yet, history has not been kind to either theorist. Aron (1996) has noted that in the history of psychoanalysis, "as soon as analysts dissented too much, mainstream psychoanalysis excommunicated them from the analytic community" (p. 32). Nowhere has this been truer than the reaction to the pioneering work of Sandor Ferenczi and Karen Horney. Aron documents the extent to which Ferenczi's pivotal work, *The Clinical Diary of Sandor Ferenczi* (1932), had been suppressed for over half a century. This was a great loss to the profession.

An equally great loss to the profession has been the disenfranchisement of the remarkably prescient work of Karen Horney (1939; 1945; 1950). Her entire work has been groundbreaking. She was the first psychoanalyst to offer a comprehensive critique of Freud's neo-biological orientation (1939), directly challenging the panoply of his psycho-sexual theories involving the oedipal complex, penis envy, and castration anxiety. Although Aron does not adequately integrate Horney's work, he does make the important point that the feminist movement of the last few decades has had a profound effect on current psychoanalytic thinking and practice. Of course, it was Horney who provided the first thorough feminist critique of classical theory. For a detailed examination of Horney's crucial impact on today's practice, see Chodorow (1989) and Westkott (1986).

In sorting out various dynamic contributions to our field, it may be helpful to organize our thinking around the metapsychological assumptions of the classical school versus the Ferenczi/Horney school or, to be more current, the recent derivatives of these traditions. It might be constructive to think in terms of post-Freudian contributions versus both post-Ferenczi and post-Horney contributions. While the former use the language of ego, guilt, and objectivity, the latter use the language of self, shame, and subjectivity. Thus it becomes easier to see self-psychology, intersubjectivity, and relational schools as three legs of a stool created at great cost by Ferenczi and Horney. Among other goals, our intention is to reground post-Freudian advances in the work of the two voices that stood up to question Freud's biological, psychosexual theories. Sadly, until recent times, the price of their challenge was to be black-balled from mainstream theoretical development. In the words of Jessica Benjamin (1991), "Horney's work . . . deserves to be rescued from the disparagement it received at the hands of the psychoanalytic establishment" (p. 278).

With the evolution of self-psychology (Kohut, and others), the evolution of intersubjectivity (Stolorow, and others), and the evolution of the relational school (Mitchell, Aron, and others), we invite readers to see for themselves how much of these modern positions can be elegantly traced to the challenges laid down by Ferenczi and Horney. In particular, with a bit of updated language, we draw attention to Horney's systemic contributions to understanding the complex interplay between the authentic self, the over-idealized self, and the self-hating self. No less do we highlight her emphatic positions on subjectivity and on the vital relational and cultural influences on human psychic development.

Horney's characterological understanding has yet to be fully integrated into our current clinical work. It represents the moment-to-moment appreciation of the dialectical balance between the obstructive and constructive forces within the personality, which inevitably involves the clash between the authentic self and the mechanisms of disavowal, depersonalization, derealization, splitting, dissociation, and fragmentation. Holding the dialectical tension between the obstructive and constructive has powerful implications for treatment, adding to our ability to hold ever greater degrees of complexity, both intrapsychically and interpersonally. Horney highlighted how various parts of the individual self align or cannot align into a cohesive whole. This view of a self split against itself constitutes a clear theoretical paradigm shift originating over a half-century ago. We have found that Horney's descriptions of overdetermined character solutions are unmatched in their intensity, depth, and comprehensiveness. She was ahead of her time in locating narcissistic injury in relational failures of attunement which fuel seemingly disconnected feelings of acute shame and vulnerability. Horney's courageous efforts to promote important political progress are solidly and deeply grounded in psychodynamic thinking and practice. Perhaps, like Ferenczi, it is time that Horney be given the credit she is due. Both Ferenczi and Horney have paid a large price professionally and personally for their courageous positions.

PART-WHOLE THINKING

A foundational cornerstone of this manual is the importance of understanding the concept and technique of part-whole thinking. We will refer to part-whole analysis throughout this book, but a more detailed coverage of the topic can be found in chapters 4 and 5. The process of part-whole thinking is fundamentally non-linear since there are multiple parts and multiple wholes with no straight lines between them. The linearity of time and space are cognitive impositions of psychological reality. Unfortunately, they are often assumed to define that very reality, not simply approximate it in familiar terms. Think of the timeless and spaceless qualities of the dreaming mind and of the dream state itself. Dreams inform us of psychic reality but the qualities of the dreaming "process" also educate us on the inherent nature of the therapeutic exchange. This is precisely the nature of systemic thinking, which can be defined as a part-whole process of absorbing seemingly disconnected realities. In the clinical hour integrated attention depends on simultaneous awareness of "opposites" or simultaneous awareness of seemingly disconnected splits that, notwithstanding appearances, are dynamically connected in non-linear ways.

Given the non-linear connections involving emotional and cognitive splits, empathic immersion becomes a vital methodological tool in understanding the role of the part and the whole. This is not a type of learning that has been emphasized in much of Western education. It has been assumed that the intuitive process is a constitutional given and, since it cannot be reduced to linear connections, it cannot be reliably taught. However there is nothing about part-whole understanding that is not teachable, once space is created for it outside the confines of the linear line.

If we can think in terms of circles rather than straight lines, we are already training ourselves to see that objective knowledge is insufficient to constitute a systemic whole. As we have mentioned both objectivity and subjectivity are parts of larger whole. It is for this reason that dynamic psychotherapy cannot proceed very far without due attention to subjective learning, subjective attunement, and a subjective capacity for immersion, a key component of which involves part-whole thinking.

If we applied part-whole thinking to the process of understanding how dynamic psychotherapy unfolds, we would first begin to conceptualize psychic reality as mutually non-exclusive, interacting circles having multiple feedback loops. Acausal and systemic in nature, these ever-widening circles serve to integrate culture, family, interpersonal, and intrapsychic into a single dynamic theory. Most important, as mentioned, these are not just individual factors (the "parts") but the connections and interactions between them must be seen in the context of the whole structure (the "whole"). These are non-linear relationships being described, ones that establish the realm of subjective experience, allowing us to open up a method of processing clinical information that can simultaneously hold and contain seemingly unconnected "opposites." Opposites such as intrapsychic/relational, self/other, inner/outer, self-hating/self-idealizing, cognitive frame/affective frame, one person/two person, health/illness are important examples of critical dissociations, yet, all of the above splits, once contained, can be seen to fit into a larger systemic whole. Or put otherwise, using this metapsychological framework, we have moved from a posture of subject-object splitting to a posture of subject-object healing.

As a concrete example "ego" has been logically abstracted as a mental construct but only a "self" can experience pain, only a self can process self-hate, and finally only a self can grow. Thus, it follows that "[as] one more fully grasps the reality of the self, the interplay of health and illness can be more fully engaged. The [therapist] becomes more able during this process to 'feel' the in-born capacity for growth in all patients, in all people, and in ourselves. As these constructive movements deepen, selfness itself becomes a centering experience and selfhood a centering concept" (Danielian, 1988, p. 20). A prime example involves what may be called the artificial theory-mandated split between cognitions and affects, a split to which we have already made reference. Clinical data can be interpreted *cognitively as structure* or *affectively as process* and hence are not mutually exclusive categories at all but different ways of looking at the same data.

INCREASING THE CAPACITY OF THERAPEUTIC LISTENING

The art of therapeutic listening is not just about attending to what's being said but includes giving careful attention to content, body language, tone of voice, and affect. Deeper levels of listening require that and more. While one is attending to all of the visual and verbal cues, it is important to analyze *what is not being said* as well. Moving the therapy forward requires that the therapist must dedicate some degree of attention to themes and patterns, what themes and patterns mean, and why they repeat themselves. As we begin to listen in a more non-linear fashion, wondering how parts connect to other parts and to the whole, and on a content level wondering about what makes sense and what doesn't seem to quite fit, we can begin to see what is being hidden when a patient glosses over statements in a matter-of-fact way. What do patients want us to discover or uncover about themselves? What wishes or longings are they too embarrassed to admit? What negative affect or desires are hidden from view?

Presentness, or what some have called moment-to-moment phenomenological receptivity, is sometimes taken as a given in psychotherapy, something that automatically goes with the "listening professions." However, experience has shown that "listening" cannot be achieved by a simple cognitive recognition of its need. Actually, it develops in steps over time, as the therapist learns to "hear" without needing to resort to clinical extrapolations such as a therapeutic diagnosis, interpretation of meaning, or methods of relieving patient urgency. These extrapolations are phase-appropriate but they can only have a chance at therapeutic gain if a therapist has already become reasonably comfortable with the patient's experiential reality. Because "presentness" is not a given, it can sometimes require an unexpected period of time to achieve a degree of mastery of the many forms of therapeutic listening.

We have found that listening has been understressed and understudied in the listening professions. This situation has created an undue hardship for therapists, especially beginning therapists, because therapists already, and almost automatically, expect themselves to be able to "listen" to patients. Listening is supposed to be what any good friend can do and professionals are assumed to be professional not merely because they know how to "listen." Rather, professionals are assumed to be professional because they know how to *intervene* therapeutically with understanding and skill. To assume otherwise can make one feel that not enough is being done professionally or that the patient will judge us negatively, assuming either that we are insufficiently trained or that we lack the qualities of a good therapist.

The capacity for listening can indeed be deepened and refined over time, and the pressure to "do something" can be modified with the help of good supervision. A case in point is the following illustration of a trainee session. Here we see how the impact of "solution-focused" techniques may have created a less than subtle pressure to produce results in a seasoned therapist. In the case illustration that follows we see a trainee who presents a case involving a woman who complains about her husband's lack of interest. The trainee's strategies around working with this patient involve offering suggestions regarding what the patient might say or do to gently confront her husband. As you can see the patient becomes more and more frustrated as the exchange proceeds.

Patient: My husband doesn't seem to pay any attention to me anymore.

Therapist: What happens between you?

Patient: Well, I talk to him about my day, and he just ignores me. Or I ask him to go away for a romantic weekend, and he'd rather plan a fishing trip with his buddies.

Therapist: Have you tried asking him to alternate between doing things with his fishing companions and with you on the weekend?

Patient: Yes, but he just gets irritated. All he wants to do is be on the go constantly. I think he's lost interest in me.

Therapist: Have you asked him whether he still loves you?

Patient: No, I'm too afraid to ask.

Therapist: Do you think that you could bring him into one of our sessions? Perhaps, we can focus on getting him to be more expressive.

Patient: I don't know if I'm ready for that. He's really a nice guy, you know. I don't want him to feel pressured in any way (Begins to cry). I don't know why this therapy business is so difficult for me.

Although this trainee knew that she had a tendency to "try to fix things," she hadn't quite connected this with how the exchange reached an impasse, stating, "Why was it that my patient always seemed to end up in a bit of a struggle with me by the end of the hour?" When asked what she thought the struggle might mean, the trainee was at a loss. She worried that her own anxiety had affected the patient because she couldn't offer more helpful suggestions. She was at a loss as to any other reason that might have caused the patient to cry.

When asked if she thought there might be a transferential communication within this therapeutic exchange, the trainee didn't quite know how to respond. It was if she knew she was at the edge of her own experience and expertise, recognizing the somewhat precarious position she was in with her patient but did not know what her next move should be. When asked if she could see the transferential opening in this exchange, the trainee admitted that moving into a dialogue *about* the transference made her very nervous. Essentially, we concluded together, that this was because she didn't have any idea about *how* to intervene and how to enter into a phenomenological tracking process.

As a way of beginning the consultation, we talked about the fact that there were a number of possible interventions if we stayed within the phenomenological present and allowed ourselves to slowly track the process. For example, she could go back to the initial articulation of the patient's complaints about her husband, and then try phenomenologically to track exactly when the patient's mood changed. She could then ask the patient at what point in their conversation did she feel she had to defend her husband to the therapist? Alternatively, she could wonder out loud with the patient about what was making her cry, asking if there was something she might be afraid to say to the therapist. Finally, she could name the unspoken tension that had been building at the end of several sessions, wondering if the therapist's suggestions were in any way overwhelming, or when her suggestion no longer felt helpful.

One of the classic mistakes that therapists often make is to try to bypass transferential exchanges because they believe that any comment might create undue discomfort for the patient (or the therapist). In these instances many therapists secretly wish that if they simply ignore a transferential comment they might be able to dispel or distract from the tension and make the transferential reaction disappear. Even seasoned clinicians are not immune from missing opportunities to move the treatment forward because they have either missed transferential cues or they are afraid to stay in the dialogical present in a way that allows them to convey a deeper understanding of the patient's subjective experience. The avoidance of *presentness* can often be recognized when we see a therapist making attempts to "fix" a situation or a problem.

Rather than jumping to make an intervention, a posture of *presentness* would require that therapists try to immerse themselves more fully in the position of the client—in this trainee's case to immerse herself in the patient's feelings and concerns about her spouse's lack of interest in her. Immersion (sometimes referred to as empathic immersion) means not just a fleeting recognition or comment about the patient's concern but a more prolonged process involving overriding any tendencies to judge or "fix." If the therapist does not stay in the phenomenological present, it may trigger an unconscious collusion with the patient's need for the therapist to "cure the problem." If/when this unconscious collusion does occur, the focus of the treatment now becomes dependent on the patient's *urgency* to define how the therapist must proceed.

In the above case example, the trainee quickly felt adrift because the patient did not seem to respond with relief to the suggestions that were offered. Instead the patient exhibited discomfort, tearfulness, and ended up in "a bit of a struggle" with the therapist. Because of the urgency of the patient's wish for the therapist to "do something," the therapist responded by trying "to be helpful" which in turn foreclosed deeper inquiry and deeper listening. We can presume that because the patient did not feel sufficiently heard or understood, she then rejected the "fix" by saying that her husband is "a really nice guy."

This transferential dilemma could have likely been avoided simply by staying in the phenomenological present. Using the same case, here is an example of how to use an inquiry process of empathic immersion that maintains an alignment with the patient's affective state and illustrates how to adopt a posture of *presentness*.

Patient: My husband doesn't seem to pay any attention to me anymore.

Therapist: What happens between you?

Patient: Well, I talk to him about my day, and he just ignores me.

Therapist: What happens after you start to tell him about your day?

Patient: He gets up and just leaves the room sometimes. I used to follow him around, but now I've given up. It just feels so awful and so lonely.

Therapist: Can you describe the loneliness?

Patient: I feel worthless. I don't feel desirable anymore.

Therapist: Loneliness and worthlessness feel like the same thing . . . and if you could just be more desirable it would take both the loneliness and the sense of worthlessness away?

Patient: Well, yes, I mean, no. I guess I connect feeling desirable with being loved. My mother always used to tell me that no man would ever love me over the long haul unless I was sexy and desirable.

Therapist: So if you're not sexy, you feel worthless?

Patient: Yes, when I say it out loud is sounds pretty foolish. I guess that puts a lot of pressure on my husband to keep proving to me that I'm worthy.

As you can see, this form of phenomenological inquiry takes the dialogue in a different direction. When the therapist suspends problem-solving and stays in the present, the patient is able to reveal more of the underlying source of her discomfort in terms of her husband's lack of attentiveness. Some of what the patient fears may have less to do with her husband and more to do with the patient's internalized sense of what her self-worth is based upon. There may also be relational issues within the couple system, but until we discover the affective link to self-worth, any suggestions about how to improve the relationship may fall on deaf ears. Empathic immersion through staying in a posture of *presentness* may take more time but can lead to more lasting insights.

The major function that therapeutic *presentness* plays is to help us to suspend such linear solutions, thereby opening up the possibility of a more prolonged immersion in what the patient is experiencing. Thus, if anything, immersion in the present is a more sophisticated intervention than the contemporary solution-focused mindset. There is nothing about such understanding that is not teachable, once space is created for it outside the confines of the linear line. Again, if we can think in terms of circles rather than straight lines, we are already training ourselves to see that "objective" knowledge is insufficient to constitute a systemic whole. Both objectivity and subjectivity are parts of a larger integrated system.

Fine-tuning cannot be achieved without an empathic ongoing connection with the patient. In turn, an empathic connection with the patient is difficult to sustain without the creation of a subjective space. The reader will recognize that the above language is a refinement of interpersonal

concepts and traditions long informally employed in psychodynamic therapy, although these traditions were not fully integrated into dynamic theory
until much more recently.

Empathic immersion is a quality of attention that operates within a
mutually created subjective space between the patient and the therapist.
Achieving this quality of empathic attention requires a systemic approach to
understanding and integrating both the interpersonal and the intrapsychic
components of awareness. Ideally, both the therapist *and* the patient can hold
or learn to hold this dual awareness simultaneously. Some patients naturally
gravitate between the two, sensing how both are parts of an integrated whole.
However, for many patients this systemic self-awareness is particularly difficult. For example, some patients will compulsively fix on the interpersonal
dimensions of life, and in effect create a split where interpersonal awareness
does not inform or enrich intrapsychic awareness. Some patients overly focus
on the reverse, compulsively fixing on the intrapsychic in a way that does not
allow intrapsychic issues to illuminate interpersonal problems.

When the dissociative split is intense enough, patients who are overly
focused on interpersonal issues may become prone to externalizing problems and projecting them onto others, while patient who are more fixed on
internal phenomena may become prone to a detached hypersensitivity, one
which seems to be divorced from the external world. The therapist's anticipation of these splits allows for therapeutic modeling and better integration
of how the interpersonal and intrapsychic continually educate and enrich
each other as parts of a systemic whole.

As noted, the patient's subjective reality becomes our clinical point of
entry into the patient's world. We may never fully know objective reality. All
we can do is to create better and better maps of that ultimate reality. Our
interventions are not focused on objective reality; they are focused on the
patient's subjective reality. To a greater or lesser degree, depending on our
therapeutic skill, the treatment of the patient's subjective reality will lead us to
increasing objective change. The Japanese terms for subjective and objective
may be instructive here: in Japanese, subjective is translated as "host" and
objective as "guest." Objective reality is not "something out there, independent
of our psychological processes" (Moses Berg quoted by Kelman, 1971, p. 110).
Rather objective and subjective realities remain intimately connected.

CHARACTER STRUCTURE VS. CHARACTER SOLUTION: THE IMPACT ON OUR UNDERSTANDING OF NARCISSISTIC INJURY

This book is aimed at addressing the patient population that falls within
what we are calling *the spectrum of narcissistic injury*. When we refer to

narcissistic injury, we are not using the term in a traditional diagnostic sense (as in symptoms and descriptors historically highlighted in the DSM). We are, instead, offering a way of conceptualizing narcissistic injury as *the often formidable residue of characterological damage that remains in the present due to varying degrees of trauma, deprivation, or the lack of adequate relational attunement from the past.* As such, we are inviting the reader to consider that the phenomenon of narcissistic injury occurs to some degree in all of us. Everyone struggles to overcome or compensate for some degree of injury to the self. In that respect none of us is immune from areas of vulnerability that color our ability to be completely objective or neutral.

How one determines where the line gets crossed into what has traditionally been characterized as psychopathology is not always easy to quantify. Therefore, we are suggesting that the descriptor of narcissistic injury not be used as a fixed or pejorative label, per se. Instead, we suggest that this is a dynamic concept, one that is best viewed on a continuum. Variations along the continuum of narcissistic injury range from minor wounds that don't appear to compromise much of the personality, all the way to major injuries that result in more rigidified attempts to compensate for and recover from more severe degrees of trauma or deprivation.

Anyone with a history of trauma and/or deprivation in childhood has learned to utilize some degree of defensive compensations in an attempt to maintain a cohered sense of self. The degree to which those learned, compensatory behaviors permeate the personality will determine the degree to which the development of the authentic self is thwarted. The greater the trauma and/or deprivation, the more rigidified the personality structure becomes, sometimes to the point that the only "self" that is presented to the world is the "as if" appearance of a real person. The parts of the self that contain the hurt, the feelings of inadequacy, or the longings for rescue or redemption are forced to go underground, only to operate through compulsive enactments in an attempt to hide underlying feelings of shame and inadequacy.

This construction of the overdetermined, overcompensating self is both dynamic and characterological in nature. Rather than attending to "parts" of the characterological whole by treating symptoms as they surface, or by seeing character as something that is fixed and immutable, we are suggesting that treatment must take into account the organizing schemas that comprise the *foundation of character formation.* This is a more encompassing picture of how one's sense of self comes into being. Our view of self and development draws our attention back to what Karen Horney identified as "character solutions." Character solutions are what patients create in an attempt to compensate for inadequate or unsafe nurturing conditions in childhood.

Unlike traditional understandings of *character structure* or *character disorder*, the idea of a *character solution* opens up greater possibilities for hope in the change process. (If an overdetermined construct within the personality has been created, it can also be dismantled or modified over time). In other words the idea of character solutions can be seen as fluid and changing, whereas assumptions about character disorders are often seen as static and fixed.

Horney viewed character as "solution" not as an immutable given but as a part of the personality this is in continuing, moment-to-moment opposition with the authentic (although often hidden) yearnings of the patient. Working from the point of view of "selfhood" Horney (1945, 1950) depicted how the alienation from self, stemming from an unfavorable and unpropitious childhood, is the root cause of narcissistic disturbances. The vulnerable self, unbeknownst to the person, splits into warring factions that must be kept dissociated from each other, lest their collision lead to a dissolution of any sense of self-integration.

What are these sub-system splits? A most damaging split is the self-hating self (condemning any reasonable assets or achievements) divorced from the self-idealizing contempt of anything short of perfection. These splits involve an intimate connection between the interpersonal and the intrapsychic. They are compulsively driven and therefore remain largely out of awareness. Note that character solutions should not be confused with current practitioner usage of the term solution-based therapy. A visual diagram will help to illustrate the change process as follows:

Therapeutic Fluidity of Character Change

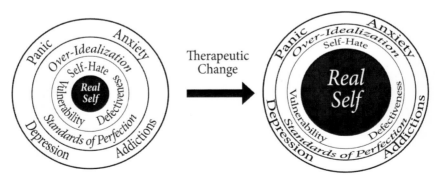

Figure 1.1 Therapeutic fluidity of character change.

Figure 1.1 is a depiction of the influence that psychotherapy has on the change process and the expansion of the real self. When a patient enters treatment the real self is often hidden or tentative, as the constructed parts of the overcompensating as-if self work to defend against feelings of vulnerability, self-hate, or defectiveness. These attempts at overcompensation often take the form of overidealized standards and the wish for perfectionism. However, as this is a constructed solution, it can never be a "permanent" fix, and we see that symptoms and/or forms of acting out behavior threaten the wished-for stability of the "as if" construction. Each circle is tightly woven into every other circle, comprising a larger integrated whole. As you can see, if therapeutic interventions only address the outer circle of this diagram, the remaining characterological influences remain untouched and untreated.

As such the premises that inform this book, our approach, and the Four Quadrant model are based on a paradigm shift that moves our thinking away from seeing symptom reduction as cure and away from viewing character structure as immutable. It shifts our thinking toward a non-linear, more comprehensive and fluid view of character as something that can be influenced and changed in the present and over the course of time. This non-linear, more fluid view of character change as a treatment approach for individuals with narcissistic injuries opens up doorways for the treatment for narcissistic injuries that are more optimistic and respectful. A more detailed description of character solutions as they pertain to our model can be found in chapters 2 and 3.

SUMMARY

Our manual introduces concepts and terminology that build in a step-wise fashion. From the basic introduction of our Four Quadrant Model in chapter 2, to various techniques and ways of listening that are highlighted in the remaining eight chapters, each chapter has been chosen to represent a critical aspect of clinical work. We begin in chapters 3 and 4 by introducing understandable frameworks and techniques necessary for deeper immersion in listening techniques. Chapters 5 through 10 will build in complexity, introducing concepts and techniques that are typically more challenging in terms of understanding and mastery. Though each chapter builds upon the preceding ones, they all present a combination of theoretical content coupled with questions and clinical discourse from our trainees. This combination of theory, technique, and questions and answers is meant to help therapists improve their skill sets. Regardless of your theoretical orientation or level of clinical expertise, we hope that the material will be both clear and understandable, and presented in a way that will challenge the expansion of your thinking and practice.

In this first chapter we have provided an overview of key concepts that anchor the theoretical framework of the text as well as providing a description of and justification for the paradigm shift that we believe is already occurring within our field. Furthermore, it is our belief that a systematic and rigorous approach to training is imperative if we are to consolidate the theoretical contributions and gains that have been made over the past several decades. Our field is not short on methods, opinions, and approaches when it comes to the practice of psychotherapy. We *are,* however, at risk of losing our metapsychological underpinnings unless training institutions and practitioners begin a dialogue around building in some degree of uniformity in the preparation of future generations of practitioners.

As mentioned we will be presenting a diagrammatic four quadrant model that will offer a more systemic process for conceptualizing and tracking the components of the psyche as the therapy unfolds. The model is also meant to help practitioners understand the non-linear manner in which integration, consolidation, and change occurs over time. The underpinnings of the model rely on an understanding of personality development based on attachment and attunement, as well as the sober appreciation of the damage that occurs as a result of trauma and/or deprivation. It is out of these narcissistic injuries or ruptures of attunement that we have designed our model. As has been mentioned, the model is based on what we refer to as "character solutions," which are basically the various ways in which individuals compensate and overcompensate for injuries or damages to the psyche.

Understanding *how* and *why* these solutions are necessary creations in the first place is one of the keys that can help unlock the puzzle of healing narcissistic injuries. Not only do these "solutions" help stabilize the personality when early parental care or the environment is inadequate or unsafe, they also help ward off feelings of shame and inadequacy by keeping painful or overwhelming feeling states at bay. The task of therapy is to help connect all of these component parts to the whole, uncovering old wounds in an effort to mitigate the overdetermined compensatory mechanisms, while encouraging the often quiet but valiant efforts of the authentic self to finally have a chance to emerge. This is the field and ground upon which the process of dynamic psychotherapy takes place. Our intention is to highlight and clarify this process even further.

Although we have spoken about the clear need for a paradigm shift, from linear to non-linear modes of listening and reacting, we also want to say that this is a very exciting time for the field. All paradigm shifts need to be approached with attendant feelings of anticipation and uncertainty. The development of a growing awareness of greater degrees of complexity demands that of all of us. In spite of the variability in our field, we are optimistic about the prospect of greater alignment within our current theories and greater sophistication and efficiency in our practice. We remain dedicated to efforts that advance training throughout the professional life span of the dedicated clinicians who practice this craft.

CHAPTER 2

An Overview of the Therapeutic Model

What is interesting . . . are the meta-theoretical issues: how are the different theories put together and what do they have in common? What are the real differences? What are the real potential points of convergence? These questions are very interesting to me. In a way, it's an area that has been almost, until recently, undeveloped in psychoanalysis. People out of each tradition are too religiously devoted to their particular theories to be able to sit back and say what are the assumptions here? Are we and they talking about the same thing but maybe in a somewhat different language with different deities? This is what relational means in its best usage: there's a more encompassing way of looking at a set of concepts that are often expressed in different languages.

—STEPHEN MITCHELL, FROM AN INTERVIEW
BY JACK DRESCHER, M.D., PUBLISHED IN
THE WHITE SOCIETY VOICE (1994)

THIS CHAPTER begins with an explanation of the "The Four Quadrant Model." We will present a systemic explanation of the model as a whole, followed by a detailed description of each of the four quadrants. In addition we will also provide a way to conceptualize aspects of each quadrant on a continuum, ranging from relative health to severe pathology. Clinical case studies will follow, providing an analysis of how to use the model in the service of deepening our therapeutic listening skills. Each of the subsequent chapters will focus on a particular aspect of treatment, connecting each of these aspects to the application of The Four Quadrant Model and part-whole analysis.

As an overview this chapter will help therapists identify aspects of the personality that comprise the characterological whole. The four quadrants present a visual illustration of how patients' organizing schemas and/or expectations of self and other relate to symptoms, behaviors, and the degree of relational connection or disconnection. Therapists can draw upon this model to enhance diagnostic assessment as well as increase proficiency around treatment interventions throughout the course of therapy. As a way of operationalizing the concepts presented in this chapter, we will use a combination of clinical vignettes combined with questions from our trainees that help clarify how the model can be used throughout the course of treatment.

The structure that constitutes the underpinnings of the Four Quadrant Model evolved in a quite organic fashion and uses both visual and linguistic referents as a way to synthesize the complexity of what it takes to listen more deeply. What do we mean by listening more deeply? As introduced in chapter 1, advanced therapeutic listening is an evolving process that involves learning how to become more attuned to hearing splits during a dynamic exchange. In other words one must both attend to the micro-level and macro-level of communication simultaneously. This type of attention allows for better recognition of the dialectic tension that exists within the self-system and between the parts and the whole. No single part of the systemic structure of the personality is immutable. Character organization, itself, cannot be fully understood without holding all parts of the whole simultaneously.

Our attention and our listening can be developed as we understand greater degrees of systemic complexity within our clients' unfolding stories. We are suggesting that over time clinicians have a tendency to pay attention to certain aspects of therapeutic dialogue more than others. For example, some clinicians have a tendency to focus on content more than process. Others attend to early history and intrapsychic frameworks at the expense of interpersonal or cultural factors. Some move to quick solutions, trying to fix or relieve a painful situation as opposed to staying deeply in the moment, learning more about the patient's dilemma or suffering. Most of us have varying degrees of comfort with how much or how often to attend to subtle transferential cues and actively bring them into the therapeutic dialogue for discussion. Given the pressures of the last decades to produce quick results through solution-focused therapies promising symptom relief rather than internal repair and integration, there runs a risk that therapists will fall into the trap of over-attending to content, which in turn runs the risk of putting ourselves in a reactive or co-opted position.

We believe that with a systemic approach to understanding the complexity of psychic functioning, process interventions can become more explicitly prioritized. For example, most modern-day theorists accept that dissociative mechanisms are heavily driven by a variety of shame dynamics. Shame and shame derivatives are some of the most painful emotions a patient can face. Accordingly, through detailed clinical examples, we will illuminate how allying with the patient's subjective experience can allow entry into painful dissociated splits which experience-distant approaches can easily close off. Put otherwise, the centeredness of the therapist allows the decentered aspects of the patient's self to come into greater focus, greater focus for both the therapist and the patient. We will demonstrate how this greater focus allows the past to flow systemically from the characterological present, rather than the classical reconstruction of the present from the past.

Although we hope to elucidate the organic process of what it means to actually do the work of therapy, we also hope to create a tracking system of how to watch and listen. As an organic process, it is something that can be well understood only if the therapist can hold the dynamic tension between objective theory and the subjective experience of our clinical work. All theoretical terms are meant to be held lightly. As soon as you make any model static, you lose the understanding of the "process moment."

Historical Foundations for an "Experience-Near" Paradigm

The most non-static and experience-near descriptions of narcissistic phenomena we have found are in the writings of Karen Horney, a German-born psychoanalyst who immigrated to the United States in 1932. Horney describes in often excruciating detail how people give over healthy, genuine, spontaneous satisfactions to compulsive drives, which by their very nature, create vicious circles of unattainable goals. These unintegrated splits render the patient helpless, bereft, and fragile as if under the clutches of a toxic drug. Beginning interpersonally and working her way to the intrapsychic, Horney described three dominant narcissistic trends, each with the power to lead to greater and greater depletion of the self. In interpersonal terms these are called, with elegant simplicity, the human tendencies now extending to the pathological: *moving toward people, moving against people, or moving away from people.*

All of us possess all three trends but, under the weight of psychic conflict, one trend with its associated splits will typically become paramount, constantly driven by the unconscious attempt to achieve safety. Compulsively driven, these trends are inevitably accompanied by, and sustained by, unintegrated splits between self-contempt and unattainable perfection. These self-sustaining "solutions" perhaps implicate temperament but most certainly involve family environment, cultural conditioning, and psychic conflict. Needless to say, the degree and pervasiveness of the split determines the level of pathology and/or symptomatic thoughts, feelings, and behaviors.

The Movement toward People

The "movement toward people" Horney calls the "Love Solution" as well as the Compliant or the Self-Effacing Solution. For example, a patient may feel presumptuous to have an opinion of her own; she may feel love will conquer all. Both the patient's conscious assumption and her unconscious wishes will denigrate her own true assets and accomplishments. She dismisses them with the belief that it is only due to luck or another person's good will ("It was only because my teacher liked me") that she will be allowed to achieve her longings and ambitions. Such a person, Horney (1950) says, whether male or female, grew up in the cloud of someone else's shadow, most often a parent or sibling. Affection was attainable but only at "a price . . . of a self-subordinating devotion" (p. 222). Thus self-worth becomes defined in terms of being liked, needed, or wanted.

The Movement against People

The "move against people" Horney calls the "Expansive Solution": The Appeal of Mastery." Such a person openly covets self-sufficiency, ambition, aggressiveness, superiority, and triumph. Failures or rejection of these expansive efforts lead to corrosive self-hate and self-contempt equally as intense and debilitating as in the case of the self-effacer challenged by her or his naïve optimism. The corresponding naiveté in the "move against people" may be called the naïve belief in the magic of "greatness." In childhood such a person was destined to believe that true affection was impossible to attain. Therefore, he or she coped with this lack of affection by becoming more and more convinced that not only was it "unattainable . . . but that it does not exist at all" (p. 202). Here self-worth is defined as becoming categorically invulnerable to others and being the self-righteous master of one's life.

The Movement Away from People

The third major trend of "moving away from people" was called by Horney "Resignation: The Appeal of Freedom." This is perhaps the least well understood of the characterological solutions and warrants some additional explanation. In the first characterological type Self-Effacement is paramount and Expansiveness is suppressed or altogether beyond awareness. In the second, the reverse is true: Expansiveness is dominant and Self-Effacement is buried. In Resignation however both of these major trends have been seemingly forsaken. Instead a third solution is pursued through the compulsive drive to arrive at a state of freedom and independence impervious to outside influence. The resignation from active living creates a person who fears attachment to anyone in his life, tries to avoid having wishes or needs, or in Horney's words (1950) "Nothing should be so important for him that he could not do without it" (p. 264). A profound aspect of such a personality is his exquisite sensitivity to being coerced, a sensitivity that is so pervasive as to include moral indignation at someone invading his "space," animals being confined in a zoo, or shoes cramping his feet.

How does such a person relate in psychotherapy? Horney describes a patient who will "comply with the obvious rules, such as being on time or saying what is on his mind, but assimilates so little of what is discussed that the work is rendered futile" (p. 278). But the one passion that provides an opening in therapy is the powerful appeal, psychologically or philosophically, that *freedom* has for him. True, he wants to remain "himself" and fears being chewed up in the cookie cutter of psychotherapy; but at the same time his inner life, often relegated to dreams, can be full of a "world of conflicts and passionate feelings under the smooth surface" (p. 289). Of course such a patient can talk about his dream symbols as if he were talking about an engaging production; but given time, commitment, and therapeutic patience, characterological change is possible. In childhood such a person was likely coerced by tangible or intangible forces, extremes of attention and abuse, or a marked reversal of child-parent relationships. But once the entire characterological solution can be visualized, the treatment process can be constructively engaged.

The reader will notice that Horney's descriptions are rich not only in clinical detail but in the vitality of their "presentness." The intimacy of her cases reveals a subjective singularity that can only be achieved through an active immersion in the patient's deepest needs and struggles. This is the great value of maintaining an experience-near posture and being empathically in touch with the moment-to-moment specificity of the treatment process. It is no accident that the reader may feel a sense of embarrassment at reading such vital and intimate descriptions of characterological splits, when these splits have often been assumed to be just part of "normal" life.

Thus, our experience-near model takes much of the foundational work of Horney, using her descriptions of "sub-system splits," and illustrates how the interpersonal and the intrapsychic are interconnected within the dynamic unfolding of the therapeutic exchange. Because all defensive postures or solutions are compulsively driven and remain largely out of awareness, the major objective of the model is to illustrate how sub-system splits interact and reinforce a homeostatic, systemic balance. In turn, this model illustrates how and where the therapeutic dialogue can create leverage, thus having an impact on dismantling homeostatic splitting in the service of integration and healing.

Although we have drawn upon the theoretical underpinnings of Karen Horney's macro and micro understanding of the self, the utility of this model is that it can serve as a template to help track the intersubjective exchange between the therapist and the patient in any given moment in the present. Therefore, using this model as a way of *staying in the intersubjective present* grounds theory more firmly in the phenomenology of experience. We see it as a natural unfolding of a process of historical and personal integration.

The Experience-Near Four Quadrant Model

In an attempt to illustrate how we might capture a three-dimensional grid of the conscious, dissociative, and unconscious interplay between various parts of the self, we have devised a quadrant system where various components of the psyche are broken down into syntonic and dystonic, conscious and unconscious (and varying degrees of partially conscious states in between). The model suggests that we can hold each of these dimensions of the psyche simultaneously. Listening is not just art or intuition, nor is it merely interpretation of content based on a theoretical framework. Rather it is a dialectical holding of both.

Although this model is set up as a grid, it is in no way meant to be used in a linear fashion. For example, Quadrant One does not necessarily lead to a focus on Quadrant Two. Rather, we are suggesting that all quadrants or aspects of the psyche are connected to each other and that therapeutic entry can occur at any time within any quadrant. As a preview to the model we have listed five overarching questions to keep in mind that are meant to help track the unfolding process and progress of the therapy:

- How can we listen both for what is being said and what is not being said within any given therapeutic exchange?
- How can we leverage the positive transference while listening for and palpating the negative transference in ways that are both subtle enough to approach the negative transference, but also direct enough so that we don't inadvertently collude with the patient's avoidance of disavowed material altogether?
- How can we use the technique of moment-to-moment tracking of the dialogue in a way that exposes the patient's hidden longings, wishes, and fantasies, both syntonic and dystonic?
- How can we begin to move the inquiry in the direction of unearthing and articulating the hidden or unconscious material in ways that the patient can tolerate?
- How can we attend to the glimmers of the buried traces of the authentic self and help those aspects of the self emerge and grow stronger?

By using these five questions as building blocks for thinking about the therapeutic relationship, we can become better able to use the model and hear underlying themes that are expressed within each quadrant. In other words, we can develop a deeper understanding of how splits function and thereby capture the dynamic unfolding of vertical splits within the therapeutic process. We achieve this through the self-questioning process of moment-to-moment tracking.

Let us take a moment to clarify this further. A common misconception about dissociative splitting is that we have come to define it as a primitive defense, often associated with more severe character pathology. Thus, we have been trained to believe that repression occurs in less severely disturbed patients and is used in the service of blocking uncomfortable affect or memories in an attempt to maintain a homeostatic balance in the psyche. However, dissociative splitting is just as common as repression. Understanding how this is so is a matter of shifting our perspective. Although it is true that the more extreme forms of dissociation are the result of severe trauma, leaving deep scars on the psyche, this picture is only one point on a continuum of the dissociative spectrum. When viewed on a continuum, Elizabeth Howell (2005) states that we are able to understand the subtle nuances of dissociation that occur in the normal population, not only in severe psychopathology (p. 5). All points on the dissociative continuum involve splitting off aspects of reality from awareness and behavior.

To illustrate this point, let us take the example of shopping. On one end of the continuum, there are many people who go into a store to buy something that they really don't need, but they tell themselves its harmless or they deserve it. Moving along the continuum, many people may convince themselves that it's okay to buy something by telling themselves that it will make them feel better. What they block from awareness in that moment is the memory that this strategy has never worked in the past. Further along the continuum, you may see people who buy something in hopes of feeling better, knowing that they don't have enough money in the checking account to cover the expenditure, but such people magically reassure themselves that money will come in before the check clears. Even further along the continuum, we see greater degrees of dissociative splitting in the form of buying an item and lying to one's spouse, saying that a friend had given them a present in hopes that this will prevent another argument about their spending. Finally, we see even more extreme forms of dissociation where people enter a store with the conscious intention of shoplifting. They tell themselves that this is harmless in fact, or they use some form of rationalization to justify their behavior. Perhaps, the most extreme form of massive dissociation takes the form of amnesia around the shoplifting behavior altogether.

At the beginning of the continuum, we see how the more subtle forms of splitting are defense mechanisms we all use from time to time. Our supervisees have come to call the subtler forms of vertical splitting as "splitting lite." In a general sense dissociation can be seen as any behavior that restricts, foreshortens or fragments experience as a result of feeling pressure of anxiety, guilt, shame, or the need to retain important relational ties. According to Wachtel (2008) another way to understand the concept of dissociation is to see that "it's not so much what we *don't know* about ourselves, but what we *both* know *and* don't know, or the ways in which we 'know' do not seem to exert much influence over the actions we take or how we feel" (p. 143).

For example, a client begins her session by recounting a trip she had taken to the city with her partner. She received a call from a sick friend, asking her to stop by for a couple of hours. Her partner initially agreed that she should go. When she returned at the appointed time, she reported that he was in a "foul" mood, and she felt as if he were trying to punish her. She tried to soothe him, suggesting things they could do together for the remainder of their long weekend, but he continued to sulk, refusing to do anything other than watch TV. The client reports that she was secretly annoyed with his childish behavior.

In the same breath, the client then begins to describe how they were getting ready for the upcoming holiday. She says, "He has been so warm and so kind. It's really fun to be around him." When asked how she was able to make sense of the weekend they had just experienced and her description of him as warm and kind, she looks confused and puzzled. "Can you hold these two experiences that you have described about your partner at the same time? They seem to present two very different pictures." She responds matter-of-factly by saying, "Yes, but that she would rather think about him as being warm and kind." She knows he has an unpleasant side, but she doesn't want to think about it because it makes her feel confused and anxious.

As we can see from this example, the conceptualization of *both/and* in terms of working with the spectrum of dissociation is useful in terms of how we listen for the degree of severity or pervasiveness of a client's use of splitting. Using the framework of *both/and* is also a way to integrate our understanding of vertical splitting. As clinicians it is our job to measure the *degree* of pathology, the *pace* that the therapeutic unfolding must occur, and the underlying *intensity* of affect that the individual is defending against. In that regard our model is in part meant to be used as an assessment tool in terms of each of these above measures. By breaking the psyche into four distinct quadrants, we can begin to see the systemic interconnection of the sub-systems, as well as the patient's capacity for the integration of the dissociative splits. The more cut off the patient is from awareness of each of the other quadrants, and the more intensely the patient holds the various aspects of each quadrant, the more fragile the personality and more delicate the pace of therapy must be.

How does our model juxtapose shame versus guilt? What is the significance of that juxtaposition? As we have noted earlier, guilt has long been considered the bedrock affect of psychopathology. Yet this theoretical assumption has been coming under increasingly intense scrutiny as our therapeutic efforts have focused on dissociative splits associated with narcissistic disturbances. In such splits, often called splits which are "known and not known" all at the same time, the splits are characterized by in-and-out levels of consciousness of shame. Traditionally, guilt has been considered the undisputed primary affect and shame a secondary affect. There is pressure in our field to reverse this hierarchy, to see shame as the primary affect and guilt perhaps a variant of shame.

When self-psychology introduced the term *vertical splitting* to describe dissociative splitting, Kohut was contrasting these defense mechanisms with Freud's traditional repression barrier between conscious and unconscious, referred to as *horizontal splitting*. There are theoreticians who now say that if interventions applied to vertical splitting are conducted properly, then the repression barrier between conscious and unconscious is also loosened. This is an intriguing possibility, but in our current early state of knowledge in the field we are advised to work with both sets of dynamics as they surface in the patient. We can best address these therapeutic needs as we understand the splits in an integrated systemic approach.

We wish to make one further point before launching into an explanation of The Four Quadrant Model. This diagram represents a schematic of the interconnected sub-systems that comprise what Karen Horney has called "the idealized self," that is the self that was constructed as a result of failures in nurturing along the life span, ones that began in childhood and then were increasingly solidified into a working whole as the developmental trajectory of experiences continued into adulthood. In other words, this schematic represents a visual grid of the dimensions of the psyche that form a composite of overdetermined, compulsively driven attempts at keeping the self cohered.

In terms of assessing the level of health and pathology in any given client, it is important to pay attention to the level of *flexibility versus rigidity* that is reflected within any one of the four quadrants. The degree of rigidity and flexibility that the client exhibits both within and between quadrants is diagnostically significant in terms of our ability to assess the fragility of psychic organization. For example, clients may describe their standards around performance expectations in language that reveals their attempts to achieve a state of perfection. Then, if we follow this with the question wondering whether anything short of these standards would measure up, we can assess the degree of rigidity contained *within* Quadrant One. A question aimed at assessing the degree of rigidity or disconnection *between* quadrants might be to wonder whether the patient has thought about what these standards might cost him/her with regard to self-care, symptom formation, or the quality of relational satisfaction. In this way we can measure the permeability (or level of conscious awareness) that exist between the Quadrants and thereby begin to assess the extent of splitting or disconnection between the various parts of the whole.

In studying figure 2.1 you will note that the left side illustrates both conscious and unconsciously held material that is syntonic in nature. We are defining syntonic to mean *any and all associations that are identified as acceptable, congruent, or at least tolerated in terms of one's sense of self.* The right side of the diagram contains the dystonic aspects of the self which are defined as *any and all uncomfortable, negative, or foreign thoughts, behaviors, or emotions that are threatening and cannot be contained or incorporated within the self-system.* In terms of the visual construction of the diagram, although we have divided these quadrants into conscious and unconscious, acceptable or intolerable, they are not meant to be viewed as a fixed or static picture of the psychic construction of the self. Instead, they are meant to be

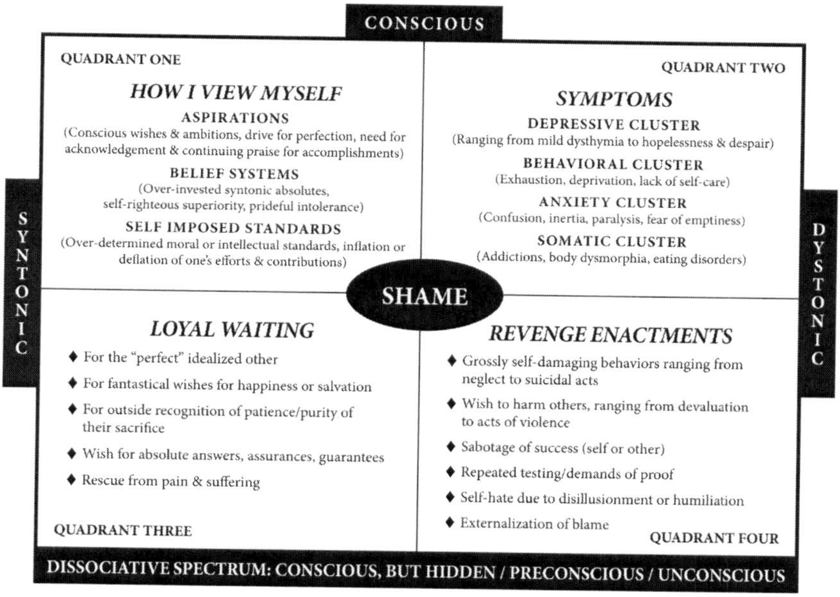

CONSCIOUS

QUADRANT ONE

HOW I VIEW MYSELF

ASPIRATIONS
(Conscious wishes & ambitions, drive for perfection, need for
acknowledgement & continuing praise for accomplishments)

BELIEF SYSTEMS
(Over-invested syntonic absolutes,
self-righteous superiority, prideful intolerance)

SELF IMPOSED STANDARDS
(Over-determined moral or intellectual standards, inflation or
deflation of one's efforts & contributions)

QUADRANT TWO

SYMPTOMS

DEPRESSIVE CLUSTER
(Ranging from mild dysthymia to hopelessness & despair)

BEHAVIORAL CLUSTER
(Exhaustion, deprivation, lack of self-care)

ANXIETY CLUSTER
(Confusion, inertia, paralysis, fear of emptiness)

SOMATIC CLUSTER
(Addictions, body dysmorphia, eating disorders)

SYNTONIC

DYSTONIC

SHAME

LOYAL WAITING

♦ For the "perfect" idealized other

♦ For fantastical wishes for happiness or salvation

♦ For outside recognition of patience/purity of
their sacrifice

♦ Wish for absolute answers, assurances, guarantees

♦ Rescue from pain & suffering

QUADRANT THREE

REVENGE ENACTMENTS

♦ Grossly self-damaging behaviors ranging from
neglect to suicidal acts

♦ Wish to harm others, ranging from devaluation
to acts of violence

♦ Sabotage of success (self or other)

♦ Repeated testing/demands of proof

♦ Self-hate due to disillusionment or humiliation

♦ Externalization of blame

QUADRANT FOUR

DISSOCIATIVE SPECTRUM: CONSCIOUS, BUT HIDDEN / PRECONSCIOUS / UNCONSCIOUS

Figure 2.1 The experience-near four quadrant model.

seen as changeable at any given point in time, given both the client's subjectively experienced external environmental variables, and given the power of the therapeutic process to make inroad into the healing or integrative change process.

At the center of the diagram is a circle with the word "shame," which represents the driving force that underlies the connection to all four quadrants. From the perspective of narcissistic injury, the experience of vulnerability is associated with memories of fragility, inadequacy, and defectiveness. For individuals with less than adequate childhoods, association to one's own vulnerability is not a neutral or benign experience. Others are not to be trusted, and it is from this place of mistrust and disappointment in caregivers that a sense of alienation from others is born. At the core of the injured self is an unconscious and compensatory attempt to create a solution of self-coherence that attempts to bypass any encounter with one's own inadequacy as well as any need for reasonable and realistic reliance on others.

Scheff and Retzinger (2001) consider shame to be the *master emotion* because shame may interfere with the effective management of other difficult feeling states such as fear, grief, and anger. In the absence of shame, it is possible to detect, express, and work through such feeling states. However; for individuals with an internalized sense of inadequacy, *any* painful or uncomfortable emotion can be associated with shame. Therefore, painful emotions themselves become a reminder of one's vulnerability and inadequacy, and the conscious awareness of this reality is unbearable and shameful. All of this becomes a vicious circle, where the eruption of shame threatens the coherence of the idealized construction of the self. (See chapter 6 for further elaboration.)

In its most basic sense this model is best understood as a fluid diagram, one that is more circular in nature as opposed to envisioning a picture of the personality that is linear and fixed. In presenting *the parts of the whole* in quadrant form, we are not suggesting that a person should be viewed as a composite of attributes and defenses that simply can be understood as divisions between the horizontal or vertical dimensions of this diagram. Rather, we are presenting parts of the whole as a subjectively created composite, one that is ever-changing, or at the very least, is capable of change. All individuals, regardless of the degree of their damage or the rigidity of their defenses always bring elements of their *authentic potentialities and health* into their defensively constructed organizing schematics that were created in childhood to establish some semblance of safety and stability. The reason our patients come into therapy is that those learned, defensively driven schemas are no longer working, or perhaps the more buried aspects of the real self are in a struggle with the compulsively driven self, lying in wait for the opportunity to be recognized, hoping to emerge.

Viewed from a circular, fluid perspective during the unfolding process of psychotherapy, each of the individual quadrants contains relative and changing degrees of conscious and unconscious awareness, as well as relative degrees of health and pathology in any given attempt at self-expression. For example, elements from any of the four quadrants can be experienced either consciously by the patient, consciously but with elements of the quadrant that must be kept hidden from view, or the patient may experience material both consciously and unconsciously simultaneously as Wachtel (2008) described earlier. Finally, the more threatening aspects of the psyche do remain completely buried or unconscious until other aspects of the real self can mobilize resources to handle and metabolize these more shameful or vulnerable components of the self and to do so without running the risk of increasing self-fragmentation.

It is the slow and methodical process of psychotherapy that allows for the integration of these split-off aspects of the self to come into greater awareness and communication with one another. Prior to the work of psychotherapeutic integration, however, it must be said that both of the dystonic quadrants (Two and Four) will initially be regarded as foreign or threatening to the self. Therefore, any intensified eruption of feelings or thoughts from either of these quadrants is likely to be associated with concomitant feelings of shame and discomfort as they threaten the equilibrium of the overdetermined, overidealized self-system. Patients often come into therapy, for example, being consciously aware of symptoms they are experiencing in Quadrant Two. However, their consciously expressed wish as they begin therapy is to "get rid of the symptoms" rather than to understand them or to connect them to incidents, beliefs, or behaviors that may have triggered the eruptions of symptoms in the first place.

Often the unwanted experiences that stem from disappointments within Quadrants One and Three are directly connected to an increase in the conscious awareness of elements contained within Quadrant Two or Four. Generally, the manifestation of symptoms experienced in Quadrant Two are due to some disappointment in the relational sphere of Quadrant Three or the disappointing attempts to achieve recognition for efforts contained within Quadrant One. If disappointments in either of the syntonic quadrants are severe enough, this may result in break-through feelings that are buried within Quadrant Four. Before going any further in terms of understanding how the four quadrants are connected, let us take a moment to describe each in further detail.

Quadrant One: Conscious/Syntonic

Quadrant One contains aspects of the personality that are within conscious awareness and are considered by the patient to be normal, resulting in a congruent sense of the person being able to say, "This is who I am." This sense of congruence varies, however, and can range from an overly exaggerated sense of greatness to an overly exaggerated sense of inadequacy. In this model the measure of pathology is not simply determined by whether one is confident as opposed to insecure. It is measured by *the amount of effort the individual must exert* in order to maintain a sense of "this is who I am." Less healthy individuals on either end of the idealized spectrum often appear to have a more fixed, stubborn, or rigid attachment to the sense of who they are and have difficulty taking in feedback that runs counter to their rigidly internalized self-image. In contrast individuals with a healthier sense of self often present with a more flexible, spontaneous, and adaptive quality to who they are. For example, they are willing to consider how certain beliefs or views about themselves may cost more than they are worth. They are able to consider alternative feedback and incorporate this into their ideas about themselves and their world view. Healthier individuals are able to maintain a sense of the curious, and they are interested in change and growth. More rigidly organized individuals are more likely to say, "This is the way it is, I can't help it, I'm not interested in changing, other people don't understand who I really am."

In terms of clinical assessment, we must determine whether the consciously exhibited strengths, standards, and aspirations in Quadrant One are overly determined or if they are well grounded in reality. We can accomplish this by assessing the degree of intensity or overdetermination of these internalized standards, and we can begin to wonder with our patients what happens if they fall short, make a mistake, experience roadblocks in their path. In addition we can begin to assess the balance between self-care and personal aspirations, noting which relational dynamics and/or conflicts come into play when the patient attempts to balance interpersonal needs with personal ambitions or what symptoms begin to emerge when the patient experiences roadblocks or disappointed aspirations.

As a means of providing further clarity, we have provided a continuum of attributes and beliefs found with Quadrant One, ranging from relative health to pathology. We have offered a range of specific examples from both ends of the continuum as well as a mid-point as a way of illustrating the movement from authentic self-appraisal and confidence to compulsively driven measures the individual will take. These compulsive measures are an attempt to preserve the illusion of the constructed picture of the self

QUADRANT ONE

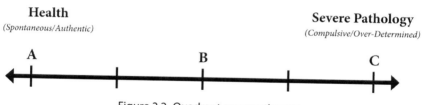

Figure 2.2 Quadrant one continuum.

whether that picture is a reflection of a grandiose overidealization or a distorted devaluation of self-worth.

Example A

Realistic appraisal of one's self-worth and accomplishments, able to remain curious about one's values and ideals, able to modify and expand one's ideas to include greater and greater degrees of complexity, able to see mistakes and receive constructive criticism as an opportunity to learn and grow, maintain a sense of spontaneity, perspective, balance, and sense of joy and satisfaction in one's accomplishments.

Example B

Aspects of the real self can be activated as evidenced by displays of spontaneity such as sense of humor or some capacity for grief; ability to see some shades of grey, yet secretly holding the belief that one's own view is correct, and others are simply not as well-educated or informed. Has some difficulty receiving constructive criticism or admitting mistakes, but is willing to intellectually consider that everyone makes mistakes, does not actively try to retaliate when others point out negative feedback, but vows to achieve perfection the next time.

Example C

All aspects of the self are compulsively driven, overdetermined, and rigidly held. There is a sense of absolute certainty in the correctness of ideas and beliefs. It is difficult, if not impossible, to admit to mistakes; personal failures and/or disappointments are explained as someone else's fault or due to external circumstances beyond one's control. If there is a sense of humor, it is generally derisive, directed toward poking fun of others. Demands respect and acknowledgment from others and takes self very seriously; rigidly holds onto standards of perfection and believes in the ability to achieve more than is humanly possible; has difficulties accepting limitations of any kind.

Quadrant Two: Conscious/Dystonic

Quadrant Two focuses on symptom formation. You will notice that we have organized this quadrant into a number of symptom clusters. Each cluster presents a slightly different manifestation of how individuals experience and attempt to cope with ruptures or threats to the coherence of the self. These coping strategies can range from how patients attempt to manage episodic breakthroughs of anxiety and/or depression, to the degree to which they attend to basic behaviors of self-care such as bathing, exercise, sleep, and nutrition. The cluster that encompasses addictions (behaviors ranging from substance abuse to eating disorders) can be assessed in terms of the individuals' attempts to achieve a numbing of painful affect and/or feelings of emptiness.

If we understand addictions as attempts to regulate and/or control overly intense, painful, or unwanted feeling states, we are not only able to track the pervasiveness of these behaviors but the underlying meaning of said behaviors as well. In this way we can assess underlying affect dysregulation and the degree of fragility of the coherence of the sense of self. With addictions it is as if feelings in general become the enemy and must be mastered through self-destructive numbing agents. A further dimension of understanding Quadrant Two is to determine whether the eruption of symptoms is consciously or unconsciously triggered by disappointments experienced in Quadrants One and Three. We might ask ourselves, "Do symptoms episodically appear based on disappointments experienced in the syntonic quadrants," or "Are addictive coping strategies used prophylactically as a means of 'self-medicating' through the numbing of feelings altogether?"

Two additional points must be mentioned in terms of understanding the overall scope of Quadrant Two. The first pertains to the relationship between genetic vulnerability and affect regulation or dysregulation as measured by the intensity and degree of symptomatic feeling states. The second pertains to understanding how acute or chronic conditions of trauma have an impact on one's ability to regulate feeling states. This would include episodes of trauma and abuse suffered in childhood as well as acute or repeated episodes of trauma due to war or genocide. Recent literature suggests that whether one is the direct victim or participant of these experiences of trauma or one is merely a witness to "second-hand" abuse, the damage to one's ability to regulate affect can be greatly compromised, thus threatening the stability of the person's underlying psychological make-up. Contributions from neurological and medical research have enhanced our understanding of the complexity and fragility of our neurological circuitry and what seems to affect the neuroplasticity of the brain. Various other models and theories offer additional understanding in terms of the treatment of individuals with a genetic predisposition to depression and anxiety as well as how severe trauma can create a state of hyperarousal leading to an inability to regulate affect and reduce symptoms.

Based on patient reports and our own clinical observation, we can begin to assess the degree to which patients are able to manage and metabolize feeling states as opposed to masking or dissociating from painful feelings. Concerning the latter, a person with debilitating anxiety may experience symptoms as a shameful sign of failure, whereas patients with eating disorders may view their lack of concern over maintaining adequate nutrition as proof that they have control over both their bodies and their environments. Symptoms offer us a window into the source of split-off material and how patients attempt to maintain that split. Our aim when focusing on this quadrant is to gather information in order to understand how beliefs or fears that are held within other quadrants work to maintain a homeostatic balance. It is through the disruption of this balance, through the emergence of symptoms, that we are allowed greater access to seeing how the parts attempt to preserve the existing status quo.

QUADRANT TWO

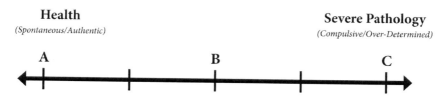

Figure 2.3 Quadrant two continuum.

Example A

Symptoms are generally acute and short-lived, due to external factors such as loss of a relationship, the diagnosis of a physical illness, losses in capacities, either through the aging process or a major life transition. After an initial period of adjustment, however, individuals are able to come to terms with the change in lifestyle or relational supports; they find a place of acceptance, resolve, or peace. Overall functioning during these periods generally remains relatively stable.

Example B

Symptoms are more chronic in nature, ranging from mild to moderate discomfort with a history of repeated episodes of symptomatic complaints throughout the life span. Generally, recovery from disappointments or losses takes longer, and these individuals can resist life transitions such as retirement or the empty nest. They have feelings of being unfairly singled out and often wish for symptoms to "magically" disappear without having to exert the effort to alter their lifestyle or make accommodations for their own physical limitations. This can be accompanied by feelings of resignation fueled by the secret belief that some people never have to suffer painful emotions, or loss. If symptoms are coupled with the lack of adequate supports, the symptoms can turn into more entrenched belief systems and become directly linked to Quadrant Four.

Example C

Symptoms are experienced with more intensity with feeling states threatening dysregulation and a fragmentation of the coherence of self. Affect dysregulation is often coupled with behaviors or wishes that have a self-destructive flavor, such as suicidal thoughts or gestures or addictive escalation. The underlying desire is an attempt to numb or eliminate painful feelings altogether. Severe breakthroughs of symptoms are generally accompanied with feelings of shame and self-loathing. If the therapist suggests medication or other means of support, this is typically seen as a sign of failure and further evidence of the individual's inability to control his or her own feelings.

Quadrant Three: Loyal Waiting—Unconscious or Consciously Hidden/Syntonic

Quadrant Three, "Loyal Waiting," is the quadrant where we most clearly see how feelings, values, beliefs, and ideas are organized within the context of relational expectations. First, let us take a moment to clarify the difference between healthy loyalty and what we are calling "loyal waiting." Healthy loyalty is something that is considered to be a strength, a capacity that is a component of the authentic self. Healthy loyalty is grounded in a realistic appraisal of the relational dynamics between people, dynamics that are based on mutuality and fairness. "Loyal waiting" is a term meant to describe dimensions of relational dynamics that reflect an overdetermined and over-idealized self. Such "loyalty" is not grounded in reality. It represents a manifestation of wishes and hopes for an idealized version of perfection that is projected onto others. Or, it represents the wish for salvation or rescue from one's own pain and suffering.

Loyal waiting is a fantasy construction, originating in the imagination of a child in an attempt to compensate for a depriving, inconsistent, or unsafe home environment. Loyal waiting that is carried into adulthood remains archaic and alive as a fixed structure, one that encapsulates unrequited wishes carried forward from childhood. These wishes may be organized in a number of ways, each reflecting some dimension of compulsively driven strivings. We have provided the following examples of loyal waiting as a means of illustrating how overdetermined loyal waiting might manifest within the patient population.

- An attempt to achieve restitution for early childhood injuries and/or deprivation. In this variant the individual holds on to the fantasy of waiting for "the perfect other" with the belief that perfection exists. The insistence behind this expectation is that the idealized other will make-up for all that was lost or missed in childhood. Often these expectations include the wish to have someone's undivided attention, to never be challenged, to never be disappointed, and to have every need met without having to ask.
- A reenactment of childhood messages that were internalized in the form of parental demands that then become translated into one's idea of the "rules" around what it means to be a loyal person. For example, a parent may say, "I'm your father. You must show me respect," or "No one will ever love you as much as your family," or "Who do you think you are acting like you're smarter than the rest of us." Each of these statements instructs the child that there is something shameful or frightening about moving into the authentic self, and authenticity will cost you relational connection. In each of these examples there is an implicit contract around loyalty that includes some degree of sacrifice of the authentic self in order to preserve one's relationship to others.
- An attempt to be rescued from a belief that the self is defective or worthless. Often individuals who manifest this form of loyalty have internalized negative messages about self-worth from parents. They believe that they don't really deserve anything better than what they experienced in childhood. Because of the paucity of real care, they may

come to doubt that healthy, kind-hearted people even exist. Although the *belief* may appear resigned, the *hope* for rescue from this relational inadequacy is still kept alive. Therefore, the manifestation of this conflict between hope and belief is recapitulated by picking a partner who is less than adequate, and then convincing themselves that the person is their ideal. When faced with disappointments in reality, individuals remain in a position of "loyal waiting" because they secretly believe that they have the power to change their partner into a person who will love them unconditionally if they just say or do the right thing. When faced with disappointments where this does not work, these individuals are apt to blame themselves to preserve the idealized image of the other and therefore to keep the hope for rescue alive.

At the core of each of these pictures of *loyal waiting* is the story of the patient's relational past. It is within this core narrative that we discover the patient's hidden values and cognitions, the wish for absolute answers, and for rescue by the perfect "other." Within this position of loyal waiting we often discover the compensatory motivations behind self-sacrifice or a seemingly passive stance.

Patients essentially remain entrenched in a position of *loyal waiting* because they cannot move beyond an expectation of what is owed to them. The unconscious message seems to be, "I'm not going to move from this position until I get what was missing from my life"; or "I'm not going to move forward in my life because if I do, it means that the person who disappointed me or harmed me will get off scot-free." Often patients choose real relationships that seem to fall short of the mark. Out of their disappointments, we can observe how patients often create fantastical belief systems to help maintain internal comfort, hope, and homeostatic balance. We may observe a martyred stance, or we may find that over time *loyal waiting* turns into a feeling of distain for people who fall short of the idealized standards they themselves are held to.

QUADRANT THREE

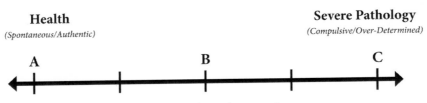

Figure 2.4 Quadrant three continuum.

Example A

Healthy loyalty is the foundation from which long-term relational commitment is born. It has a degree of perseverance as opposed to stubbornness.
It is grounded in reality and a sense of mutuality. It can manifest in many
forms ranging from feelings of love and compassion to a sense of fidelity to
the greater good, or faithfulness to realistic goals such as equality or non-
violence, even if those goals are unreachable in one's lifetime.

Example B

There is either a quick, reflexive tendency to blame others when expectations around perfection are disappointed or there is a tendency to take the
blame back onto the self when disappointments in relationship do not produce the results they had expected. This quick reflex to either internalize
or project blame is less rigidly fixed within the personality in so far as they
are able to maintain an intellectual perspective that is more balanced and
based in behavioral reality. However, this healthier observational perspective seems to be split off from having any effect on the person giving up the
position of loyal waiting. In other words the idea of real relationships that
can be "satisfying enough" does not hold the power to enable the person to
let go of the idealized wish for rescue and/or perfection.

Example C

Beliefs about the perfect, idealized other are rigidly held, with greater
degrees of sacrifice of reality being made in order to maintain the wished for
other. Extreme examples include the type of loyalty that borders on fanati-
cism, either for the perfect person, for salvation, or for sacrifice to a "loyal"
cause. Displays of martyrdom or self-righteousness are not uncommon.
There is an all-or-nothing quality to the relational attachment, whether that
is to an ideal, a partner, a leader, or a religious figure.

Quadrant Four: Unconscious/Dystonic

Quadrant Four captures the part of the psyche that is often buried or unacknowledged. It is the quadrant where shame and anger are tightly interconnected and where prohibitions against the direct expression of negative
feelings are most strongly legislated within the self-system. When negative
feelings or revenge fantasies *are* consciously acknowledged, it is generally in response to what the patient believes is a justified disappointment,
which in turn helps to normalize feelings of revenge or the wish to destroy
or devalue another. Often personal feelings or wishes for retaliation are

justified under the guise of believing that a perceived religious or moral code has been threatened or is about to be violated. Fueled by this moral rationale (or "cultural permission"), individuals allow themselves to be absolved of any feelings of shame or guilt because they are acting in the service of the "greater good."

If the expression of feelings of anger and frustration had been inhibited or punished in childhood, often we will witness those feelings of anger or revenge turn against the self, rather than being outwardly expressed. The person will exhibit self-damaging behaviors or may express feelings of self-hate, self-loathing, severe self-judgment or criticism. Healthy self-esteem or the expression of a more authentic sense of self is virtually absent. As a result, patients fall into behaviors where they constantly test others or ask for proof of their value, or question the trustworthiness of their relationships. It is out of this enactment that negative transferential reactions can also erupt in the treatment. The disavowed or unacknowledged anger, mistrust, and wish for retaliation are projected onto others and eventually onto the therapist if aspects of this quadrant are not addressed directly or sufficiently.

It should be noted that as our culture becomes more polarized and vitriolic, the conscious taboos against acting on impulses and feelings generated from within Quadrant Four appear to be lessening. Lashing out or expressing shaming comments against others is becoming more accepted by the culture at large. The desire to act on one's anger, rage, or disappointment is becoming more conscious and more permissible. No longer is the wish to strike back at another met with an internalized sense of horror or shame. Rather, it is as if the person feels entitled to express disappointment and outrage, something he or she wears with pride and a sign of strength.

QUADRANT FOUR

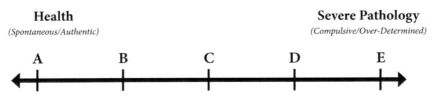

Figure 2.5 Quadrant four continuum.

Example A

Strong feelings such as anger or resentment are appropriate and in the service of self-protection when the authentic self is threatened, under attack, or undermined. There is little shame, guilt, or fear associated with these feelings. Nor does the individual come from a place of self-righteous indignation when expressing negative emotions. Rather, negative emotions are the response to events or behaviors that the individual knows are unfair and undeserved. Negative feelings are expressed directly and transparently, yet there is also an attempt to reach understanding and resolution whenever possible. If negative outbursts do occur, the individual will routinely express feelings of remorse and a wish for reconciliation whenever possible.

Example B

Negative feelings are experienced and expressed with an accompanying sense of guilt, shame, confusion, or ambivalence. Often these feelings are buried, acted out indirectly, minimized, or turned against the self. There is either a denial around these feelings or there is a passive-aggressive quality to the expression of negativity. When negativity erupts, the person may experience an exaggerated sense of guilt. Retaliation may take the form of subtle devaluing, competitiveness, or complaining without offering solutions. In the latter case this is often accompanied by a lack of personal responsibility for looking at one's own contributions. Negativity may also be expressed by testing others, where individuals believe in the right to demand continual proof.

Example C

Strong negative feelings are associated with victory and a sense of enjoyment. Retaliation toward others for feelings of disappointment is experienced in extreme forms, such as feeling a sense of betrayal or outrage. Disappointments are often expressed as a sense of "injustice" as if perfect justice were possible. With all of these extreme frameworks around negative feelings, patients then feel a sense of self-righteousness indignation with respect to their disappointments. This in turn becomes the rationale or justification for retaliation. These individuals believe that rageful acts of retaliation are in the service of some greater good.

APPLICATION

If we focus on this model from a systemic perspective, we can begin to see how each quadrant is helping to hold a homeostatic balance in place, maintaining psychic equilibrium and thus the status quo. Moving from Quadrant One to Quadrant Two may be initially uncomfortable as the exposure of inconsistencies between aspirations and symptoms are being brought to the patient's attention. Over time, however, if one remains curious about the dilemmas or inconsistencies at play within the visible domains, the therapist can subtly prepare the patient to tolerate and articulate material from Quadrant Three and eventually Four.

Within the course of treatment once we begin to sense a patient's developing readiness to tolerate material from one of the two unconscious quadrants, a method can be used to bring this material to the surface, a method we have called *forecasting*. Through the subtle use of language, introducing a word or idea helps frame the emergence of dissociated or unconscious material that had previously been too "hot to handle." Often this can set the stage for the patient to slowly develop a growing curiosity about how to take ownership of previously hidden feelings and wishes.

An example of this might be to begin to introduce the concept of "loyalty" around patient dilemmas about every-day choices, such as a decision to voice one's preference, or set a limit because of feeling overextended. Pairing these struggles around every-day choices and linking them to the concept of loyalty telegraphs permission to become more curious about how one understands the connection between commitment, responsibility, autonomy, and choice. Normalizing these conversations around decision-making and loyalty, we can then leverage further curiosity by wondering whether one must remain loyal forever, or we can wonder if the patient ever experiences any drawbacks or limitations to remaining loyal. In this way something that was previously seen as fixed now becomes subject to discussion, leading to personal revision, fluidity, and integration around one's authenticity.

In designing the Four Quadrant Model, the reader might wonder why we chose the frameworks of *loyalty* and *revenge enactments* as a part of our model. We chose these themes because we believe they capture core struggles within the narcissistic character structure—the defense against vulnerability, the exposure of shameful feelings, and the wish to retaliate when shameful feelings come to the surface of consciousness. The concepts of loyalty and revenge are in many respects the flip sides of a coin, expressing potentially shameful material while also attempting to compensate for the exposure of feelings of vulnerability, of unrequited longing, and shame.

Through the diagram we see how seemingly opposite feelings of self-hate are linked to idealized aspects of the self-system. The Four Quadrant Model illustrates how the hidden aspects of loyalty can erupt in the obstructive wishes for revenge if loyal waiting is not rewarded. Similarly, if wishes for revenge do not result in some restoration of homeostasis, these vindictive urges can turn against the self as reflected by eruptions of acute acting-out behaviors. Finally, we can further understand how a positive transferential position of the patient can quickly erupt into negative transferential feelings if the patient experiences some secret longing or wish as not being gratified by the therapist.

Case Examples That Help Illustrate the Model

Case Example 1

An example of the push/pull tension between symptoms, loyal waiting, and the breakthrough of anger, devaluing, or revenge is illustrated in the following clinical vignette.

A long-term patient who suffered from persistent bouts of anxiety and depression coupled with underlying feelings of shame and inadequacy began one of her therapy sessions by saying that she was furious with the therapist for how she had treated her in their previous meeting. When the therapist asked what triggered this reaction, the patient became vague and elusive and was not able to come up with anything specific. Rather, she reported that she was so upset that she didn't know how to talk about her feelings without harming the relationship in some way.

Upon further inquiry, the patient said that she felt that the therapist had been dismissive in the last session, stating that she felt that she had trivialized her fears about losing her looks. She informed the therapist that she was tired of talking about her father's detachment and mother's dependency. She refused to believe that her flirtations with a recent male acquaintance, an older married man, had anything to do with the intense resurgence of her feelings of self-loathing, anxiety, and emptiness. The patient said that she was fed up with connecting everything back to "issues from her childhood."

She said, "We've been through all of this analysis before. I know it by heart. If you can't have a real conversation with me in the present about my real feelings about losing my looks, then perhaps the therapy has outlived its usefulness."

The therapist responded by saying, "You say I could be more helpful to you if we stayed focused on your very real concerns about aging? Is there something more that you would like to share with me now?"

With that invitation, the patient began to talk about aging, how her beauty had always given her a sense of power that she was able to use it to get attention and to feel special, but that now these strategies didn't seem to be working very well. Furthermore, she stated that she didn't think that the therapist seemed to be interested in how much looks really matter in this world. "Why don't you understand that? You're an aging woman too." As she talked, rather than feeling better, the patient began to become more agitated, saying that this talk was making her feel worse. Then, in exasperation, the patient expressed the wish that her therapist would do something.

When the therapist asked what she would like her to do, the patient eventually revealed that listening and talking are not enough. She admitted that she wanted the therapist to make her feel better by saying just the right thing. "I guess I still keep hoping that one of these days you're going to fix me, give me a magic pill that will take away all of this emptiness inside of me. At the very least you can tell me that it's ok to have plastic surgery."

The therapist's reply was to say, "And when that doesn't happen, you feel that the therapy is no longer useful, and that somehow if I can't do something to take this pain away, then I am not being effective."

At this point, the patient breaks into a slight smile, catching herself in old, unrequited longings, and says, "I'm not saying that. I just get so frustrated sometimes. Why does this process take so long?" (With this comment, it should be noted that the negative transferential tension had been temporarily broken, and the patient and therapist could begin to process what happened together).

One of the comments the therapist made to the patient at that juncture centered on letting her know how important it was that she was able to express her anger and disappointment directly. The therapist told her that it showed that on some level she trusted their relationship enough to begin to reveal uncomfortable feelings more directly. The therapist also wondered aloud if the patient was worried that the therapist might become angry or retaliate in some way. By raising this fear in the form of a question, the therapist could voice a hidden fear and dilute the transferential tension even further. The therapist followed this question by reflecting on the contrast between how they were able to 'weather this storm' vs. what her parents' typical response would have been. The patient was then able to volunteer that, yes it was quite different, reflecting that her parents would turn a cold shoulder or withdraw whenever she made a request of them or tried to express her frustrations.

Case One Analysis

In this brief clinical vignette we see all four quadrants at play. The patient's former reliance on her looks (idealized standards of perfection from Quadrant One) was now beginning to be threatened as the patient gradually confronted her aging. Symptoms of anxiety, fear, and irritability (Quadrant Two) became a threat to the patient's emotional equilibrium as she struggled with the loss of her looks which she equated with her own feelings of power and control. In this session the progress of the therapy reveals that the patient has moved past the relational position of depression at the beginning of treatment and has entered into a more affectively charged transferential communication with the therapist. For the moment she has lost her patience and has given up her position of "loyal waiting" (Quadrant Three) for her therapist to "do something." The defensive split between loyal waiting and her wish for revenge, as expressed by her anger at the therapist (Quadrant Four), is now beginning to teeter. The homeostatic balance between syntonic and dystonic is disrupted. This signals the beginning of unpermitted feelings of rage as her formerly unconscious/dystonic wishes to retaliate begin to break through. The mounting intensity of these feelings has begun to overshadow and overtake her daily efforts to remain perfectly controlled and to be seen as desirable in the eyes of her romantic love interests. As mentioned, in her youth this had been an effective distraction from her feelings of emptiness.

The primary posture of this patient and the principal thrust of the therapy up to this point had been the focus on her debilitating symptoms of depression (Quadrant Two) as well as her sexually provocative behavior enacting unrequited wishes and longings. By connecting the timing of the eruption of symptoms with her self-destructive provocative acting out (Quadrant Four turned against the self), the therapist was able to set the stage for a partial integration of a split. With this session the dawning realization that her old coping strategies were no longer working began to be integrated into conscious awareness. As we can see, the patient's impatience and anger vigorously manifest and begin to unfold through the transferential communication. It is here that we see the hidden wish beginning to emerge—if the patient can no longer rely on her old strategies, then the therapist must step up to the plate and rescue her from her feelings of disappointment, grief, and emptiness. What remains at this point is to continue to track dystonic unconscious dynamics, to continue to try to keep them "in the room," and to make the connection back to the symptomatic pain that the patient has been suffering. By holding all of these parts simultaneously, eventually the patient will hopefully discover that the authentic aspects of herself can grow and replace her old pattern of self-destructive acting out.

The therapeutic challenge when negative transferential responses emerge is to understand that it is usually because of some disappointment in Quadrant Three that has not become consciously manifest as a part of the treatment. Articulating the wishes contained within Quadrant Three often has a mitigating effect on the negative transference reaction without confronting it directly. Only after several dynamic exchanges in this quadrant can we, as therapists, gain purchase with language that more closely names the affective wish for angry retaliation in Quadrant Four. Using language to name negative feelings and wishes helps to normalize those responses and invites them into conscious awareness and dialogue. In this way we can begin to tackle deep seated issues of deprivation and longing directly.

In addition once we truly understand the connections and the interrelationship between the quadrants, we are then able to hold a more dynamic and complete picture of the patient. We are also able to more effectively use the "moment-to-moment" tracking of material presented to facilitate a deeper level of inquiry eventually leading to the integration of the splits. This is what we mean by staying in the *phenomenological present*. Using language to help "forecast" negative feelings, in addition to addressing negatively charged comments or feelings when they erupt in the treatment, demonstrates the therapist's comfort with handling material contained within Quadrant Four. This also indirectly conveys to the patient that all parts of the self are welcomed, that it is possible to not only understand but also normalize much of what used to be considered taboo.

Case Example Two

A second clinical example illustrates a breakthrough in the treatment in terms of penetrating and then neutralizing the negative feelings and wishes contained in Quadrant Four. With this patient the old homeostatic balance preserved the split between over-exaggerated pride (Quadrant One) coupled with a profound wish for rescue (Quadrant Three) used as a defense against humiliating disillusionment and disappointment. In this case vignette we begin to see a shift toward a more realistic appraisal of self and others.

Note the shift that is beginning to occur in the patient's thinking, particularly with regard to how she holds the relationship between her standards for performance, her wish for rescue, and her harsh self-appraisal. This vignette exemplifies a partial resolution of the split contained between these quadrants.

Patient: I think that it is finally dawning on me that it's really, really hard to be a single parent. I don't know what I was thinking before, that this should be easier for me than it was. And I've also been realizing that maybe the reason I resented my kids was that they reminded me of the reality of just how hard it is to be a good parent. I kept hoping that Jeffrey would pick up the pieces, especially when it came to parenting his own son, a son who needs a male role model so desperately. But, I guess I can't keep waiting for him to miraculously change, and I can't keep making excuses for him either. I'm so mad at him! Why did it take me so long to see this? But, you know, the funny thing is while I feel more anger at his failures, I also feel so much more distance from him. It's clear to me now that it's time to move forward with the divorce. I know that this will mean that I have so much more on my plate, but I guess I will just have to buckle down and do it. And I will do it.

Therapist: You know as I listen to you, I hear less rage against this unfairness, not that the situation isn't terribly unfair.

Patient: I know what you mean. I do feel less rage, but I think it's because I've given up on him. I've given up on the hope that he will ever really be able to rescue me. I have to do this on my own, and nobody else can do it.

Therapist: Well, just because you're seeing that rescue was never really an option doesn't mean that you are without support or that you must shoulder all of this alone. In fact, you have already taken steps to get more support for your son with the school guidance counselor, his teachers, and a tutor. Remember, we have talked about support and rescue not being the same.

Patient: I know, I know. And I did feel a sense of relief when I called the school and reached out. I also feel that I finally have a solid group of friends that I can be myself around which is really exciting. But, even with all of that, I know I have to buckle down and do my work. I feel more focused even though so much more has been dumped on my plate. But, I also have been able to tell myself that if I'm tired, I'm entitled to take a half hour nap if I need to.

Therapist: Yes, so we can see that when you used to try to minimize the reality of your situation, it was actually that misappraisal of the reality of your situation that helped fuel your feeling of failure. So, when you are able to anchor yourself in the reality that is before you, this is what actually allows for the birth of gentleness toward yourself.

Patient: Yes, you're right. That's pretty amazing, don't you think?

Case Two Analysis

In this clinical example as contrasted with the first, we see some of the rewards of persistent moment-to-moment tracking, bringing dissociated/

unconscious material to the surface both in Quadrant Three with loyal waiting and also in Quadrant Four. Part of the breakthrough occurs after repeated tracking of the connection between increased symptomotology (Quadrant Two) and increased self-damaging thoughts and behaviors (Quadrant Four) whenever she became disappointed in her own failures to meet performance standards, the very standards that she set for herself and secretly for her husband in terms of her wish for rescue.

By understanding the inter-relationship between the quadrants and repeatedly pointing out this connectivity to the patient, she is gradually able to let go of her unrequited longings. The extent of the integration can be measured by the decrease in severity of symptoms and self-harming thoughts and behaviors. In addition we see an increase in healthy functioning with an increase in efficiency around her use of time, an increase in hopefulness, and a more realistic appraisal of self and others.

The two case examples above are meant to offer a beginning familiarity with the model and how it can be used to understand what it takes to uncover and heal splits within the self-system. This model illustrates a visual representation of "meta-process in action," or how one can operationalize the macro- and the micro-attention required through part-whole analysis. When we frame our understanding of how change occurs through visualizing the entire self-system at once, we are better able to see the connection between contradictory communications on the part of our clients. Using the Four Quadrant Model, for example, allows us to see how a patient can both strive for a rigid standard of perfection and hold a hidden longing for rescue at the same time.

This macro-level of understanding self-systems is also a non-linear framework, one that enables clinicians to open up the possibility of micro-level processing of clinical material through the technique of moment-to-moment tracking. It is rare for a theory of character pathology to become so immediately useful in "experience-near" terms. If the practical application of theory is to be effective, the proof is in the application.

SUMMARY

The model presented in this chapter provides a macro-level of the entire snap-shot of how the characterological self-systems are interconnected to form a tightly woven homeostatic balance. Using the tools of *moment-to-moment tracking* and *forecasting* allows us to become more adept at tracking the contextual details of the micro-level process that unfolds within the therapeutic exchange. Through this use of moment-to-moment tracking of material contained within the four quadrants, we have the essentials of a *process methodology* to help us become more proficient in experience-near therapy, particularly increasing our understanding of how splits function in the psyche. When we become clearer about recognizing splits as well as understanding how they function, we can become more adept at attending to the integration of the splits in the unfolding relational exchange in the present. Our aim in this chapter has been to provide a model that can be replicated and applied in experience-near terms. This is our understanding of how theory meets practice.

Questions from Trainees about the Model

As a means of reviewing the application of this model and the concepts covered in this chapter, we have provided a list of questions that our trainees have recorded. Hopefully, their questions and our responses will shed more light on a means of helping to further explain the model of how one holds the dialectic tension between self-systems in a non-linear way.

Question: In terms of application, which character pathologies or diagnoses most apply to the use of this model?

Response: The model isn't meant to be used in the same way we diagnose character disorders according to the DSM. Rather, we invite you to conceptualize character pathology as a means of recognizing fault lines in the personality. The greater the number and the depth of the fault lines, the more damage, trauma, or deprivation that has occurred; therefore, the fragility is likely to be reflected in the functioning of the personality. One could use the quadrant system as a way of assessing the *intensity* of the position the patient holds around the construction of the character solution, which in turn is reflected within the relationship between the quadrants. In short, assessing the level of intensity is a way that the model can be used to understand character formation.

In terms of listening in the present we could use the model in a slightly different way. For example, if we focused on Quadrant One, we might begin by paying attention to how rigidly the individual holds his or her standards, aspirations, and beliefs. When a patient talks about his aspirations and accomplishments, we might begin to wonder about what is not being said. We also might begin to wonder how he feels about making a mistake or falling short. Or we may try to link the patient's aspirations with symptom complaints. This gives us an entry point into a deeper level of inquiry. By asking a question in this way, we have illustrated an example of what we mean by "forecasting," an inquiry technique where we ask questions or use language to begin to create bridges to help the patient "connect the dots" and promote integration.

Question: Does that mean that we are to start with Quadrant One and then move to Quadrant Two, and so forth?

Response: No, not at all. Listening is a circular process. The model is seen as a circular system, where the therapist can enter any quadrant without following any particular order. Part of how we achieve the circular fluidity that the model illustrates is to stay as closely immersed in the present as possible. We ask questions based on the content or affect that the patient provides in the session. That is what is meant by phenomenological or moment-to-moment tracking. Our aim in staying in the phenomenological present is to go deeper, to get more information, a fuller context, in order to immerse ourselves in a more complete understanding of the patient's subjective experience.

Of course, it is tempting to try to reify or rigidify any new model or any translation of theory into practice, which is something we have to guard against. In this case one way we can recognize our tendency to drift toward reification is when we begin trying to apply the theory or model in a linear fashion. Linear thinking as it applies to listening generally misses the mark. We do not challenge ourselves to see therapy as an unfolding process. The model reminds us to hold the intrapsychic, interpersonal, and systemic picture in a way that is fluid. What we're talking about here is trying to find a way of holding the *spirit of the model*, rather than nail down a set of absolute rules.

Question: I guess I don't see the simultaneous intrapsychic, interpersonal, and systemic. I see the first two parts, but not the systemic piece.

Response: A systemic perspective allows us to see how each quadrant and each aspect of intrapsychic and interpersonal are parts of an interconnected whole. This allows us to see both the part and the whole simultaneously. In other words, we can ask ourselves, "How rigidly held is the homeostatic balance between internal and external, how rigid are the intrapsychic rules and the person's interpersonal rules for external engagement? Is there tolerance for difference or disagreement between people without stirring up powerfully negative feelings? Is there room for fluidity, curiosity, introspection, and self-reflection within the psyche?

We often think about these questions in terms of a measure of ego capacities if we are looking through an intrapsychic lens. But they can also be seen as forming a systemic, homeostatic balance that is relationally glued together. We can ask ourselves whether there are any limiting exceptions to the degree of functionality. For example, can the patient's response and organizing schematic be triggered by a given situation, the setting, socio-cultural influences, or external stressors in the environment?

Question: The decision-making process about which quadrant to focus on is still confusing to me. I assume that each quadrant can be invoked by the content material that comes up in a session, correct? How do I know when I am speaking to an issue too quickly for the patient to process meaning-fully? Sometimes it feels like trial and error, and at times, I end up saying "oops, that was too soon, or that didn't work because it seems to provoke a defensive response."

Response: Some of what we do *is* a trial and error process. Some of it is also an issue of timing. Moving to an interpretation too quickly or toward solu-tions or suggestions often results in further entrenchment into a defensive posture on the part of the patient. When this occurs, we do have the oppor-tunity to notice the reaction and possibly offer a comment or observation in a gentle way about the patient's reaction. This may be all that is needed to get us back on track. It offers us the opportunity to gather more informa-tion from the patient about what just happened, or it may move us into a transferential situation. It's difficult to say without having a specific example. However, in a general sense, staying within the syntonic side of the model and getting as much information as possible helps us to move into asking questions about what is not being said or what is being muted or ignored in terms of the patient's reactions or responses.

Question: I'm having a hard time keeping the model in my head during the session. There's too much going on, too much to pay attention to as a fairly new therapist. I find that when I think about the session afterwards, how-ever, I find that I can use the model as a learning tool. Sometimes I can see what I missed or a different direction I could have gone if I think about the case in terms of the complexity of the model. Will this ever change? Will I get quicker at this?

Response: Yes, to all of the above. Understanding the complexity of the parts and the whole takes time. It takes time and practice. Thinking about your sessions after the fact and trying to apply theory is always helpful. Even with more seasoned therapists we find that thinking about the various dimensions of the person, where there are splits, where the patient is able to integrate aspects of the self into a unified whole, is a difficult formulation process.

However, the model seems to be particularly useful when clinicians feel as though they are "stuck" with a case. Generally, what we find is that when a clinician is feeling stuck, he or she is being drawn into an over-focus on one quadrant. Often what happens is that an unwitting collusion begins to occur. One way to think about this is to understand that collusions essentially are unconscious agreements not to talk about areas of the psyche (or other quadrants) if we sense that this makes the patient (or ourselves) uncomfortable. Shifting back to thinking about the other quadrants outside of a session is a useful way of helping us get "unstuck."

Initially it is hard to understand the complexity of the model on a systemic, intrapsychic, and relational level simultaneously. It is also difficult to achieve a sense of mastery in using the model as a way of deepening the inquiry process of uncovering hidden or unconscious or split-off material out of which integration can occur. Finally, there is the question of the therapist's style or personal blind spots. Even the best therapist can fall into a drift of joining the client in one area of communication and introspection and avoiding others. The model, in this particular instance, can serve as a useful way to help pull us back to a more balanced, complete, and dynamic view of the person.

(Note: A final question came from a first year supervisee in our training program whose background was primarily cognitive-behaviorally based. He presented a fairly pointed challenge to us.)

Question: Why should I take the time to learn this dynamic model of yours? Can you give me a good reason why I should pay attention to the unconscious, much less the various components of unconscious communication? What risk do we run by only trying to address conscious solutions to problems?"

Summary Response and Our Reflections: This trainee's questions are good ones, and unless we can provide straightforward, practical answers to new clinicians in the field, the power of long-term dynamic therapy is at some degree of risk. Our answer to his question actually directed him back to the culture at large. We asked, given the polarizing drift toward absolutes, the increased demand for the quick fix and simple answers, isn't it the job of the therapist to remain a voice that champions the value of understanding the complexity of issues? Isn't it our job to help people build their capacities of reflection and introspection, healing split-off parts of the psyche and integrating them into a richer whole?"

We said that we believed that working with the unconscious or split-off parts of the psyche was important and suggested that persistent double-binding from childhood creates out-of-awareness, compulsive, and self-sustaining "solutions" which short-circuit growth. We then asked him if cognitive-behavioral interventions are able to address double-binding. Of course, his answer was no.

In terms of our training institutions and the preparation of new generations of therapists, it is critically important to shift our focus back to a reference point where we understand and are able to map the various domains of the psyche, both conscious and unconscious, looking at both historical factors and present conditions that inhibit or impinge upon growth. Remaining with this foundational stance gives the therapist a greater chance to see the whole picture and move out of a reactive position. It also serves as a chance to protect long-term integrative therapy from becoming a dying art.

CHAPTER 3

Compulsive Resolutions
Idealization, Loyalty, and Revenge Enactments

Among the drives toward actualizing the idealized self, 'the need for perfection' is the most radical one. It aims at nothing less than molding the whole personality into the idealized self. Like Pygmalion in Bernard Shaw's version, the neurotic aims not only at retouching but at remodeling himself into his special kind of perfection prescribed by the specific features of his idealized image.

—KAREN HORNEY (1950, P. 24–25)

DIFFERENTIATING BETWEEN THE
AUTHENTIC AND OVERIDEALIZED SELF

The development of the authentic or "real" self is an inherent outcome of the individuation process: an inherent outcome, that is, if certain relational conditions are in place. Those conditions essentially require adult caregivers who possess the capacity to nourish and support a child's unique qualities in an environment that provides the right amount of safety, love, and consistency. As a result of these relational conditions having been met, the child is then able to consolidate a sense of unconditional love paired with fair, reality-based expectations and consequences, ones that encourage the child to achieve his or her full potentialities while simultaneously teaching a sense of mutuality and respect for others.

Clients come to us because one or more of these conditions were missing from the relational equation of their development. Through the therapeutic process, the road to the discovery and integration of the client's authentic self is something that we bank on, for we know well in advance that the hard work of therapy is a journey that ultimately can bring more than its fair share of rewards. For those of us who bear witness to the fruits of this labor, we find that facilitating deep, reparative work acts as its own confirmation, one that enables us to guide the therapeutic process in patient and quiet ways.

Ultimately, our empathic immersion into the unfolding of the stories of our clients' lives results in a shift in their ability to experience and hold their own vulnerability. Rather than associating pain and uncertainty *simply* as a source of weakness or shame, they come to realize that it is out of this well-spring of vulnerability that they are able to develop the capacity for tenderness, compassion for others, and an open curiosity that lead to growth and creativity throughout their life span.

Exposure to one's emotional vulnerability seems to be a fair price to pay in exchange for the benefits that come as a result of perseverance, introspection, and the willingness to learn from the therapeutic process. Equipped with these tools and the compassionate support of the therapist, individuals find that over time they are able to discover their own unique potential, achieve a sense of healthy mastery, appreciate their vitality, discover an internal sense of well-being, and feel a deep sense of love and connection in relationships. From this vantage-point of an authentic, relationally connected self, it is often painful to see the compulsive drive toward what Karen Horney calls "neurotic perfectionism." And yet, this is where so many of our patients begin.

On the surface authentic self-expression and the compulsive strivings for perfectionism may look very much the same. After all, ambition, hard work resulting in a sense of accomplishment, and a desire to leave one's mark are part of what we are taught defines a successful life. When it comes to identifying what is at the core of those motivations, however, Horney, as well as Winnicott, DeRosis, Rubin and others, make a clear distinction between the type of ambition that leads to the healthy development of our potentialities *vs.* a pseudo-resolution to the self-actualization process. Horney describes this form of overdetermined ambition as something that is driven by nothing short of perfectionism or what she has termed "the search for glory."

The search for glory is an apt and quite succinct description of the continuum of the narcissistic struggle and the varying degrees of injuries which impede the development and emergence of the real self. The phrase itself telegraphs a picture of a dynamic process that captures both the *motivation and the energy* required of individuals who were not able or allowed to develop real self-confidence and inner strength.

What are the conditions that constitute the failure of a fuller emergence of the real self? Generally, these conditions can be traced to early parental failures, ones that span the continuum of mild to severe trauma and deprivation, or some combination therein. The free and spontaneous development of the authentic self becomes gravely compromised as the child resorts to mechanisms of self-protection that form compulsively driven organizing schemas regarding self and self-in-relationship. The shift away from the development of a reality-based authentic self and a move to the creation of the "idealized self" will have a major impact on the course of the individual's entire development. As this shift from the real to the ideal progresses (Horney, 1950), it "exerts a molding influence upon the whole personality" (p. 24). The process of how the idealized organizing schemas come into being will be discussed at a later point in this chapter.

There are numerous other theorists, using slightly different language, who have identified how the construction of the idealized self comes into being. Winnicott (1960) coined the term "false self" to describe a process where the real self becomes buried in an attempt to manage tensions within the psyche and in relation to the external environment. He states that if the mother's adaptation to the child's needs is "not good enough," a corresponding withdrawal on the part of the child begins to take place. "In practice the infant lives, but lives falsely. The protest against being forced into a false existence can be detected from the earliest stages" (p. 146).

Winnicott goes on to state that as the child matures, this presentation of the false self extends into building up a false set of relationships. Individuals become so good at this, that the presentation even attains a show of being real. Winnicott (1960) states:

> A particular danger arises out of the not infrequent tie-up between the intellectual approach and the False Self . . . The world may observe academic success of a high degree, and may find it hard to believe in the very real distress of the individual concerned, who feels 'phoney' the more he or she is successful. When such individuals destroy themselves in one way or another, instead of fulfilling promise, this invariably produces a sense of shock in those who have developed high hopes of the individual (p. 144).

Generally, this creation of the idealized or false self becomes so fixed or all-encompassing that the individual seems to have no way of regaining access to the real self. As observers, we may have a visceral reaction to such individuals, an intuitive sense that what the person is presenting to us is "not real," not the whole picture. We may experience a mild annoyance or mistrust, and may even be able to sense some degree of anxiety and/or uncertainty that permeates these individuals' lives.

Louis DeRosis (1974) used the term "the invented self" in reference to the "false self" or the "overidealized self." He states that the seeds of the invented self emerge as a result of a struggle within the personality that first begins to take shape in childhood. He states that all children develop in an "emotional greenhouse," one in which the moment-by-moment environmental influences of the child's caregivers and peers form a pattern of relating that helps shape the child's sense of self-agency and self-worth as well as the sense of self in relation to others. The quality of parental attention, the degree of distortions and expectations that are passed from parent to child, become the parameters and the reference points out of which the child's sense of self begins to emerge. If this greenhouse environment contains a number of contradictory influences that are imposed on the child, and if these contradictory influences are too severe or unsafe, the child loses his way and begins a separation process from the real self. This is an unconscious attempt to mitigate the suffering and internal tension he experiences as a result of being engaged in these relational contradictions (p. 109–10).

The development of the idealized self is not to be confused with ideals, aspirations, and values that healthy individuals possess. Horney highlights the difference between normal aspirations and overdetermined ideals by presenting a number of noteworthy traits or behaviors that help organize and consolidate a picture of the idealized self. In chapter 2 we presented a continuum of behavioral examples ranging from the healthy expression of one's desires, aspirations, and ambitions vs. the compulsively constricted expressions of the narcissistic injury that result in the creation of the overidealized self.

Because each of us is likely to have learned at least some compensatory mechanisms of self-protection in terms of our interactions with others and the development our own potential, the list of traits that are described below may sound familiar or hit somewhat close to home. They are meant to capture qualities or degrees of overcompensation. Where the line is crossed into compulsively driven disturbances is, again, a matter of how much of the psychic energy is used in the service of maintaining the idealized self-image, how much of reality must be sacrificed in order to maintain the insistence of the individual's defensively driven world view.

A LIST OF TRAITS THAT COMPRISE THE CONSTRUCTION OF THE OVERIDEALIZED SELF

First and foremost, these individuals are *compulsively* driven to express their idealized selves, to prove it in action if you will. Whether that means being the best at everything they do or achieving recognition or reward, this compulsion lives out in the person, not as a conscious choice where one can turn away from his or her overdetermined strivings at will. Rather, the idealized self must *prove his or her ambitions in order to avoid danger* (Horney 1950). The formation of the idealized self at its core is compensatory, an attempt to escape painful feelings of anxiety, shame, or fears of annihilation. In contrast, persons who manifest an authentic self will express ambition and the desire to reach their potential in more spontaneous, light-handed ways. Authentically grounded individuals seem to be able to balance their personal ambitions with other needs that are equally important, such as the need to grow as human beings and the need to achieve fulfillment in personal relationships. Therefore, *the degree to which a person can balance personal ambition with a respect for others or a desire for intimate connection* becomes a determining factor in terms of assessing the degree of health and pathology.

Second, persons with narcissistic injury tend to enact their compulsive pursuits in ways that appear to be *insatiable, indiscriminate, and short-lived*. Recognition or admiration may produce a momentary glow of elation, but the feeling of elation becomes difficult to hold in memory, as if the feeling has an elusive quality, one that tends to evaporate very quickly. The excitement about a job promotion, the purchase of the new car, new vacation home, for example, is quickly followed by a letdown, as evidenced by despondency, a sense of emptiness and confusion, or feelings of franticness or irritability. In an attempt to overcome or avoid these difficult feelings, these individuals quickly search for the next person, the next goal, the next distraction to keep these buried feelings of inadequacy and emptiness at bay.

A third way persons struggling to compensate for narcissistic injury can be identified is through the measure of their reaction to *frustration and disappointment*. The more intensified the reaction, the greater the compulsion that drives the idealized self. Any mistake, any sign of failure is met with feelings of shame or disgrace, coupled with harsh criticism or rage that may be directed either at the self or at others. Fears around disappointment are generally anticipated with an acute hypervigilance that stems from an effort to avoid painful feelings at all costs. Any disagreement with ideas, any feedback that is short of absolute praise is met with contempt and anger. Feedback for these people is generally heard in absolute terms. A negative comment, even constructive criticism, results in a crushing blow to the idealized self. It is difficult for these individuals to balance negative feedback in the context of the whole picture or message that is being delivered. Instead, they interpret any need for improvement as a sign of being worthless or a complete failure.

For example, if an eighteen year old son asks his mother to stop interrupting him when he is talking to his father, the mother may respond by saying that her son doesn't love her, or that she must be a lousy mother. As a result of the mother's internal pressure to achieve an idealized status in her son's eyes, she is apt to hear his simple request as a criticism, a blow to the idealized image she sets for herself. Needless to say, these individuals are hypersensitive to criticism, block feedback that runs counter to their own expectations, and have difficulty modulating their own disappointments. They often demand proof of loyalty through tests requiring others to live up to idealized standards. If others fall short, they become the target of the individual's contempt or rage. Conversely, they may revert in an attempt to get sympathy, hoping to return to the old status quo of relational interaction where the child must comply to maintain mother's approval. Any failure to live up to the idealized standards then makes the one who "failed the test" worthy of derision, a target for punishment or retaliation.

The fourth personality feature found in narcissistically damaged individuals is that they have a tendency to believe that *whatever they think, feel, or do should not carry any adverse consequences.* They know that there are laws, for example, but somehow don't really believe that laws should apply to them. They may become outraged when they get a speeding ticket, get caught by the IRS for not paying their taxes, or become puzzled and hurt when a colleague is upset by their negative outbursts at work. Although these individuals believe that they have the right to express themselves freely, including voicing anger, distain, or contempt of others, they become enraged and/or wounded if they are slighted in any way. This is not to say that most people don't experience *some* degree of frustration over receiving a speeding ticket or feedback that is difficult to hear. However, it is the *degree of entitlement* and the *intensity of the reaction to minor slights and disappointments* that reveal the precarious foothold the idealized self has over maintaining its special status. When threatened, one's entire sense of equilibrium is punctured. This is clearly evidenced when real adversity or hardship occur. It seems to shake the very foundation of the idealized self, throwing these individuals into a state of momentary panic, collapse, or psychic fragmentation.

A fifth feature of individuals with narcissistic injury is their *insistence that life should be filled with unlimited possibilities.* As Horney points out, the drive for the *absolute* and the *ultimate* are so stringent in these individuals that the reality checks that most of us come to accept in terms of the concrete limitations of life are absent. The wishes and fantasies of these individuals are fused with their severe narcissistic vulnerabilities. The idealized self, in other words, uses imagination in the service of detachment from any impingement, as if the desire to keep all options open will some-day result in a state of ultimate perfection and bliss. Any checks and bal-ances on the idealized expansiveness of imagination are experienced as an irritation, as individuals come to expect ultimate success, perpetual vitality, and enough wealth that they will never have to put a limit on their desires.

For all of us the very act of having to make a choice naturally precludes the possibility that all other options remain open. In an attempt to avoid the experienced constriction of facing this reality, narcissistically damaged indi-viduals will often employ delay tactics to circumvent *taking the responsibility of making clear choices*. This may manifest as a pattern of having problems making a commitment. These individuals often enter into relationships in a "dance of ambivalence," displaying a push/pull pattern, voicing irritation around feeling pressured to commit. However, when they fear that their partner is about to end the relationship, feelings of overwhelming anxiety may compel them to make promises of fidelity that they later cannot keep. In addition these individuals often regret *any* choice once it has been made. They will also describe a feeling of restlessness in terms of where to direct their focus of attention. When the choice that they eventually make fails to bring the fulfillment expected, they begin to second-guess themselves, won-dering if a different alternative would have brought them more "perfect" contentment.

Whether the early family environment was one of deprivation or over-indulgence, these individuals come to associate limitation with defeat, depression, or constriction, all of which threaten to expose underlying feelings of emptiness or despair. In extreme cases, even benign limitation, such as coming down with an illness or becoming fatigued because of lack of sleep are associated with signs of weakness. It is as if the idealized self is striving to surpass his or her humanness by becoming super human. Even basic physical requirements of self-care feel like an annoyance and ought not to apply to them. At the same time, these individuals do not take personal responsibility to fulfill their hopes and dreams. They expect that other people should provide what they need, or pave the way to pointing out strategies that will lead them to the "perfect solution." Therefore, when faced with disappointment, they are quick to blame others for their unhap-piness and spend little if any time on self-reflection or learning from mis-takes in order to do better the next time.

A sixth feature has to do with *how these individuals attend to feedback from the outside world*. With a fair degree of regularity they attend to envi-ronmental feedback in ways that are *not well-grounded in reality*. Instead of taking in a more or less complete picture of available information, "red flags" about others or situations that may prove to be risky, these individuals seem to pick and choose what information gets acknowledged, only taking in information that already confirms their existing beliefs and/or wishes about self and others. For example, if persons hold a harsh, internalized standard about their performance, it may be extremely difficult for them to believe positive feedback from others about their work efforts. Or, these individuals may only attend to factors that underscore *their* greatness, searching for examples of performance that highlight other peoples' limitations. As mentioned, while searching for the idealized other, these individuals are often prone to miss obvious red flags of concern. Instead, the change process itself becomes idealized.

A seventh manifestation of the compulsive neurotic strivings of the idealized self is measured by how *these individuals attempt to gain a sense of self confidence or achieve a state of contentment.* Confidence is measured by proving oneself, and is, in fact, dependent on it and the feedback received. In terms of contentment, these individuals often complain of feelings of restlessness or boredom. There are no islands of respite, nor is there security in the knowledge that they are loved. They seldom feel a sense of peace when they are at rest and have difficulty enjoying something that is completely outside of themselves, such as the accomplishments of others or the beauty of nature.

Overall, for individuals with an overdetermined sense of the idealized self, accomplishments are not experienced with a sense of true joy. Instead, all nuance of feeling is conflated into a feeling of pride. Because feelings of pride are dependent on accomplishment and praise, failure to reach one's goal often produces a deep sense of self contempt. In fact, all feelings and motivations seem to fluctuate between two extreme alternatives—an inflated sense of pride and a deep sense of self-hate. When the individual's pride is wounded, there is an extreme swing toward self-contempt or self-hate that may or may not also become displaced and projected onto others. Both the overinflated sense of pride and the experience of self-loathing work together as a system to keep the authentic self from emerging. One of the ways of understanding the Four Quadrant Model is to picture each of the quadrants working in conjunction to keep the pride system in place.

For example, people with highly perfectionistic standards take great pride in trying to attain a state of "flawlessness." Although impossible to attain, they will persist in trying and will also insist that others live up to these same standards as well. When others fail to do so, they will be despised or disparaged; thus, perfectionists can externalize their own self-condemnation, keeping their sense of pride intact. The construction of the idealized self can be viewed as an individual attempting to manage the tension points between his or her inflated expectations, which manifest in the form of pride, and the shattering of those expectations, which results in the self collapsing into feelings of self contempt. An apt description of this dynamic tension is described by Horney (1950) as one entity, which she has termed the *pride system* (p. 111).

Others have referred to this concept as *systemic pride*. From a systemic perspective idealization and contempt are parts of an interlocking whole. Each is dependent on the other when assessing how one "measures up" relative to others. When the standards one uses to assess personal worth and value are overdetermined and compulsively driven, we can be sure that the experience of shame is at the core. The creation of the idealized self is the individual's attempt to control his world and thus avoid shame. Contempt is what follows if the individual's attempts fail to produce perfect mastery. It is proof that being shamed is what one deserves.

In an effort to avoid shame the construct of overidealization, whether manifesting as the illusion of the perfect self or the wished-for perfect other, is a compensatory solution. It is a fantasy born in the imagination and created at the expense of truth. If we appreciate the daily challenges that deprived or traumatized individuals face in childhood, we come to understand that children have little recourse or resources to escape unbearable tensions of the home environment. They have very little choice when it comes to preserving the spontaneous expression of self. The internal conflicts resulting from the contradictory influences imposed upon them force them into a double-bind between perceived safety and authentic self-development.

As the child moves into adolescence and adulthood, the ability to develop cognitively and emotionally continues to be compromised. Progressively learned developmental capacities, such as the ability to discern the complexity of a situation, or the ability to negotiate one's own needs while appreciating the needs of others, can be severely hampered. Instead, as these narcissistically injured individuals enter the playing field of adulthood, one of the ways they can be recognized is by noting the degree to which the quality of their thinking is prone to exaggeration. They tend to exhibit an organizational style that presents beliefs and solutions to problems in absolute, all-or-nothing terms. In more extreme forms, sometimes these individuals distort reality to the point that they have difficulty distinguishing between genuine feelings, beliefs, strivings, and their artificially constructed desires about the way reality "should be." As a consequence they will too quickly mistrust the feedback from others, or conversely they will too willingly sacrifice their own intuitive sensibilities when they have placed their hopes for rescue in an all-powerful other.

To summarize, the schematic that the Four Quadrant Model is based upon is grounded in Horney's description of "character solutions." We have found her descriptions of the compensatory efforts of individuals with narcissistic vulnerabilities to be some of the most vital and compelling descriptions in the literature. Her theoretical formulation of the idealized self captures not only an intrapsychic picture of the self, it also describes the interpersonal and systemic features that complete a metapsychological picture of the self-system, a picture that unifies an understanding of both the parts and the whole simultaneously. A summary of the key components and behavioral features that comprise the underlying structure of the narcissistic character solution is provided below:

- These individuals seem to be *compulsively driven* to express their idealized self, to prove it in action. They often need praise or reassurance to affirm this overidealized image of their accomplishments.
- The pursuit of their perceived needs and goals takes on a quality of being *insatiable, indiscriminate, and short-lived.* This is accompanied by a feeling of restlessness, irritability, or emptiness, followed by the desire to achieve the next goal or satisfy the next need.
- The reaction to *frustration and disappointment* is more intensified than warranted by circumstantial triggers. The greater the compulsion that drives these individuals to prove their idealized sense of self, the more intense their reaction to frustration or disappointment.
- They have a tendency to believe that *whatever they think, feel, or do should not carry any adverse consequences.* They are surprised or offended if others have a negative response to their self-serving behaviors.
- They hold to a stringent belief *that life should be filled with unlimited possibilities.* They often avoid commitment or have difficulty taking personal responsibility for their decision-making.
- They attend to external feedback in ways that are *not well-grounded in reality.* Instead, they pick and choose pieces of information that confirm their convictions and world view.
- Feelings and motivations seem to fluctuate between two alternatives, *an inflated sense of pride and a deep sense of self contempt.* When the individual's pride is wounded, there is an extreme swing toward self-contempt or self-hate. Both the overinflated sense of pride and the self-loathing work together as a system to keep the authentic self from emerging.

Each of these above descriptors enables the therapist to assess the client's strengths and vulnerabilities. When taken together, these seven components form a composite that helps in diagnosing the level or degree of compulsive strivings. Clients come to us with overdetermined wishes stemming from the construction of the idealized self as well as with inherent needs to actualize their given authentic potentialities. Yet, in the early stages of therapy, clients will typically have marked difficulty differentiating between the two.

Entry Points into the Phenomenological Inquiry Process

The components that organize and drive the narcissistic defenses may be used as entry points into the therapeutic inquiry process. What do we mean by entry points into the inquiry process? An entry point is a therapeutic opportunity to delve into the phenomenological tracking process. It is a way of questioning patients to learn more about *how they think, what they perceive and what they fail to perceive, the affective meaning of a given event, the intensity of frustrations and disappointments, and the speed of their reactivity to a situation*—in other words, how the idealized self system is organized. By listening to the phenomenological present and directing patients back to the present, we invite them to pause with us and become more curious about habituated patterns and responses. By going back to statements that they have made, ones that reveal a belief or construct mentioned above, we obtain a window into how the idealized self is maintained. By asking thoughtful, pointed questions that force the patient to explain what he/she takes for granted or believes without question, we begin to open a doorway to curiosity and self-reflection. Over time, this creates an opening for the real self to begin to emerge.

Daniel Stern (2004) describes phenomenology as the study of things as they appear to consciousness, "the mental landscape we see and are in at any given moment" (p. 8). Therapeutic change occurs in the intersubjective field between the therapist and the patient which is occurring at the micro-level in present time. His research directs our attention to the "small but meaningful affective happenings that unfold in the seconds that make up now" (p. 8). In order to make best use of the therapeutic unfolding, the affective and cognitive exchanges that comprise therapeutic dialogue, one must *slow the process down enough* to be able to pursue different and multiple paths that will open up for exploration, as long as the therapist does not move to interpretation too quickly.

In other words our attention to process increases in importance as we pay attention to the micro-level of our patients' subjective experience in any given moment. This immersion, through the phenomenological tracking process, helps us learn more about their subjective experience and helps us to better understand how patients have organized the parts of their experience into a unified whole. Rushing to interpret threatens to foreclose opportunities to learn more about our patients' relational organizing schemas. Also, imposing our subjective meaning through interpretation onto the therapeutic moment may run the risk of shutting down our patients' own self-discovery process or their ability to verbally articulate an important feeling or insight for the first time.

As an example, if a patient matter-of-factly states that he doesn't feel appreciated at work, the therapist may use this as an entry point to gently begin the phenomenological tracking process in the present moment. The therapist may gently begin to probe into the patient's assumptions around what adequate appreciation would look like and follow this with asking the patient how the feedback he did receive fell short of the mark. We could than ask how the patient is feeling in this very moment describing this experience of disappointment. As patients are able to tell us why and how responses from others fall short of the mark, as well as reveal the feeling states that accompany disappointments, we are able to have a window into their idealized wishes and longings as well as their expectations from others to live up to these standards. We are also able to join patients on an affective level, expressing our resonance of holding the disappointment together within the subjective interpersonal space.

Through the phenomenological inquiry process, we also begin to understand more fully the amount of space that the subjective, overdetermined idealizations occupy in the psyche. Does the need for praise occupy the bulk of the patient's psychic energy, where any slight or omission threatens to throw him or her into a state of frustration and anxiety? Or is the need for praise only limited to certain situations, such as the work arena where the patient may reveal to us the degree of rigidity of his standards around performance? In terms of assessing how much of the personality is compromised by the compulsive drive to *prove* the idealized self, we may follow-up by asking if the patient also feels underappreciated at home or if he ever felt underappreciated by the therapist. In this way we begin to get a better sense of how much of the psyche is compromised by the patient's compulsive drives.

As a point of further clarification as to how to use the phenomenological tracking process, three brief case vignettes are offered to illustrate entry points into the idealized organizing schemas of individuals who fall within the spectrum of narcissistic vulnerabilities.

Case Example 1

Patient: I had a hard time at work this morning. Nobody seems to appreciate me, and I feel like I'm invisible in that "Good Ole Boy" network. My project is about to be launched and do you think that I got a thank you from anybody?

Therapist: What were you hoping would happen this morning?

Patient: I thought that at least my boss Larry would have popped his head in to tell me that the website looked great.

Therapist: Did Larry say anything to you at all about the project?

Patient: Nope. He was behind closed doors with the big wigs.

Therapist: I thought that you had told me that Larry brought you into his office last week and told you that he was glad that you were a member of the team and that he "had your back" in terms of the leadership team?

Patient: Yeah, but I'm not sure I believe it; otherwise he would have invited me into the meeting today to talk about the website.

Therapist: You hoped that he would bring you into the meeting with the big wigs, and when he didn't you assumed he was only giving you lip service?

Patient: Pretty much. I feel like he's continuing to set me up. You know, I didn't have enough time to make that website spectacular.

Therapist: So, you have your own worries about not living up to the standards that you set for yourself, and you believe that your boss thinks you failed to meet those same standards?

Patient: That's right. I could have done so much better if I had the time.

Therapist: I'm a bit confused. I thought you had said that you knew going into this that you weren't going to have adequate time, and Larry said that this was just a preliminary launching. And yet, it seems that in spite of hearing these reassurances, you can't let yourself off the hook. You have an idea of what you want, and anything short of that seems to make you feel like a failure.

Patient: But, I know that I could do more than what was sent out to the public.

Therapist: Yes, but at what cost to yourself? It seems as if your expectations of yourself didn't include the realities of the time you were given to complete the project.

Patient: You're right. Why do I always keep putting that kind of pressure on myself?

Therapist: Do you think that we can pause, and together look at what happens when you do keep driving yourself with these standards of being absolutely perfect. It's so automatic for you. When you jump to this automatic response, it seems to cloud your ability to remember a very positive meeting you had with your boss just last week, where he gave you reassurance that you were doing a good job, and that you were a valued member of the team.

Patient: Yeah, you're right. Maybe I should cut myself a break for once.

Therapist: If you think about it in that way, are there any aspects of the project you can feel satisfied about?

Patient: Yes, actually, there are many features of the website that are going to work much more smoothly in terms of our customers being able to place orders. Gosh, I'm feeling better already.

Here the therapist focuses on the patient's harsh standards around his performance expectations and links this with the patient's inability to remember reassuring feedback from his boss. This link creates an *entry point*, one that highlights real, positive feedback, and grounds the dialogue in reality in an attempt to penetrate the patient's compulsive pattern of maintaining the idealized standards of perfection. Notice that by slowing down the automatic assumptions that have led to a high degree of agitation, the therapist is able to use the moment-to-moment tracking to help link two competing statements the patient has made in the two previous sessions. By introducing the reality-based evidence of the boss's support, the therapist challenges the patient's assumptions. It is at this point that the patient is then able to relax his standards and think about his performance in less absolute ways. In addition, this momentary repair of the split-off parts helps contain the anxiety and the self-contempt that springs from a deflated sense of pride around a disappointed wish for overdetermined perfection.

Case Example 2

A second case illustration highlights a patient's compulsive pursuits in a way that reveals the insatiability of her desires and her letdown after the initial excitement.

Patient: I think that my husband and I are going to buy that vacation home in Aruba. I finally convinced him.

Therapist: I know, you were talking about it for weeks and you were really excited about it. How did you feel once he said yes to you?

Patient: You know, it was the funniest thing. I didn't feel much of anything.

Therapist: Didn't feel much of anything?

Patient: I guess I felt a little deflated, let down.

Therapist: Can you tell me more about what you mean by deflation?

Patient: I guess it felt a little empty.

Therapist: Do you mean you felt empty inside?

Patient: Yes, and then I started to get nervous.

Therapist: Can you describe that nervousness?

Patient: It's like I don't exist, like I don't have anything to focus on. Then, I noticed that I started getting irritated at my husband. He's so irritating, especially the way he clears his throat all the time and says, "Now we're cookin'." I guess he thought he had made me happy.

Therapist: It seems as though you shifted away from feeling nervous and empty inside to feeling irritated with your husband.

Patient: Well, he's irritating.

Therapist: How much time went by before you noticed that you shifted from feeling empty and nervous to focusing on your irritation with your husband?

Patient: I don't know. I think it just shifted without me thinking much about it.

Therapist: Did you remember being aware that a shift in your feelings had occurred?

Patient: No, not until we started talking about it like this. That is a little strange isn't it?

In this case example we see how the therapist is working with the feature of insatiability and the short-lived satisfaction once the patient was able to convince her husband to purchase the house in Aruba. Using this as an entry point, the therapist uses the phenomenological tracking process to help the patient consciously remember the moment-to-moment unfolding of the sequence of her feelings. The therapist's questions are directed to help the patient learn more about what is underneath her "non-feeling" reaction. By the therapist asking for more detail, the patient is able to identify feelings of deflation, which in turn connect with feeling empty inside. We see that the patient defends against feeling more intensified anxiety by shifting her attention to her irritation with her husband.

Here we see the overidealized standards functioning as a way of restabilizing the patient. She is able to move away from her painful feeling state of deflation and emptiness by focusing on her irritation with her husband. By experiencing him as failing to live up to her idealized expectations, she is able to recover by making him the defective one. In this way she is able to avoid any conscious penetration of her feelings of emptiness and inadequacy.

Case Example 3

This third case illustration highlights a person who has difficulty accepting limitation, seeing it as an impingement on life, one in which he must prove his invincibility.

Patient: I've been having this stomach pain that sometimes keeps me up at night.

Therapist: Have you been to the doctor to have this checked out?

Patient: No, I'm fine. I don't believe in doctors.

Therapist: When was the last time you had a physical?

Patient: Not since my mother forced me to go when I was sixteen.

Therapist: That was 35 years ago.

Patient: Like I said, I don't believe in doctors.

Therapist: When you imagine yourself going to a doctor, what would you think that would mean?

Patient: They're a bunch of pill pushers. I know if I make an appointment for a physical, they'll try to get me onto some medication. Besides, people will think I'm weak. I take good care of myself. My body can heal itself.

Therapist: You think that people would think you are weak for getting a consultation around why you might be having stomach trouble?

Patient: It's not that bad. I don't want to be calling to complain willy-nilly about every little thing.

Therapist: So making one call feels like you would be seen as a complainer?

Patient: I'm fine, I'm fine. You're starting to remind me of my mother.

Therapist: Hum, I'm wondering how my concern about something you brought up about your health seems to create a feeling of irritation in you, that somehow my questions are starting to sound like your mother.

Patient. I'm not irritated. You don't understand. My mother was a hypo-chondriac. She was at the doctor's office every other week, and then she started dragging me in.

Therapist: That must have felt embarrassing for a sixteen year old boy.

Patient: No, it just made me more determined. I told myself I'm never going to be like her. I don't need to get attention that way. I have more important things to do with my time rather than wasting it in some doctor's office.

Therapist: And yet, you take the time to come here, and you took the time to let me know that you must be just a little concerned about your health.

Patient: Yeah, but I don't want you to make a big deal about it.

In this case vignette we see how any sign of physical ailment comes too close to threatening the patient's wish for invincibility. Although the patient begins the session with the statement about stomach pain, at the first sign of the therapist's concern, he experiences her question as an attempt to expose a weakness or vulnerability in him. When she wonders about the patient getting additional support from the medical community, he displays an attitude of mistrust. Further phenomenological tracking reveals that the patient does fear that other people will see him as weak, or they will try to take advantage of that weakness by pushing pills at him.

When the therapist persists in the inquiry process, we see the first signs of transference erupting, as the patient reveals that the dialogical exchange is starting to remind him of his mother who historically had been very controlling with a history of hypochondriasis. Again, the therapist continues to track the feelings that were triggered by the transference breakthrough, and the patient is able to reveal a vow that he has made to himself, to not be weak, to not be like his mother. He will not have to need anyone as proof of his invincibility. It is at this point that the therapist reminds him of his willingness to come to therapy and that on some level he trusts her enough not to feel completely controlled or weakened by another person offering help. The patient consents to a willingness to tolerate some penetration into his defense of invincibility, but must remind the therapist that she must proceed slowly by "not making too big a deal" out of it, thereby allowing him to save face for the time being.

In the above case examples we have illustrated how phenomenological tracking can be used in the present moment of any given exchange between the therapist and the patient. This slowing down process, attending to nuance and detail, not only allows for more information to be revealed, it allows for the intersubjective experience between the therapist and the patient to be deepened toward greater levels of trust. Furthermore, it is a way of creating an entry point into the construction of the idealized self system, where the therapist can learn more about the nature of the compulsive drives that bind the parts together into an idealized whole. Understanding entry points through the phenomenological tracking process is a way of conceptualizing how therapeutic dialogue can be used to dismantle and heal splitting within the psyche. The rush to interpret often runs the risk of foreclosing too quickly, acting as further entrenchment, in fact, of the maintenance of the idealized self system.

ENVIRONMENTAL FACTORS CONTRIBUTING TO THE DEVELOPMENT OF IDEALIZED IDENTITY FORMATION

The neurotic solution described by Horney is fundamentally the result of parental failures in the area of support, nurturance, the creation of a sense of safety, and mirroring back to the child the parents' value and appreciation of his or her unique attributes. When these essential mirroring functions are absent, the child must then manufacture through fantasy and imagination an idealized version of self, one that is overdetermined, absolute in its standards, and compulsively driven.

Louis DeRosis (1974) captures the dilemma of children who grow up in environments of contradictory, confusing, or traumatic influences beautifully.

> In his effort to cope, to present at least a seemingly solid, seemingly whole front to the world, and to himself, the child generates a precariously balanced, stress-filled, easily disturbed order. In this delicate state he is kept divided from the operation of spontaneous tendencies which are naturally his, really himself. This separation is the beginning of neurosis, and neurosis is the cause of our suffering. We suffer not because we are involved in contradictions, for the ability to be so involved is crucial to our development. Rather, we suffer because we become 'caught' in contradictions. It is in being so caught that the child loses access to his spontaneity. That loss hurts and injures us the most, for in the freedom to respond to our deepest being there is a quality of life we crave, however dimly we may be aware of it. We all seek to satisfy this hunger, though we may deny it or have it denied by some insistent influence around us (p. 110).

The "insistent influence around us" that DeRosis is referring to is the parental influence and is comprised of messages that we receive about ourselves and the world around us. This daily interpersonal exchange results in the development of organizing schemas and associations that come to give a particular definition to the intersubjective field. DeRosis describes the development of this intersubjective field as an "emotional greenhouse" of moment-to-moment environmental influences. He further states that there are a number of key factors that contribute to an emotional greenhouse where children are forced to choose the "neurotic solution" as opposed to the development of their authentic self. Those factors are:

- The quality of parental attention—safe or unsafe, loving or critical
- The degree of distortions and expectations that are passed from parent to child
- The number of contradictory influences that are imposed on the child

If there are too many factors that thwart or discourage the development of authenticity, the child loses his way and begins a process of alienation from the real self. We have highlighted four key types of parental influence that constitute a precarious emotional greenhouse compromising the fuller development of the real self. They are:

- The Trauma-Filled Environment: Trauma-filled environments are usually chaotic and unpredictable, and include some degree of verbal, physical, or sexual abuse. Children are either the direct target of abuse, or they internalize the damage of secondary abuse from witnessing a sibling or parent being physically or verbally threatened. Parenting is irresponsible and disorganized. Verbal dialogue with children is filled with harsh and volatile exchanges, confusing, and inconsistent standards, and ready criticism when children fall short of the mark of parental expectations. Innocent mistakes, such as a child spilling a glass of milk, can be dealt with severely. In general, parents exhibit a frequent loss of emotional control, usually in front of or at the expense of the child. The child becomes the target of the parent's emotional dysregulation and is often blamed for causing the parents' outbursts of rage or loss of control.
- The Depriving/Neglectful Environment: This environment is more difficult to pinpoint and what occurs within these environments often remains invisible to the outside world. Because of this, children who grow up in these conditions remain lost and confused, as there is less likelihood that outside help will intervene on behalf of the child. In such a picture of parental failure, the child's basic needs for support, mirroring, praise, comfort, and love remain overlooked and under-attended. Children who come from these types of family environments are likely to feel invisible. They are either left to their own devises, or they are put in charge of younger siblings. Very quickly they learn that any legitimate need they have must be subjugated to the needs

of others. Yet the wish for attention and nurturing is not eradicated. It merely goes underground, sequestered in the child's fantasy world where the use of imagination helps to create the growing pattern of idealized wishes and longings. Later, in adulthood, these illusions are expressed in terms of overdetermined ambitions for recognition or overidealized wishes for the perfect other.

- The Envy/Hate-Filled Environment: This environment is often filled with parental communication that expresses an overt or covert show of contempt whenever the child attempts to express his or her needs, desires, or emotions. One child can be singled out as the target of parental envy and contempt, whereas other children are seen as valued members of the family. For the child who becomes the target of envy, this becomes demoralizing and unfair because other siblings are able to receive parental praise and acceptance, or are even encouraged in developing their authenticity. The targeted children are apt to internalize the projected contempt and see it as evidence that they are doing something to cause this hurtful treatment. In adulthood we find them making extreme efforts to overcompensate to be recognized as valuable and prove their self-worth. Often this is paired with self-punishing behaviors and an increase in symptom-formation when efforts for recognition also fail to bring the acceptance they long for.

- The Overly Rewarding/Overly Driven Environment: Here we see an environment where the child is used in the service of explicitly narcissistic projections of the parents. The failure of this particular parenting style is one where the child is not seen as a separate person with boundaries. Instead, the child becomes a screen upon which the parents project their fears, wishes, or ambitions. The child learns that in order to be seen and validated he or she must do something to win the parents' approval or meet a parental need. For example, children who have overly anxious, ambitious parents tend to be pushed to excel and to perform in the limelight so that the parent can stand out and be praised. The drive for excellence will be played out through pressuring the child to be the brightest, most attractive, most desired of all friends and classmates. These children are either pushed to excel with excessive demands placed upon them, or they are praised lavishly for every little accomplishment. Children learn that their own dreams and ambitions must be subjugated to the parents' desires and come to expect excessive praise at the slightest efforts made. The unfortunate consequences are an inadequate appraisal of their own actual talents and the efforts required to achieve authenticity.

What each of these relational environments has in common is that there are insufficient opportunities to experience loving support by parents who have a genuine interest in the development of the child's unique potential as a person. As a result, children who come from any of these environments are left with an *inner sense of being weak, invisible, or defective* with a fragile grasp on negotiating the real challenges and opportunities of life. Instead, these children have learned that in order to manage their fears of disappointment, abandonment, or annihilation, they must take extraordinary measures to remain safe. In childhood they learned to attend to the parents' needs in hopes of escaping criticism or abuse, thereby maintaining some semblance of safety. The price was to subjugate their inner feelings, hopes, and dreams in a desperate search for approval, recognition, and acceptance. They repeat these relational patterns in adulthood coupled with the attendant hope that *this* time their efforts will make a difference.

This overattention to the needs of others creates a posture of defensive vigilance, which in turn produces one-sided development. Because the growing child's inner strength has been sapped by the need to please others and maintain a semblance of safety, the child's course of development puts him at a distinct disadvantage. These children learn that expressing their needs is either dangerous or futile. Conscious awareness of their needs and their vulnerability eventually becomes associated with shame and despair, and on some level these individuals come to realize that they are less well equipped for life than other people.

In sum these failures of empathic attunement on the part of caregivers provide the fertile ground out of which the neurotic solution of the idealized self is born. Paris in his introduction to *Karen Horney: The Therapeutic Process* (1999) has summarized this dynamic as follows:

> Neurosis arises . . . from the behavior of parents who treat the young child inconsistently and fail to give it 'the feeling of warmth and protection' it needs to counteract its sense of helplessness. Feeling frustrated, intimidated, and confused by a 'mixture of indulgence and harshness,' the child responds with a 'rebellious hostility.' This provokes a 'renewed intimidation' that forces the child to suppress its antagonistic behavior. The child's hostility can be lived out only in violent fantasies, but these are so threatening that they have to be repressed, and the child develops vague fears of both its buried explosive affects and possible retaliation from others. All this creates 'anxiety states' . . . against which the child defends itself by developing 'certain character trends,' the function of which is to avoid

fear-arousing behaviors. The child, and later the adult, adopts 'protective measures' that result in inhibitions, emotional impoverishment, and loss of flexibility, but that provides a feeling of safety in an unreliable world. The protective measures may work smoothly for a while, but 'situations will easily arise' in which they are ineffective . . . and then the individual is flooded with anxiety (p. 6).

Because the real self was never supported and valued by the caregiver and because the child has an inner sense of being weak and/or defective, any semblance of limitation is fought against and denied. In addition feelings of vulnerability come to be treated with disdain, including the vulnerability one experiences in real relationships. Therefore, the need for relationship is often experienced with mixed feelings of longing and an intense fear of dependency. As early emotional deficits are sufficiently buried in the unconscious or split off from an integrated sense of awareness, the idealized image of the self becomes further ingrained in the personality. It is the "idealized solution" that comes to be believed as the one thing that will make up for past parental failures.

It is, therefore, this idealized solution that is projected onto every relationship in present-day reality, fraught with all of the accompanying overdetermined standards and wishes for perfectionism. Based on the simultaneous interpersonal and intrapsychic wish for the idealized solution, we can come to understand the function of loyal waiting and the desire for retaliation when wishes for rescue or change do not happen. Here is where our therapeutic training model comes into action as a tool to help move the compulsive, idealized solution into a more integrated, reality-based perspective. This in turn allows us entry into deeply buried cravings as clients search to access their authentic selves.

Quadrant Three: The Function of Loyal Waiting as a "Longed-for Perfect Other"

Most individuals with narcissist vulnerabilities hold very high if not impossible standards and expectations of others. As a result they engage in a pattern of relationships where others often disappoint them, never quite being able to live up to the very standards that they place on themselves. However, when it comes to understanding how these idealized standards play out through Quadrant Three of Loyal Waiting, a very different picture initially emerges. This is often initially confusing for the therapist who may see a client who presents with low self-esteem.

We would normally associate a person with compulsively driven standards to be quick to express disappointment in the shortcomings of others, with an accompanying attitude of contempt and devaluing. These individuals may show understanding or express an apparent ability to forgive others for their "shortcomings" but that forgiveness or that understanding comes from a superior position of judgment. A person with narcissistic vulnerabilities might say to a therapist that the therapist couldn't possibly understand the complexity of his line of work because it is so technical, or he may accuse the therapist of following cookie cutter solutions that the therapist learned out of a text book. Both of these are predictable ways we have come to understand how individuals with narcissistic vulnerabilities consciously or unconsciously try to gain the upper hand by throwing the therapist or others off balance.

A specific picture of how overidealization manifests in more hidden ways is found through our understanding of the position of loyal waiting. Here we see how part of the wish for the idealized solution is projected in fantasy onto the "longed for perfect other." Essentially, the position of loyal waiting is a communication and a resolution that both consciously and unconsciously can be summarized by the following statement. "I didn't get what I deserved in childhood, and I'm going to hold out until I get it." Individuals with less than optimal childhoods, but who have some measure of their authentic, spontaneous self intact, are able to learn from the deficits of childhood and pick partners who are better equipped to fulfill their realistic needs for love and affection in adulthood. However, individuals whose authentic self was consistently suppressed move into adult relationships with an overdetermined wish that disappointments in childhood can be rectified through an unwavering insistence that a perfect person exists, someone who will never disappoint them. Or they secretly believe they have the power to change the person whom they are with into that perfect, all-fulfilling other.

One of the ways we can recognize this longing for the idealized other is by noting a pattern of entering into relationships *as if the patient doesn't see the short-comings of others*. Because idealization functions to the exclusion of being anchored in behavioral cues tied to reality, these patients have a tendency to ignore unfavorable aspects of the other and only attend to the features that fit into their idealized image. What is remarkable, however, is that much of the time they pick people who actually possess many of the limitations and shortcomings of their parents. They are either blind to this fact or are convinced that they can get the other person to change. For example, a young man continued to pick cold, distant, or unavailable women to fall in love with. When the pattern was pointed out to him that each of the last four women fit the description of his mother, he would insist that this time the person he had picked was different. This time, his patience and perseverance would pay off.

What is often confusing for therapists treating these individuals is that patients will often focus on the glowing attributes of their partners, while in the same breath complain about a slight or mistreatment. There is an evident disconnect between the positive attributes of the person and the complaints they are making about that person, sometimes in the same sentence. If the therapist tries to point this out, an excuse is quickly made, or the patient will quickly take on the responsibility for contributing to the other person's shortcoming. In this way we see the repetition and the insistence upon their illusions of perfection in an attempt to keep hope alive. Their hope contains the belief that they can achieve their idealized longings because they secretly possess the power to change the object of their desire—to make them into the image they want them to be. Because of this compulsive drive to keep the illusion alive, both within the self and within the other, the result is a history of relationships that are fraught with endless waiting, self-image issues, and symptomatic complaints disconnected from any disappointment in the relationship. All of this is in an effort to keep the illusion from being shattered.

Needless to say, relationships where individuals assume the position of loyal waiting are often one-sided in terms of satisfaction or mutual support. Of course, the degree to which persons hold onto their passive posture of loyal waiting for the idealized, rescuing other is dependent upon the pattern of relationship with adult caregivers in their family of origin. This pattern, a type of repetition compulsion to create a more satisfying relational experience, is one that will inevitably show up within the transferential dynamic once the therapeutic work begins to unfold.

Case Example of Loyal Waiting Using the Four Quadrant Model for Analysis

Marsha is a thirty-seven year old woman, married for thirteen years with two children in elementary school. She entered therapy through a physician referral due to issues of weight gain with resulting complications of borderline diabetes and high cholesterol. Early in the therapy Marsha articulated vague symptoms of depression and extremely low self-esteem. Identifying herself as a caretaker, she spent a great deal of energy attending to her two sons, determined that they would excel in sports and academics in order that they could "take advantage of every opportunity." Marsha's childhood family environment was one of trauma and neglect. She had an abusively alcoholic father and a mother who was distant and withholding. Marsha remembers being embarrassed by her family and tried to spend as much time at friends' homes as she could. Her husband came from a very affluent family and Marsha proudly described that she "married above herself."

Initially, Marsha reported that her relationship with her husband was "blissfully happy." However, as the therapy continued, she admitted that her husband exhibited early signs of substance abuse while she and Jack were dating in college and that occasionally he would lash out at her in hurtful ways. After the children were born, Jack became increasingly irritable, often criticizing her about her weight, that she had let herself go, and that she should go back to work and "get a life." Marsha followed that advice, went back to work when her sons were in school full time and then received multiple promotions at work. Her husband, on the other hand, recently lost his job and has been doing part-time work and odd jobs as a handyman.

This session takes place approximately one year into the therapy. Marsha begins her session with complaints that Jack continues to be irritable and critical of her, but she reports that she has followed through on her goal to lose weight.

Patient: I'm happy to report that I'm taking better care of myself, and I'm also trying to observe more of what is going on at home with my husband.

Therapist: What have you noticed?

Patient: I've been noticing how often my husband criticizes me or tries to pick a fight. I've been able to walk away more of the time and not take the bait. I'm also trying not to forget these incidents and I'm trying to keep them in my memory.

Therapist: That's good.

Patient: I'm not sure how I'm going to use them or when, but I feel that it's making me stronger. For instance, the other day he tried to blame me for putting a dent in the new refrigerator, but I just walked away from him. I'm recognizing he's a mean man; I've known it for a long time, but I'm just walking away.

Therapist: So, when you walk away do you feel better?

Patient: No. It gnaws at me.

Therapist: So, how is that going to make you stronger?

Patient: Good point. I guess I don't know. (looks confused)

Therapist: Are you hoping that if you get stronger, you might be able to make him become nicer to you?

Patient: Yes, in my heart I think that can happen. In reality, I don't know anymore. I wish he could be different, would be able to change. Maybe I'm wrong.

Therapist: What would you be wrong about, exactly?

Patient: That I'm not accepting reality, that I'm confused about what's real anymore.

Therapist: What part of reality do you think you're not accepting?

Patient: I'd like to believe that the guy I married isn't that mean. I'd like to believe that the person who says he loves me would treat me better. For instance, how can he come downstairs in the morning and be so loving to his children, giving them a hug, and walk right by me, and then turn away from me when I try to give him a kiss? How cold is that?

Therapist: Are you trying to say that part of what you're struggling to accept is that you think that your husband is cold to you and not other people?

Patient: That's what I'm not sure about. I get confused.

Therapist: Where are you confused?

Patient: Does he really not love me or was he never taught how to show affection?

Therapist: You just told me that he is quite able to show affection to your children.

Patient: I just don't want to believe it.

Therapist: You don't want to believe . . .

Patient: It goes back to what we were talking about last week, about my mother and my father's relationship. My mother loved my father, chose him over me. Even on his death-bed, she loved him. Maybe I just can't love. You know, in sickness and in health . . . Maybe, I just don't know how to love.

Therapist: How did you make a switch to yourself just now—when we had just started to talk about your husband's coldness toward you? (long pause) Where you aware of that switch? You began describing his coldness, and then you suddenly began to blame yourself for not knowing how to love.

Patient: Boy, you're tough. I guess I don't want to see it. It's easier not to see it.

Therapist: Is it easier not to see something that you don't want to see?

Patient: Ok. I don't want to look at it. Bingo! There's the key, isn't it? I don't want to see what makes me feel uncomfortable.

Therapist: I'm wondering how all of this might connect back to your mother. Do you think that because your mother never left your father that she was somehow more loving than you?

Patient: No, in reality I know that I'm a very loving person. I love my kids, I have great friends. My mother never really showed me love, and she really didn't have any friends.

Therapist: So, you're not struggling in the same way with issues of loyalty when you try to sort through your feelings about your husband?

Patient: What do you mean?

Therapist: Well, your mother never left your father; do you think she was somehow stronger than you because she was able to stick it out?

Patient: No, I always thought I was much stronger than she was. I made a life for myself that was much better than hers.

Therapist: Does that include a better relationship with your husband than she had with your father?

Patient: (long pause) It's like I married my father, isn't it? But, I can't believe that. Jack is a much nicer man than my father. We live in a nice house, I have two beautiful children, and he has a large trust fund.

Therapist: Yes, those are real differences that make the quality of your life much better today, but, how about the quality of your relationship? When you think about your relationship from the vantage-point of how you are treated by Jack, is it similar to your mother and father's interactions or does it feel different?

Patient: I can't believe it. I won't believe it. I couldn't have possibly repeated this pattern. I hated my father.

Therapist: This must be very painful to be talking about with me right now. Does your discomfort make you want to push it all away by telling yourself that you won't believe it? Are you telling me that a part of you chooses to ignore the parts that make you feel uncomfortable? That's quite a tough choice.

Patient: It's something I learned to do to make me feel stronger.

Therapist: But I thought you said when you came into our session today that staying in the present, being observant, and remembering what you observed about your husband would make you stronger.

Patient: It doesn't make any sense, does it. It's like there are two parts of me warring inside myself.

Therapist: If you did let yourself stay with the complexity of all the parts of what you are seeing about your relationship with your husband, what would that mean?

Patient: It would mean that I'm a failure, that I made the wrong choice. I made a mistake and I'm stuck with it, for better or for worse.

Therapist: So, when you make a choice, regardless of how young you were, you're stuck. There's no turning back, no learning from insights gained.

Patient: I'm not supposed to make mistakes. Other people can make mistakes. I couldn't afford to. That's how I survived my God-awful family. This is too painful. I hate it. (begins to cry)

Therapist: Yes, I know, it's very painful, (long pause) . . . but I'm wondering if there isn't a part of you that's a little bit relieved to be talking about all the parts that have been a struggle for so long.

Patient: I am relieved. I've been keeping this inside for so long, it's making me tired. Maybe that's what's giving me the strength to walk away from the fights with my husband. It takes too much energy. (long pause) Do you think that this might be part of why I've been feeling a little stronger lately?

Analysis

In this case vignette we see an example of the organizing principles contained within Quadrant Three around Loyal Waiting and also the initial emergence of aspects of the patient's overly driven standards for herself that reveal aspects of Quadrant One. As noted in the history, the patient offered an idealized description of her relationship with her husband, describing them as "blissfully happy." As the therapy evolved, however, the patient was able to admit that she saw early warning signs of her husband's critical nature, even during their dating relationship in college. Here we see a breakthrough of the patient's authenticity beginning to emerge. However, we also see her deeply entrenched devaluation of self by her comment that she had "married above her station." In this statement we also get a glimpse into her overidealized longings, as the affluence of her husband's family money is an important clue to the extent of her desire for rescue.

The therapy session begins with what appears to be signs of progress that Marsha has made in terms of more proactive attempts at self-care. She reports that she is less prone to lapsing into a self-destructive pattern of overeating when she and her husband have an argument. Instead, she is trying to take care of herself while maintaining a stance of *observing and remembering* the quality of her husband's comments to her on a daily basis. She states that by maintaining her powers of observation, this will make her stronger, even though she is not yet sure how she will use these observations on her own behalf. This communication telegraphs to the therapist that some aspects of her fixed position of loyalty are beginning to lessen, and that there is a growing capacity of observation anchored in reality that is beginning to emerge.

However, when she moves to the point of verbally articulating that her husband is cold and mean, we see the more entrenched, defensive pattern of loyal waiting re-assert its hold. Here the struggle for reality-based aware-ness runs counter to her wishes around loyal waiting. We see these wishes play out within the unfolding therapeutic dialogue. For example, when the therapist makes a point about the patient getting stronger and won-ders aloud whether the patient hopes to use this strength to change her husband's behavior, it is here that we see the patient's ambivalent struggle re-emerge. The patient first agrees with this observation, then says that she doesn't know, and finally says she doesn't want to believe this painful part of reality.

When the therapist asks which part of reality the patient does not want to believe, she shifts to talking about her mother and father's relationship. Here we see precisely how the family rules around loyalty were instilled on a systemic-inter-generational level. The patient describes her mother as having the *strength* to remain loyal "until death do us part." Even though the patient has admitted earlier that her father was an abusive alcoholic and that she hated him, her feelings about her father are split off from the family rules about loyalty. Loyalty, therefore, is measured in terms of having the strength to stick it out regardless of the circumstance.

As a phenomenological tracking illustration, it should be noted that just prior to the shift where she reflects upon her mother's loyalty to her father, she had just revealed an observation about her husband that was nega-tive and hurtful to her. From the position of loyal waiting, this statement of growth and emerging authenticity cannot be tolerated. It will threaten the old homeostatic balance. Suddenly she now must become the one who doesn't know how to love. If she threatens to challenge the existing loyalty contract within her family by speaking negatively about her husband, this is the equivalent of being told by her family that it is *she* who does not know how to love. Her unconscious wish seems to be that if she could just get strong enough, it would be possible to somehow exert her influence over her husband in order to get him to change. If she could accomplish this, she could maintain her old loyalty contract *and* get her needs met.

It is interesting to note that when the therapist points out this switch from talking about her husband to self-recrimination, the patient's response is, "Boy, you're tough." Here the patient is telegraphing a transferential com-munication to the therapist. It is as if she is saying, "Don't mess around with my family's loyalty system. Why are you forcing me to take a look at that?" When the therapist continues to direct her to the loyalty bind, it is then that we see the signs of the Overidealized Standards in Quadrant One begin to surface. Here the client says that if looking at reality includes admitting that she made a mistake, this is not something she will tolerate. It is not permissible. She must be above making mistakes for this is how she learned to survive. It is a source of strength and pride that the idealized self is holding and does not want to relinquish. So, it is in this way that we come to understand how patients who present with low self-esteem and a high degree of loyalty from a seemingly passive position actually harbor secret overidealized expectations about their ability to change people, in spite of evidence to the contrary.

This relationship between loyal waiting and the often secret belief that the individual has the power to change another is an example of parts of the self working in unison to keep the idealized self-structure in place. We also see beginning entry points for dialogue where the therapeutic relationship can begin to act as a bridge, helping the patient create new schemas around how the patient might experience new ways of defining self-in-relationship. By examining loyalty in more depth, there is an opportunity to make room for healing the split between authentic desires and what healthy loyalty contracts might look like. Again, immersion into the deeper understanding of loyalty dilemmas is what allows the patient to explore alternative ways of connecting, initially within the context of the therapeutic relationship, and eventually in her real relationships in the outside world.

VINDICTIVE RAGE AS A RESULT OF DISAPPOINTMENTS IN LOYAL WAITING: HOW THE FOURTH QUADRANT COMPLETES THE PICTURE OF THE PART-WHOLE PERSONALITY STRUCTURE

Perhaps, the most destructive component of the overidealizing self-system has to do with understanding the function of Quadrant Four and what part it plays in maintaining the homeostatic equilibrium of individuals with narcissistic vulnerabilities. As it relates to the compulsively driven ambitions of the overidealized self, Karen Horney refers to what we are identifying in Quadrant Four as *the drive toward vindictive triumph*. The way in which Quadrant Four relates to the passive stance of loyal waiting is through the individual's attempt to reestablish the frame of the archaic homeostatic solution. For example, feelings of rage enter into maintaining the solution, either in the form of rage against another (including the therapist) or *rage turned against the self* for even questioning the old homeostatic rules around fairness and loyalty. Again, how we hold the elements of this quadrant in the context of the whole self-system is a matter of the degree to which the compulsive drive is aimed at vindication and the intensity of the vulnerability that the individual is attempting to defend against. What determines the degree and intensity is largely due to several key factors:

- The degree of shame the child had to endure due to feelings of personal vulnerability or literal shaming messages that were directed at the child from parents and other adults.
- The degree of anxiety the child suffered caused by deprivation or lack of safety in the home environment.
- The degree of conflicting messages given to the child by the parents through their inability to tolerate the emergence of the child's real self.
- The degree the child was used to fulfill the parents' own needs and ambitions.
- The degree of permission *vs.* envy the child experienced in out-performing parents or having a better life than the parents.

In each of these circumstances the motivating force behind revenge enactments stems from a wish *to make up for or to enact revenge for* feelings of humiliation suffered in childhood. The drive toward vindictive triumph manifests as a relationship between the parts of the self expressed in Quadrant One and Quadrant Four. For example, when attempts to achieve over-idealized goals and ambitions fail, the individual must make someone else suffer for his or her disappointment as a way of preventing feelings of shame and inadequacy from emerging. By lashing out at others, this rectifies the momentary defensive rupture that is threatened when the feelings of the individual's own shame begin to emerge. Over time, disappointments, themselves, become associated with shame and once shamed, the individual is justified in retaliating. For some, this pattern even becomes associated with feelings of pleasure.

In terms of revenge enactments that are turned against the self, we see a somewhat different picture. If attempts to produce change in the idealized other are not rewarded through loyal waiting, patients offer up an explanation for their disappointment as something that occurred due to a personal failure. This distortion has an important function in terms of preserving hope that the idealized solution is possible. As in the above case example with Marsha, each time she was confronted with disappointment due to cruel or unloving behavior on the part of her husband, it threatened to collapse the hope that she had the power to change him. Rather than face this reality, she resorted to self-blame as a way of preserving *both* the wish for the idealized other *and* the hidden conviction that the idealized self has the power to change another. Whenever she is faced with the reality of her disappointment in the present moment, she resorts to self-punishment or self-doubt as a way of preserving hope that her idealized expectations will come true eventually. In other words, it could not be Marsha's husband that fell short. It was *her* inability to be strong enough, loving enough, otherwise he would have treated her in a more loving manner. In Marsha's case, her self-punishing behaviors took the form of overeating and lack of exercise to the point that her health was at risk. Her husband's comments only added confirmation to her sense of failure, providing "proof" that she deserved to be humiliated. In this way her husband's criticisms acted as further verification that his rebuffs were due to her failure at self-care efforts.

HOW REVENGE ENACTMENTS ARE DIRECTED TOWARD OTHERS: USING THE FOUR QUADRANT MODEL

To illustrate how revenge enactments of Quadrant Four are directed toward vindictive triumph against others when the idealized self is slighted or disappointed, the following case vignette is provided:

A patient begins his session extremely upset with a business associate who did not respond in a timely manner to a dinner invitation. This patient has a long history of disappointed relationships that follow a fairly typical sequence. The pattern often begins with the patient awkwardly reaching out in some way, extending a friendly offer of friendship or an invitation for social connection. However, there is an unrealistic, self-defeating quality to his invitations, where something he has failed to anticipate seems to set him up for disappointment. The inability to accurately assess what might be reasonable or realistic in terms of his expectations continually baffles him and seems to remain outside of his awareness. Many times the patient will push the boundaries of relationships in subtle ways, either overly sexualizing a friendship, waiting until the last moment to extend an invitation, or bending over backwards to do a special favor for someone he barely knows. In each case when the other person does not respond in a favorable manner with an adequate amount of appreciation or reciprocation, the patient experiences extreme disappointment that becomes further amplified with every subsequent exchange between the two parties. Rather than taking the time to reflect, he is quick to blame others and has difficulty looking at any part that he may have played in contributing to the disappointing outcome.

At the initial moment of any given disappointment, the patient experiences an intense feeling of shame followed by momentary anxiety. This anxiety seems to be a secondary reaction to being humiliated and, therefore, thrown off balance. He attempts to recover by lamenting over the fact that he even has such a pathetic need for companionship in the first place. However, the most prominent feelings he is left with are intense anger coupled with shame. Rather than trying to seek resolution or understanding through these contacts, the drive behind these communications seems to have a quality of wishing to get even. We begin the session as follows:

Patient: I've decided that Julia is pretty selfish and preoccupied. I'm beginning to feel more like she's using me to make herself look good at work, and that she's not interested in a friendship like I had hoped.

Therapist: What do you mean? What happened?

Patient: As you know, we've been involved in this business project for some time now, and I've spent the bulk of my time meeting when it's convenient for her. Just this once I asked her to come to dinner on Friday to work on the project and then catch up socially, and she said that she had other plans.

Therapist: You asked her to come to your home? When did you ask her?

Patient: Just yesterday. (with an irritated and impatient tone, he states) I know, she might think I'm trying to confuse business with pleasure. But she could have cut me a little slack. I wasn't going to put the moves on her. What does she think I am, stupid? She could have realized just how much I wanted to get this project done. I wasn't going to do anything to jeopardize *that*.

Therapist: How do you think she interpreted your invitation?

Patient: I shouldn't have to clarify myself. She should just trust me as a friend and remember who is doing the bulk of the work on this project. She couldn't grant me a little favor by coming over for dinner? Why is it that I'm the only one who has to be aware?

Therapist: Have you talked to her about how you feel—that you believe that the work load has been unfairly distributed? It seems as though your invitation for dinner was an attempt to rectify the situation without having to talk about the fairness issue.

Patient: I don't know what you're talking about. Things should not have to be this complicated.

Therapist: It seems as though you are upset by two separate disappointments, that you have two different agendas that need to be addressed, your wish for a more meaningful friendship, and a more equal working alliance.

Patient: I did raise the work issue last week. She seemed a bit surprised at my reaction and said she would try to work extra on one part of the project that was giving me a hard time. She didn't apologize though and didn't seem to be as troubled as I would have thought. So, Big Deal!

Therapist: Why do you say "big deal"? Wasn't that an attempt to address and correct the situation?

Patient: It wasn't good enough.

Therapist: What would have made it enough?

Patient: I know that she wasn't sincere. She looked at me kind of funny. I know she was just trying to placate me to make herself seem like a reasonable person. But, I know the real story. She's self-centered and a bit narcissistic.

Therapist: I can hear that you're disappointed, but do you think that asking her to dinner in your home to work on a business project on a Friday night might have been setting yourself up for disappointment? We've talked about this before.

Patient: You don't know this person. You can't possibly see what I now see about her. She goes out to lunch and dinner with lots of people at work.

Therapist: I know you are angry about being disappointed. Did you feel that I was siding with Julia just now, letting her off the hook when I asked about the nature and timing of your invitation?

Patient: No, I'm not saying that. Will you please stop overanalyzing this? It's not that big of a deal. Can't we move on to something else? I have more important things on my agenda today.

Therapist: (gently) I'm spending time talking with you about this because you brought it up, and you seem to have a lot of feelings about it.

Patient: I know I'm right, and I have a right to protect myself from people who can't meet my needs. Isn't that what you have said?

Therapist: Of course. That is one of the important factors we're looking at in terms of your relationships. But are all disappointments equal? What do you make of your stance of maintaining your position of disappointment even after you received a promise to help you on a difficult piece of the project? That seems to be a bit different than other people you have spoken about, people who never responded to you.

Patient: It's too late.

Therapist: Are you saying that once the disappointment happens, there's no recovery? (long pause) What about in here? You've been disappointed with me, even very angry with me. How did we recover from those ruptures?

Patient: Well, we talked it through, and you seemed to tolerate my anger without retaliating.

Therapist: And so, if someone can tolerate your anger, you can let go of your disappointment.

Patient: Yes, I guess so.

Therapist: Does it ever seem as if you need to punish someone for disappointing you *before* you can forgive them?

Patient: Well, yes. (reluctantly) There's some satisfaction in getting even. It actually feels good. Then the scales are balanced.

Analysis

In this case example we see how the Fourth Quadrant of Revenge Enactments functions in the service of "saving face" by the patient striking back when his colleague Julia's behaviors fall short of his expectations. The patient's disappointment quickly shifts from a feeling of emotional vulnerability into a cognitive posture where he makes a number of assumptions. He concludes that Julia is no longer trustworthy because she failed to meet the patient's request for dinner. Based on these assumptions, the patient is then free to express his anger and wishes for retaliation through pejorative comments, such as calling his colleague selfish and narcissistic. Correct or not, there is little if any room left for self-reflection on the part of the patient to wonder whether his own standards and expectations are reasonable or fair.

When the therapist asks him to think about whether the timing of his request was in some way a "set-up" for disappointment, the patient turns his anger on the therapist telling him that he is wrong, that the therapist *couldn't possibly know what he knows*. Again, we see the subtle strike of retaliation by devaluing the therapist's knowledge base. However, in this instance, the therapist does not waiver or back down from the retaliatory remark. Nor does he strike back in kind. Instead, the therapist persists by asking if the patient felt as though he took sides with Julia because he didn't join the patient in his anger. When presented with this clear, verbal articulation of the patient's either/or organizing schema, the patient backs down. However, he doesn't answer the therapist's question about the timing of his invitation as a possible set up for disappointment. Instead, he shows his impatience with the phenomenological tracking of the therapist's inquiry process and asks to change the subject because he has "more important things" on his agenda today.

Again, the therapist stays calm in the heat of the deflection and gently reminds the patient that it was he (the patient) who brought up the matter and, in fact, the topic still seems to be highly charged with affect. By staying with the client in this affective space in the spirit of neutrality and curiosity, the therapist is telegraphing to the patient that he can tolerate the patient's feelings emanating from Quadrant Four. This sitting in the moment with negative, accusatory, or devaluing statements shows the patient that his feelings can eventually be metabolized and worked through. As per the patient's former pattern, the therapist is telegraphing that they will not be resolved through avoidance.

Yet again, the patient attempts to get the therapist to join him and agree with his position of angry outrage by equating his anger with his need for self-protection. He reminds the therapist that it was he (the therapist) who brought up the topic of self-protection when his needs weren't getting met. Again, the therapist refuses to move into an all-or-nothing position with the patient and wonders instead if all disappointments are actually the same. Is a disappointment followed by an attempt to make restitution different than no action at all? In response to this question we see the patient reveal more of the fixed structure of highly idealized standards. Once you have disappointed him, it is too late. In order to preserve the ideal, the hope that there is someone out there who will *never* disappoint him, the patient must cut the person off altogether.

This is where the therapist moves more deeply into the relational capital that has accrued between them. He reminds the patient that he has also been disappointed in the therapist in the past and that they had weathered those storms. The therapist then wonders what made the difference in these instances. The patient then reveals that the therapist was able to tolerate his anger without retaliating in return. Although this is an important component to the reparative work that must happen within Quadrant Four—having the patient experience that he can express feelings of anger without being harmed in return—there is more yet to be done.

The therapist then uses this leverage or entry point to ask the question that directly reveals *the patient's desire to punish before he can forgive*. It is here that the patient lets the therapist know that it feels satisfying to be able to punish. These feelings, so deeply buried or hidden from view from the therapy, only were able to come to the surface after working repeatedly with transferential eruptions that led to the exposure of aspects of material contained within Quadrant Four. It was the sturdiness of the therapeutic relationship over time that allowed the patient to then reveal the fact that it sometimes feels pleasurable to punish. Once the patient is able to admit this deep secret, a shift toward greater authenticity will be possible. Now, much of the integrative work within the other three quadrants, in terms of softening the compulsive stance can follow suit. Up to this point the idealized self-structure had been dependent on the protection of the revenge enactments following loyal waiting to remain intact.

SUMMARY

In this chapter we have discussed the various ways of recognizing the organizing schemas of the idealized self-system as it is differentiated from the authentic or real self. We have also highlighted the childhood environmental factors that are responsible for the creation of the compromised solution of overidealization as a way of maintaining self-coherence. In terms of the idealized self, the Four Quadrant model is a way of capturing a picture of how the parts of this complex, interconnected system work to form a compulsively driven, although tightly woven composite of the whole. By illustrating how the interconnected parts work together, we hope to have given therapists a way to begin using aspects of this model as entry points into dialogue that over time will allow the conversation between patient and therapist to reveal the more hidden territories of these organizing schemas.

There was little discussion given to Quadrant Two in this chapter. That is because Symptom Formation can appear at any time, and patients routinely come to us leading with complaints that stem from this quadrant. Generally, we understand symptom formation as an acute manifestation or communication that lets patients know that something has broken down in their drive to achieve overidealized longings and wishes. Acute symptoms are one of the few ways that the patient experiences how the other parts of the self-system become overtaxed or overburdened. Without symptoms, there would be no need for the idealized organizing mechanisms to be questioned or changed. Symptoms, in one sense, give birth to consciousness and curiosity.

For example, if the efforts contained in Quadrant Three of Loyal Waiting bear no signs of hope that the idealized other will change, patients often develop acute symptoms partially as a way of avoiding the reality of their disappointments. In this sense symptoms can also function as a distraction from disappointment, helping patients to maintain the wish for the idealized other. Yet, in another sense, symptoms also alert patients that something about their approach isn't working and, perhaps, they need to seek help in figuring out a better strategy for finding a satisfying relationship. If we examine the function of symptom formation in terms of feelings of retaliation that are generated from Quadrant Four, when feelings of self-destruction or the wish to harm others become so intense that they threaten to break through in actual self-destructive acts, symptoms of anxiety may become more acute, providing a balancing mechanism or a way to manage and quiet outbursts of rage.

The concomitant forces of anxiety and depression essentially can be viewed as flip sides of a single coin. Each symptom is often accompanied by the other, and both are a response to some fracture or disappointment in the idealized self-system. If one imagines multiple fractures or disappointment on a daily basis, some other mechanism must be put into place to stabilize the system. Here is where "The Pride System" comes into play.

In an overall sense, the Four Quadrant Model is used to capture a *picture of systemic pride in action*. What we mean by this is that as therapists it is our job to distinguish between the pride that comes as an outgrowth of healthy self-esteem and which is in the service of growth and the actualization of the authentic self vs. pride that masks vulnerability, an overcompensation for feelings of inadequacy, emptiness, and a fragile core. As a way of concluding and summarizing key points in this chapter, the following chart is provided.

	QUALITIES OF **Healthy Pride**		QUALITIES OF **Over-determined Pride**
1	Celebrates other people's accomplishment as well as one's own	Vs	Feels resentful and envious of other people's accomplishments
2	Does not feel threatened by or have a need to undermine others' accomplishments	Vs	Feels threatened by other people's accomplishments and needs to undermine or destroy them
3	Holds an accurate perspective of one's own contributions relative to the larger whole	Vs	Holds an inflated sense of one's own accomplishments relative to the accomplishments of others
4	Is able to maintain a sense of humility in the face of external achievements	Vs	Craves praise and rewards for external achievements
5	Can receive constructive feedback without becoming defensive	Vs	Becomes defensive and angry in the face of constructive criticism
6	Learns from mistakes and can readily admit them	Vs	Has difficulty admitting mistakes or learning from them.
7	Takes responsibilities for one's actions, both successes and failures	Vs	Blames other for mistakes and often defers responsibility onto others
8	Gives credit to others when credit is due	Vs	Takes credit for other people's ideas and accomplishments
9	Keeps a balanced perspective and can walk away from a project when it becomes too much	Vs	Is driven to achieve success at all costs and has difficulty knowing when to stop
10	Comfort in sharing intimate feelings, including the awareness of appropriate boundaries	Vs	Difficulty in sharing intimate feelings, including no apparent ability to understand mutuality and reciprocity

Figure 3.1 Qualities of pride—authentic versus idealized.

Questions from Our Supervisees

Question: Could you say a little more about why the overidealized self needs to be created in the first place? Also, what purpose does it serve in adulthood? Doesn't the person know on some level that he or she isn't being authentic?

Response: Idealization is a life saver for the child because in childhood the sense of self is in danger. Why does this happen? Because there is a breakdown in empathy and validation from the parental environment that gets experienced as an insult to the child's needs. This is basic empathic failure on the parents' part, pure and simple. Babies and children need a continuous, loving connection, and when that connection is broken, a part of the child gives up and becomes parched. It's as if there isn't enough oxygen in order to thrive, so the idealized self is a direct outgrowth of that breach. It is the child's attempt to create more oxygen. The child does this to keep safe. So, the seeds of the idealized self occur in response to failures in parental love and safety. The child in a creative response to that actually finds a way to replace the parent with a fictionalized version of what he needed from the parents, how he wishes he would have been nurtured. He is doing it all by himself. He's become both himself and his parents to avoid feelings of abandonment and panic.

Question: Is that why these overidealized standards that some adults set for themselves are so extreme, for example the need for perfectionism? Is it because these organizing schemas were formed in childhood and therefore the structures or ways of experiencing the self and the expectations placed on others has to be exaggerated—because this is still a reflection of childlike thinking?

Response: Yes, that's an interesting observation and it's correct. It goes further, however. As the child grows, the idealization both feeds and fuels itself. It gets chiseled and refined. For example, a child may want a parent to be "Superman" and creates super hero scenarios in his mind to help him feel safe and protected from the dangers in the home or his own inadequacy. All children do this in play to some extent, but the narcissistically damaged child refuses to let those fantasies go. They never get transformed or attenuated into a more reality-based version of self and others. Instead, he must become "Superman." He must be the best, the strongest, the most successful—perfect in other words. In our adult patients we see them holding onto these idealizations at all costs.

Question: Why can't they let go of those created images about themselves? They must realize on some level that they aren't based in reality.

Response: Yes, and no. They realize it on some level, in an intellectualized way, perhaps. But secretly, there is a stubborn refusal to give up the fantasy. Here is where we see the vertical split. Fantasy is split off from reality, but co-exists side-by-side. For example, some individuals never give up on the fantasy that they will find the perfect partner. Therefore, they enter relationships—often with healthy individuals—but they can never commit. At the first blush of disappointment, there is always the secret belief that somewhere there is the "perfect" other who will *never* disappoint them. At some point they begin to see this as a pattern, may even get that feedback from others that this is the case, but it doesn't seem to matter. It fades from view or pales in comparison to the wished for fantasy.

Response 2: Also, if they did give up on the hope that is preserved in fantasy, there is a grieving process involved. They seem to be saying, "This was something I needed. It was my friend, and now you're telling me I have to give it up?" Grieving is avoided because it reminds them of an internal weakness associated with their presumed defectiveness threatening to tumble them into feelings of shame. In a sense, the defense against feelings of shame interferes with the grieving process. It is grief that will set the authentic part of themselves free.

Question: Why do they want to hold onto the idealization so tightly? As we do the work of therapy, aren't we really acknowledging the real self, encouraging authenticity to be present?

Response: Yes, this is what we are doing. It is the aim of therapy, but it is a long-term process. In terms of why they hold on so tightly, let us imagine that the child has built a prosthesis. The question is after some time in therapy, the adult now begins to wonder if he still needs it. If you gradually dismantle the prosthesis of overidealization in therapy, the patient wonders whether his own leg will grow and be healthy enough to provide adequate support. Imagine all the thoughts and feelings that would come up. He might be thinking, "Why should I trust you? Other people let me down, that's why I had to build this in the first place. It works. I made it. Why give it up?"

Question: Don't they realize on some level that it's not real, how inefficient it is to keep the idealization going?

Response: If they give it up, they will have to grieve. Giving up the idealizations and wishes for rescue immediately throws the patient into reality. There they have to face how much of their life was lost, how unfair the hand was that was dealt to them, how the majority of their adult life has been built around these self-created idealization. The amount of grief, and also rage for that matter, can often seem overwhelming to the patient.

Response 2: Another part of the resistance has to do with the fact that on some level patients realize if they let go of wishes for restitution or rescue, their parents will be let off the hook. On some level the child part of the self is still saying, "I was the one who suffered. You (parents) get off free and clear with no apology, no guilt or remorse on your part? No way!" In part the stubborn refusal to give up the idealizations is an unconscious expression of anger at the parents, anger for having had to build the self-protecting prosthesis in the first place.

CHAPTER 4

Resonating between Part and Whole
Therapeutic Systemics

> In every living thing what we call the parts is so inseparable from the whole that the parts can only be understood in the whole, and we can neither make the parts the measure of the whole nor the whole the measure of the parts; and this is why living creatures, even the most restricted, have something about them that we cannot quite grasp and have to describe as infinite or partaking of infinity.
>
> —GOETHE (1785, P. 195)

IF WE WERE to take a pulse using contemporary culture as a barometer, at first blush it may appear that we have completely lost an interest in understanding complexity. The demand for immediate answers, the promise of a quick fix, make it so much easier to form snap judgments rather than trying to understand how various parts connect to a larger whole. If we merely point to shifts in our attitudes toward education funding or to how information is disseminated through the media and advertising, we find more than enough evidence of a narrowing of focus, oversimplification, and reactivity in our thinking. Reductionistic sound bites now pose arguments in either/or terms, offering them up as truth or proof. Intellectual curiosity and critical thinking are framed as elitist or unnecessarily complicated. The desire and the effort it takes to hold greater and greater degrees of complexity, and therefore a larger grasp of how various parts comprise an interconnected whole, seem to be diminishing from the collective cultural landscape.

And yet, an interesting and equally compelling trend also seems to be present. If one were to simply examine the line-up of television shows week after week (as one meager barometer of cultural trends), it is astonishing to see the amount of programming that is dedicated to crime solving, intricate analyses performed by a long list of detectives and forensic investigators, details that are painstakingly spelled out for the viewing audience. Our admiration for protagonists such as Sherlock Holmes, Hercule Poirot, and now a flock of modern day detectives and forensic analysts seems to be universal and apparently timeless.

What is equally curious is that these star sleuths are often paired against other agency officials who are quick to rush to judgment, making assumptions based on superficial evidence and personal bias. We react with contempt at the officer who rushes to a premature conclusion; and we identify with the intellect, patience, and the perseverance of Sherlock Holmes. We try to figure out how he puts the pieces of the puzzle together and are often surprised at the end, when Poirot or Holmes methodically bring into alignment each piece of evidence until a clear picture of the whole emerges. In spite of ourselves, it appears that some part of the psyche is trying to understand and master part-whole analysis. Intuitively, if we are to advance, perhaps we know that cracking *this* DNA code lies in our ability to create a method of understanding part-whole systemics.

Creating the Context

The concept of "parts" making up a "whole' greater than the sum of its parts has been accepted as a truism for centuries. Philosophers have weighed in on this. Spinoza spoke of connecting the "least parts and the greatest wholes," and Goethe noted that parts are "so inseparable from the whole that the parts can only be understood in the whole." In fact, Fairley (1947) notes that Goethe was so deeply committed to part-whole process that the philosopher-scientist felt that both truth and beauty were derivatives of it. Contemporary social scientists have concluded that "[h]uman communication is so complex and ambiguous that in order to understand it, participants must constantly be shuttling back and forth between the smallest moving parts, the words and gestures, and the largest wholes: not only the whole conversation of which the exchange is a part, but the whole relationship, family, society, and civilization out of which each utterance has grown" (Scheff, 1997, p. 204).

However, the acceptance of the truism has not led to a clear or uniform understanding of how such a dynamic process unfolds psychologically. The difficulty in operationalizing part-whole thinking is that the process involved is acausal and hence does not lend itself to linear thinking, linear definitions, or linear logic. With linear logic, after all, if 1 and 1 equals 2, then how can the whole of 2 be greater than 1 and 1?

Part-whole systemic analysis empowers the therapist with a non-linear method of processing information, one that allows us to see how the various parts of the psyche are dependent on other parts, each tightly woven and interconnected to comprise a homeostatic balance within the personality. By using a non-linear approach to therapeutic listening, we find that we are better able to anticipate what might be missing from the picture at any given moment, as well as what might happen if we attempt to "alter" one part of the personality matrix that comprises the whole.

From our perspective, using a non-linear method of processing information does not do violence to the dynamic connections within the psychic process; rather, it expands our ability to see those connections. It easily embraces both conscious and unconscious factors as well as relational and contextual influences that have an impact on an individual's psyche. As highlighted in chapter 1, the relationship between part and whole is both reciprocal and reflexive, each enriching the other in a continuing systemic circle. When someone comes into our office, they come with a history from a particular family, a particular community, and with stresses and discomforts within their present lives that may surface in the form of symptomatic complaints. The part-whole analysis that we are offering allows the therapist to listen across these complex and divergent experiences to see how they relate, where to intervene, and how intervening may affect any one of the experiences (parts) or a more fundamental way of being in the world (whole).

The Four Quadrant Model presented in chapter 2 is essentially a visual representation of how one might begin a non-linear approach to part-whole analysis. In other words this diagram is a tool to help organize and categorize component parts of the self in a way that begins to track where integration and connectivity flow easily between the various parts of the self. On the other hand, where there is disconnection or dissociation between the parts, the compensatory, defensive, or dissociated responses becomes obvious. We see these connections and disconnections through:

- An analysis of the consistency or inconsistency between words and behaviors
- An analysis of the consistency or inconsistency between values and actions
- An analysis of what is being said and what is not being said within the treatment hour

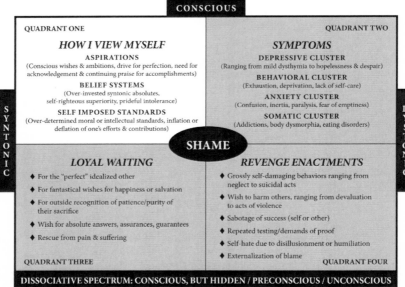

Figure 4.1 Four quadrant model—illustrating part-whole connections.

The various components that are highlighted in the model can help us become better organized at capturing a snapshot of both the intrapsychic organizing schemas and interpersonal motivations of the psyche simultaneously. Our ability to traverse between these perspectives is what allows us to see part-whole analysis in action. Structurally, the Four Quadrant Model is a picture of an "open system," where each part can be seen as a subcomponent, but each part can also be viewed as *partially* autonomous. Parts serve both each other and the larger system which comprises the whole.

We can understand how Quadrant One can be viewed as *partially autonomous* by narrowing our line of inquiry to this subcomponent of the psyche that describes the overidealized construction of the self. This subcomponent is divided into further parts—one's ambitions, belief systems, and standards. In terms of therapeutic inquiry each of these parts within Quadrant One requires further examination in order to understand the detailed composition of each sub-part of the individual personality.

The various sub-parts within Quadrant One will vary from individual to individual. No two individuals' overdetermined aspirations, beliefs, or standards will look the same. Our job as therapists is to understand how the details of the various sub-parts *within* Quadrant One operate in a unique manner with each patient. In addition, the part-whole analysis must be expanded *between* quadrants, as well. By observing how the individual with overidealized standards interacts with other people in his or her environment, we are able to see how Quadrant One connects with Quadrants Three and Four.

It is only when we think about the connectivity between the parts that we are able to see the relationship to the whole. It is only when we measure the person's ability to strive for success in conjunction with how that same person treats others in relationship that the larger systemic whole begins to emerge. For example, if we are able to link the patient's internal capacity for self-awareness to interpersonal triggers of disappointment and ask what meaning this might have in terms of how the person views himself, are we able to assess the level of resilience or rigidity of the individual. Through part-whole analysis we are able to attend to both the intrapsychic and interpersonal aspects of psychic organization simultaneously. Therefore, the Four Quadrant Model becomes a visual tracking devise, helping us shift back and forth until the parts fall into an alignment of a systemic whole.

Having said this, it is important to mention that the Four Quadrant Model does not present a *static* picture of the self. As therapy unfolds we are able to see how parts resonate with other parts and with the whole, and the whole in turn resonates with the parts and with (possibly yet unknown) greater wholes. In other words the picture is constantly evolving and changing. Simply by entering into a therapeutic dialogue where two people are engaged in a discovery process, the existing homeostatic balance of the personality will be altered.

It is a general truism that systems are continually in a state of flux, either moving toward growth or toward entropy. In terms of the therapeutic process, although there may not be a complete integration of all of the various parts into a "finished product," it is important to emphasize that the composite parts of an individual upon *entering* into therapy will not look like the same composite of parts upon *leaving* therapy. Ideally, the end result will produce a more "open system," one in which more aspects of the personality will be freed up to be brought into alignment with the authentic self, which in turn allows the individual greater access to present attention, creative thinking, and further growth.

The ability to slow down the listening process, paying critical attention to the details of the dialogue in the *present* actually changes *the quality of what we are capable of observing*. By tracking the moment-to-moment unfolding of the various parts that comprise a whole, we are able to slow things down enough that we can suspend our judgments, our preconceived notions, our rush to foreclose or interpret, so that *something new can emerge*. This is precisely how and why the change process in therapy actually works.

Authors in the field of organizational dynamics (Kim, Senge, Scharmer, Jaworski, Flowers, Block, Schein) and others highlight the importance of the process of part-whole analysis from an organizational systemic perspective. Through careful observation and reflective participation in the study of part-whole analysis with groups, work and leadership teams, these systems' analysts were able to make the determination that, "Until people can start to see their habitual ways of interpreting a situation, they can't really step into a new awareness" (Senge, et al., 2004, p. 45). They conclude that part-whole analysis allows us to suspend our thinking, and train ourselves in a way that we can begin to shift our attention, between field and ground, between what is in the background and what is in the foreground, to the point that eventually we are able to see "the dynamic living process" that is contained within all systems.

Applying Part-Whole to Create Leverage Points for Deeper Inquiry

When an individual enters therapy, the dialogic process begins in an attempt to create leverage points within the existing homeostatic balance of part and whole. This in turn can evolve into a connection or integration of parts, which then transmutes into a larger system whole. Since every part of a system is resonating with every other part of the self-system, as well as the external environment, the homeostatic balance is never really at rest.

The following case example illustrates what we mean by reflexive resonance between parts into an increasing awareness of a larger whole.

Patient: No matter what kind of shoes I buy, they always bother my feet. It's crazy.

Therapist: Do you mean your feet are cramped?

Patient: Yes, all the time.

Therapist: Can you go with that feeling?

Patient: What feeling?

Therapist: The feeling of being cramped.

Patient: I don't know. It makes me feel like pressed ham.

Therapist: Like you're being jammed into a shape that's not yours?

Patient: I guess I feel I can't be myself, like there is always some pressure against me.

Therapist: It reminds me of the dream you had a couple of weeks ago that people were trying to talk you into renouncing your values.

Patient: Yes! It's the same thing, I guess. I want to be me and only be me, not anyone else. Am I too touchy about this?

In order to understand how parts are both reciprocal and reflexive, we begin by first identifying several of the parts contained within a dialogue and then try to see the reciprocal nature between them. In this example the patient begins by saying that his feet always bother him. The therapist tries to expand the inquiry process by changing the word *bother* to *cramped*, and then tries to link this with a feeling state by suggesting that the patient "go with that feeling." This invitation initially goes over the patient's head because he's not connecting the part (his complaint about his feet) to anything else. At this point it represents a split-off part. However, the therapist persists and repeats the association of being cramped with a feeling state. Now, we see that the patient is able to volunteer more information saying, "It makes me feel like pressed ham." You will note that the patient has made a shift to a more expanded metaphor and couples this with a feeling association. Here we are able to see how moment-to-moment inquiry that remains involved in the patient's *present* state produces a clearer picture of the whole coming into focus. *The process of moment-to-moment tracking is a way of both staying in the present and slowing down the inquiry process so that we may gather a more complete picture of the psyche.*

Attending to this level of contextual detail is an example of how non-linear or "extra-linear" processing of information can expand and enrich our understanding of the patient. In this case because the patient has volunteered the image of "pressed ham," the therapist is able to connect being jammed into a shape that is not his and also connect it with a dream the patient had about people trying to make him conform to values (or a shape) other than his own. It is at this point that we are able to see the whole as a characterological picture of detachment. The patient feels the world is trying to change him, and he fights by taking a position of resignation.

As we can see from this brief therapeutic exchange, narcissistic character solutions are internally highly woven systems although the "weave" may not be visible for some time. The process of part-whole analysis needs to be open to remain resonant. This is because we are depending on an open system to educate us on "parts." A system remains open when it is not concretized or reductive, not reified, and not foreclosed or preordained. In other words an open system welcomes feedback, is able to assimilate new information, which allows for the possibility of integrating existing parts and new information into a greater whole.

One of our goals as therapists is to find leverage points of inquiry in order that we increase the patient's conscious awareness and curiosity about automatic thoughts and assumptions that have worked in the service of maintaining a closed-system. Opening up the system to new information first involves the therapist's immersion in the present in order to better understand the already existing homeostatic balance, both in the other and in oneself. It is only through our understanding of the details of the parts and how they function to maintain a delicate balance, that we can slowly create the leverage required for change.

As therapists we are required to call upon all our senses to identify cognitive-affective elements that may later be seen to be important constituent elements of an organic whole. In order to uncover, amplify, and understand elements of the organic whole, a method of trial and error is entirely appropriate. Psychotherapy is remarkably forgiving of a therapist's listening faculties as treatment quickly moves from moment to moment. If we trust in this truth, it takes some of the pressure off of the assumption that we must be "perfectly" attuned to any given exchange. This in turn allows us to begin to trust our own developing intuition, once we slow the clinical process down to ask about a possible "part." Slowing the patient down automatically slows us down. Conversely, slowing ourselves down can open up important phenomenological insights into the treatment process.

How to Access Part-Whole Analysis through "Entry Points" in the Dialogue

Often an emotionally laden word or phrase early in a session will turn out to be a "part." How then might we turn this word or phrase into an entry point that will lead us into an exploration process that goes deeper? For example, if a patient says, "*It seems that a lot of people always try to take the easy way out*," we can treat this as an *entry point* and an opportunity to slow down the process in order to gain further clarification into our understanding of the meaning of this simple statement. As a way of going deeper, the therapist may zero in on the phrase *easy way out* and ask if the patient has been seeing this sort of thing frequently, or she may follow with a question wondering whether it seems as if other people aren't carrying their fair share of the load.

This opens the dialogue to wondering whether the patient feels overburdened, or isolated, or unable to ask for help. Depending on how the patient answers the initial question, the therapist will follow the patient's lead, tracking the unfolding exchange in order to get a clearer picture of how that particular part connects to the greater whole. In doing so we are able to see how the phrase *easy way out* may reveal a personal standard that the patient holds for himself in Quadrant One and how this standard is measured in terms of relational disappointments in Quadrant Three. Then, we can begin to wonder what might happen next. Will the patient develop symptoms in Quadrant Two or express his disappointment in a vindictive way in Quadrant Four? Seizing upon a word or phrase as an *entry point* allows us to track the patient's immediate response, which in turn will lead us into further investigation as to meaning. A more complete understanding of meaning can only occur when we are able to see how the connection between the parts of the psyche lead to an alignment with the whole.

Thus, from the beginning of treatment, this is *how* we enter into a process of engagement with the patient's phenomenological "present." By staying close to the emotionally laden word, we begin to see the forces and assumptions behind "innocent" statements and how these statements lead us to greater understanding of what drives the part. The great advantage of experiential learning through immersion is that there are no *a-priori* rights and wrongs. The emotional truth reveals itself in the intersubjective space through many fits and starts but always as a co-created product of the patient's contributions and the therapist's ability to listen. Immersion need not be, cannot be, and ought not to be governed by any imposition of "accuracy." Theoretical presumptions or rushed interpretations may foreclose an open discovery process. Process is the ultimate arbiter.

Many theorists aspire to an "experience-near" approach of integrating the interpersonal and intrapsychic dimensions into a systemic whole but fall short of it, being unable to sustain the integration experientially. (It is only with a systemic perspective that "inter" and "intra" can be seen as two sides of the same coin, not separable in theory or practice). There are of course notable exceptions. Beebe and Lachmann (2005) specifically start with the premise that "self-regulation and interactive regulation are continuously affecting each other" (p. 223) thereby allowing therapists to access a "focus on process" (p. 223). Similarly, Wachtel (2008) recommends attending "in meticulous detail to the patient's *experienced* subjectivity" (p. 148) while Stern (2004) calls for a new form of consciousness which he calls "intersubjective consciousness" (p. 125).

Frequently Asked Questions

Many of our therapists in training ask, "How can I tell when a word or phrase is a part of a larger whole or whether what the patient is saying is simply a minor comment?" Although there is no precisely correct answer, perhaps we can gain further understanding by clarifying how we are defining entry point. *An entry point is any word or phrase that strikes your own subjective awareness to the point that it gives you pause.* In other words you may be struck by the tone in the patient's voice, or a pronouncement she delivers that contains an expectation or shared assumption, or perhaps you detect an undercurrent of a feeling even when one is being denied or not quite articulated. In some instances the patient may make a statement that contradicts other factors that were previously reported. For example, a patient with a known history of being abused may say, "My mother was a saint." Obviously, at least two pieces of information (or parts) do not seem to be lining up. You may not understand why at this point. However, it is this lack of understanding that gives you an indication that you have hit upon an important entry point that requires further investigation.

Your choice in that moment might be either to ask the patient about her statement, or to wait for a more opportune moment because you sense a fragility within the patient, with emotional undercurrents of shame. Whether you act on the entry point in that moment or file it away until the patient is more able to tolerate potentially uncomfortable feelings that may emerge is a judgment decision. What is important is thinking about the parts you are observing and whether they seem to be connected to or dissociated from each other and from the whole.

As an exercise based on the example of this entry point, what are some of the questions you might begin to wonder about in terms of connecting part to whole when you hear the patient say, "My mother is a saint"?

- Would you wonder about what is not being said?
- How might you ask a question that would go in the direction of what might consciously or unconsciously be omitted?
- Would you follow-up on the patient's choice of the word "saint," and if so, what might you say next?
- What could you ask that would not offend the patient or throw the patient into a defensive position of over-loyalty and/or embarrassment?

Regardless of what line of inquiry you choose, the overarching goal is to gather more information about the highly charged word that powerfully telegraphs that there is more to the story. Using the part-whole inquiry process will eventually lead us to greater and greater systemic awareness, which in this example contributes to the totality of the patient's character structure.

A second frequently asked question by therapists-in-training is "where and when do I intervene in a therapy session and how do I come to that decision?" The therapist has something in mind to say but is not sure the intervention is consonant with the therapeutic context or the patient's mood. Or, perhaps, the therapist is concerned about the patient's readiness to go deeper. Issues of timing or the possibility of triggering a negative transferential reaction are important factors to consider when using the patient's exact language as an entry point for further inquiry. Furthermore, "entry points" are easier to see in a case presentation after the fact, but they are considerably more difficult to identify in the midst of a perhaps tense therapy hour. However, when a therapist begins to understand how parts connect with the whole, answering questions as to *what to say* and *when to say it* become easier.

As an example, when a patient says, "I can't say anymore," the therapist may realize that this is a point of "saying and not saying," thus allowing possible therapeutic entry. In the above statement what appears to be the closing down of an exchange *can* be an opening leading to further inquiry. Following the patient's statement of "I can't say anymore," the therapist may ask for further elaboration by saying, "Can you imagine being able to say more if we just sat quietly together for a moment?" This statement from the therapist does several things. First, it telegraphs to the patient that the therapist knows there is more to say but that there is no need to rush the process. This in turn gives the patient a sense of permission to regain control over the pace of the unfolding therapy. Second, the therapist's comment models a slowing down of the process by being willing to wait comfortably in silence, trusting that something more will emerge. Third, the therapist is "forecasting" that she trusts that the patient has the capacity to go deeper, sensing that perhaps there is possibly a hidden "loyalty" issue or sense of shame or inadequacy behind the phrase "I can't say anymore."

As you can see from the above example, when the therapist decides to intervene in such a way, it is often to simply ask for elaboration. However, this seemingly simple act affirms the value of the *present* for the patient. As well, the patient understands that the therapist's willingness to wait until the patient is ready to say more is an invitation by the therapist for greater self-immersion by the patient in his or her own experience, which further conveys to the patient the importance of the "moment." If the entry point turns out to highlight a constituent part of an organic whole, then the patient has a chance to educate both her or himself (and the therapist) on an important clinical area, important both for the moment and for the future of the therapy.

THEORETICAL SUMMARY POINTS

Pathogenic character structures cannot dismantle themselves until the dissociative splits keeping the constituent parts disconnected from each other can first be identified. Unconscious components, semi-conscious disavowal, and dystonic feelings can certainly all be involved in such splits between over-idealized (perfectionistic) standards and massive self-negating thoughts. The two ends of the split fuel and reinforce each other in a pathological spiral and constitute the systemic whole of a compulsive character "solution."

However, because reality constantly impinges upon us, the overidealized (or closed) system is without relief. Individuals or groups that exist in closed systems initially attempt to maintain a compulsively driven homeostatic balance by pushing away information that is threatening to the existing status quo. The level of denial, degree of blind spots, and increased rigidity/fragility, however, point out that the system is in a devolving spiral. In other words in a closed system what *appears* to be in homeostatic balance is actually in a state of entropy. If new information or feedback from outside sources is resisted, the system cannot correct itself or accommodate important feedback that would help move the growth process. Pathological spirals are the reason why we can say, if we are not getting better, we are getting worse.

It may be important to point out that although all compulsively driven (and therefore overdetermined) character structures are tightly integrated with visible and invisible parts, this fact does not define the seriousness of the narcissistic disturbance. The seriousness of the disorder is determined by how much of the patient's *healthy* resources have been co-opted by the compulsive structures, how much attainable needs get superseded by unattainable needs, how much real self has been sacrificed to "false self," and how much health has been invaded by non-health. Thus, all of us will appear on a continuum of narcissistic character vulnerability but differ in how much the compulsive solutions have invaded our spontaneous resources.

We have described how parts operate eventually to reveal their organic connections to each other and their organic connections to a larger whole. Organic connections are always interconnections; witness the human body. These are moving dynamic parts that may appear to be utterly disconnected but, with wider and wider framed circles, begin to shape a systemic whole. We have also mentioned that parts can only be tentatively identified pending continuing empathic immersion in the patient's experience.

Each part is subject to continued scrutiny as new parts come into view. For example, a patient says, "I can't focus" but later says, "I'm everywhere and nowhere." The latter puts the former in a larger frame. Parts are on "trial" until a whole can be identified but of course even a whole can be superseded by a wider systemic frame, rendering the former "whole" now a "part." This process does not end and indeed cannot end. In sum, part-whole is an extra-linear open system of processing information, building on itself as it proceeds.

Integrating an Understanding of the Four Quadrant Model with Part-Whole

Case Example 1

Note: The following supervisory exchange occurred with beginning level therapists shortly after teaching them our Four Quadrant Model. At this point we had had three sessions with the group. The first two sessions were spent explaining the theoretical underpinnings of the model as reflected in the first three chapters of this manual. Some of their questions that pertain to the integration of concepts are recorded in chapters 2 and 3. In our third meeting we offered a sample case vignette as a way of practicing and applying what they had learned thus far. This also offered us an opportunity to assess their level of understanding and integration of theoretical material as well as providing further opportunities for questions and discussion.

The exchange that follows occurred in our fourth meeting with the group, which meant that this dialogue was recorded after a total of only 4½ hours of group supervision. It should be noted that when we began with this group of three, they had difficulty understanding concepts such as "syntonic" and "dystonic" and weren't certain how relevant it was for them to pay attention to the unconscious if the therapy were short-term. What surprised us as supervisors was how quickly this group, who were virtually untrained in dynamic therapies, could pick up part-whole dynamics. Not only were they able to think about cases in fairly sophisticated ways, they demonstrated that they could begin applying aspects of our Four Quadrant model with their patients.

Patricia: We wanted to get back to a question you had posed to us earlier. You had asked if this model could apply to short-term therapy. I guess we would say that it would depend on how short-term, who your general client population is, and what expectations and resources particular clients are bringing to you. In a general sense, however, we want to begin by saying that this model certainly is a useful tool diagnostically with either short-term or long-term treatments. In many instances it can be used in short-term therapy but in a more modified way. Sam, you were telling us earlier about a client you are seeing in brief therapy where you began to apply some of the concepts from the model, and it really had an impact. Do you want to tell us about that?

Therapist: Yes, that would be good to help me think it through a little more. This is a young man, age twenty-three, single and in graduate school. I have seen him for five sessions thus far. He began this session by telling me about an incident that happened where he was frustrated with a classmate, and he was ready to just write-off the friendship. Apparently, he had asked his friend to meet him for coffee to go over an assignment in a class they were taking together, and the friend said that he couldn't because he had to study for another exam but would be happy to meet him later in the week. My client began his session by saying that he was very disappointed and had immediately become very depressed. At prior points in his life, this client had reported that he occasionally had fleeting suicidal thoughts when he experienced disappointments in relationships. Today, he said that he was tired of being so affected by people and wanted to talk about how he could figure out a way to not let these situations get to him like this.

Now, normally, I would have immediately begun with a cognitive intervention to bring him some relief from his symptoms of depression, such as trying to help him problem solve ways that he could build up a larger social network. I'd connect this with how he wouldn't feel so vulnerable to rejection if he could call on more than one person whom he counted on as a friend (which is his overall pattern.) My strategy would have been to try to change the outcome in order to alleviate and ultimately prevent disappointment and symptomatic reactions. This time I started thinking about the Loyal Waiting Quadrant and the Overidealized Self Quadrant and decided to explore whether any of his symptoms of depression stemmed from over-idealized expectations he had of others living up to his standards.

Jack: Excellent formulation. So, how did you introduce this line of inquiry?

Therapist: Well, I asked him to tell me the outcome of their initial phone conversation. I asked whether he followed up on his friend's offer, and how he resolved his disappointment. I remember thinking that I needed to slow things down, get as many details as I could—I was trying to practice phenomenological tracking (laughs).

Patricia: Great! So tell us about the exchange between the two of you.

Therapist: So, he tells me that he did agree to meet for coffee a couple of days later, and I asked him, "How was that for you?" He had a look of frustration or disgust on his face and said, "It was worthless." I remember thinking that this was a pretty extreme reaction, so I thought about his overidealized standards and expectations of others. I also should say that he has a family background where both of his parents would drop everything whenever he had a need or request. Regardless of whether they were in the middle of something or not, they would stop what they were doing and respond to his requests.

So, then I thought about that continuum under each of the four quadrants, and I asked him whether his expectations of others were being connected or in any way measured against how his parents treated him. I wondered with him out loud if there were any other ways people could "measure up" in terms of proving that they cared about him. I asked him if he could think about a "continuum of care." We then began talking together about what a 10 out of 10 would look like, then what would an 8 look like, or a 6 on that continuum.

My client started getting pretty excited and actually got into the exercise. After we identified some specifics about what other behaviors might look like further down the continuum, he was able to say, "You know, maybe someone's 8 for me is really their 10. Maybe, this is all they can do or give. Maybe, that's okay." I know that some of this was working on a cognitive level, but I realized that the difference is that the line of questioning wasn't in the service of fixing or symptom relief.

(Therapist turns to us) What was amazing for me about this is the guy wasn't depressed at all after that. He actually said he felt better and he looked energized. But, I don't know where to take it from here. I know that there is some stuff that is buried in Quadrant Four, but the guy never gets angry. He has had these overidealized expectations, but where is the anger?

Jack: Ok, first of all, let's look at how far you've come. You've already started to link up the parts with the whole. You heard dialogue from Quadrant One, and you linked it to Quadrant Three in terms of loyal waiting for others to meet his parents' standards. By moving into the territory of relationship being connected to loyal waiting, you gently suggest that there might be a way to maintain friendships other than by adhering to this perfectly idealized standard. At some further point you might want to ask your patient if his parents ever gave him any messages around how he should expect others in the world outside of family to treat him. But, you would want to wait for a bit longer timing-wise before asking that question because it might threaten his sense of loyalty to them. For now, you did just the right thing entering Quadrant Three in the manner that you did.

Patricia: Also, do you notice how you are already moving around the quadrants pretty organically? You knew that there was something that "wasn't being said" when you began to wonder about Quadrant Four. You also noticed that there was something unusual about having that level of idealization without any apparent manifestation from Quadrant Four. But, I would like to suggest that your patient did reveal a bit of Quadrant Four when you asked him how it felt to meet with his friend two days later. He said that the experience was "worthless." Do you hear the devaluing that is contained within that statement? Yes, there is disappointment, but there was also more than disappointment. He was devaluing the experience because it didn't live up to his expectations, and he was also indirectly devaluing his friend by calling him worthless. In other words, if you don't live up to my standards (and my parents' standards) you are worthless.

Therapist: Wow, you're right. Now, I see it.

Jack: You know, there is such a thing as over-solicitous care. You can begin to wonder for yourself, why did his parents have to drop everything every time their child had a need? What were they afraid of? What were they trying to prevent? How might this patient have picked up on their fear, which may explain some of the shame that is underlying his disappointment in others? For example, does he feel unworthy unless others drop everything as a sign of proof? Does he secretly believe that his parents thought he was fragile or inept?

Therapist: Yeah, if a parent never lets you struggle to find your own answers, meet some of your own needs, or delay gratification, where is that child left? There's no chance to develop a sense of one's own mastery.

Patricia: Yes, and you just described the difference between overgratification and being given the right amount of gratification and attention to let the authentic self emerge. People can be stifled and boxed in just as much by over attention as under attention, especially over attention coupled with anxiety.

Jack: All of what Patricia and I are talking about right now is a cluster of questions that you would keep in the back of your mind, for future harvesting in the therapy

Supervisee One: You know, as I'm listening to you all, I can now see more clearly how this model could be very useful with short-term work. It's not as if you'll have a chance to get all of it done. Maybe there won't be time for "future harvesting" if you will. But, Sam provided value to his client in the short run. Who knows what an impact that will have?

Jack: Yes, some patients are able to use short-term therapy if they penetrate sufficiently into the conscious/ unconscious, syntonic/dystonic whole. It's as if they recognize on some level that you see them, that you get the whole picture even if you only do a small portion of the excavating.

Supervisee Two: Can we go back to the diagnostic piece for a minute? I'm thinking about how this patient had feelings of suicidality in the past. What does that say to us in terms of how far we go with the excavating if we know its short-term work?

Jack: Good point. Some of what we have to keep in mind when we hear information like this is monitoring the pace of the therapy, how much to be mindful of and what we contain as well as open up. However, if we can make inroads to the patient's level of extreme overidealization, perhaps some of the tension around the intensity of disappointment might be modulated and, therefore, suicidal thoughts may diminish. It is very difficult to know for sure unless the patient comes back into therapy.

Patricia: And, I would predict that if this patient came back to therapy, he would remember you and think to call you back. This is unlike many people who go from short-term therapist to therapist. They will tell you about former treatments, "Yes, the therapy was okay. It was supportive, but I want to try something different this time." I guess what it boils down to is if you understand what you're listening for in the patient's presentation on a dynamic level, seeing all four quadrants simultaneously, it's a little bit like doing laser therapy rather than using a scalpel.

Supervisee One: You mean rather than using a Band-Aid (laughs).

Analysis of Case Consultation

At the time of the recording of this supervisory dialogue, these beginner-level clinicians had not had the opportunity to read this chapter. Therefore, they did not have the opportunity to study part-whole analysis or the opportunity to integrate these concepts. What we were struck by in the above supervisory exchange, however, was that when clinicians began to develop a working understanding of the Four Quadrant Model, their thinking about what they were hearing in sessions *naturally* led to part-whole analysis. This organic unfolding confirmed our assumptions that if trainees were presented a clear, visual picture of multiple aspects of the dynamics of the therapeutic exchange, as reflected in the four components of the patient's psyche, they would automatically begin to anticipate what was missing from the content of the dialogue, both intrapsychically and interpersonally. This proved to be the case with Sam.

When we can begin to recognize *what is missing* as well as *what is being expressed* in any given exchange, this is when we begin to see the power of deep immersion early in the therapeutic process. As noted, these trainees asked whether a dynamic understanding of clients could be applied in short-term therapies. We see from this case illustration that the answer can be a *qualified yes*. Sam talked about how he heard his patient's complaints differently—from the vantage point of loyal waiting. Because of that, he saw *the part* emerge more clearly in what his client was reporting. In turn he was then able to direct his line of inquiry in a different direction than he would have if he had simply used a "solution-focused" intervention. Sam admitted that a solution-focused strategy would have taken him in a direction where he would explore with the patient how he could possibly avoid disappointments in the future. For example, he noted that he might have suggested that the patient should call on more people rather than banking on one friendship to meet his needs, or perhaps if the patient hadn't waited until the last minute to make a call, he could have prevented his disappointment.

Although Sam drew upon cognitive techniques to help him phrase questions for his client to reflect upon, he *paired* these questions with an understanding of the power of loyalty. He was able to connect the client's present-day expectation of others to the behavior of his parents, where they dropped everything to meet his needs. Sam was able to explore with his client how his parents' behavior had instilled unrealistic expectations in him that then became the test he used to see if present friendships could measure up to his ideal.

By penetrating the patient's less than conscious assumptions around loyalty, Sam was able to break through some of the overidealized standards around the experience of disappointment in relationships. Rather than seeing relationships as either "all-gratifying" or "worthless," his client was able to express a more measured, modulated definition of his expectations. In this session Sam was able to move his client out of all-or-nothing, black and white thinking that reflected his idealized standard of others, to an appreciation of the limitations of others viewed from a more compassionate vantage point.

As future sessions unfold, we can hope that Sam might be able to leverage this insight about others to the exploration of expectations that Sam's client places on himself. Much more work is needed to delve into all four quadrants, but we can begin to see that a partial exploration and integration is possible in short-terms therapies. In this case a short-term therapy may help with a lessening of the rigid expectations placed on others, but the resolution of those expectations in terms of the patient's own expectations of himself may remain fixed and tightly held. It is also unlikely that opening up feelings of anger and retaliation contained within Quadrant Four may bear much fruit if short-term work is limited to twenty sessions or less.

In summary one might view this short-term therapy as laying a foundation for further work at some future point in time. Making inroads on multiple parts connecting to the larger whole is where we see how long-term treatment becomes the modality of choice to work through deeper and broader aspects of the overidealized construction. Without this deeper and broader penetration, we can expect that symptoms will reemerge at some point in the future, requiring further working through. Or we can assume that there is some risk of backslide into old patterns and assumptions, as, in our experience, the wished for ideal is difficult to relinquish.

Case Example 2

An intermediate level therapist comes into supervision stating that his patient seems to be "stuck in her life and in her therapy." He tells the supervisor that he sees the situation as "tragic and so unfair." The relevant case history is then reported. A woman, age fifty-two, who has been in treatment for approximately a year, has recently been diagnosed with early stages of Parkinson's disease. She has been in an unsupportive marriage throughout their relationship, but now her husband has become even more critical and irritated with her because her disease is compromising her ability to function. The husband complains that the patient "can't keep up with him like she used to" and that "their life is becoming boring." The patient reports that she believes that her husband is in denial about her illness because she states that he has told her that he thinks she's "faking it to get sympathy."

The therapist admits to being quite angry and "charged up" about the situation. He points out that the husband lost his job over five years ago and doesn't seem interested in contributing to the household or pulling his own weight. The patient continues to work full time and ends up doing all of the cooking and cleaning. He wonders with his supervisor why his patient just doesn't leave him. He also states that the woman's sister and her friends keep giving her advice, telling her to leave. However, when the therapist asks her why she stays, she reports that it doesn't really bother her and offers the statement, "I'm used to it. I had to take care of my father and brothers when mother died. All men are alike; they're all helpless."

When asked what the therapist did around this particular entry point, he stated that he had tried to make the connection between her husband's expectations and her former role in her family of origin as a caretaker. He also asked the patient if she thought she was so used to being in this role that she had resigned herself to doing nothing because her strength is not what it used to be. However, the therapist then reported that these questions didn't seem to be getting them anywhere. He also stated that he has tried to explore any fears she might have around her husband's inability to take care of her if she gets any worse, thinking that perhaps this might explain her lack of movement. Again, he reported that these questions seemed to lead nowhere.

Analysis

Here, we have an intermediate level clinician who is frustrated by an unfair situation and where he is possibly overidentified with the patient's recent news of the diagnosis of Parkinson's disease. To begin, we might ask ourselves, "What is missing from this picture in terms of the patient's presentation?" One obvious answer is to note that there appears to be a noticeable absence of anger on the part of the patient with regard to her "unfair" situation on a number of levels, her illness, her marriage, the amount of support she is getting at home. Consequently, everyone around her who cares about her is carrying some of the dissociated affect—her friends, her family, even her therapist.

The therapeutic question is, "How do we get to the hidden affect?" How do we facilitate a process that will help the patient make better decisions around planning for her future and self-care as she declines in health? As we can see, the therapist's direct approach has not worked. Questions such as, "Why do you stay, why don't you leave" get nowhere. Therefore, we go to the patient's comment, "It really doesn't bother me. I'm used to it. I had to take care of my father and brothers when mother died. All men are alike;

they're all helpless." Any of the above statements is a powerful entry point. By understanding more fully what it was like for her when her mother died can produce a wealth of information. By exploring what the patient means by "all men are helpless," the therapist is allowed entrance into assumptions about helplessness, her need to be self-sufficient, and her possible feelings about her male therapist as being helpless.

The therapist's interventions to this point were either attempts to come up with solutions, or attempts to direct his patient toward an interpretation prematurely. Both interventions shifted *away from the present* and away from deeper inquiry as to how the parts aligned with the whole. The patient will not be able to feel her sadness, her loss, her fear, or her anger until these parts are brought into more conscious awareness and alignment. Once doing so, affect is generally a natural outcome.

Questions from Our Trainees

Trainee: I'm not quite sure that I see how part-whole analysis and entry points fit into the Four Quadrant Model. Are the four quadrants different parts in themselves, or are there parts contained within *each* quadrant?

Jack: The answer is that it is both. Each quadrant has multiple parts that are unique to each individual, and each quadrant is a part of a larger whole. For example, we can focus on patients' sense of themselves, how they would define themselves, what is important, etc. There are multiple aspects or parts to a person's conscious sense of self. However, we then want to see how this links up with the person's interpersonal world, whether their words and ideas about themselves match their behaviors, how connected or disconnected they are to any inconsistencies that we might be observing in the moment.

Trainee: I'm not sure what you mean by non-linear or "extra-linear" processing of information. I'm not clear on how this expands our thinking *or* our inquiry with the patient. What do you mean by all of this "enriching the continuing systemic circle"?

Jack: A non-linear (or some people call it extra-linear) method of inquiry is a way that we begin thinking about what it is that we are actually hearing. It's a way of processing information without simply taking what a patient is saying at face value. It's a way of putting pieces of a puzzle together. We can do that in a number of ways: slowing the dialogue down between the patient and the therapist; examining our own subjective reactions to what a patient is saying; seeing if there is something that doesn't make sense, or doesn't connect; and then tracking the disconnection by asking follow-up questions to get more clarity.

Trainee: Is this what you mean by moment-to-moment tracking?

Jack: Yes, and the way we track moment-to-moment is by trying to locate "entry points," words or phrases that don't seem to fit, or words or phrases that will give us further pieces to the puzzle.

Patricia: We would also be wondering about a number of other possibilities. (1) Is the patient contradicting himself without being aware of the contradiction? (2) Does the patient seem to be either self-indulgent or overly critical? (3) What is the patient's attitude toward making an effort to achieve his goals? (4) Is the patient able to hold in memory conversations from previous sessions, or is there a feeling that you have to start from square one each time?

Jack: Yes, Patricia is listing other considerations besides thinking about what the patient is saying and we could also use them as entry points. For example, after noticing several omissions of a piece of history or forgetting what had been discussed in a former session, we can begin to ask the patients what they make of these omissions or lapses in memory.

Trainee: It's as if what we're talking about now is identifying where these lapses or omissions occur. By identifying these areas, is this where the fractures in the personality are located?

Jack: Yes, lapses and omissions can be entry points as we are trying to identify some part that is split off. For the patient, omissions or "forgetting" are a strong indicator that a part is being dissociated from another part. Over the long haul, our task is to help the patient see how the parts are connected. Using part-whole analysis, we're looking for where things line up, where pieces of the puzzle seem to be omitted, exaggerated, out-of-conscious awareness, or completely dissociated.

Patricia: Another way to think about entry points is by seeing them as the *tip of the iceberg*. So often with beginning therapists or with short term therapy techniques for that matter, we're trained to only respond at the tip of the iceberg level. We never see the whole picture that way, and if we aren't responding to the whole picture, often symptoms will reoccur or the initial complaint will be absorbed into the overidealized organization.

Trainee: So, slowing things down and staying in the present helps to correct that?

Patricia: One of the most important things we can say about the power of slowing the inquiry process down is that you are communicating to patients that what they are saying is important, *that it matters to you*, and you want to take the time that patients deserve to get all of the important contextual details and to understand them more fully.

Slowing the process down and staying in the present is one of the most powerful ways that we can convey to our patients that they aren't alone, that they don't have to hide their secrets, their embarrassing thoughts or wishes. We are there to offer quiet, thoughtful, careful companionship. This is at the heart of intersubjective treatment. This may be one of the first times our patients may ever feel this level of companionship in their lives. It is what helps the healing and integration process.

AT-HOME QUESTIONS FOR REVIEW

1. Discuss how the Four Quadrant Model is actually a visual grid that will assist clinicians in part-whole analysis.
2. Take one of your own cases and try to apply part-whole analysis using each of the Four Quadrants. Think about your client from the following vantage-points: (a) an intrapsychic vantage-point; (b) an interpersonal/relational vantage-point; (c) a systemic vantage-point.
3. Notice how each part-whole analysis brings different elements of the personality into view. Discuss how this model helps to bring a three-dimensional picture of the person into view.
4. Can you see any splitting or dissociative processes that are at play? Discuss how these splits may be in the service of (a) maintaining the idealized self; (b) preserving hope in the idealized wish for the perfect other (or change in existing relationship); and (c) keeping feelings of shame from flooding the personality.
5. Discuss options for how you might start an inquiry process with your patient that will help you create entry points for gaining more information about each part.

CHAPTER 5

The Four Quadrants
and Part-Whole
Uncovering Dominant Solutions

I]t is not the parts that explain the meaning and significance of the whole but the whole that explains the meaning and significance of the parts . . . The student must from the beginning try to do both things at the same time.

—HEINZ KOHUT (1984, P. 127)

The key to 'seeing from the whole' is developing the capacity not only to suspend our assumptions but to 'redirect' our awareness toward the generative process that lies behind what we see.

—PETER SENGE ET AL. (2004, P. 42)

IN THIS chapter we will continue our discussion of part-whole analy-sis using Karen Horney's framework of "neurotic solutions" as a way of connecting the Four Quadrant Model to a theoretical framework. Part-whole analysis is a way of visualizing the whole and penetrating the parts in the service of repairing and integrating split-off parts of the self. Hor-ney's character compulsions are essentially descriptions of typical solutions that derive from an individual's attempts to resolve conflicts between the "pseudo-self" and "real self." The greater the disturbances, the more the pseudo-self has usurped the healthy energies of the real self. The question that puzzles many clinicians is how then does the patient keep himself from experiencing the immobilizing vulnerabilities from such splits?

Individuals attempt to contain their distress by developing what Hor-ney called idealized solutions. These compulsive creations buffer against dystonic or painful emotions and maintain a protective internal homeo-static balance. The "solution" binds a certain level of anxiety but unfortunately additionally creates a much larger psychic burden. *(If I cannot meet the demands of my ideal perfections, how can I not judge myself?)* As a counter-point, an equally demanding form of self-contempt may also develop when idealized standards are not met, a self-contempt that does not yield to debate or rational argument. Compulsive creations are inherently unstable. They cannot deal adequately with the true realities of life and end up with internally warring factions. *I hate myself because I am not able to be perfect, but if I could become perfect I would not need to hate myself at all.*

In its attempt to reinforce itself, the pseudo-self generates continuing psychic splits, now between compulsively created idealizing and self-hating sub-systems. In character disturbances (that is, the pseudo-self), the pathological disconnects we have discussed above (and as we have depicted in the Four Quadrant Model) are always present. These disconnects represent the damaging dissociative splits that can occur between idealization and self-hate. However, each solution yields up its own particular compulsive "witches brew" of perfection.

For training purposes, we will describe treatment sessions from three individual cases, each representing a characterological solution corresponding to Horney's three interpersonal trends. We will illustrate the use of part-whole consciousness in each case, including the special beliefs each patient possesses and each patient endows with unconscious, or less than conscious, meaning. We will see that each of the three trends has evolved its own susceptibility or, as we might say, its own witches brew of compulsivity.

The particular solution may not at all be obvious at the beginning of treatment and may take weeks, months, or even years to reveal itself. Although patients certainly have layers of solutions which can gradually come to light in treatment, one solution is likely to usurp the greatest amount of resources of the real self. The three "dominant solutions" as we have noted earlier are defined as:

- Detached Resigned Solution (movement away from people)
- Overattached Self-Effacing Solution (movement toward people)
- Self-Inflating Expansive Solution (movement against people)

To somewhat simplify the identification of solutions using part-whole systemics, we have restricted ourselves only to "dominant" solutions, and we have further restricted ourselves in those cases to dominant solutions which, if not immediately identifiable, are still not deeply hidden. We identify and track in moment-to-moment time the likely constituent parts which can lead us to an identification of the particular dominant solution. The reader may notice that the part-whole resonating system bears some resemblance to our own clinical intuition. Why not stay with the simpler and more familiar term? The reason is that it is difficult to imagine how one would teach or train intuitive processes in a written manual. When we use part-whole analysis, it allows us to operationalize the power of intuition, breaking it down into steps of consciousness which lends itself more readily to a teaching format.

As early as 1950, Karen Horney herself had seen the teaching value of part-whole dynamics in communicating her psychodynamic understanding of character mal-structure. She wrote, "a whole organism [is] one in which every part is related to the whole and interacts with every other part" (p. 179). Part-whole analysis facilitates the clinical process as the therapist begins to resonate between parts and whole in a reflexive way. The resonance helps to "unpack" what the patient is both *saying* and *not saying*, a decided advantage in identifying or encompassing the larger whole. Note that our Four Quadrant Model and part-whole dynamics are based on the same non-linear principle: a systemic understanding of how each quadrant/part resonates with every other quadrant/part and coalesces into an idealized solution or pseudo-self (the whole).

DETACHED RESIGNED SOLUTION: THE APPEAL OF FREEDOM

This solution to intrapsychic conflict involves converting oneself into an "on-looker" on life, especially an on-looker on one's own personal being. There is a marked difference between a life lived and a life merely observed. When posed with decision-making (which forecloses the wish for limitless possibilities), the individual finds that he cannot escape an endless internal debate, eventually self-defeating, about how a movement in any direction might compromise his "integrity" and change him in ways that could alter his "individuality." In an attempt to guarantee that he will not be influenced or coerced by outside forces, such a person desperately aspires not to accept any one need over another need.

The solution is to experience no needs *at all*. In his youth he has already been coerced into dealing with conflicts beyond his tolerance. He has given up his struggle to maintain his toehold on active living, settling for a "peace without conflict." But unfortunately as the solution grows, it becomes more self-perpetuating in its compulsive detachment. *If only people understood the sensitivities of coercion, as he does, the world would be a much better place in which to live.* In the therapy situation, such an individual fears that the therapist will want to convert him into a preconceived therapy type. With his hypersensitivity to coercion, his freedom to be himself constantly seems to be in danger of being compromised.

In the following case of Michael, note how a number of parts, seemingly unconnected, begin to coalesce into a comprehensive characterological whole. As the constituent parts and whole resonate between each other, the dominant solution becomes thrown into clearer relief. The dissociated splits outlined in our Four Quadrant Model will be seen in therapeutically useful moment-to-moment real time. The parts we want to *see* and *hear* are overdetermined beliefs in freedom, independence, detachment, and the hypersensitivity to coercion.

Case Example of "Michael"

Michael is a forty-five year old married male with two children ages ten and twelve. His wife is a similar age and they moved from a major industrial center for a "simpler life." Michael has been in treatment for one year. He presented at the behest of his wife who said, and continues to say, that his high level of stress is affecting the family. She most recently has asked that he start on medication which he opposes, but is considering, given her request.

His youngest daughter has been diagnosed with a psychological disorder and is in treatment. The girl is not liked by her peers and is frequently obstinate and perseverates on being right. Michael states that it is impossible to do anything with her without a conflict. With respect to his wife, Michael reports no fights and he will not raise any disagreements with her, feeling that either his wishes would be criticized and ignored, or that they are unreasonable.

Michael has an advanced computer software degree and has had several successful start-ups. He has shared that he and his wife are financially well off, with his wife also being a successful consultant. For the last few years he has traveled to North Carolina for a week or two at a time for work. He reports he likes these trips in that they are to some degree an escape from family life.

Michael describes his father as well-liked by others but possessing a bad temper at home, critical of his mother, and demanding of both Michael and his brother. Mother was constantly stressed, and though she could occasionally be warm, seemed negative and depressed. Michael excelled in school and quickly felt superior to others academically, although he had few to no friends until late high school. He described paralyzing shyness but he is proud that he could force himself to not completely give in to his shyness in high school. He has no adult friendships.

He describes that he was awkward-looking in appearance and the formal clothes style he had as a child, forced by his parents, did not match the style of his peers, making him stand out even more. He reports that his parents enforced a rigid and early bedtime that did not lessen even as he transitioned into his teen years. Michael says that he has always been most awake in the evening, and he frequently reports being awake until 1–3 am, wishing to sleep late, but required to get up to tend to his children. He does make time for his children but feels conflicted about being a good father, not enjoying the role.

Unlike most clients presenting with anxiety, Michael does not present with an overt sense of guilt, shame, or insecurity about himself; rather his presentation is more irritable, overwhelmed, frustrated, and helpless. He reports rare feelings of excitement or pleasure but neither does he report feeling depressed.

When the therapist asked Michael about his vision for family life, he could not come up with one. He has few interests except watching the news and woodworking projects. What appears to cause him stress and anxiety are firmly held beliefs about how life should operate. He is libertarian in his political views and likes the idea of not depending on others. Michael wishes everyone were as conscious as he is in not crossing anyone's boundaries, and he also wishes that others would work harder at knowing what he needs without his having to ask. His feelings/views complicate family life in that he has high demands that his children should never be out of control and that they be highly intellectual and exceptionally polite, which they are not.

His therapist says, "I often find Michael uncomfortable to be with." She states it is hard to convey how emotionally distant the patient is: "I have noticed I can tend toward an intellectual way of relating with him as it feels the only way to connect. He has a great difficulty identifying feelings or seeing any worth in exploring them, a topic I have suggested which might be helpful to better understand. He shared once that he identified with the description of Asperger's, something I have wondered about, though he demonstrates empathy, can relate to me with some feeling, and seems to understand that much of what he experiences comes from how he sees the world."

When Michael starts a session he stares at the therapist with a great sense of doubt as to how to start, often just saying, "I don't know." Michael then presents a list of physical ailments and current stressors, none of which seem addressable to the therapist, that is, a deadline at work or demands by his children. Michael comes to treatment regularly and has teared up a few times mainly around his wish to feel closer to his children. The therapist's fantasy is that Michael will just end one day saying therapy has not done anything for him. Currently, Michael just shows up and then thinks something will happen.

Part-Whole Analysis of the Case

- *The couple moved from North Carolina to find a "simpler life."* We entertain the idea that the pursuit of a "simpler life" is an overdetermined "part," a possible entry point. Questions about what the couple was hoping for in this change may contribute to further information relevant to "part-whole" analysis.

- *Michael presented at the "behest of his wife."* Clinical experience tells us that this can be a problematic motivation for change, although not necessarily so. Again, we entertain possible meanings of this history: (1) Is the patient passively complying with his wife's wishes because he fears his wife's anger? (2) Does he submit because he feels his wife is more knowledgeable about such things?

- *Michael's wife most recently has asked that he start on medication which he opposes, but is considering, given her request.* Here we learn that even though he doesn't agree with another's judgment about his life, he may offer no resistance and simply accept it. This is another likely entry point. Again we pose the two basic questions we ask earlier about why the patient submits.

- *His daughter has been diagnosed with a psychological disorder and is in treatment . . . not liked by her peers and is frequently obstinate.* Here we wonder about genes *vs.* environment, and we also wonder how each parent is processing this information. Father and daughter are both in treatment, but we hear nothing about wife/mother participating. Note: As the case proceeds, you may see that it gets easier and easier to find parts and entry points. Try to locate parts and entry points on your own as you read the rest of the case.

- *With respect to his wife, Michael reports no fights, and he will not raise any disagreements with her.* Michael seems to not "fight" with his wife either because he is afraid of her or he thinks his reasons may be ill-considered. If he fears her, his submissiveness speaks to a conflict around aggression, wishing to assert himself but too fearful to do so. If he thinks his reasons may be ill-considered, then his self-doubts become more comprehensive: he is questioning whether he is "in the world" enough to have a valid opinion.

  Note: As a clinician what would you say is the characterological difference between these positions?

- *Michael has a software degree . . . he and his wife are financially well off.* At this point, we wonder about the reasons why the couple has so much difficulty blending family and work responsibilities.

- *Michael travels to North Carolina . . . to some degree for Michael an escape from family life.* This statement begins to shape several previous "parts" we have wondered about. The investment in distancing sheds light on Michael's unwillingness or inability to hold his own with his wife on their disagreements and his seeming readiness to accept her advice uncritically. We begin to understand how his interpersonal posture contributes to his automatic deference to his wife's expectations, despite fleeting moments of concern.

- *Father was well-liked by others but possessing a bad temper . . . mother was constantly stressed.* The dysfunctions of his family are consistent with the patient's interpersonal posture. From the information gleaned so far, the patient appears to be unattuned or unresponsive to the needs of the children; most likely he is adultocentric, reflecting the history of his own family of origin.

- *Michael excelled in school . . . paralyzing shyness . . . no adult friends.* The "parts" are beginning to accumulate of a highly intelligent, well-educated and successful individual who cannot psychologically sustain himself with family, children, or peers. His "shyness" is beginning to look like a dynamic outgrowth of a walled-off frozen emotional posture, making interpersonal reciprocity painful and unsatisfactory.

- *The formal clothes style he had as a child, forced by his parents, did not match the style of his peers.* He coped with such coercions by giving up and detaching, leading to his fears of the "hazards" of human attachment. In treatment, as outlined in chapter 2, such a client fears being chewed up in the cookie-cutter of psychotherapy. He fears abdicating the "resigned posture" compulsively created so that he can inure himself to any attachment to people, which of course would include attachment to the therapist. Involvement would compromise his unconscious need to eliminate the "intrusions" on his ideal definition of himself. Thus the patient's treatment will involve how the patient has constructed "space" as a compulsive solution to dealing with the conflicts of his life and how this characterological compulsion is intimately involved in his anhedonia.

How to Proceed Moving Forward

In this case presentation the therapist had reported that the patient presents in a somewhat passive manner at the beginning of each session. This is echoed in the way that he comes in at the behest of his wife and is willing to consider medication despite being against the suggestion. Through part-whole analysis we are able to *make sense of his passivity,* understanding it as a way of maintaining his "resigned solution" in hopes of achieving freedom from being controlled by others. Therefore, any attempt on the part of the therapist to confront the passivity directly will likely be met with resistance.

Using logic or reason as a way to problem-solve current dilemmas will be met with equal resistance through stonewalling or intellectualization because the patient experiences the act of making a choice as equivalent to the loss of his freedom.

In many respects this puts the therapist in a bind as to finding any neutral direction in which to move. Therefore, we must go back and ask ourselves, "What is the solution in the service of?" As we see from the Four Quadrant Diagram, shame is the overriding emotion that is being defended against. In this man's case shame was first experienced in childhood through over-controlling parents who made demands on him that both limited his options and embarrassed him in front of his peers. The one place in treatment that this patient showed authentic signs of emotional expression was when he talked about the pain his own daughter must be feeling being ostracized by her peers.

In order for the treatment to develop traction the therapist must move out of joining the patient in intellectualized conversation and look for entry points that can move into *any display of feeling* on the part of the patient. Although the therapist reports that she has tried to explore feelings and explains that there are benefits in doing so, the patient has shown little interest in focusing on this line of pursuit. Nevertheless, the therapist can stay with her intuitive hunch that this might be an entry point to begin dismantling the compulsive solution, and remain focused on opportunities to connect intellectualized reporting with a feeling. This can be accomplished in a number of ways.

- First, she can wonder if he had *even a fleeting* feeling when his wife asked him to take medication. This question is an invitation to slow the process down, allowing for moment-to-moment tracking, the pause that is needed to introduce curiosity and self-observation to the patient's own processing of information.
- Second, she can suggest that *most* individuals would have at the very least a slight reaction on a feeling level when someone else tries to tell them what to do. This telegraphs to the patient that it is okay with the therapist for feelings to be present without fear of reprisal or control on her part. It also begins to help normalize negative feelings for the patient.
- Third, the therapist can connect content that the patient brings in terms of his present day relationships back to his relationship with his parents or struggles that he had with his peers. Making this connection models for the patient that the past is linked to the present which then can pave the way for seeing how unresolved issues or conflicts from the past are alive in present relationships.

- Fourth, the therapist can *name* feeling states and attach them to intellectualized reporting by the patient. For example, if the patient states that he has no adult friendships, the therapist can ask if that feels lonely sometimes. If the patient responds in the negative, the therapist can follow this with a question, "How have you managed not to feel lonely?" This question allows greater access into understanding how the solution works and fits in with other parts of the whole.
- Fifth, using the same example of no adult friendships, the therapist could wonder if the patient ever wishes that his shyness as a boy could have been overcome so that his life would be different in the present. This statement connects isolation in adulthood with shyness. It bypasses the solution of "wished for freedom through resignation" and goes directly to the feelings of shyness, the struggles around shyness, and suggests that there may be an *alternative* solution.

In this case example we have shown how by understanding both the "compulsive solution" and how it evolved from the parts that comprise the whole of the resigned solution, we are able to use these same parts as entry points into the therapeutic inquiry process. The parts create the whole and the whole then defines the entry points. Thus, it is by first understanding the power of the resolution and the function that it serves that we are able to begin the slow process of integrating painful memories and feeling states. This in turn frees up more psychic energy to be utilized by the authentic self.

THE OVERATTACHED SELF-EFFACING SOLUTION: THE APPEAL OF LOVE

In this attempt to solve interpersonal conflict, the individual seeks security through the participation of the gains and accomplishments of significant others in his or her life. Personal autonomy has been thwarted, and self-credit has come to be associated as something negative. Personal achievement, if it occurs, does so by luck, happenstance, or someone else's interventions. Salvation comes from others, but like all solutions, the self-effacing solution is compulsive in so far as no actual amount of love, concern, or approval fills the need. The patient is thus continuously subject to self-doubts, self-reproaches, and self-denigration. *If my loved ones cannot be made whole, then I am at fault by not being giving enough.* In childhood, the effacing individual had to compromise any demonstration of the authentic self in exchange for love and attention. Love might possibly be available but only at the cost of subordinating oneself wholly and devoting oneself to a needy parent or ill sibling. Horney (1950) describes such a person as one who "grew up under the shadow of somebody" (pp. 221–22) or, more specifically, under the shadow of someone who needed or demanded full devotion. It is in the shadows that "protection could be gained by pleasing and appeasing" (p. 222).

In the treatment situation, the patient tries hard to be liked, appreciated, and admired by the therapist. The therapist can take on God-like qualities which, however, will eventually result in disappointment as the patient discovers that her or his wishes for the therapist are also unsustainable. The phenomenon of loyal waiting takes the form of waiting for the therapist to "cure" through acknowledging admiration for the patient's devoted sacrifices. The admiration may require testimony of the therapist's "special" feelings for the patient.

In the following case of Diane, as with the preceding case of Michael, note the eligible or likely "parts" as the session proceeds. And note how, through the resonating "meanings" of these parts, the solution of Self-Effacing Overattachment (the "whole") gradually begins to reveal itself. Once it does, note how the whole both dynamically connects the parts and simultaneously deepens their meaning, both consciously and unconsciously.

Case Example of "Diane"

Diane has been in treatment for six months. She is a forty-eight year old mother of two who, five years ago, returned to graduate school to become a psychotherapist. She is in private practice and specializes in psychosomatic illnesses. Diane initially presented with bouts of unexplained sadness, anxiety, fatigue, and loss of self-confidence.

Patient: I've been thinking about what you said that being a therapist can be stressful.

Therapist: Yes?

Patient: There are certain cases I can't get out of my mind. I take the feelings home with me and my husband is getting tired of me being so upset.

Therapist: Certain patients do this to you?

Patient: I'll tell you about one. I feel so sorry for him. He lives alone, has Crohn's disease and he is so frightened to go out for fear of having an accident. He actually likes coming to therapy because he knows I understand, and he can leave abruptly and use the restroom if he has to. It just bothers me so much.

Therapist: How does it make you feel?

Patient: Like I'm impotent to do anything for him. What can I do? I thought of suggesting a support group, but I know he'll refuse that. He's too ashamed.

Therapist: He's ashamed of his condition?

Patient: He's ashamed of his condition, he's ashamed of himself, he's ashamed of talking to people, everything.

Therapist: I see. What happens when you try to talk about this kind of problem with your husband?

Patient: He doesn't want to hear about it. He says I'm getting carried away with my job. He shows no sympathy at all.

Therapist: You mean sympathy for the people you treat or sympathy for you?

Patient: Both. I mean, I'm not a robot, of course I feel for my patients.

Therapist: Did he ever have to take care of anyone?

Patient: No! His sister did it all for him. When his parents needed care, his sisters were the ones who stepped in.

Therapist: How did he care for the children when they were young?

Patient: He did just enough to get by. On good days with the children, he was front and center. When they were having a bad day, it was all on me . . . I didn't really mind it . . . after all I was the mother.

Therapist: Was it like that in your family too?

Patient: I said before how my mother was the peacemaker and my father the hothead. He embarrassed her. My two younger sisters and brother rebelled, but I didn't have that luxury. I tried to help my mother when she would break down and cry.

Therapist: You were the caretaker.

Patient: Yes, I guess I've always been the caretaker. I can't stand people suffering. I guess it's not just physical suffering I can't stand; I can't take mental suffering either.

Therapist: You mean like your patient?

Patient: Yes.

Therapist: You mentioned the shame he feels. Is that part of it?

Patient: That's the worst part. He feels so ashamed, and I can't help him.

Therapist: Do you feel the shame yourself that you can't help him?

Patient: It bothers me terribly (patient chokes up). It's a shameful situation, and I can't do anything.

Therapist: I hope you don't feel you are failing your profession. Are you embarrassed by it yourself?

Patient: (now openly crying). I can't help it, I can't help it.

Therapist: I know. This is terribly hard for you.

Patient: I can't help him, and I can't help myself.

Therapist: But you've told me about other patients you have helped.

Patient: (pause) What makes me continue to feel that I'm not doing enough?

Therapist: You've tried so hard all your life to fix things for other people.

Patient: I guess I've always thought that I'm a failure if I can't help someone in need.

Therapist: Even if their situations can't be fixed? With your mother you were a mere child yourself and you were trying to fix the problems of an adult. And now you are faced with a patient who has severe Crohn's disease.

Patient: And I can't fix that.

Therapist: Right, you can't fix that. It seems what's happening is that the other person's pain or shame takes you over and makes you feel you aren't doing anything, no matter how much you give of yourself, no matter how much you sacrifice. Can you still be a good person if this doesn't take you over?

Patient: You mean if I'm not Mother Theresa, then I feel I'm not good enough?

Therapist: Yes, something like that.

Patient: I know I need to be taking care of myself. They told me that in training, but it just passed over my head.

Therapist: If we are taking care of other people and not taking care of ourselves, that sacrificing may not be good for either of us.

Patient: They said that too, that we need to help ourselves before we can help someone else. Next time I want to talk about this.

Part-Whole Analysis of the Case

Diane has been in treatment for six months. She is a forty-eight year old mother of two who, five years ago, returned to graduate school to become a psychotherapist. She is in private practice and specializes in psychosomatic illnesses. Diane initially presented with bouts of unexplained sadness, anxiety, fatigue, and loss of self-confidence.

We wonder how significant Diane's choice of sub-specialty is and whether it has any connection to her late entry into clinical work, her own symptoms, or to larger issues in her life.

Patient: I've been thinking about what you said that being a therapist can be stressful. [Note: As a clinician, begin to ask yourself, "What thought process could be involved in the therapist making such a statement?" Try to identify advantages and disadvantages. What meaning can we attach to a patient immediately starting her session with such an earlier observation by the therapist?]

Therapist: Yes?

Patient: There are certain cases I can't get out of my mind. I take the feelings home with me and my husband is getting tired of me being so upset. [At this juncture we can begin to wonder if this is part of a larger characterological issue linked with Diane's choice of work and choice of sub-specialty. Note: As a clinician, what comes to your mind? At this point, do any "parts" seem connected?]

Therapist: Certain patients do this to you? [The question focuses on the condition of Diane, bypassing its effect on her husband. What are the advantages and disadvantages of a decision to stay with Diane's condition, rather than with its impact at home? Note: As you read this, what response would you have made?]

Patient: I'll tell you about one. I feel so sorry for him. He lives alone, has Crohn's disease and he is so frightened to go out for fear of having an accident. He actually likes coming to therapy because he knows I understand, and he can leave abruptly and use the restroom if he has to. It just bothers me so much. [We now see what appears to be the beginnings of a countertransferential issue ("I feel sorry for him" and "he knows I understand"), which in turn can connect "parts" of Diane's presentation to a larger clinical picture, a more encompassing dynamic "whole" of her personality structure. Transferentially, the Crohn's patient is creating a "split" between visits to his therapist and visits to other places. We can "feel" him placing his therapist on a pedestal of unconditional trust verses unconditional distrust of others. We now ask ourselves if unrecognized evidence of transferential issues and Diane's response to it connects possible "parts" we marked earlier in this analysis: choice of sub-specialty and persistent symptoms of being overwhelmed. Note: As a clinician, you might begin to ask yourself,

"Is Diane's choice of work overdetermined? Is she trying to resolve her own characterological issues through her chosen field of work?" What might these issues be?]

Therapist: How does it make you feel?

Patient: Like I'm impotent to do anything for him. What can I do? I thought of suggesting a support group but I know he'll refuse that. He's too ashamed.

Therapist: He's ashamed of his condition?

Patient: He's ashamed of his condition, he's ashamed of himself, he's ashamed of talking to people, everything. [We sense here a powerful entry, a major "part" unfolding, which makes us want to re-interpret the past and to start to predict the future course of psychotherapy. For example, whose shame are we talking about?]

Therapist: I see. What happens when you try to talk about this kind of problem with your husband? [Note: As a clinician how do you assess the timing of this question? What are the advantages and disadvantages of this moment for bringing Diane's husband into the dialogue?]

Patient: He doesn't want to hear about it. He says I'm getting carried away with my job. He shows no sympathy at all.

Therapist: You mean sympathy for the people you treat or sympathy for you? [The therapist connects elements of a triad for the first time but does so in a non-specific way. It seems the therapist is "palpating" the transferential issue for Diane but does not want to weigh too heavily on it. As we immerse ourselves into the therapist's statement here, we can "feel" ourselves in an open-ended situation. The therapy also seems to be moving into heavily charged uncharted territory with three people (Diane, her patient, and her husband) now coming into focus.]

Patient: Both. I mean, I'm not a robot, of course I feel for my patients. [Diane creates a union of sorts between the unsympathetic world her Crohn's patient faces and the unsympathetic attitude of her husband toward her. This immediately seems to liberate her to express anger and a sense of unfairness that her husband expects her to be "like a robot." The term "like a robot" also sounds like a strong "part" resonating with other parts noted earlier and with a larger whole: a cold and lonely world in which people selfishly do not respond to other peoples' pain.]

Therapist: Did he ever have to take care of anyone?

Patient: No! His sister did it all for him. When his parents needed care, his sisters were the ones who stepped in.

Therapist: How did he care for the children when they were young?

Patient: He did just enough to get by. On good days with the children, he was front and center. When they were having a bad day, it was all on me . . . I didn't really mind it . . . after all I was the mother. [The therapist, following Diane's anger, has chosen to pursue her husband's very limited past assumption of responsibilities with their children and within his own nuclear family. Diane willingly engages in the dialogue with the therapist but abruptly reverses course that she didn't really mind his irresponsibility because "after all, I was the mother."]

Therapist: Was it like that in your family too? [Here the therapist hears the reversal, decides Diane's ambivalence is being mobilized, and switches to the safety of the past and to a more cognitive level. Considering the split-off idealizations of self-sacrifice and self-renunciation emerging within Diane about her Crohn's patient and how these issues extend deep into her childhood, we can cohere the seemingly disparate and seemingly contradictory parts into a larger organic whole, namely, the patient's characterological solution of self-effacement and compulsive overattachment.]

Patient: I said before how my mother was the peacemaker and my father the hothead. He embarrassed her. My two younger sisters and brother rebelled but I didn't have that luxury. I tried to help my mother when she would break down and cry.

Therapist: You were the caretaker.

Patient: Yes, I guess I've always been the caretaker. I can't stand people suffering. I guess it's not just physical suffering I can't stand; I can't take mental suffering either. [Here the patient is able to reconnect with her resentment about her own family trials with a conflict-avoidant mother ("a peacemaker"), an affectively unpredictable father ("a hothead"), and all her siblings rebelling except her ("I didn't have that luxury"). The word "luxury" seems to be announcing the split between a painful self-loathing and a prideful self-renunciation. The characterological whole of compulsive "movement toward people" continues to gain confirmation. The overdetermined role of "caretaker" becomes more vividly clear as we see it in her family of origin, with her husband, and with her patient. Is there evidence of the transferential role of caretaker with Diane's therapist?]

Diane is describing her painful split between her idealized self-renunciation and her bitterness at not having the "luxury" of being free to choose or not to choose to be a "caretaker." It is the split between being compelled to help all sufferers and being unable to sustain the unexpected painful repercussions of the need. Her siblings (and husband) are of no help. Yet, is the mental suffering imposed on her or has she imposed it on herself? Of course it is both, one from the past and one from the present.

Having arrived at a characterological whole, we now can "see" reflexively deeper meanings of the" part" described by Diane. We arrived at the whole from the parts but the whole now gathers up a much larger pool of critical parts, parts that we were unable to identify earlier. This is an example of the systemic use of part-whole thinking and systemic thinking itself can be thought of as a part-whole process of listening.

Note that the characterological "present" can now not only illuminate the past but also the future. The non-linear path forces us to use terms like "reading," "hearing," and "immersing." And the future being illuminated includes a beginning grasp of the patient's future course of therapy.

Therapist: You mean like your patient? [At this point, the therapist decides to return to Diane's "caretaker" role, linking it to the affectively laden present.]

Patient: Yes.

Therapist: You mentioned the shame he feels. Is that part of it? [She promptly agrees, leading the therapist to an even more loaded question. If we stand back we can see that these are critical links in the therapy. How should the therapist react?]

Patient: That's the worst part. He feels so ashamed, and I can't help him.

Therapist: Do you feel the shame yourself that you can't help him? [Note that this was a pivotal question that the therapist asked.]

Patient: It bothers me terribly (patient chokes up). It's a shameful situation and I can't do anything.

Therapist: I hope you don't feel you are failing your profession. Are you embarrassed by it yourself?

Reflections and Analysis

The therapist senses that an emotional dam is breaking and that the patient is facing a deep level of despair and emotional pain. He offers needed support but maintains an important momentum toward uncovering Diane's shame. Shame is intensely present, but it is not exactly unannounced. The therapist appears to have been waiting for the opportunity to connect Diane's patient's shame to Diane's own shame. Every visceral experience of shame indicates progress in the treatment.

With narcissistically derived splits in the psyche, shame has been increasingly accepted as a key emotion. Diane's strong reaction reflects the acute stress of shame but also reflects the beginnings of the healing of the dissociated split between reality and Diane's idealized construction of it.

The remainder of this therapy hour does not add anything significantly new to our understanding of part-whole process or systemic re-construction. The reader may again wish to review the final statements in the above session to get a "feel" for the process of change as it unfolds moment-to-moment in the painful yet key area of shame. As we can see, the therapist continues reassuring, confirming, and extending Diane's insights within the scope of the intersubjective space which has opened up.

How to Proceed Moving Forward

With this breakthrough in the treatment, Diane is beginning to connect her feelings of despair and emotional pain with the shame she viscerally experiences in working with her own patient. We see that the therapist has begun to create a bridge, giving the patient permission to explore feelings of shame more directly. In addition there are other opportunities for follow-through in future sessions based on our part-whole analysis of the content revealed within this session. These identified parts can begin to be connected back to the whole in a number of ways.

- The therapist can invite the patient to wonder how her feelings of helplessness are basically synonymous with feelings of shame and/ or unworthiness. This could be followed with questions that would explore how these associations derived from learned responses stemming from childhood. (Gaining more detailed information along these lines will give the therapist a window into how the "compulsive solution" was formed.)
- The therapist can connect symptoms from Quadrant Two (where the patient initially presented with bouts of unexplained sadness, anxiety, fatigue, and loss of self-confidence) to her feelings of helplessness and to her internalized belief that her ineffectualness produced the symptoms in the first place.
- The therapist can also connect feelings of helplessness to the buried wishes contained within Quadrant One. For example, if the patient is able to see how her wish to be a "perfect enough" caregiver is connected to the pressure she places on herself to be a "better" therapist, she may have a window into her wish for the perfect solution – (*If she is perfect enough, she will be able to get people to change, and if she can get people*

to change, she can prove her value and worth.) Insight into this vicious cycle is the first step in breaking the cycle.

- At some point further into the treatment, the therapist may also begin to explore the motivations behind the patient's career choice in mid-life and wonder whether this was an extension of her desire to expand her care-giving role beyond motherhood.
- The therapist should be thinking about how all of this ties into Diane's feelings about her relationship with her husband. The patient has already shown evidence of some eruptions from Quadrant Four by voicing contempt for her husband's lack of ability to show true interest in her needs.
- Rather than moving directly into Quadrant Four, the therapist may wish to explore underlying wishes (contained within Quadrant Three) of loyal waiting. How might the patient begin to express her desires for her husband to do something more, to change into a more loving partner? How might the patient be experiencing shame over the thought of waiting so long for her marriage to become more satisfying?

Exploring the feelings contained within Quadrant Three will naturally lead to some expression of the underlying feelings contained with Quadrant Four. Here we see how the model works in conjunction with part-whole analysis. Loyal waiting both prevents the direct experience of shame and allows feelings of anger and frustration to remain suppressed. When the treatment moves toward the direct awareness of shameful feelings, a part of the compulsive solution is broken, allowing a new homeostatic balance to emerge. This homeostatic balance is moving in the direction of integration, freeing up larger aspects of the psyche to spontaneous self-expression. This in turn may result in further ripple effects in the form of gains as well as unintended consequences. As the patient gains confidence in her authentic self-expression, it may put new pressure on the marriage. If the patient begins to make demands of her spouse that he is incapable of, or disinterested in accommodating, adjustments in the marriage may occur.

SELF-INFLATING EXPANSIVE SOLUTION: THE APPEAL OF MASTERY

This solution is the most consonant with Western culture, a situation that can likely create specific problems for both the patient and the therapist. Historically idealized, the qualities of *masterful, triumphant, ambitious, assertive, and self-sufficient* are buried deeply in the American psyche. In the expansive solution we find individuals who primarily identify with the grandiose or glorified self. The appeal of life lies in mastering situations and bending them to their will whether that is through the power of their intelligence, ambitious pursuits, or through vindictive triumphs over others who are perceived to be adversaries.

Often they will carry an attitude of superiority, although this may or may not be conscious. Their superior stance may manifest in a variety of ways, ranging from being consciously aware but hidden from view, through subtle devaluing, through extreme condemnation and judgment, or through being in a position of authority where they have the power to select who are the chosen ones and who are banished from favored status. Generally, this banishment is not based on any rational or logical consequence of misdeeds. It is based on the whim, the mood, or the failure to gratify the expansive person's wishes.

The reason that this character solution presents a challenge in treatment is that there is a shared unconscious cultural avoidance in looking at the underbelly of this dynamic solution, which in turn makes it more difficult to treat, much less contain. Rather than adopting a position of curiosity as to the costs as well as benefits of behaviors that manifest out of this character solution, we have come to frame triumph over others as part of the competitive spirit, something that makes us strong and successful. However, when this solution goes unchecked and is not tempered or balanced with other values we hold to be precious such as treating others as we would wish to be treated, *we create a cultural climate where grandiosity is given a pass until a crisis hits.*

When individuals come into treatment with the expansive character solution, they may balk at the therapist tampering with their "formula" for success. By the same token, the therapist may be more tentative and may feel uncomfortable dealing with such culturally sanctioned behavior. In such a patient, the pseudo-self, unlike in other solutions, may openly embrace the more grandiose aspects of the self. There is less open discomfort with the solution, and the patient seldom experiences symptoms contained within Quadrant Two until some fall from grace or loss of power is experienced. The split that is observed occurs between the pursuit of respect and the pursuit of love, with respect commanding the greatest admiration and love reflecting a possibly risky display of weakness. The early years of an expansive personality are likely to have been harrowing. The possibility of love or tender ministrations, for whatever reasons, carried a risk. And being "lovable" would likely have been met with ridicule or contempt.

In treatment, a major difficulty with a self-inflating person is that he can feel humiliated accepting the role of patient *vis-à-vis* the therapist. It can stir up feelings of weakness rather than reinforcing feelings of mastery and self-sufficiency because underneath the grandiosity often lies a fear that all of the accomplishments and displays of confidence are a bluff. Therapy, itself, may signal a breakthrough into consciousness that the bluff will be exposed. Thus, many practitioners have seen far fewer of these patients. Often the patient comes into treatment only after he has suffered a severe loss in his life. The therapist on the other hand is often intimidated by the aggressiveness of the patient, thus encountering countertransferential impediments to the treatment.

To illustrate this solution, we have presented the case of "Rupert." We again ask you to note the likely "parts" leading to the "whole." As well, try to assess what your own reactions might be if you were treating this patient.

Case Example of "Rupert"

Rupert is a sixty-two year old engineer who before retiring at fifty-five was the owner of a major industrial plant. He is married with five children and has been in treatment for six weeks. He sought help because of recurring dreams of having to stand by helplessly while his economic fortunes declined. He has been on anti-depressant medication for one year.

Patient: Something has happened to affect me. I was always a take-charge guy who knew what the situation demanded. These dreams just won't go away. They seem to be worse on the nights before I come here.

Therapist: How do they get worse?

Patient: Last night I dreamed my company was facing a hostile take-over and they were directly challenging my vested interests. I was in a frenzy trying to prevent the take-over. This is not me.

Therapist: They were jeopardizing your complete security?

Patient: They acted like they owned the operation and were just waiting for the right moment to take it over. I was screaming at them but nothing was coming out of my mouth. Is this talking making it worse? I don't want to talk; I want to fight.

Therapist: It's almost as if they were taking advantage of your not being there.

Patient: (angry) You're damn right it feels like that.

Therapist: And you were trying to fight them and no words were coming out.

Patient: Damn it, I was the CEO. None of these guys would have dared to challenge me like that. The dreams are a freak. Can't you see? I feel I should never have retired. I can't stand this feeling of being taken over.

Therapist: Did you recognize any of these guys?

Patient: No, they were a bunch of losers playing big-shots.

Therapists: Did anything like this ever happen in real life?

Patient: No, never, never. I was on top of every situation and saw a crisis before it happened. That's how you build a top-notch company. In business being respected is more important than being liked.

Therapist: And they did?

Patient: You betcha. If they didn't, they were gone. Some people said I was too hard on them but business is cut-throat, you know what I mean? If you can't hack it, you'd better not be competing.

Therapist: How does it feel being retired, I mean not being a CEO.

Patient: (solemnly) I was made for the job. I ate it up. Now I just hang around the house and get in the way. It's a great house, but I don't feel like the same person.

Therapist: What do your wife and children think about this?

Patient: I don't tell them. I don't want them to see me this broken-down. It's not right. If they know what I'm going through, they'll see me differently.

Therapist: But that leaves you all alone, like in your dream. You couldn't talk at work despite the crisis there and you can't speak at home because you are afraid they will see you as weak. You said you didn't want to talk; you want to fight. But the only way to tackle this crisis and fight it is to talk about it. Do you understand?

Patient: So I should come here and just keep talking about it?

Part-Whole Analysis of Case

- *I was always a take-charge guy who knew what the situation required. These [recurrent] dreams won't go away. They seem to be worse on the nights before I come here.* Early on in this session we are confronted with a stark split between an "in-charge" guy now suffering from frightening dreams of losing his entire portfolio. It seems Rupert is right that something has happened to him. But neither the patient nor thus far the therapist knows what has triggered these outbreaks of fear. The patient has been on anti-depressant medication for a year but notices worse nightmares on the nights before sessions. This speaks to a high level of stress about his appointments due, we surmise, to his dread of unbidden thoughts or the fear of exposure of his vulnerability. If this line of reasoning is correct, then we can identify a significant "part" involving his acute fear of unbidden events and unbidden emotions.

- *I was in a frenzy trying to prevent the take-over [of my company] . . . I was swearing at them but nothing was coming out . . . Is this talking making it worse? . . . I don't want to talk; I want to fight.* This is only the sixth session and the patient is heavily immersed in his unwelcome dreams. He raises doubts about the talking process and whether it can make his condition worse. He does not connect his suspicions about talking to the terrifying matter of his utter muteness in his dream. The issue of "talking" is becoming another resonating part of a larger picture of a take-charge guy who is feeling helpless.

In response to questions by the therapist attempting to connect real-life with Rupert's dreams, Rupert registers his strong disagreement that any connection can be made. He buttresses his point with a ringing statement of philosophy of what makes a good CEO ("Some said I was too hard . . . but business is cut-throat . . . If you can't hack it, you'd better not try to compete").

Reflections and Analysis

In this brief clinical exchange we can begin to see how, as this client's "compulsively driven solution" is breaking down, he reveals parts that are emerging more clearly and resonating more strongly. Thus, we have a picture of a man whose stability his entire life has depended on his ability to maintain control at work. His "mastery" has begun to feel unsafe for reasons not yet clear at this early stage in the treatment: his not-working, his advancing age, other factors? Also not understood are the reasons right now for the violent kickback in his dreams which depict him losing what has always been most precious to him, his financial success.

Having arrived at the structural whole of an individual who had always been driven to control his own destiny, his loss of control, for whatever reason, has overwhelmed and humiliated him. The more he dreams, the more he feels out of control. Yet, he is apparently allowing himself to be out-of-control for the first time in his life, which we can understand as a beginning step toward health. The therapist asks about Rupert's family trying again to connect Rupert's outside world with his internal conflicts. Rupert reveals that he doesn't tell his family anything ("I don't want them to see me this broken-down. If they know what I'm going through, they'll see me differently").

The stark revelation confirms the enormous shame patient feels in having unwanted thoughts and feelings. It allows the therapist to establish the point that, both at home and in his dreams, Rupert is unable to talk, and it is this situation that needs therapeutic attention. Unlike many others with a similar character make-up, Rupert appears to be distressed enough, but also resourceful enough, to accept the therapist's clinical understanding about the importance of talk to his condition. He seems to agree to continue in therapy. As therapy progresses, we expect to hear about areas of present characterological concern (for example, issues of control, will-power, and respect) as well as the further unfolding of feelings of loss, grief, and shame.

How to Proceed Moving Forward

For individuals who have had success using this character solution to navigate the world, it becomes difficult for therapists to touch the grandiosity at first. Instead, providing gentle assurances, as this therapist has done, to help create a link between the patient's continuing in "talking therapy" and patient *not being alone,* as his dream was highlighting, is a way to forge an initial bond or connection with the patient. It also subtly telegraphs to the patient that there may be alternative approaches to how he might tackle the challenges before him at this phase in his life.

Along these lines, the therapist may also attempt to explore other windows of opportunity revealed through the part-whole analysis of the dialogue. A place to start may be to focus on his relationship with his wife and grown children. For example, when the patient says "*They'll see me differently,*" the therapist may wonder exactly how the patient expects that they will see him differently. This may open a door for the patient to speak more about his family and reveal more about his fears of weakness, loss of status, or loss of control. The therapist may wonder if they might see him in ways other than weak, such as seeing him as more approachable or accessible.

For example, is the relationship with his wife reciprocal in terms of giving and taking, or is he in charge and has she played a more deferential role? Asking these questions can be diagnostic. Based on how the patient responds, this will give the therapist an indication of how pervasive the patient's need to exert control has been. Are there areas in his life where he can reveal more of his authentic self, more of his sense of dependence or brokenness without experiencing an overwhelming sense of shame? Additionally, these same questions will create further entry points allowing us to see the particular configuration of how this patient's "parts" connect to the "whole."

Areas for further exploration might include focusing on phrases such as "jeopardizing complete control," "feeling of being taken over," and "I was on top of everything." Each of these statements in a sense acts as a "lightning rod," opening up more than the patient had probably intended to reveal. Here, care must be taken in terms of how far to prod or question before pulling back. Too much focus on words such as *jeopardizing, being taken over* runs the risk of unmasking excessive shame. It will also either semi-consciously or unconsciously telegraph to the patient that he has been exposed, threatening the patient's stability and self-control within the therapist's office. However, asking the patient to elaborate on what he means by *being taken over* might offer further insight into a part.

This case study can also deepen our understanding of the Four Quadrant Model. Rupert either feels it is too personal to discuss loyalty, too obvious to talk about, or not high on his values, other than to a sense of his own beliefs. The latter would make the loyal waiting of Quadrant Three problematic. In the full-blown version of this character solution, triumph over adversaries is paired with a sense of pride. Devaluing and retaliatory behaviors would be experienced as more syntonic than dystonic. Therefore, challenging the "pride system" too early may lead to a negatively charged transferential response directed toward the therapist, in an effort for the patient to try to reassert the homeostasis of self-control.

These are opportunities for inquiry and connection by staying focused on content material that comes from Quadrant One. In terms of the material contained in this vignette, focusing on the patient's statement at the end of the exchange where he says, "I don't feel like the same person" could be an important (benign) entry point. In asking for more information as to what he means, the therapist can try to link the dystonic aspects of his changing sense of self with his former syntonic assumptions about who he is in the world. We also wonder about the relative lack of time spent on describing symptoms (Quadrant Two) other than dreams. Does Rupert feel talking about his symptoms to a therapist is a further sign of weakness and loss of control? Is he hoping to "will" them out of existence? Or, in the more extreme instance, are they so dystonic that they exist in a partially or wholly dissociated state? These are potentially important transferential concerns for the therapist as the treatment proceeds.

Some of the risks we have seen in working with this character solution are that therapists will either challenge too quickly, or they will not challenge enough. Challenging too quickly can take the form of going prematurely toward the aggression contained in Quadrant Four, possibly resulting in a negative transferential response, generally resulting in an abrupt ending to the therapy. A very different form of "doing too much" is to move toward finding an "answer" too quickly, such as brainstorming ideas about what he can now do with all of his free time in retirement. It is also possible to be somewhat in awe of the individual's success and essentially join the patient in supporting his or her idealizations. This may cause the therapist to not challenge enough when the opportunity presents itself. An example of how to "enter" into this solution at an appropriate time would be to slow the patient down and have him respond at greater length if he were to say that his wife prefers to be deferential or if he were to say that people have always been deferential to him.

The reader may have noticed that this patient, judging by the criteria we have outlined for the self-inflating expansive solution, does not fully qualify. Both the nature of his dreams and his almost instantaneous reaction to them speak to a weakening of his pride system and his life-long characterological solution. After all, he has not experienced these blows; he is just imagining them in his dreams. Why this is occurring currently in his life we do not know, but it will certainly be an important part of his therapy as the treatment unfolds. Rupert's dream-work is operating against his character solution, a favorable prognostic indicator in this type of patient.

CHAPTER 6

Shame, Splitting, and Trauma
Vicious Cycles

We live in times made more dangerous by our misunderstanding of shame . . . Shame is the hidden power behind much of what occupies us in everyday life . . . The general reader may be surprised to learn that until quite recently shame has been almost totally ignored by the various schools of psychotherapy.

—DONALD L. NATHANSON (1992, PP. 9–21)

However good your reasons for going into treatment, so long as you are an adult speaking to another adult to whom you are telling the most intimate things, there is an undercurrent of shame in every session.

—HELEN BLOCK LEWIS (FROM R. KAREN, P. 10)

IN RECENT years therapists have given more serious weight to the incipient, often painfully difficult experience of shame. This much-delayed attention to the etiology of shame reflects our expanding awareness and understanding of the role dissociation plays in patients' attempts to *integrate, regulate, and avoid* disconnected aspects of their life experience. As outlined in chapter 2, the Four Quadrant Model places shame front and center as the driving force behind both the dissociative spectrum of the unconscious as well as the overdetermined assumptions of the idealized self. Viewed from this perspective, we can begin to see how disavowed or unacknowledged shame is what connects the parts of the injured self to a whole, a whole that has forsaken the authentic self in exchange for the construction of an overidealized, compulsively driven identity. As Michael Lewis (1995) says, "Narcissism is the ultimate attempt to avoid shame" (p. 2).

Forsaking the authentic self is easily understood in light of the pain one suffers when encountering feelings of shame. Shame and its associated affects, humiliation and self-mortification, constitute some of the most difficult emotions a patient can face. Citing Bromberg (2001), "no words can capture the assaultive intensity of the experience" (p. 296). Through clinical observation we have come to understand that the direct experience of shame often poses a psychic threat, flooding the system in ways that may result in momentary fragmentation of the personality. As such, our patients obviously need to be safeguarded from traumatic hyperarousal of these overwhelming, often dysregulating emotions. Although we intuitively know that we must proceed with caution when it comes to shame, it is also important to remember that shame cannot be therapeutically bypassed.

The cost associated with bypassing shame has unintended consequences both culturally and therapeutically. Often the wish to avoid shame is what propels individuals into a lifestyle of overload in hopes of appearing more important than they really feel, or in hopes of extinguishing the very curiosity that would eventually afford introspection, modification, and relief. In his landmark essay Robert Karen (1992) observed that shame has been "so thoroughly neglected that it might be considered psychology's stepchild" (p. 40) and he offers us a clinical and cultural reminder:

> As painful as shame is, it does seem to be the guardian of many of the secret, unexplored aspects of our being. Repressed shame must be experienced if we are to know ourselves more fully, to build an identity that is more than a complex of compliance with and rebellion against cultural standards and constraints, and to come to terms with the good, the bad, and the unique of what we are (p. 56).

As clinicians if we begin our assessment process by asking how shame might impact the *motivations and defenses* behind our clients' actions, beliefs, and symptoms, we discover that simply *starting* with this question has the power to shift the "field and ground" of how we anchor ourselves, which is both a diagnostic and procedural shift. When we connect the parts to the whole, and focus on the avoidance of shame as the underlying motivator, clarity of thought begins to emerge, an integration of our thinking if you will, that allows us to take a deep breath of fresh air. As we bring into alignment our understanding of the driving forces behind the organizing/compensatory mechanisms of the psyche, we begin to identify that which has been given minimal clinical attention and thereby has remained underground—the elephant in the room called shame.

HISTORICAL PERSPECTIVES ON THE
MINIMIZATION/CLINICAL BLINDNESS TO SHAME

Following some fitful reverses in theory development, Freud rejected the notion that trauma was a pivotal factor in the formulation of a metapsychological framework for psychoanalysis. In lieu of incorporating an *experience-near* theoretical position based on direct reports of trauma (incest) from some of his female patients, Freud chose to relegate these disclosures to the realm of fantasy in favor of a theory based on instinctual drives. These instinctual drives were linked to stages of a child's development in terms of a bodily focus on need gratification and the pursuant ability of the child to master libidinal and aggressive tensions stemming from the oral, anal, and phallic phases of development. Conflicts that appeared in adult patients were seen as intrapsychically based and were interpreted as a sign of arrested development: fixation points in the adult psyche that represented a failure of mastery of libidinal tensions in childhood. Using this metapsychological framework, Freud was able to then subsume and incorporate reported disclosures of incest within his drive-theory, connecting them to his postulations about the Oedipus complex. In this way reports of sexual trauma were able to be interpreted as distorted memories, stemming from the child's sexual desire for the opposite sex parent and his or her concomitant fear of retaliation by the same sex parent.

Thus, trauma and the underlying feelings of shame were trumped by guilt and anxiety as the predominant affects that became the focus of psychoanalytic treatment. Shame was assigned to pre-Oedipal stages of development, seen as a "primitive" feeling state, more passive in nature, whereas guilt was viewed to be a more *evolved* emotion. According to Broucek (1991) Freud viewed shame as "reactive, inhibitory, and prohibitive, opposing the pleasure principle and leading one to abstain from certain (more natural) behaviors; man's primary condition is shameless or unashamed" (p. 11).

Freud's metapsychological theory focused primarily on the intrapsychic aspects of development. Therefore, the systemic and relational factors that we know to have a significant influence on an individual's psychological make-up seemed to have fallen off of Freud's radar screen. This is largely because variables such as relational attunement, the influences of culture, and our subjective assumptions and values do not easily fit into Freud's attempts to create a "scientifically objective" theoretical model based on instinctual drives. When we try to incorporate such variables as relational attunement and cultural bias into his model, a conceptual block develops.

The foundation stones of his theory begin to crumble when we try to align the various parts of the whole into his theoretical model. Because of this, trauma and the attendant feelings have had a difficult time receiving their rightful place in the practice of classical analytic therapy as well as many post-Freudian dynamic therapies that followed.

Because shame has been so neglected in the literature, we have chosen to document at some length existing theoretical positions on shame and the self, including the similarities, differences, compatibilities, and contradictions. A case in point is the impact of Freud's metatheory on relatively recent theorists, specifically Kohut and Kernberg, both of whom have addressed narcissistic character pathology and both of whom attempted to incorporate their observations into a framework that was at least partially grounded in drive theory. Both theorists identified the grandiose self as a key component of individuals with narcissistic vulnerabilities. However, they disagreed as to the etiology and the treatment of narcissistic patients. Kohut (1971, 1977) described narcissist grandiosity as the natural original state beginning in infancy, and he saw adult narcissism as a fixation of an archaic "normal" primitive self, whereas Kernberg (1975) took exception with Kohut's view stating that the grandiose self was a pathological structure that evolved separate from normal infant and child development.

For Kohut (1966) disturbances of narcissistic balance in the adult patient were referred to as "narcissistic injury" and were most readily identified by "the painful affect of embarrassment or shame which accompanies them and by their ideational elaboration which is known as inferiority feeling or hurt pride" (p. 243). Although Kohut's theory was a movement away from drive theory, per se, his description of shame shows vestiges of straddling the fence between an object relations framework and drive theory. Defining the origin of shame, Kohut (1966) states,

> A firmly cathected, strongly idealized superego absorbs considerable amounts of narcissistic energy, a fact which lessens the personality's propensity toward narcissistic imbalance. Shame, on the other hand, arises when the ego is unable to provide a proper discharge for the exhibitionistic demands of the narcissistic self. Indeed, in almost all clinically significant instances of shame propensity, the personality is characterized by a defective idealization of the superego and by a concentration of the narcissistic libido upon the narcissistic self; and it is therefore the ambitious, success-driven person with a poorly integrated grandiose self-concept and intense exhibitionistic-narcissistic tensions who is most prone to experience shame (p. 253).

As you can see from the above quotation, Kohut locates the origin of shame within an ego that has difficulty discharging the exhibitionistic libidinal energy, language that is largely grounded in drive theory referents. Although Kohut elaborated extensively on "empathy," his description of shame does not easily lend itself to empathic attunement. The language itself seems to create a dispassionate, objectifying distance from a patient's suffering. Self-psychology *does* address relational failures, specifically around parental nurturance as a cause of narcissistic injury. However, Kohut anchors his understanding of shame through the framework of Freudian metatheory where the discharge of libidinal energy takes precedent over relational attachment and the consequences of ruptures in attachment.

Although Kohut does focus on trauma as an important factor in a child's development and attempts to address traumatic ruptures in treatment through the reparative function of the mirroring and idealizing transferences, he positions traumatic events within the context of the child's primary narcissism not the development of the child's authentic sense of self. Trauma is described as a condition which occurs when the balance of primary narcissism is disturbed by maturational pressures and painful psychic tensions that stem from failures of mother's ability to nurture. These maternal failures result in feelings of shame, which interfere with "a proper discharge for the exhibitionistic demands of the narcissistic self" (p. 253).

In general Kohut's self-psychological theory offers advances to the body of theoretical knowledge insofar as he draws our attention to the importance of empathy as a therapeutic posture, and he cautions practitioners to take care when offering interpretations to individuals with narcissistic injuries. However, his attempts to bridge the gap between classical drive theory and ego psychology/object relations theory using language that is anchored in drive theory actually muddy the waters around our understanding the importance of shame relative to the development of the authentic self.

Kernberg's views on narcissism (1974) position the development of pathological narcissism as a distinct entity, one that is separate from the normal trajectory of healthy development. Taking issue with Kohut's position of viewing narcissistic exhibitionism as the "natural original state of infancy," Kernberg (1974) states,

> Pathological narcissism can only be understood in terms of the combined analysis of the vicissitudes of libidinal and aggressive drive derivatives. Pathological narcissism does not simply reflect libidinal investment in the self in contrast to libidinal investment in objects, but libidinal investment in a pathological self-structure. This pathological self has defensive functions against underlying libidinally invested and

aggressively invested primitive self and object images which reflect intense, predominantly pregenital conflicts around both love and aggression (p. 218).

Not only does Kernberg take issue with Kohut's theories on the etiology of narcissism, he disagrees on Kohut's approach to treatment. Kernberg states that one cannot adequately treat narcissism with empathic interpretations or the focus on self-object transferences alone. According to Kernberg, it is the interpretation of the aggressive components of the pathological self-structure that leads to a complete treatment of narcissistic disorders. One should note that Kernberg's (1974) definition of narcissism is one that primarily focuses on the grandiose aspects of the pathological self-structure as evidenced in the manifestation of "chronic, intense envy, and defenses against such envy, particularly devaluation, omnipotent control and narcissistic withdrawal, as major characteristics of their emotional life" (p. 215).

Like Kohut, we find Kernberg's object relations orientation steeped in the language of drive theory, particularly with reference to the discharge of libidinal and aggressive drives. Although Kernberg does separate normal development from a narcissistically pathological trajectory, he falls short in his description of the spectrum of narcissistic behaviors. Kernberg's focus on the manifest aspects of the grandiose self fails to adequately address *shame as the key component* behind envy, devaluation, and the wish for omnipotent control. Horney (1950) would take exception with Kernberg's limited focus. Importantly, she viewed grandiose pride and toxic self-hate as the flip sides of the same coin. Horney viewed both as defensively driven postures that attempted to keep feelings of shame at bay.

Upon closer examination Kernberg's depiction of narcissistic grandiosity seems to mirror Horney's description of the "expansive type" of narcissistically driven character solution. On the other hand, Kohut's description of narcissistic grandiosity seems to capture the description of Horney's "self-effacing type." As you can see, identifying the various manifestations of narcissistic overcompensation, Horney's description of character solutions offers a more encompassing perspective than either Kohut or Kernberg. It is for this reason that we chose to design the Four Quadrant Model in a way that theoretically mirrors a Horneyan understanding of both the intrapsychic and interpersonal shame components of the psyche, thus, visually providing a more three-dimensional picture of the self. Because this model directly addresses how compensatory mechanisms attempt to ward off feelings of shame through the various character solutions, it affords us a more comprehensive scope with regard to the treatment of narcissistic disturbances.

To illustrate the potential limitations of using too narrow a scope, let us apply our Four Quadrant Model to Kernberg's approach to the treatment of narcissistic disturbances. If we apply Kernberg's definition of narcissism to the Four Quadrant model, it appears that if one simply focuses on Quadrants One and Four, the clinician would have a complete picture of the narcissistic dynamic. Because Kernberg primarily focuses on the grandiose aspects of narcissism, connecting them to devaluing behaviors that are a component of the grandiosity, his recommendation is to encourage therapists to expose the patient's devaluing or aggressive behaviors as a way of dismantling the narcissistic defense structures. *Notice that the mention of shame and treatment interventions that attempt to counter-act shame are bypassed altogether.* In Kernberg's model shame is virtually rendered invisible in the therapeutic encounter. Again, the mechanistic language of drive theory clouds the picture of what constitutes ruptures in the development of a healthy sense of self. It is only by elevating shame to a more critical place of concern that we are able to weigh the risks involved in premature interpretations contained within Quadrant Four. If the therapist interprets before an alliance is well established, this may actually contribute to a deepening sense of shameful inadequacy in the patient.

In summary Kohut and Kernberg represent a dichotomous split in the treatment challenges faced by clinicians treating individuals with narcissistic vulnerabilities. In order to hold all of the pieces of the whole, one must address the dialectic tension between the various parts of the personality simultaneously. This requires a model that is robust enough to handle the "experience near" situations we encounter in treatment, as well as allowing for a perspective that encompasses the depth and breadth that would allow us to hold simultaneously the intrapsychic, interpersonal, and systemic aspects of a patient's life. We believe that the Four Quadrant Model addresses the dichotomous split, advancing the treatment of narcissistic injuries in a more holistic and systemic fashion. The case analyses at the end of this chapter will more fully illustrate how the Four Quadrant Model addresses shame through the configuration of holding a more complete picture of individuals with narcissistic character solutions.

Before leaving vestiges of drive theory behind with regard to the treatment of underlying shame, let us turn our focus to the writings of Robert Stolorow. Stolorow (1986) speaks directly to the problem of straddling the metatheoretical fence between drive and object-relations theories. Stolorow references theorists who address narcissistic disorders (Arlow and Brenner [1964]; Kernberg [1970]; Oremland and Windholtz [1971], and Kohut [1971]), and he states that the above authors "seem unwilling to take the ultimate *metapsychological* step of freeing the concept of narcissism from an *economic* [classical] definition which it has outgrown, and redefining narcissism in functional terms" (p. 200). Referencing Kohut in particular, Stolorow states that Kohut's metapsychologogical view of narcissistic object relations as defined by "the nature or quality of the instinctual charge. . . . [i]n a narcissistic object relationship the object is invested with narcissistic cathexes" (p. 200). Stolorow rightly asks, "But what is a narcissistic cathexis" (p 200)? For many practitioners, this continues to be unclear. Instead, Stolorow invites us to simply define narcissism from a *functional* perspective, and offers a definition of narcissism as follows: "a narcissistic object relationship [is]one whose function is to maintain the cohesiveness, stability and positive affective colouring of the self-representation" (p. 201).

As we can see from Stolorow's definition, he invites us to take a complete leap and leave the mechanistic model of drive theory behind. In our view this theoretical leap lands us very close to Horneyan metapsychology. From the beginning Horney took into account external factors that influenced the developing self, factors such as parental misattunement and larger systemic and environmental influences that would create a sense of trauma and isolation. Because Horney broke from Freudian doctrine early in her career, her writings are not conceptually muddied by trying to fit experience-near observations of treatment into mechanistic language. The simplicity and elegance of her framework must not be mistaken for being reductionistic or simplistic. There is a non-linear precision to her metatheory that is holistic and comprehensive. Horney is able to hold the dialectic tension between grandiose pride and self-hate; for example, she speaks to the tension between relational self-effacement and the hidden belief that the patient has the grandiose power to change or control the other. In this way she is able to integrate the descriptions of both Kernberg and Kohut, viewing their theories as parts of a more complex whole that more accurately captures the variants of narcissistic injury. Finally, Horney well understood the debilitating power of shame as the etiological source of the creation of the grandiose self. She also understood the concept of *wholeheartedness* as not simply the opposite of grandiose narcissism, but rather the manifestation of an authentic self. As Danielian (1988) states,

> The shift away from subject-object splitting and toward a tolerance and containment of opposites (i.e., toward a goal of wholeheartedness and empathic immersion) becomes healing on several levels, constructively addressing splits between inner/outer, active/passive, self/other, and health/illness. Guided by such a paradigmatic shift, Horney (1950) developed her innovative concept of health ("real self" she called it) as it unfolds in an ongoing relation to illness, a

concept of health in a non-static, indeed dialectical, relationship to illness (p. 20).

One cannot adequately treat shame that is at the core of narcissistic vulnerabilities unless we find language to speak about the theory that informs our interventions. The theory cannot replicate the pre-existing splits within the treatment paradigm. One cannot provide adequate treatment if our theoretical underpinnings contain language that is distancing, objectifying, and removed. In this regard Horney's description of the "real self," juxtaposed against the various compulsively determined and compensatory character solutions, is intuitively more understandable.

As well, the underpinnings of her theory are much more in alignment with recent discoveries around the treatment of individuals with trauma histories. Cast from a relational vantage point, one can more easily connect Horney's theory of personality development to trauma as we understand how ruptures of parental attunement are at the basis of most individuals with histories of trauma and its attendant narcissistic and borderline disturbances. Problems of hyperarousal, affect dysregulation, and feelings of shame can then be contained within this experience-near metatheoretical framework. To that same end the Four Quadrant Model lends itself to working with neuropsychological approaches that draw upon attachment theories as their metatheoretical foundation.[1]

OTHER PERSPECTIVES ON SHAME

As we have indicated, sociologists Scheff and Retzinger (2001) considered shame to be the *master emotion,* an emotion that undermines other difficult feeling states. Highlighting the presence of shame in clinical encounters, researcher Helen Block Lewis (1971, 1988) made a critical distinction between acknowledged and unacknowledged shame. Through her review of hundreds of psychotherapy session transcripts, Lewis analyzed moment-by-moment interactions between patients and therapists and found that patients were *often* in a feeling state of shame in the treatment hour. More importantly, Lewis noted that these states were virtually always overlooked by the therapist. Her conclusion was that this was generally due to the "low-visibility" of shame, where patients themselves were apt to describe their feelings as embarrassment, self-consciousness, or guilt. Influenced by the work of Goffman (1959, 1963, 1967) who stressed that unacknowledged pride and shame are part of the undercurrents of all human encounters, Lewis speculated that therapists (like patients and other adults) are accustomed to ignoring the manifestations of these emotions.

Perhaps, the most helpful aspect of Lewis's work is her observation that shame usually occurs as part of a sequence of emotions. Drawing from her treatment transcripts, Lewis noticed that if a patient imagined being seen in a negative way by the therapist, there was a brief registering of shame followed by guilt over a flash of anger the patient directed toward the therapist. Guilt, in this case, was understood to be a secondary response, if you will, to imagining the self in negative terms. Lewis noted that this entire sequence occurs rapidly, lasting only fifteen or twenty seconds. Thus, Lewis's analysis suggests that guilt and shame are closely tied and are seen as *shame-anger* variants. Guilt is experienced as the choice point in the sequence where anger is directed back at the self. Resentment, therefore, would be the outgrowth of the shame-anger sequence where the anger is directed at the other, rather than back onto the self.

DISTINGUISHING HEALTHY SHAME FROM PATHOLOGICAL SHAME

As mentioned, Lewis drew attention to the difference between acknowledged and unacknowledged shame and the impact of each on understanding approaches to treatment. John Braithwaite, basing his comments on the work of Scheff and Retzinger (2001), places shame in a broader relational context by elaborating on three sequences of interaction.

- The first is a *relational sequence of approval.* This involves an interaction between two people where the social bond between them is cemented or strengthened. Each feels respect for the other and a sense of pride based on their connection, lending the two parties to greater cooperation, less misunderstanding, and hence less potential for aggression.
- The second is a *relational sequence of disapproval—where shame is acknowledged consciously.* In this sequence the disapproval occurs when one person's actions are insensitive or hurtful—for example, Braithwaite uses the example of drinking too much and his wife giving him feedback that "he behaved like an ass." The comment may invoke feelings of shame in him, but since he knows that his wife loves him, he can hear the feedback in a constructive way. If the two individuals can engage in a healthy dialogue, shame will have been a vehicle for constructive conflict resolution. Braithwaite makes the point that constructive conflict (which includes delivering negative feedback) can actually strengthen bonds between people.
- The third is a *relational sequence of disapproval—where shame remains unacknowledged.* Let's say that a stranger comes up to someone at a party and tells the person who has had too much to drink that he's

making a fool of himself. Because the guest who is delivering the feed-back is a stranger, the first individual may take offense and respond in anger. Instead of registering any feelings of shame, he tells the person to mind his own business and stop being a prude. Sequentially, this may be countered with an even stronger retort, thus triggering an escalating spiral expressed through angry retorts and retaliation that may unravel into a vicious cycle of violence.

Scheff and Retzinger (2001) make a distinction between the second two types of disapproval. They state that when people possess a positive self-concept and feel secure or "attuned" in their relationships overall, they have the internal strength to acknowledge shame without having it destroy their feeling of worth and security. They can admit mistakes, laugh at doing something stupid, and apologize when they have done something wrong. They can also defend their own position without disrespecting dif-fering beliefs of others. However, people with secret feelings of inferior-ity and insecure social bonds are more likely to deny or repress feelings of shame, may be quick to anger and retaliate, and are often ashamed of being ashamed. By bringing shame to the fore, both Braithwaite and Scheff and Retzinger are articulating what we have highlighted as the driving force behind our Four Quadrant Model. In our model, the need to create an over-idealized character solution is in the service of allowing shame to remain unacknowledged. It is only through this disavowal that shame can take on the destructive and compulsive forces seen in the interplay between the four quadrants.

Karen (1992) also speaks to the phenomenon of repressed shame and states that the dynamics underlying this type of shame are very different from what sociologists, religious historians, and pastoral counselors have identified as "normal" shame. In past centuries and even well into the first half of the 20th century, shame was more typically associated with a sense of shyness or modesty. Bragging about one's accomplishments was seen as exhibitionistic, undignified, or in bad taste. The *capacity* to feel shame was seen as providing an important social function—a barometer if you will for maintaining social standards of mutuality and respect. Karen (1992) quotes the sociologist Thomas Scheff, "Normal shame is just like breathing air: it's necessary. Personalities and civilizations coexist, even thrive, with normal shame. But unacknowledged shame is a pathogen. It kills" (p. 42).

Following Scheff's caution with regard to unacknowledged shame, the term *shamelessness* has been used to describe a willful rejection or denial of shame, with associated attempts to extinguish the experience altogether. Attempts to eliminate shame appear to be increasing in our society. Implications both socially and clinically must be underscored. When shamelessness becomes regarded as a sign of strength of will or adult maturity, the danger of more pervasive splitting coupled with a decrease in compassion for self and others is an unfortunate consequence. Clinically, we assess shamelessness to be a counter-phobic mechanism, brought into play with the specific purpose of avoiding any conscious experience of shame or humiliation.

Based on the earlier writings of Freud who purported that shame inhibited the fulfillment of the pleasure principle and was not a "natural" state of being, many theorists and the general public alike have been influenced to view shame as an exclusively pathological emotion. Citing the pastoral counselor, Carl Schneider (1977), Karen (1992) concurs that "contemporary culture . . . has tended to dismiss shame as the mark of a timid and unfree person" (p. 42). This shift in our association to shame reflects a concomitant shift in attitude in the culture at large, a shift toward tolerating more violent eruptions of shaming and devaluing of others. It also may reflect what we are willing to overlook by turning a blind eye to enforcing sanctions against opportunistic success at any cost. Perhaps, it is the confusion around normal vs. pathogenic/repressed shame that has allowed us to translate actions such as grandiose exhibitionism and aggression against our neighbors into something we call "personal freedoms and liberty" or the "expression of healthy self-esteem."

Given this confusion, perhaps we can begin to understand how there has been a steady increase in violence in our culture, and an exponential increase in the bullying of our children with no universal public outcry or effective strategies for enforcement or containment. Perhaps, this is also why grandiosity and questionable ethics in business and industry in the last several decades have been overlooked and even handsomely rewarded. Perhaps, it is our confusion about the dangerous ramifications of repressed shame going unchecked that overwhelms us to the point that we don't even know where to begin. Or perhaps our own internalized sense of shame and unworthiness has inhibited our sensibilities, leaving us tentative and timid around voicing a call back to fairness, mutuality, and upholding common sense rules of social decency.

COMMON MISCONCEPTIONS WITH REGARD TO SHAME: FOUR CONTEMPORARY VIGNETTES

Each of the vignettes illustrated below reflects some degree of confusion as to how to deal with potential issues of shame, and each of the attempts at preventing shame actually may have exacerbated the problem.

Case Vignette 1

An associate recently reported that she was asked to facilitate a consultation with an organization that had reached an impasse in its negotiations between team members. The leader of the team reported that he felt that his hands were tied because he believed that he couldn't draw attention to a team member's underperformance for fear that he would shame her. When the consultant asked the manager why this overconcern about shame, he replied that the team member took everything personally and twisted his conversation around her performance into a personal attack. The manager felt paralyzed to take corrective action because he said that he had been taught that shaming an employee in a performance evaluation was bad management practice. The result of the manager's avoidance had left his team walking on eggshells around this woman, and in meetings the consultant observed that you "could cut the tension with a knife." The consultant also had observed that the problem employee was masterful at directing unrelenting attention to her victimhood, claiming that a stressful home situation and chronic health problems interfered with her ability to concentrate. Any attempt to get this employee to pull her weight was met with accusations that people were being cruel, insensitive, abrupt, or cold-hearted.

Analysis

In this first vignette, the manager's fear of creating a shame response in the employee actually may have emboldened her entitled grandiosity. The manager is within his rights to direct any employee back to the performance standards expected of everyone on the team. Drawing attention to fair and equitable expectations is not the same as shaming an employee. This employee might be better served by being referred to an EAP counselor. Doing so would send a clear and well-bounded message to the employee about performance expectations while giving her a different avenue to pursue personal difficulties that may be interfering with her work.

Case Vignette 2

A parent enters therapy due to difficulties with her twelve year old son. She states that she had been brought into the school because the teacher and principal had observed her son ridiculing and threatening a girl in his class to the point of bringing her to tears. When the mother asked her son if he had threatened the girl, he responded, "No, she's exaggerating. She's a whining, complaining, stuck-up brat. I asked her if she wanted to be my girlfriend, and she rejected me." The mother immediately came to her son's defense and complained to the principal that the girl had humiliated her boy by rejecting him. She explained to the therapist that his behavior was understandable because he was just trying to recover his self-esteem. She refused to ask her son to apologize because she thought it would be a further humiliation to him. It appeared that she had entered therapy hoping that the therapist would side with her and intervene with the school on her son's behalf. However, when the therapist tried to educate the mother that there may be other ways to teach her son how to express his disappointment, she became furious with the therapist and dropped out of treatment.

Analysis

In the second example the mother's defensive overprotection of her son's aggressive, retaliatory behavior in the face of his embarrassment may actually *create* a sense of entitlement in her son as well as narcissistic expectations of others. Part of the developmental mastery of self/other relationships includes learning how to handle disappointment and rejection without experiencing a total collapse of self-esteem. Clearly, the mother's narcissistic vulnerabilities and her own sense of entitlement are being projected onto her son in an attempt to protect him from feelings of shame.

Case Vignette 3

A father shows irritation with his seven year old son for crying on the playground in front of his peers. The other boys in his class laugh at his son whenever he cries, calling him a baby and "a girl." The father, in an attempt to prevent further shaming of his son, tells him he just has to get tough and fight back. When the son starts to cry saying that he is afraid, the father begins to pressure him, raising his voice saying, "No son of mine is going to be pushed around. Now, buck up and fight back like a man." The son tells his father that he will try, but recently teachers have noticed that the boy appears more and more withdrawn and is asking to stay in the classroom during recess. He also has begun to wet the bed at night. His father asks him why he can't control himself and insists that the son change his bed himself each night he has an accident. When the boy's mother tries to intervene, the father accuses her of making the problem worse.

Analysis

In the third example the father's own shame is being triggered by his son's reaction to being bullied on the playground. The father then creates a further shaming experience for his son, compounding the problem rather than helping the son master the situation in a manner that is more suitable for his temperament. Adults need to intervene within school environments in order to maintain a climate where all children feel safe. The father's solution, to send his son in to do an adult's work, is essentially a failure of attunement. A seven year old is not capable of solving a problem that appears to be more systemic in nature. Therefore, it is a set-up for failure and further shaming.

Case Vignette 4

A therapist reports to his supervisor that a female patient of his, a graduate student in psychology, asked for his email address because she often came across continuing education opportunities that she thought that he might like to attend. His response to her was to say that the office email was only used for appointment scheduling purposes by all of the practitioners in his group. The patient then asked if she could send information to his home email, and he responded that he had a policy not to give out his email address to patients. At this point the patient became visibly angry and asked why the therapist had to be so rigid and "always play it by the book." The therapist simply responded that this was his policy. When he told his supervisor about the incident, the trainee stated that he felt justified holding a firm limit with her as she had a history of pushing boundaries in other relationships. He was, however, a bit puzzled by the intensity of her reaction.

Analysis

In the fourth example although the therapist was correct in setting limits and holding the therapeutic framework with his female patient, there was *possibly* a missed opportunity, where the therapist could spend additional time on the patient's experience of rejection in an effort to expose, understand, and help her recover from her feelings of shame. This example is similar to vignette two, where disappointments around rejection or limit-setting can be understood in less than absolute, black and white terms. The patient is struggling with her refusal to accept that all relationships have certain boundaries. As long as feelings of shame triggered by disappointed requests can be adequately processed, both adults and children can learn to manage those disappointments. They can preserve self-esteem and relational connection rather than experiencing every disappointment as a shameful rejection that must be defended against.

USING THE FOUR QUADRANT MODEL AS IT IS APPLIED TO SHAME

As you can see from the above vignettes, misconceptions around shame or the disavowal of shame lead to misunderstandings or missed opportunities around the treatment of shame. Using the Four Quadrant Model, we have provided a breakdown of key factors that we consider essential for the treatment of individuals with shame-related defenses. Specifically, we address:

- The ideal therapeutic posture for dealing with issues of shame
- How accessing shame becomes more possible by staying in the present
- Understanding how underlying shame reinforces the defense mechanism of splitting
- How to recognize and acknowledge shame verbally in a way that the patient can tolerate
- Therapeutic "mistakes" that often trigger shame
- How the Four Quadrants connect to form a unifying mechanism to defend against shame
- How to use the Four Quadrant Model to unearth and dismantle the debilitating aspects of shame

Adopting an Intersubjective Therapeutic Posture When Dealing with Issues of Shame

As long as we try to maintain a position of "objective certainty" as clinicians, we cannot hold the dichotomous tension between the parts and the whole which is necessary to adequately understand and treat shame. Listening compassionately to the patient's derivative and ultimately direct experience of shame is the way out of this dilemma. Also, when we familiarize ourselves with our own vulnerability to shame, it allows us to move into the deeper "experience near" territory of empathic immersion. From this subjective relational vantage point, we are better able to listen for clues as to how our patients learned to defend against shame, whether that be through the creation of grandiose overidealizations or whether that be taking a position of loyal subjugation to an idealized other, the latter being a subjugation designed to elicit rescue from the excruciating pain of shame-filled memories from childhood. Working with shame, more than with any other feeling state, requires close attunement to the nuances of the therapeutic relationship because shame is born out of failures in primary relationships. As Stephen Mitchell (2000) reminds us, "[h]uman beings *become* human beings through attachments to and internalizations of their caregivers and the particular culture they embody" (p. xiii). Therefore, the experience of shame within treatment will unfold in the intersubjective relationship between the patient and the therapist.

How to Access Shame by Staying in the Present

As with so much else in psychotherapy, access to shame becomes more possible the more we can stay in the *present*. Shame is an experience-near affect and as such holding it subjectively and relationally is best captured in the present moment. Because shame is so difficult to locate, often masked by the patient's defenses, it is often missed or misinterpreted by the therapist. Empathic immersion in the present offers us our best opportunity of unearthing underlying or disguised communications of shame derivatives. Slowing down the communication process in the present allows for moment-to-moment tracking of content material that may contain vague or veiled communications of shame. These feelings may be briefly registered by the patient, only to be quickly disavowed or minimized. Or, the feeling may remain unconscious, only to be expressed through off-handed comments. It becomes an important task of the therapist to look for veiled communications as an opportunity to consciously identify and neutralize the dread associated with hidden shame.

Understanding How Shame Reinforces the Defense Mechanism of Splitting

In much of her writing Karen Horney (1950) identified the relationship between omnipotent idealized images and how they co-exist in a non-linear relationship with (corrosive) images of self-hate. Together they fuel in the patients a systemic sense of false pride. False pride and its accompanying "systemic shame" are critical factors in the damaging splits that maintain a tightly homeostatic systemic balance. As noted, a frequent split exists between the "glamour" of one's illusions and insidious self-denigration. Shame and splitting constitute a *vicious cycle* where each reinforces itself and the other, and in turn is reinforced. For example, I am ashamed of being ashamed and I am also ashamed of the ever-increasing vulnerabilities that are associated with my sense of defectiveness. The result is that compulsively constructed compensatory aspects of the self can move into the increasingly debilitating cycles of further conflict, which is to say, further shame and further splitting. Without therapeutic intervention, this spiral can escalate and create feelings of hopelessness and despair. By listening for statements that appear to contradict one another, the therapist can begin to notice the dichotomy aloud and wonder with the patient how these apparent contradictions might reinforce one another.

How to Recognize and Acknowledge Shame Verbally in a Way That the Patient Can Tolerate

Shame can go by many different names—discomfort, awkwardness, embarrassment, ridicule, fear, disconnection, disrespect, stigmatization, loss of face, hurt, or humiliation. Each term forms a useful continuum for the therapist to help approximate a patient's subjective moment. Shame is an emotion that often cannot be frontally identified, or often even named. However, as the therapy proceeds and as greater levels of attunement become possible, the patient will increase the vital intensity of expression of feelings. What started out as a feeling of awkwardness may step by step graduate to embarrassment, disrespect, hurt, and humiliation. Often this growing affective intensity will reflect growing tolerance of acknowledging disassembled characterological splits. As a patient's feelings of shame become more "normalized" the therapist can notice that the patient will begin to relinquish standards of perfectionism as a method of assuring self-worth. Furthermore, the patient will also begin to more freely acknowledge traumatic memories and/or feelings of humiliation from childhood without re-experiencing intolerable feelings of shame in the retelling.

How to Use the Four Quadrant Model to Unearth and Dismantle the Debilitating Aspects of Shame

When therapists have a narrowed view of how individuals with narcissistic injuries present, they may miss the various nuances of characterological solutions that patients create in an attempt to defend against shame. By holding the systemic whole, we can see how the parts configure to connect into a dynamic whole. In any intervention, when the therapist overemphasizes one quadrant, the therapist automatically underemphasizes other quadrants. For example, when a patient is highly successful or ambitious, often a therapist will miss how this organizing schema is an elaborate defense against experiencing feelings of shame. Patients may present with symptoms (Quadrant Two) that they experience in a split-off manner from ambitions or successes (Quadrant One). These symptoms appear to have *mysteriously* arrived, unconnected to any of the other quadrants. This is an attempt to maintain the split in the service of keeping feelings of shame at bay. If a therapist is "seduced" by the patient's very real successes in the world, he or she may also foster and/or collude with the patient's splitting, leaving the compulsively driven characterological solutions unaddressed altogether. Part of the value of the Four Quadrant Model is to see how overdetermined idealizations and overidealized relational dynamics are attempts to "magically" bypass underlying feelings of shame or other disturbing symptoms.

In our experience the unfortunate path of least resistance for many therapists is to revert to linear thinking to handle the often overwhelming, hidden feelings of shame. Witnessing this painful affect is often uncomfortable for the therapist. However, the dismantling of shame requires patience and deep listening rather than letting discomfort move us prematurely to find solutions. Adequate treatment of shame requires a holding of the complexity, connecting the parts to the whole, which eventually allows for the neutralization and dismantling of the narcissistic defense structure.

CLINICAL AND CULTURAL IMPLICATIONS: ONGOING PERSPECTIVES

One can wonder if therapists have avoided looking at shame because of its contagious qualities. Clinical experience has demonstrated that shame is a ubiquitous emotion; yet, when people encounter the feeling of shame, it seems to place them in a seemingly paradoxical position that looks much like a dissociated limbo state with no way out. We experience it and yet don't experience it, we see it and don't see it; we feel it and don't feel it. Furthermore, shame itself appears at times to be everywhere and yet nowhere. Many survivors of shaming say that no words are adequate to describe such an experience.

For contemporary psychotherapists recently trained, shame has moved to the forefront as a critical issue in childhood. One might say that a child's principal concern growing up is to avoid being shamed. School at all ages has been called an "incubator" of shame. "Am I clever or smart enough, do I look good enough, am I popular enough, will I be left out?"[2]

How prevalent are messages of unrecognized and unacknowledged shame? How equipped are parents to recognize and protect their children from these often accepted, normalized incubators of shame? Optimally it would be the experience of intermittent "pin-prick" exposures of shame coupled with the recovery from shame in the form of a reassuring word or some form of empathic support from parents. Unacknowledged shame at home can be an intensely hurtful and clinically damaging experience. When a parent habitually places a child in a double-bind situation from which there is no escape ("if you loved me, you wouldn't do that"), the experience of the child is to feel alone, exposed, and trapped.

When the constellation of symptoms is met with intensified shame (in the interest of getting the child to "perform"), the stage is set for further descent into self-destructive acts or suicidal ideation. When the rage is externalized, the mutually reinforcing denial of child, parent, and society can lead to unexplained and seemingly random acts of violence ("I messed up her face because she refused to go out with me"; "he 'dissed' my friend so I threw him out of my car, I was only going 30 miles an hour").

In the adult world, cumulative unacknowledged shame is no less ubiquitous, nor less paradoxical. In the case of Diane discussed previously, we see how a therapist's shame can be powerfully mobilized by the effects of her patient's desperate efforts to ward off shame from his Crohn's disease. From whence does shame derive its mysterious power of insidious contagion? Again, words fail us in describing deep experience. Much still remains to be understood about this phenomenon. In our experience shame has the power to undo emotional bonds, which is to say, shame renders one disconnected from other human beings. Shame thus possesses the power to create a state of alienation from self and other, and to create an ominous, debilitating panic around abandonment.

Is shame also implicated in the more dysregulated borderline conditions? Nathanson (1992) holds that not only narcissistic but also borderline patients are "shame-bound people loaded with self-dismissal and self-disgust. Often their entire character structure is . . . deeply entwined with . . . complex forms of shame . . . The importance of shame in these cases is rivaled by few clinical conditions encountered in the practice of psychotherapy" (p. 183). Since therapists have seldom been trained in shame dynamics, they are unaware of "shame-related complaints, so 'borderline' patients frequently go from one therapist to another in search of relief" (p. 183). Inherently challenging, the treatment of the borderline condition is made even more difficult by the neglect in the literature of any mention of the serious issue of shame.

Our experience in the treatment and supervision of these conditions certainly parallels Nathanson's observations. As we write, the dynamics of shame have yet to be adequately integrated into the structural understanding of the borderline condition. Consider the following case taken from a longer study of negative therapeutic reaction (Danielian, 1985).

> Ruth blamed men for taking advantage of her need to please. She stopped accepting dinner dates with men because she couldn't escape from a sense of obligation that she must sexually accommodate them. She described these men as obtuse, exploitative, and arrogant . . . More generally her fear was that a male [therapist] would be placed in conflict between his "male" feelings and his "therapeutic" feelings (p. 111).

One can see in the above case that both the specific sexual material and the more generalized need to comply were suffused with painful, yet unrecognized shame, shame which led to frightening abandonment to incipient "forces" over which she had no control. One sees also the overwhelming power of Ruth's characterological solutions and how they can progressively invade the therapeutic relationship with transferential consequences. Without transferential monitoring and appropriate intervention, and immersion in the shame-drenched experiences of the patient, these more extreme characterological states can build on themselves and escalate into negative therapeutic reactions.

CASE EXAMPLE: INTEGRATING SHAME INTO THE APPLICATION OF THE FOUR QUADRANT MODEL

Case Vignette 5

As a way of applying the Four Quadrant model to the moment-to-moment tracking of shame, the following case vignette offers a description that employs the technique of using entry points in a way that leads to accessing feelings of shame. Note the seemingly sudden breakthrough of affect and the insight generated by the breakthrough. This case example, an excerpt from a trainee dialogue, illustrates the specific power of working with part-whole analysis and how the past and present are interwoven. In this case dialogue we see how the past exists in the present and the present exists in the past.

> I had a pretty amazing session that I want to share with you all. I've been seeing this guy for a little over a year. He's never shown any display of feelings in my office and stays very much in his head. He's a pretty successful guy, but he has somewhat of a compulsive quality about him. What I mean by that is that whenever someone asks him to do something or puts something on his desk at work, he reports that he has to do it immediately. He describes it by saying that if he doesn't follow through with any request, a light keeps flashing in his head not letting him rest until he completes the task. It's probably also important to mention that he also seemed very shy at first. His head dropped down whenever he spoke. It took him months to actually make eye-contact with me.
>
> In terms of his background this thirty-five year old man came into treatment because he was having difficulties with sexual intimacy. He couldn't get aroused unless he visualized himself dressed in women's clothing. He never cross-dressed in public. In fact, he presented in a somewhat conventional manner. My thoughts on this were not to pursue the homosexual associations per se because this didn't seem to be his concern, and given what I knew about his history, the presenting "symptom" seemed to indicate that he was struggling with issues of claiming his own identify in many areas of his

life. I knew that he had a very narcissistic mother and passive and unavailable father.

Eventually, I reflected to him that when it came to having sexual relations, it seemed as though he couldn't fully be himself. It was as if he could only enjoy himself if he became someone else—and I wondered out loud if who he really was as a person had to disappear. I used the word "disappear" intentionally because of what I knew about his parental failures. A few sessions later I tried making a connection with him using the word "disappear" in another context. I reflected to him that when he described his relationship with his mother, it seemed as if the only time he could get attention and love from her was if he made his "needs disappear." I didn't connect this statement back to what I had said earlier, associating his disappearing when having sex, but I'm not sure why (pause). It just didn't feel right.

What was interesting, though, was that by my saying this, he became more able to talk about his relationship with his mother. He shared with me that when he was a little boy the only way he experienced affection was when he had pleased his mother, usually by giving her attention or meeting a demand she had made of him. I noticed that then he jumped away from talking about his mother and started to connect this to the pressure he often feels when having to please people at work. When he started to go off in this direction, it felt like a distraction. I remembered our conversation about entry points and there was something that struck me in the way he said "little boy" that made me want to bring him back to that point. So, I repeated the phrase and said, "Can you think of any other ways your mother was able to show you that she was pleased with that little boy?" He thought for a long while and said, "No. There was nothing about me that she ever noticed."

It was then that he began to cry. I asked him what that was like not being noticed, and he said that it was like being in total darkness. I asked him, "Do you mean like floating in dark, empty space, like you're totally alone?" He whispered, "Yes," and began to sob deeply for about five minutes. Then, he looked up at me and asked, "Why wasn't anyone there for that little boy?" Again, he began to sob deeply.

It was so powerful. But, what's confusing is that in the next session he came in and said he didn't know why he cried in the last session and emphatically stated that he was just being a big baby. I wasn't sure what to do next, what this reversal quite meant. So, here's my question back to the group. Did it flood him? Did he experience shame over being in a "weakened," vulnerable state? Why did he seem to completely disconnect and discount his feelings from the week before?

Feedback

Jack: First of all, this was an amazing breakthrough. You intuitively seized upon an entry point by tracking the phrase "little boy." It allowed him to shift the focus onto himself, to talk about what disappearing felt like to this little boy. Not only did you get more information, you were able to uncover the affect that the little boy had bottled up for so long. If we were to try to analyze why this happened now, all I can say is that we can never under-estimate the value of building up this degree of trust. The fact that your patient relinquished his feelings of guardedness and shame to reveal his emotions to you is a sure sign of progress. Of course, we would anticipate a compensatory attempt to recover from this display of vulnerability. In cases like this a breakthrough of affect is often experienced as shameful after the fact. There is little relief at admitting the truth at first, only confusion and embarrassment because there is no organizing schema as yet to reference the experience any other way.

You framed the presenting problem—how the patient presented sexually—as an issue of his real self not being able to be present which was quite good. It allowed you to bypass the repeated triggering of patient's shame around cross-dressing while sitting with you in session. It also struck to the core of the dynamic between himself and his mother without hav-ing to give a direct interpretation, which would have likely increased the patient's defensiveness this early in the treatment. Connecting his present-ing problem to the parent-child constellation allowed you to see how fail-ures of attunement had created the overcompensation of the compulsively driven sexual behaviors. This is part-whole connection in action; so, well done. And it is a breakthrough in the treatment in spite of what you wit-nessed in the following session.

Trainee: I thought so but wasn't quite sure why, and also why the behavior was so completely the opposite in the next session. I guess I don't know where to go next.

Patricia: Before we talk about that, let's try to understand what happened by integrating the Four Quadrant Model into what unfolded in these two sessions. What do you think happened here?

Trainee: I definitely think that his repressed emotions around abandonment came up and he was able to feel them for the first time. I think it surprised him, and it surprised me with its power and intensity, and I think it scared him. Actually, I think it brought up further feelings of shame in relation to me. This is where it gets tricky. His statement in the next session seemed like he was trying to justify his manhood in front of me by associating his tears and sadness to being a baby.

Patricia: Okay, so what does that tell you? Which quadrant is coming into play and how can we connect that response to what else had been triggered in that session?

Trainee: Well, I saw him attempting to reassert his sense of self from Quadrant One. I guess what he's letting me see is the harshness of his own standards, his attitude toward being weak in front of another man. Then, that would connect with Quadrant Four. Because he had failed to keep it all together, he was beating himself up. So we see some potential for anger that may have been stirred up around his realization of how alone he was as a child. Rather than directing it toward his mother, he immediately turned it against himself. I wonder if his mother did exactly the same thing to him if he ever showed his feelings that directly.

Jack: Yes, good question. So, we've raised the question of anger, and this is something you can be on the look-out for in the future. It would be important to notice where the anger begins to surface in the next weeks and months. It may continue to be turned against himself, or he may begin to tell you about something that irritates him at work. By the way, how does he express anger?

Trainee: He doesn't. He's very mild-mannered, soft-spoken. When he gets close to being disappointed, that's when he speeds up and tries to do things, to fix things for other people.

Jack: I see. So, in terms of your question of where to go next, just keep tracking this because we are likely to see changes here.

Patricia: I think we need to spend time focusing a bit about what was going on in Quadrant Three. By repeating the phrase "little boy" you were able to not only see a great deal of affect being released, he also communicated a powerful realization when he said, "Why wasn't anyone there for that "little boy?" For the first time, I'd guess, he was able to articulate a statement of *disloyalty* to his mother for not being available to him, realizing that she was responsible for his feelings of loneliness and isolation. He felt sadness and perhaps the beginning twinges of anger, but definitely it was an expression of compassionate concern for himself. This is huge.

Jack: And because it broke such a powerful taboo, we are bound to see a reconstitution of the old organizing schema to reestablish the homeostasis.

Trainee: Okay, but what do I do about holding both of those states of awareness? How do I move forward?

Jack: Don't put pressure on yourself trying to make sure you maintain the gains. Once something like this happens, there's no going back for the psyche. The power of doing this work lies in tracking the process. The process will take care of itself if we just keep tracking and connecting the parts to the whole.

Patricia: Yes, and what you could do the next time might be to wonder with him about the two parts you witnessed in the two prior sessions—compassion for the little boy one week and calling himself a baby the next. You can just wonder about that disparity out loud with him.

Jack: You could also reframe his crying. For example, you might suggest that you consider what he did in the prior session to be very brave.

Patricia: Yes, in that way you are offering a possibility that his old way of measuring self-worth in Quadrant One does not have to be so harsh. You can introduce a new way of framing strengths and capacities that include the expression of feelings, a new standard of bravery now being equated with acknowledging deeper truths, that we all have needs, that feelings of fear around abandonment and isolation are nothing to be ashamed of, and that healthy relational connection depends on mutuality.

Jack: But all of this must unfold over time. What Patricia is talking about is just giving you a road map of what's coming. Let the process unfold and stay in the present with him. He will come back to this material. You just need to keep tracking entry points that allow you to gather more information with the attendant affect. Also, being mindful of shame triggers will help you begin to wonder about shame and embarrassment aloud. You can begin asking him to describe his embarrassment in greater detail, again getting more information about this affective part. Then you can wonder about his fears of your judgment of him which will begin to move you more into transferential material.

Trainee: This is very helpful. I can see how holding the parts of the whole contained within the quadrants, both conscious and unconscious, the old organizing schemas and new breakthroughs in treatment are what you mean by holding the dialectical tension. That's a lot to keep track of.

Patricia: Yes, but it gets easier to do over time. You've already come so far with this in a few short months.

Summary

The treatment of narcissistic and borderline conditions has taught us that both acute and cumulative, chronic trauma is often at the very root of the dissociative mechanisms of these patients. The task of treatment has now become clearer as we have realized that unspoken, unacknowledged, or unconscious shame is the prime affect that links trauma to these increasingly common disorders. We must conclude that much conceptual work remains yet to be done to adequately integrate trauma into our theories of psychopathology. Historically, the early classical tradition created a blanket myopia about trauma which practitioners and theoreticians are only in the early stages of lifting.

A theory connecting narcissism, borderline dynamics, shame, humiliation, and trauma has yet to be created. Much work remains to be done: a better understanding of our field, a better understanding of ourselves, and a better understanding of our patients. Because of the theoretical vacuum in our field, we have decided to include several different views on shame, trauma, and dissociated splitting in our therapeutic manual. At the current stage of development of theory in this area, our observations probably can be seen as a "progress report." While a treatment manual cannot replace supervised experience, what has been learned needs to be taught. We invite our readers to participate in an open-ended process of learning about trauma, and thereby contribute to lifting the lid of denial on these deeply disturbing currents in modern life. In this regard it is the practitioners who are the ones breaking new ground and moving our awareness beyond many established, pre-existing theories which seem to be lagging behind.

Questions and Comments on Shame from Our Clinical Trainees

Comment: What really made sense to me in this chapter was framing shame as the *master emotion*. The Four Quadrant Model makes so much more sense to me now. I just realized that people who have an internalized sense of inadequacy can experience any emotion as a trigger for shame. To me, this explains an organizing principle around all emotions. I now understand why some of my clients have so much trouble asking for help or have fears around needing something. It's all just a reminder of their inadequacy. Now, I understand why so many people push feelings away altogether.

Response: Yes, when we see shame from this vantage point, it becomes the *portal* to opening up all affects. Our understanding of the power of shame allows us to have more patience and empathy with our clients' defensive character solutions. It also raises our own awareness in terms of paying more attention to what we say and how we say it, specifically interpretations we might make that can trigger shame. One way to look at shame is that it is the blanket that covers all other painful affects. Associations individuals have around needs become synonymous with neediness. Shame needs to be gently identified so that it can be dismantled. Need states can then become normalized and incorporated into the authentic self.

Question: One of the things that struck me in this chapter was the places where shame was characterized as indescribable—"no words to describe the experience," etcetera. It occurred to me that the essence of the therapeutic encounter is in the narrative—when a patient describes a moment that was felt to be shameful, the therapist listens, hears, and identifies it as such. The experience of shame resonates with the attuned therapist, and though the emotion may defy description per se, the empathic attunement of the therapist to the nature of the encounter, in the naming of it, is what helps heal, like a witnessing. The shameful feeling is not conveyed through a description of the emotion, but in the description of the relational encounter and the shared experience of what its impact would have been. I see more of what you mean now by the shared, subjective experience in dealing with shame. Can you say something more about what the therapist might say in those moments to acknowledge the shame experience, and then what is in fact healing about the shared awareness of that shame experience?

Response: Yes, you raise excellent points. The words often fail us, but it is the naming and acknowledging of shame that is at the core of our ability to treat shame. If words are inadequate to heal the experience of shame, how much less effective would a linear approach be? This is why we believe that the Four Quadrant Model can help us hold and contain the unnamable. When the timing isn't right to speak about the shame directly, you can go back to the Four Quadrant Model and try to move more deeply into any one of the quadrants to gather more information that hopefully will lead you to the underlying shame. For example, you can probe into the idealized performance standards and wonder what would happen if the patient fell short of achieving his or her goals. Or, if a patient is resistant to taking medication to help bring relief from symptoms in Quadrant Two, you could wonder what taking medication might mean in terms of losing an idealized expectation of being able to control his or her emotions.

Question: If shame is so difficult to locate, how are we supposed to treat it?

Response: Sometimes, we can pick up on the subtleties such as not having anything to say at the beginning of the session. These might forecast that there is a discomfort with a topic the patient is embarrassed to bring up or feelings of shame that may have gotten triggered from a previous session. At other times material that triggers shame may be discussed through derivative material, a dream perhaps, or relating an incident at home or at work where the patient either became angry, disappointed, or fearful. Often, the feeling of shame, itself, is split off from awareness, remaining unconscious. Only the derivative material will give us a clue as to how to track the feelings, assumptions, and behaviors that occurred as a result of the shame trigger. For example, if a patient comes in and reports having a fight with his or her partner, we would want to ask for contextual details of the fight. We would phenomenologically track the exchange, asking what started the fight, who said what to whom, how the patient felt during and after the exchange, what assumptions were made based on what was said, etc. In other words, we would *slow the dialogue down* enough so that we could understand how specific shame triggers operate within the patient. We would also want to keep the family relational history in mind. Are these episodes more likely to be triggered by incidents where patients are reminded of earlier deprivation? Are they likely to be more sensitive to traumatic events that have a shaming, silencing effect on them?

Question: What are the non-verbal indicators of shame? I found that after reading this chapter I started recognizing when shame came up in clients, but it was more through non-verbal recognition. I started noticing when clients would look away or put their head down or start shaking their foot.

Response: Yes, these are all typical non-verbal indicators. Notice that your awareness and attention to looking for how shame might be manifesting with your clients allowed you to pick-up on non-verbal cues that may have formerly remained undetected. This was the point that we had made at the beginning of the chapter. Drawing attention to how shame might impact the *motivations and defenses* behind our clients' actions, beliefs, and symptoms helps us discover that simply *starting* with this question has the power to shift the "field and ground" of how we anchor ourselves both diagnostically and procedurally. Drawing on Morrison (1998) "What does the infant feel who looks up eagerly and smiles at her mother, but then looks down, with furrowed brow and pinched lips, when her mother fails to meet her gaze?" (p. 58). Here Morrison is making a point based on Tompkins' work with affect where he observed that the mother's empathic failure is interpreted by the infant as the infant's own fault, the precursor to feelings of shame. Here we see how early failures of attunement leading to self-blame and disappointment can only be expressed non-verbally.

Question: Can you say more about bringing up shame without exposing the patient to a further experience of shame within the session?

Response: We would probably want to begin by using words that are less charged, words like being embarrassed or being uncomfortable. We might also acknowledge that shame is a normal human response for every individual, and that defending against the feeling or hiding it does not work very well in terms of alleviating shame. It only comes up again in the future when another trigger activates a feeling of vulnerability. Instead, we would suggest inviting the patient to try to understand how those feelings were internalized in the first place. Acknowledging the validity of our patients' pain, connecting it to their depriving, inconsistent, or unsafe home environment, are good ways to begin. This is ground that will have to be revisited over and over as the patient makes approximations toward integration. Also, the idealized wishes that the patient had used for so long are not likely to be given up easily. Therefore, patience and perseverance on the therapist's part are required.

Question: How does listening with empathic immersion to a patient's suffering help heal the excruciating memories of a trauma survivor? Don't you have to do something first to calm down the affective response?

Response: There are varying theories about this. From a neuropsychological point of view, people involved with DBT or EMDR training would say that you have to teach early trauma survivors skill-building techniques that would help to neutralize the overpowering flooding response being reactivated in the present. This is done so that the patient can begin to reclaim a sense of mastery and not experience the traumatic memory as a repeated "re-injury" in the present. You could also teach skill-building that challenges automatic assumptions, bringing reality, logic, and alternative explanations for the patient's assumptions into cognitive awareness. Working with this sort of skill-building is a way to reconnect the cognitive part of the brain with the feeling centers. It is also a way of building in new neurocircuitry.

Others, such as the more recent work of Susan Johnson (2004, 2008) from Canada stress using Emotionally Focused Therapy (EFT) with couples. The therapist encourages the couple to stay focused on the present, slowing the inquiry process down, and going more deeply into painful emotional material. This process of listening is an example of a technique that explains how phenomenological inquiry in the present can actually repair ruptures in marital relationships. As the partner witnesses the other's pain, empathic reconnection can be the result. This same approach is what we have suggested with individual clients, where the therapeutic relationship becomes the vehicle of reparative emotional understanding and healing.

Question: How might you see a therapist's unresolved issues of shame playing itself out in the treatment of a patient?

Response: That could happen in a number of ways. Therapists who are concerned about status or financial success as a way of proving their own self-worth may be enamored by patients who are wealthy or very successful.

They may have difficulty approaching the patient's narcissistic grandiosity, workaholism, or compulsive drive to win at all costs. Instead, they may collude with the patient's success and bypass any exploration that is directed toward underlying feelings of shame. Another variant might be that therapists feel intimidated by a patient's anger and actually experience a sense of their own shame as a result of the patient's subtle devaluing of them. The lack of acknowledgment of this transferential reaction may paralyze the therapist from dealing with any of the behaviors that stem from Quadrant Four of our model. Finally, a therapist may demonstrate subtle devaluing of the patient in the form of untimely or unfeeling interpretations or always needing to be in the "expert" role. In each of the above examples, the therapist's own awareness of these dynamics may be only partially conscious or substantially unconscious.

Question: I find myself shifting away from my client's pain sometimes, simply because it is so exhausting. Do you have any suggestions about how I might stay more present?

Response: One of the first things is to try to slow the process down. Often patients who wish to avoid their own feelings of inadequacy will try to speed up the process or jump away from painful affect. This can be exhausting simply trying to keep track of the dynamics. However, if a patient is able to access traumatic memories or feelings of shame, the therapist has to trust that sitting with someone who is exposing this level of vulnerability is helpful in itself. It is important to remember that previously most of these patients have had to experience these feelings in total isolation, or they were humiliated for exposing their feelings of vulnerability or neediness in the first place. Having a non-traumatizing other sit quietly and be with the individual in this space is quite powerful. On some level our patients intuitively realize how much skill and *presence* it takes to simply sit with them, and they often express deep appreciation for this level of witnessing. Too often, therapists try to jump to "fix" something in an effort to get away from their own discomfort. Giving oneself permission *not to have to do anything all of the time* actually minimizes a great deal of the "compassion fatigue" we all feel.

Comment: You know, we've been talking about shame as such a negative, but really shame is a positive. Until we understand and work with shame clinically, we can never crack through narcissistic idealizations, our own and our clients.

Response: Yes, when this all started with Freud in Victorian times, shame was something to be avoided. The whole Victorian culture was laced with shame and concomitant attempts to avoid shame. It was viewed as something that was primitive; therefore, it was underattended. Shame is no more primitive than any other feeling. The real problem was that it didn't fit into drive theory. Shame is based on relational failures, not drive derivatives. It didn't fit, so it became relegated to lesser importance. In a sense your observation is pointing out a possible blind-spot in the field—that *we* have been terribly narcissistic or narcissistically avoidant in our handling of shame. It's as if we got off on the wrong foot, but we're getting closer. There is so much trauma in the world now, it's dragging our awareness of shame up with it.

NOTES

1. In earlier work Silvan Tomkins (1963) also departed from drive theory and described shame from his research and theory based on affects. Nathanson (1987) and Kaufman (1985, 1989) built on Tompkins affect theory examining shame from a developmental time line. Each of these authors focuses on shame from the lens of the social context in which shame is triggered. The triggers for shame are a reflection of a disturbance in the sense of self as well as a disturbance in the nature of the relationship with other.

Other dynamic theorists who rely on a relational framework agree. Broucek (1991), Lewis (1971), Lynd (1958), Morrison (1986), Nathanson (1992), Thrane (1979), and Wermser (1981) essentially all place shame front and center as an affect worthy of clinical focus. Morrison (1986) states that "shame is an affect of equal importance, theoretically and phenomenologically, to guilt . . . Shame has been relegated to second-order importance in classic psychoanalytic literature, I believe, because it relates directly to a construct which until recent writings has not been easily integrated into the mainstream of Freudian concepts—that of the 'self' (p. 348). Morrison (1998) goes on to say that perhaps shame has eluded therapists for years because it is so well-disguised. Since shame is directly tied to the *sense of who we are,* it is an emotion that is most frequently hidden from the therapist and often from the conscious part of the self as well. Confirming Morrison, Nathanson (1987) acknowledges that, among patients he had been unable to understand or help, shame was the prime issue.

2. Scheff and Retzinger (2002) clearly implicate societal forces and argue strongly that "modern societies have institutionalized the myth of individualism, as well as the denial of pride and shame, as defenses against the pain of threatened bonds" (p. 15). They stress that code words such as, "[i]*nsecure, awkward* and *uncomfortable* [become] analogous to the code language for designating other unmentionables, such as sexual or 'toilet' terms" (p. 125). The authors make the stark point that of all the European languages only English does not differentiate between shame as "disgrace" and shame as "modesty"(pp. 6–7), further evidence of the socio-cultural forces operating in our society to confound our understanding of shame.

CHAPTER 7

Trauma
The Violation of Self

Trauma impels people both to withdraw from close relationships and to seek them desperately. The profound disruption in basic trust, the common feelings of shame, guilt, and inferiority, and the need to avoid reminders of the trauma that might be found in social life, all foster withdrawal from close relationships. But the terror of the traumatic event intensifies the need for protective attachments. The traumatized person therefore frequently alternates between isolation and anxious clinging to others.

—JUDITH HERMAN (1997, P. 56)

Trauma is contagious and the contagion is likely to be insidious. All who come in contact with it can come away marked, including victim, victim families and progeny, observers, bystander witnesses, advocates, researchers, and yes, perpetrators.

—JACK DANIELIAN (2010A, P. 247)

IN THE previous chapter we presented a clinical review of the etiology and treatment of shame and discussed how the dynamic of shame is the driving force behind much of what we have come to understand as narcissistic injuries to the evolving sense of self. In our own clinical experience we see shame and trauma as being inextricably linked and find that repeated, traumatic relational ruptures often produce a sense of insecurity, inadequacy, confusion, and personal defectiveness coupled with concomitant hidden feelings of shame.

From the perspective of attachment theory, trauma can be defined as *any rupture in empathic attunement that results in the diminishment of safety or the diminishment of a secure sense of self.* Therefore, the development of an authentic self is directly linked to a secure and consistent attachment with others. Failures of attunement between a child and a parent or an individual and his/her support system can be viewed as traumatic experiences. The frequency, intensity, and pervasiveness of these ruptures of attachment register as neurobiological imprints that are often associated with memories of a fractured sense of safety and therefore a compromised sense of personal agency and self-confidence.

One of the common clinical misconceptions about the diagnosis and treatment of trauma is that in order for us to label a person's history as traumatic, the events must be *severe enough* to give a person a diagnosis that falls within the trauma spectrum. In large part this is based on earlier work on trauma of van der Kolk, Linehan, and others, where the primary research was conducted on combat veterans, rape and incest survivors, and individuals presenting with disorders of severe affect dysregulation. However, in our view trauma is more comprehensively understood and treated if we think about trauma and shame as being on a continuum of injury, ranging from minor to severe. A spectrum of traumatic ruptures is illustrated below.

Trauma Spectrum:
FAILURES OF ATTUNEMENT

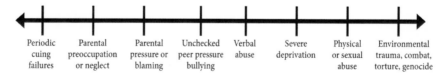

| Periodic cuing failures | Parental preoccupation or neglect | Parental pressure or blaming | Unchecked peer pressure bullying | Verbal abuse | Severe deprivation | Physical or sexual abuse | Environmental trauma, combat, torture, genocide |

Figure 7.1 Trauma spectrum.

Courtois and Ford (2009) make a distinction between "single-incident trauma" such as a traumatic accident, a natural disaster, or a single episode of abuse or assault, versus "complex or repetitive trauma" such as ongoing abuse, domestic violence, or genocide. In the latter profile of trauma, the long-term effects are often much more damaging as they often involve the fundamental betrayal of trust by someone known to the victim. Not only are these individuals more likely to develop psychological symptoms (PTSD), the effects of repetitive trauma "[m]ay compromise or alter a person's psychobiological and socioemotional development when it occurs at critical developmental periods (p. 15). Cook, et al. (2005) and van der Kolk (2005) stated that repeated acts of trauma or violence contribute to the breakdown of the healthy development of one's sense of identity, the integrity of the body and a coherently organized personality. Conclusions from their research have shown that secure attachments lead to one's ability to sustain healthy, reciprocal relationships.

In this chapter we will delve further into understanding the nuances of treatment of the often hidden feelings within the shame/trauma spectrum. Although childhood sexual trauma is included in our spectrum, the most severe cases will not be covered. Patients with severe trauma histories often require multiple interventions, brief hospitalizations, or intensive partial programs to help address feelings of safety, affect regulation, and/or co-morbid substance abuse issues. Therefore, the application of the Four Quadrant Model as it applies to the treatment of trauma will be limited to outpatient and private practice settings, focusing on client populations that do not present with severe affect dysregulation, suicidality, or a severe threat of psychic fragmentation. Individuals with histories of severe and unrelenting childhood trauma including ritualistic abuse or torture fall within a category of patients in need of wider conjoint services.

Although this can be difficult to assess initially, early diagnostic indicators of severe traumatic damage include patients who present with large gaps in memory of early childhood, a high degree of impulsivity or substance abuse, or marked fragility in overidealized relationships. Patients who fall within less severe degrees of dissociation, as evidenced by some capacity for self-reflection, or some degree of work and/or relationship stability, are the parameters of populations where our model can be best applied.

The application of the Four Quadrant Model to cases involving trauma offers a systemic understanding of *the vicious cycle of shame.* We define the unfolding sequence of this cycle as follows:

- The initial experience of traumatic relational ruptures
- An internal sense of confusion, panic, or fears around safety and annihilation
- A sense of personal inadequacy that develops, coupled with feelings of vulnerability and shame
- Followed by attempts at recovery through dissociation and/or overcompensation

By holding in awareness the various components that comprise this sequence, we can more easily see how the balance of a tightly integrated, overdetermined personality organization is used in the service of defending against feelings of shame and fears of fragmentation. Understanding the relationship between traumatic shame and disavowal/dissociation is crucial to the outcome of treatment. There are several ways shame (and underlying trauma) announces its presence:

- The client can cognitively report a humiliating event from childhood but cannot capture its affective strength ("I just decided not to think about it"). The affect here has been evicted from awareness for the purpose of achieving a dissociated balance of forces.
- The client experiences powerful affective reactions (nightmares, hyperarousal, sudden panic) but the emotions do not connect with any recognizable content. The affect is painfully present, but the client has dissociated from any connecting content ("I suddenly get overwhelmed with a terrible fear but I don't know what it is").
- Both content and affect are dissociated from awareness. The client can present with disconnected strands of bodily symptoms (nausea, choking) or blandness ("There's nothing there, I don't know what to say"). Both parts of the whole are out of awareness and both are in the service of maintaining the viability of an integrated overdetermined characterological organization.
- The client has moments of being able to connect with the cognitive content and also separately with the affective component but cannot experience them TOGETHER. When one part of the whole is in awareness, the other part drops out of awareness, and this can occur even within the same session.

In each of these clinical manifestations, we wish to emphasize that there is a *prior* disconnect (lurking behind the *current* content/affect disconnect) which maintains the status quo of the split. We can say that the earlier split, initiated unconsciously to maintain homeostatic balance, now proceeds to further usurp the personality by begetting further splits. The deeper split is fueled by abject fears of abandonment which would be triggered by the dreaded exposure of a rupture in the intersubjective space between patient and parental figures. Anxiety, sadness, anger, and fears of abandonment are kept at bay by internalized overidealized images of one or both parents. As we have indicated, this split causes the connection between affect and content to be severed, thereby protecting the threatened relational bond with the parental figures. ("I know I was hit too often, but I love my parents. They did it for my own good"). The idealizations, as we have discussed earlier, are a child's (and later an adult's) compulsive efforts to compensate for and override painful mal-attunement between patient and parent(s).

Our clinical experience has been that each of the powerful affects at play (anxiety, sadness, anger, fears of abandonment) is saturated with shame and therefore more difficult to access. The patient is ashamed of needing his parents and both proud and ashamed of his defensive (life-saving) constructions to maintain his bonds with them. The shame, unattended, multiplies on itself with the patient becoming ashamed of being ashamed.

TRAUMA: THE HISTORIC CONNECTION BETWEEN SHAME AND FAILURES OF ATTUNEMENT

Closely related to narcissistic and borderline character disturbances is the looming presence of trauma and post-traumatic stress disorder (PTSD). Military reports (epidemiological study, 2007, unpublished Veterans Administration data) estimate that 22.6 percent of army personnel returning from war zones are suffering from PTSD. Even this figure may be an underestimate because the symptoms of PTSD may take not just weeks or months to become evident but years and even decades. As well, privileged positions such as clergy, mental health professionals, or teachers have been implicated in sexual or physical abuse, sometimes in large numbers. As has been shown, bullying among school children is also a serious trauma with clear mental health consequences. In the entire range of abuse and trauma coming to light, denial has been its most conspicuous companion.

In all cases trauma can take its toll on families of the victim and on generations to come. Patients are reluctant to confide in anyone, but the "conspiracy of silence" is frequently not limited just to survivors. Families, therapists, or close friends can also be afflicted, which is a condition referred to as *secondary* traumatization. There are many forms of secondary traumatization. In families, trauma often extends intergenerationally with unrecognized symptoms in offspring appearing at any time. For psychotherapists, those who are persistently exposed to patient trauma can be unaware of its impact and can unknowingly register a numbing of pain and "compassion fatigue."

Until recent times, traditional psychodynamic theory considered the effects of childhood trauma on the mental health of children to be secondary to their underlying psychical fantasies. Paul Renn (2010) suggests that such minimization of the impact of trauma on children stems from a larger cultural bias in Western societies where children are seen as not yet fully human enough to feel pain, to grieve, to remember trauma, or to develop acute stress syndromes such as PTSD. In this deeply damaging bias, children can be seen as being not fully sentient so that pain, humiliation, or abuse will not affect them the way they would affect mature humans. Renn

(2010) points out that until recently "young children can undergo surgical procedures without anaesthetic because they don't feel pain; they do not need help with loss because they are too immature to mourn; they can be physically and sexually abused because they won't remember the abuse" ("Psychoanalysis and the Trauma(s) of History," International Association of Relational Psychoanalysis and Psychotherapy, online Colloquium Series, No. 17, Dec. 6–19). Thankfully, modern neuroscience has demonstrated that infants are born with far more affective capacity than Western science had assumed.

Trauma dynamics are a source of public alarm and confusion, as well as public denial. Breaking the socio-cultural dam parallels the delicate individual process in therapy of undoing the shame and humiliation associated with trauma. It requires the therapist to be an intimate witness to the terror lying behind clinical reenactments and other serious symptomotology. Memory is fractured so that fragments from the past and present are intertwined. The reinstatement of memory depends vitally on the presence of a "protective other" who of necessity will often be the treating therapist.

It is an accepted clinical wisdom that the greatest access we can gain to trauma-related flashbacks or reenactments is also the most dynamically challenging. The therapist's capacity to immerse subjectively in the patient's terror must be accompanied with a vigilance around maintaining boundaries. As always the immersion unfolds in the *present moment*. When immersion is achieved, traumatized patients can sense the "oneness" of the experience unfolding and be able to participate more fully. Fractured memory, a symptom of trauma, is a means to numb pain and defend against both terror and shame. The threat is all-encompassing, yet moment-to-moment awareness of the client's dread is central to the therapist's goal. The client's dread may be immediately followed by detachment or its opposite, hyper-reactivity. Both are best seen not as resistance but as an urgent form of self-soothing or an urgent form of self-protection. The following case involves a vivid example of both traumatization and secondary traumatization in a family with a history of genocide (Danielian, 2010c):

> An eight-year-old boy hears a terrifying wail emanating from a female relative visiting for coffee with the boy's parents and grandparents. The wail is followed by prolonged sobbing, which is then followed by an equally prolonged silence. The woman is a victim-survivor of . . . genocide . . . arriving in this country as only the shell of her former self. She is thoroughly trapped in the dangerous and potentially lethal world between terror and nothingness, despite seemingly involved in an innocuous social situation. Without awareness, the boy is also

trapped between hearing and not-hearing, between knowing and not-knowing. Despite [seemingly] belonging to a close-knit family, the eight-year-old does not enter the coffee room to seek explanation or reassurance from his family. And neither the boy nor his parents ever bring up the experience again. (pp. 245–46)

All the elements of trauma are present here: shame, terror, hyper-arousal, numbing, silence, fractured memory, derealization, traumatization, and secondary traumatization. Some have called the above intergenerational transmission of trauma a process of "encryption." The terror is "encrypted" in one's vital center, bypassing words, thoughts, communication, voice, or emotional rendering. Through such a wordless process memory is fractured and derealization ensues. In the face of such acute trauma, the silence can only be approached if the therapist is able to become an intimate "witness" to the visceral fear.

What is the role of theory in working with trauma? Is the "witnessing" of a patient's pain or suffering a curative factor in itself? Decades ago, Ian Suttie (1935) had told us that Freud had built a significant taboo on tenderness in his analytic theory, reducing tenderness to a component derivative of sexuality. As we have seen, there is no way to understand trauma, let alone treat it, without a major theoretical investment in the administration of tenderness. And the same must be said concerning shame. Shame cannot be understood, let alone treated, unless the therapist has processed the deeper levels of his or her shame. As therapists, when we see shame, we should look for trauma; when we see trauma, we should look for shame.

THE FOUR QUADRANT MODEL APPLIED TO TRAUMA

One distinction that can be made between simple and complex trauma is the degree of underlying shame that must be defended against in order to keep the psychic equilibrium intact. As you can see from figure 7.2, fear of annihilation/fragmentation is at the core of complex trauma, stemming from difficulties these patients have in maintaining affect regulation, bodily integrity, and relationship stability, all of which have been compromised by repeated abuse and/or failures in relational attunement.

Whereas, patients with less severe trauma histories experience a sense of underlying shame that propels them toward overcompensation and overidealization of self and other, severely traumatized individuals have greater difficulty maintaining a stable coherent sense of self. Therefore, affect dysregulation and dissociation constitute a greater degree of the core personality.

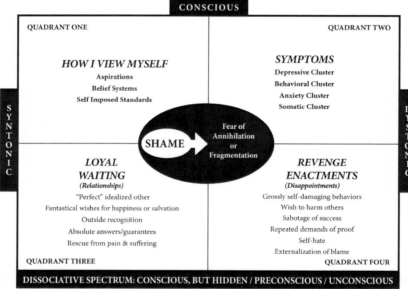

Figure 7.2 Four quadrant model—the centrality of shame.

Appling the Four Quadrant Model to individuals with complex trauma histories, it is important to note that Quadrant Two symptom formation is generally more intensified in the initial stages of treatment. Therefore, affect stabilization generally becomes one of the first goals of treatment. The organizing schematic around the underlying shame is more pervasive and extreme, taking the form of self-loathing or a view of the self that is either contaminated or unworthy of goodness. Although the dissociation and fragmentation are more severe in terms of linking affect or memory to their traumatic histories, there is usually some degree of conscious awareness that the effort it takes for them to maintain their equilibrium is greater than for other individuals. For many, simple tasks require tremendous effort and psychic energy, often leaving these individuals exhausted and depleted. In addition the performance standards that they set for themselves (Quadrant One) are often quite exacting and rigid. Harsh judgment and self-loathing (Quadrant Four) are frequent aspects of their internal dialogue whenever they attempt to dream for something more or fail to achieve those desired goals.

Relationships can be volatile or quite guarded. Mistrust of others is a major hurdle to overcome in therapy, and building of the therapeutic alliance must be done with patience over a longer period of time. Clients initially present with extreme ambivalence about therapy, coupled with magical hopes for rescue. There is also a tendency to overly idealize and/or mistrust the therapist while trying to also be "the good client." Due to the insecure attachments in childhood, victims of trauma often recreate similar versions of insecure attachments in the partners whom they choose in adulthood. The pattern in these relationships either repeats extreme volatility and/or lack of safety, or traumatized individuals will expend all of their energy attempting to please their partners at all costs.

Traumatic events or memories are often split off from consciousness, leading to mild to severe states of dissociation. Clients with trauma histories often can be identified early in treatment through a cluster of symptoms within the anxiety spectrum, including an increased startle response, social phobias, body dysmorphia, nightmares, or gaps in awareness of time. In cases where there is early childhood abuse, patients will report that there are large gaps in memory with years of their childhood missing altogether. Neurological brain research (Solomon and Siegel, 2003) indicate that the dissociated trauma of early childhood is stored in the implicit memory system. Individuals often have no way of accessing these early memories or integrating them into a working narrative that only comes with the later development of explicit memory organization.

In the following brief dream-like sequence, notice not just the physical, but the emotional absence of mother. The intimacy needs of a child are transformed into violent exploitation and sexual abuse:

- The child is engulfed in a physical and mental crisis.
- The child is overwhelmed with annihilation anxiety.
- The child painfully blames herself for the trauma.

In talking to her mother the child dissociates from the trauma, absolves the father, and makes the assumption that she has wet herself. She thought her father was asleep. Then he rolled over on her. She couldn't move, breathe, or talk. He was going back and forth, and then everything became hazy and ominous. She was going to die. Mother had gone somewhere and not come back. The child lost consciousness and disappeared into herself. Her mother returned and said, "What's the matter with you?" "Mommy I wet myself, I'm sick" she said and started to cry. The patient could never remember if this actually happened.

Because early implicit memory is often stored as a "body memory" and experienced through anxiety, hyperarousal, dissociation, fragmentation, and/or nightmares, it is often difficult for patients to find "proof" of what occurred in the blank or absent years of childhood or through vague accounts in the treatment. Understanding how dissociation contributes to psychic destabilization, psychiatrist Judith Herman (1997) speaks to how trauma often leads to a fracturing and fragmentation of the self.

> Traumatic reactions occur when action is of no avail. When neither resistance nor escape is possible, the human system of self-defense becomes overwhelmed and disorganized. . . . Traumatic events produce profound and lasting changes in physiological arousal, emotion, cognition, and memory. Moreover, traumatic events may sever these normally integrated functions from one another. The traumatized person may experience intense emotion but without clear memory of the event, or may remember everything in detail but without emotion. She may find herself in a constant state of vigilance and irritability without knowing why. Traumatic symptoms have a tendency to become disconnected from their source and to take on a life of their own (p. 34).

Fear of annihilation is a key feature of severely traumatized individuals. Because safety and attunement have been so compromised, it is often difficult to imagine the energy required to simply survive. In the following section we have included a brief description of the challenges victims of trauma had to face and how this, in turn affected their psychic organization around sense of self and other.

The Long-Term Sequelae of Persistent Child Abuse

In families where a child is subjected to traumatic abuse of long-standing, the entire family structure becomes altered. The perpetrator consciously or unconsciously holds the family to a severe code of silence about what has been seen. What is seen is said to not be seen. Members of the family understand that the price of safety is muteness. The non-offending parent often partly or fully dissociates the abuse from on-going "normality" and disowns both the memory of the event and the terror of the experience. Non-offending siblings quickly learn to do likewise adopting the same mechanisms of denial and dissociation. And the abused child, mired in the painful silence of her family, is left to take on alone the immense burden of the perpetrator's shame.

In a haunting description, Herman (1997) puts it this way: "By developing a contaminated, stigmatized identity, the child victim takes the evil of the abuser into herself" (p.105). In the face of family disconnect, the abused child finds no other way to reduce terror and maintain primary bonds between herself and others in the family. Herman continues further: "Because the inner sense of badness preserves a relationship, it is not readily given up even after the abuse has stopped; rather it becomes a stable part of the child's personality structure" (p.105).

Once created in childhood, dissociation takes on a life of its own, and similar to other pathological processes, can compound itself. Thus in the treatment process, one of the biggest obstacles for patients is the terror of re-experiencing the abuse and the "badness" of her being. If we substitute *shamefulness* for *badness*, the shame of remembering becomes the equivalent of succumbing to the perpetrator's threat to contaminate not just her past and present but her entire future. Accordingly, large gaps in the memory of children frequently occur. Because symptoms are seemingly so disconnected from each other, the clinical presentation can be confusing to even an experienced diagnostician. The body has become the repository of memory and demonstrates its violation through multiple somatic symptoms with alternating psychological hyperarousal and psychological numbness.[1]

The burden on the therapist can be daunting because while the patient wants desperately for a rescuer to "see" the true reasons for the incoherence in the narrative, the patient remains in mortal fear of being re-victimized and abandoned by perpetrator, family, and the therapist. Up to this point, the only safety the patient can muster is to create glorified images of caretakers and family. Unlike patients who have experienced less serious ruptures in the fabric of the family, patients who have sustained persistent physical or sexual abuse in childhood are much more prone to experience fragmentation and disorganization in adulthood.

Hyperidealized images become the necessary glue that holds together fragile disavowed, derealized, or dissociated parts of the personality, preventing thereby further collapse into what some have called a psychological "black hole." Idealizations are thus life-saving at this stage and need therapeutic protection. Thereafter, the long path to an increased sense of safety and the progressive establishment of a therapeutic alliance will be facilitated by the addition of conjoint group programs for safety, sobriety, abuse support, and, as needed, hospitalization or partial hospitalization.

CLINICAL EXAMPLES OF THE LONG-TERM EFFECTS OF PERSISTENT CHILD ABUSE

Case Example A

A patient calls the emergency room of a hospital with a plea for help after being raped by a man she vaguely recognized. After considerable time with the nursing staff to console her distraught condition, the medical examination finds that she has sustained cuts to her genital area. However the cuts do not fit the clinical picture of injury due to rape. The E.R. doctor asks the patient to repeat what had taken place and notices that some changes in the story have taken place. When he asks her if she has somehow inflicted these cuts on herself, the patient becomes confused, disoriented, and begins sobbing. The doctor concludes that this is a case of "malingering," prescribes a sedative, and discharges her.

The doctor has failed to realize that while the patient had indeed inflicted the wounds on herself, she was seeking help in the only way she could, hoping that the medical staff would "see through" her semi-fugue altered state and connect her symptoms and behavior to her history of chronic child sexual abuse.

Case Example B

A mother of two in her fifties presents with a bland exterior but with a variety of disruptive symptoms: vague but generalized fearfulness, difficulty controlling her bowels, swimming and bathing phobias, gagging, preoccupations with death. After several years of therapy, she feels sufficient safety in treatment to reveal that from the ages of 6–12, she had been persistently sexually abused by an influential member of the family, an uncle. She would respond to his visits with controlled panic, hiding her emotions because the uncle was so highly respected in the family. Through various ploys, he is able to get alone time with her, where a ritualized sexual abuse would take place. The patient reports this harrowing account with minimal affect, mentioning it only sporadically, and almost parenthetically, for months after.

Almost imperceptibly she begins to stay longer with her description of the abuse with gradually rising affect accompanying her descriptions. She wonders why no one had noticed her frozen and rigidly held body. She wonders also about her mother's self-centeredness and registers increasing periods of frustration and anger at her. The therapist asks at some point if she would ever consider telling her mother about the abuse. She responds, "It would do no good, and anyway she is not well."

Therapy continues with a growing therapeutic alliance and significant abatement of symptoms. The patient continues to register louder and louder complaints about her mother. The therapist supports her growing frustrations about her mother's self-centeredness, without any further reference to her mother's obliviousness to the molestation. In the seventh year of treatment patient arrives early for her appointment, promptly takes a seat, and emotionally states, "I told her the whole story, how long it went on, how much it hurt me, and how the whole family seemed to be in such admiration of him." Her mother's response is a cruel mixture of solemnity and detachment, "Oh he did that to you too?"

Making the Connection between Trauma, the Therapeutic Holding Environment, and Neuro-Physiological Brain Changes

Beginning with the research of Kardiner (1941) and Lindemann (1944) on the traumatic effects of war veterans and acute stress/grief reactions, there has been a growing interest in post-traumatic responses to combat trauma, rape, natural disasters, and the long term effects of childhood abuse over the life span. Horowitz (1978) and van der Kolk (1987) have documented that trauma creates a bimodal response system that involves hyperamnesia and hyperreactivity to stimuli. That is, a traumatic hyperarousal can occur with the reactivation of a traumatic memory and that this can coexist with psychic numbing, avoidance, amnesia, and anhedonia. van der Kolk (1987) states:

> Traumatized individuals may gain some sense of subjective control by shunning all situations or emotions related to the trauma. Often they

avoid intimate relationships, apparently out of fear of a renewed violation of the attachment bond. Avoiding emotional involvement further
diminishes the significance of life after the trauma, and thus perpetu-
ates the central role of the trauma (p. 3).

Clinicians and researchers who work with victims of trauma find that
the memories seem to leave an indelible imprint on the psyche, affecting
their ability to handle subsequent stressors and their ability to regulate affect
in general. When high levels of emotional and physiological arousal occur,
the ability to process emotions is hampered. When states of hyperarousal are
triggered, there is decreased activity in the Broca's area of the brain, the area
related to language and verbal expression. Therefore, it is not uncommon for
individuals to have great difficulty verbalizing their experience. Van der Kolk
(1994) is noted as saying that traumatized individuals are said to experience
"speechless terror," difficult to capture in words or symbols.

With advances in neuro-imaging studies of brain activity, it is now
widely understood that psychic trauma produces changes in brain chemis-
try. There is an increased production of catecholamines such as epinephrine
and norepinephrine that result in increased activity of the sympathetic nervous system. In addition there has been documented evidence of decreased
levels of corticosteroids and serotonin, the effect of which is a decreased
ability to moderate catecholamine, or the fight/flight response. In addition
to neurotransmitter and endocrine system changes, the neurobiological
effect of trauma is registered in limbic system activity, specifically in the
amygdala and hippocampus regions (Siegel, 1999). High level activation of
the amygdala interferes with hippocampal functioning and prevents our
ability to categorize experiences effectively.

In treating post-traumatic stress disorder, Danielian (2010b) has
emphasized the remarkable features of non-conscious memories:

[O]ne cannot but be impressed by how difficult it is for patients to
maintain a coherent narrative of their lives. Memory seems to connect
and disconnect without will, depending on the equilibrium state of the
patient. How could patients remember (often in excruciating detail)
and yet not remember at all? Turning to neuroscience for help, the
well-known researcher Daniel Siegel [1999] recognized that the so-
called implicit memories tied to the hippocampus in the limbic system
via neuro-pathways to the amygdala held great promise in uncovering
a neurobiological underpinning for PTSD. These are the first areas of
the brain to process emotion and short-term memory. In a state of
mind free of trauma, information flows freely to the higher cortical

levels where long-term memory is stored and where executive functions can proceed. However with exposure to trauma, the amygdala and hippocampus may not be able to perform their functions properly, becoming overwhelmed; limbic dysregulation results. Memories remain in an implicit non-conscious state, frozen in a time and space warp, just as we observe clinically in the treatment of PTSD. When a patient is unable to properly process traumatic emotions and memory, he or she may retain an astonishingly vivid and often terrifying sensory experience of the original trauma. A coherent narrative becomes nearly impossible to achieve but notice how in the study of trauma, researchers have discovered that the mind and the brain are continually and reciprocally affecting each other, and doing so in powerful ways. Thus the concept of neuroplasticity, the brain's inherent capacity to rewire itself, becomes much clearer (p. 102).

In terms of treatment one question that prompts a certain degree of debate is whether psychodynamic therapies are as effective in the treatment of trauma as are other modalities that fall under the rubric of cognitive/behavioral therapies, such as Dialectical Behavior Therapy (DBT) or Eye Movement Desensitization and Reprocessing (EMDR). What these approaches have in common is the goal of calming the hyperaroused affect in an effort to re-engage other centers of the brain that are responsible for insight, such as changes in the intensity of memory triggers, increased judgment and regulation, and the building of new mental associations to help explain potentially shaming or traumatic stimuli. The theoretical basis for these approaches centers on a belief that the patient must be able to master some degree of skill building/mastery of affect regulation before the deeper, integrative work of dynamically oriented psychotherapy is possible.[2]

Marsha Linehan (1993), originator of DBT, uses what she calls "the technology of acceptance" in all of her treatment procedures. Linehan believes that individuals with more severe affect dysregulation issues have a past relational history of *invalidation*, and thus they have not been able to learn any effective methods of coping with their sudden surges of emotion. DBT is a method that teaches skill building, while also using "mindfulness" techniques that encourage the patient to remain focused in the present. The task of the therapist is to adopt a stance of respectful acceptance of the patient and to offer skill building strategies that reintegrate cognition and insight, thus teaching individuals how to regulate their emotional states.[3]

Bessell van der Kolk et al. (1996) state that a treatment approach must address two fundamental aspects of PTSD: the treatment of anxiety and the reestablishment of a feeling of control. The aim of any therapy with trauma survivors is to help the individual move from being dominated by the traumatic memories to being capable of responding to the current moment in time. Van der Kolk, van der Hart, and Burbridge (1995) break the treatment of PTSD into three principal components: 1) processing and coming to terms with the overwhelming experience, 2) controlling and mastering psychological and biological stress reactions, and 3) reestablishing interpersonal relationships. Generally a combination of procedures for deconditioning anxiety and for reestablishing a personal sense of control will be needed in all but the simplest cases (van der Kolk, McFarlane, and van der Hart, 1996).

In both DBT and EMDR treatment modalities, the therapeutic interventions are often done in conjunction with a referral from the primary psychotherapist who is responsible for providing long-term oversight and treatment of the case. A referral is made either in the initial phases of treatment to help ground the patient in the necessary skill-building around decreasing hyperarousal of affect, or at such point in the treatment where overcharged transference issues directed at the primary therapist might be mitigated by a secondary treatment alliance. Care is used by both therapists to present a coordinated effort and avoid transferential splitting.

From a psychodynamic perspective the treatment of traumatized patients would certainly address deficits in capacities throughout the therapy, specifically with regard to affect-regulation, relational guardedness, and the cognitive capacities of introspection, sound judgment, and self-reflection. In addition to managing the level of hyperarousal, long-term dynamic treatment approaches would rely on the therapeutic relationship as a primary leverage for change. However, if we incorporate recent knowledge gleaned from neurobiological research, how we *integrate* these findings into a metatheoretical understanding of treatment is critically important. A description from Paul Renn (2010), "Psychoanalysis and the Trauma(s) of History," (International Association for Relational Psychoanalysis and Psychotherapy, online Colloquium Series No. 17, December 6-19) is instructive:

> From a trauma perspective, the patient's symptoms, destructive and self-destructive behaviors are understood as expressing unresolved traumatic experience encoded in implicit-procedural memories, as represented in confused, unstable self-other representational models. These non-conscious state-dependent memories and patterns of expectancies organize experience and emerge in the relational system or intersubjective field, being communicated directly to the therapist via the patient's discourse style and expressive behavioural display. This, in turn, activates a matching countertransferential or

psycho-physiological response in the therapist (activates the mirror neuron system), enabling the therapist to participate in the subjective experience of the patient in terms of shared attentional, intentional and affectional states of mind.

The developing intersubjective relationship with the therapist provides a good-enough safe haven and secure base from which the patient can explore his or her self-states, as reflected in the mind of the therapist moment-by-moment, thereby unlocking the affective components of their unresolved trauma. Crucial aspects of the therapeutic process consist of the repair of inevitable ruptures as these are mutually enacted in the therapeutic relationship, the interactive regulation of heightened affective moments, the provision of new perspectives, the reorganization of maladaptive patterns of expectancies, the transformation of implicitly encoded representations, and the promotion of reflective functioning or mentalization.

This is a cogent description illustrating how intersubjective psychodynamic treatment modalities can use the power of an emotionally meaningful therapeutic relationship to gradually facilitate both relational and neurological changes in patients with trauma histories. Renn explains that it is the collaborative nature of the relationship that is important, where the therapist gradually gains the patient's trust by using present based, moment-to-moment tracking of the patient's discourse, as well as the patient's behavioral and affective expressions. Through a therapeutic holding environment, the patient gradually comes to reorganize dissociated traumatic experiences, connecting them to various relational contexts.

The interactive process between the therapist and patient helps the patient learn to regulate affect, label and evaluate emotional triggers, bringing an increased conscious awareness to one's motivations and personal mastery. With these changes in the patient's sense of agency, there is an equally powerful shift in the patient's sense of self in relation to others. The therapeutic relationship over time has engendered a more secure sense of attachment and reliance on others in the present. Renn (2010), (IARPP, online Colloquium Series, No. 17) concludes,

> The enhancement of the patient's ability gradually to organize his or her self experience consists, in significant degree, of the moment-to-moment micro-repair of misattunement or misaligned interaction—an intersubjective process operating at the level of implicit relational knowing. The therapeutic process is informed by the tracking and matching of subtle and dramatic shifts in the patient's mood-state

as they narrate their story. This interactive process leads, in turn, to the recognition of the existence of the therapist as a separate person available to be used and related to intersubjectively within a shared subjective reality. . . . From a neurobiological perspective, the process of affect regulation links nonverbal and verbal representational domains of the brain. This process facilitates the transfer of implicit-procedural information in the right hemisphere to explicit or declarative systems in the left. Thus, implicitly encoded body-based visceral-somatic experience is symbolically transformed into emotional and intentional states of mind that then become available for reflection and regulation.

Here we see how neuropsychological observations can help to confirm our metatheoretical understanding of how therapeutic change is possible through the power of a shared subjective experience. This intersubjective and reparative process takes place within the dyadic relationship, where the memory of intensely painful and dreaded affect is disclosed by the patient and witnessed by the therapist. A gradual unburdening of the self takes place within the holding environment of the present. Thus, the relationship becomes the container of affective material that is too difficult to bear alone. Together, the therapist and patient can begin to bring the shattering effects of a life filled with trauma into a coherent narrative with the hope that the patient is then able to move forward into present day reality.

CASE STUDIES THAT INTEGRATE SHAME, TRAUMA, AND PART-WHOLE ANALYSIS

The remainder of this chapter is devoted to the presentation of two different case studies, exemplifying varying degrees of trauma, in an attempt to help integrate theory with practical application. We invite you to think about each of the following cases from the perspective of part-whole analysis, the trauma spectrum of relational attunement, as well as the Four Quadrant Model presented in chapter 2 that we have discussed in the manual.

Case Vignette 1

Bob is a forty-five year old male patient with a family history of physical and emotional abuse. This individual was the recipient of verbal abuse by both mother and father and was the witness of second-hand physical abuse on the part of his father directed toward his younger brother. Father was diagnosed with a major depressive disorder in adulthood but refused to take medication. Younger brother had a history of severe acting out in high school, served some jail time for an attack of his girlfriend in a bar fight, and continues to be a source of embarrassment for the family. Bob has attempted to both help his younger brother and set limits with him during the course of therapy. He has a distant and "cool" relationship with both of his parents. Bob is married with two children, but complains of a dissatisfying relationship with his wife. However, he is quite attached to his two children, and he is a good provider with a successful job in sales and marketing. In addition he has several long-term friendships that he finds satisfying.

Bob: I need to talk about something today that is difficult for me to discuss. It's about something that I did that confuses me (pause). I don't understand it. It doesn't seem like me, but this thing that I did, well . . . I did a similar sort of thing about ten years ago. Anyway, I won't get into that incident right now. Here's what happened last week. We have this staff meeting via a conference call once a week with people from various parts of the country. During this meeting I was aware, well (pause as if struggling for words), I mean, you know how sometimes when you bring something up as if you're trying to be helpful by pointing something out or asking a question, you secretly have other motivations (pause)? Well, that's what I was doing to Jim during that meeting. I don't understand why I was doing it because he's a good buddy of mine. But, I kept bringing something up to the boss that Jim hadn't done and said, "Maybe you should check in with Jim to make sure he understands the new mandate."

Therapist: Was Jim there? Was he a part of the conference call?

Bob: No, he was out on assignment, and he wasn't at the last meeting either, so I know that he didn't hear all of the details behind the rationale for the new mandate. In a way I was trying to really be helpful, but secretly I knew I also had another motivation. That's what bothers me. I don't know why I would do something like that.

Therapist: What was the other motivation you are referring to?

Bob: I guess that I wanted to make him look bad. And what was really strange is that another one of my buddies who was at the meeting pulled me aside afterwards and said, "Boy, you really threw Jim under the bus." I said, "What do you mean?" You know, because it really hadn't registered completely what I had done until he said that. Anyway, Larry repeated to me other things that I had said later in the meeting, and I was shocked. I didn't even remember saying those other things.

Therapist: What did he say that you had said?

Bob: I don't know. I can't even remember it now. But, anyway, it gets worse. Jim found out what I said and got really angry and wouldn't return any of my calls that day. Later that week Jim, Larry, and I had a scheduled business meeting that we all had to attend. When I saw him, I just kept apologizing, saying I'm sorry, I'm sorry. Then Jim started questioning me. He told me that Larry had told him what I had said about him at the end of the meeting—and I still can't remember that part of what I said. He kept asking me, "Why did you do it?" And, I said, "I don't know, I don't know. I'm sorry." Anyway, I'm glad we talked. I think we're okay now.

Therapist: How do you know that?

Bob: I don't know. We shook hands and gave each other a hug. He said, "Don't worry about it. We're all under a lot of stress."

Therapist: I'm wondering how you're feeling right now having told me about this?

Bob: I feel fine. Well, I feel confused and a little sad.

Therapist: Anything else?

Bob: No, why do you ask?

Therapist: Well, generally people don't have this much trouble remembering something that they said less than a week ago if they're just feeling sad or confused, particularly when someone repeats what you had said more than once. Do you find that a little strange? I mean, it's not like you to not remember things.

Bob: I know, that's what's so confusing.

Therapist: Well, I'm taking a guess, but I wonder if the reason you can't remember is that you're feeling ashamed about what you did, and maybe a little embarrassed to even tell me about it.

Bob: I thought shame was taboo, something we're not supposed to feel, something you're supposed to fight against.

Therapist: Where did you get that idea?

Bob: I don't know. It was something I read, I guess.

Therapist: Well, shame is one of the most uncomfortable feelings we can feel, that is true. But, I think that all of us would feel a little ashamed if we became aware that we have treated a friend badly, even if we don't understand why we did what we did.

Bob: Yeah, I guess I do feel really, really badly about it. But, I don't understand why I did it.

Therapist: No, it doesn't sound like something you would do consciously or intentionally. But, you know what I'm thinking about? I'm thinking about what you told me two weeks ago about the change in leadership at your organization and how everyone got pay cuts, and they were told they should just be thankful that they still have jobs. You took that pretty hard, and we talked about how devaluing that was, how underappreciated you felt.

Bob: (pause, stares at therapist blankly).

Therapist: So, I'm wondering if you may have unconsciously tried to align yourself with your new boss by reminding him that you were aware of the new mandate by pointing out that Jim hadn't been "following orders." I'm wondering if unconsciously you were trying to regain your status in a way.

Bob: Oh, my God. I was feeding the monster.

Therapist: What do you mean?

Bob: This new guy, this new boss is a hatchet man. Everyone knows it. He's brutal—he takes pleasure in making people feel like they're worthless, and I just fed him a bone . . . my friend. What kind of person am I? I sacrificed my friend to please this jerk?

Therapist: Okay, now let's try to slow the feelings down. You see, here's where we see the shame beginning to surface. But, let's see if we can understand this a little better, so you don't have to beat yourself up with your shame. You know, this is a pretty understandable response when people are being devalued by their superiors. It makes your behavior even more understandable given your family background.

Bob: What do you mean?

Therapist: Well, both your mother and your father humiliated you and your brothers in different ways. You told me how your father physically and verbally abused your oldest brother and that you often witnessed that abuse. And I remember how your mother repeatedly told you how ashamed she was of all four of you boys for not living up to her standards.

Bob: Yes, but I hated it and vowed I'd never be that way to other people.

Therapist: And you haven't been, really, not like they were. But, witnessing the kind of abuse that you had to witness, shaming to the point that an adult is trying to break a child's spirit leaves deep scars. I wonder if it feels a little bit like your boss is trying to do that to people at work?

Bob: Yeah.

Therapist: So, back when you were a child you survived by feeding the monster?

Bob: I always tried to please my father, to live up to his standards. I became the smartest one in my family. That's how I was able to eventually escape (begins to cry). I fed his ego, let him brag about me, take all the credit, until I was old enough to get out of there. Boy, I never knew all of this stuff was still in there (continues crying). I never, ever would have put that together— I mean what happened with my father and what's going on with our new boss (looks up). I think I need to tell Jim about what we talked about today. I think I owe it to him.

Analysis

In this case vignette there are a number of salient points worth mentioning. First, we see how shame goes underground, in part because the patient's own actions feel foreign and also because he had read that "shame is bad for one's health." Hence, the patient was struggling against acknowledging the shameful abuse, which probably also contributed to his memory loss of the feedback his friend gave him about his behavior.

Second, although the patient was aware of his actions to make his friend look bad, the true motivation for doing so remained outside of his conscious awareness. When the therapist made the connection between his boss, the cutbacks, and his own sense of feeling devalued, the patient was able to see that this might explain part of the puzzle of his uncharacteristic behavior. In order to facilitate further connections, the therapist tried to normalize her patient's wish to recover from his devalued position.

When the patient exclaimed in response, "Oh, my God, I was feeding the monster," the therapist remembered that her patient had used these words to describe his father some time ago. She was able to direct the patient back to this historical memory, connecting all of the essential parts to the whole. It was at this point that the patient was able to feel the full brunt of the affective components of his abuse, at the hands of his boss, at the hands of his father, and also what he had learned to do as a child to escape his father's shaming and debilitating rage. His vow to himself, never to become like his father, had been shattered by his recent behavior toward his friend, Jim. Here we see the patient turn that shame harshly against himself because he had broken his idealized vow from childhood.

It is at this point that the therapist uses care to reduce the shaming response against the self (stemming from Quadrant Four) and encourages the patient to join her empathizing with the boy who had no other choice but to excel at all costs to escape the devaluation. Here, we see how empathy and the integration of split-off parts of the whole can lead to insight, repair, and a more realistic approach to one's own vulnerabilities. By working directly with Quadrant One the therapist is "modeling" for the patient a way of forgiving himself for creating an overdetermined coping strategy that originated so many years ago, a strategy that has been refined and developed further in his present life. She is also putting this current incident into perspective, given the enormous amount of stress and disappointment the patient had been through in the last several weeks. Having done so, the patient is ready to make deeper, reparative amends with his friend.

Case Vignette 2

This is a thirty-nine year old female, divorced mother of two children who has been in treatment for approximately five years ("Laura"). When Laura entered therapy she was married to a very depressed man who had been out of work for several years and who functioned as a stay-at-home dad. Laura was the primary bread winner and was quite successful in her field. As the therapy progressed she admitted to having a secret affair with a coworker primarily based on sexual attraction. Over the course of treatment Laura began to become increasingly dissatisfied with this relationship and complained of "being used." She ended the relationship and also left her marriage because she felt it was a sham. Within six months she also left her place of employment and started her own business.

During this next phase of treatment Laura began to more actively reflect on her past relationships. Beginning in early adolescence, she reported that she had had an unusually high degree of sexual activity, several pregnancies and abortions, and a four year sexual relationship with a male cousin. Although Laura has never been able to remember specific incidents of childhood sexual abuse, she did remember frequently sleeping in the same bedroom with her older sister when they were between the ages of eight and ten. Laura reported that she woke up one night to discover her sister fondling Laura's genitals when she thought that the patient was asleep.

It was at the same time that Laura remembered a dream about her father sitting in a large, overstuffed green chair that was located in her bedroom. She identified herself in the dream to be approximately six or seven years of age. When she was aware that her father was sitting in the chair in her bedroom, she climbed into his lap and noticed that he had an erection. As she and her therapist processed this dream, the patient couldn't remember anything inappropriate that occurred with her in real life with her father. In fact, her father was frequently away from the home for months at a time as a ship's captain of an overseas commercial cargo ship. Laura remembers longing for her father to come home because "he was the only parent who showed me any real love and affection."

As the therapy progressed, the patient began to exhibit increased signs of strength, as reflected in her ability to expand her social networks and "grow" her business into quite a successful company. At one point her youngest sister, who was also in therapy, shared with her that she had uncovered some disturbing memories from her own childhood. The sister remembered being in a bedroom with her uncle (one of father's brothers), and he was inserting a candle into her vagina. The sister believes that this memory was quite real and wondered whether something similar may have happened to Laura.

Following this disclosure on the part of her sister, Laura had a series of dreams that spanned the course of two to three months. To date this patient has yet to recover any specific memory of childhood abuse. However, these dream fragments are included as a part of this case vignette to illustrate how fragments of potential childhood abuse can often surface through the content and affective tone of dream material.

Dream Segment 1: I am in my family home and there is this big picture window in the living room. On the coffee table there are objects that seem to be used for some sort of ritual or ceremony. These objects were quite mysterious to me, and I somehow became aware that I wasn't supposed to have discovered them. Suddenly, I look out the window and I see a huge mushroom cloud that has exploded. I am aware that a nuclear bomb has gone off, and it's the end of the world. I am panicked and don't know where to run. Then, I become aware of my father and older brother standing in the corner of the living room. They are calling out to me to come with them down a long, dark corridor to safety. Something about this did not feel right; it didn't feel like they would be pulling me to safety. Instead, I opened this small window at the top of the wall near the ceiling and tried to climb out. They were calling me to come back, but I knew I had to take my chances and get out of the house even though I knew I would be entering into fall-out.

Dream Segment 2: I am sleeping on the second floor of this house and it's dark and I'm aware that there is a man downstairs. My daughter is sleeping in one of the first floor bedrooms, and suddenly I know that he has raped her and now he's coming upstairs to rape me. I escape quietly down the back staircase and get into a rowboat at the edge of this body of water and row across the lake to a neighboring house with lights on. I run in and there are a group of women gathered in a room talking and laughing and drinking wine. I try to get them to pay attention to me, telling them that they need to come back with me to help me get my daughter out of the house and to call the police. They don't take me seriously and make no move to help me. Then, I decide to go back into the boat to try to get my daughter. There is a man at the shoreline, not the bad man in the house, and this man is trying to help me get the boat out of the water. I think that he is here to help me, but suddenly the other man comes out of the shadows, and I see that they are together. I try running back to the house but notice that they have set the place on fire. I start to scream for my daughter and find her huddled in the bushes outside, crying.

Dream Segment 3: I was chasing a man who was chasing children. I had seen him putting an arm inside their vaginas like they were puppets. At first I thought they were little boys, but I could see what he was doing to those little girls. I got so angry that I started screaming at him and chasing him. Then I finally cornered him, and he was shaking in a corner. I could see that he was holding something. They were three aborted babies (I had three abortions). The last baby I saw wasn't dead, however, and I think it was me.

After the patient related this dream to her therapist, she asked, "Why can't I let all of this go? Why can't I move on? Why can't I forgive and forget? I feel stuck. I feel stuck because I don't think I'm going to get a real memory back. It doesn't matter if it happened or not. I need to move on and get a life. But I can't move on unless I have a clear narrative. I want to know, but at the same time I don't want to know what really happened."

Analysis of Dream Segments

Each of these dream segments seems to contain a similar theme and intensity. Each is equally horrifying in content, where the patient has lost a sense of control and the ability to trust others who appear in the dream. Interpreted together, the dreams symbolize some form of violation that may potentially lead to death because the patient is alone with no one to help, no one whom she can really trust. The order of the dreams is significant, where each dream seems to build on the next in terms of specificity of content, each becoming more sexually explicit as the dreams progress.

What is noteworthy is that in each of these dreams the patient is proactively trying to help herself or she is trying to escape. In the third dream rather than running away from the perpetrator, we find that the patient is able to chase him down. When he is confronted, shaking in a corner, he produces three aborted babies. However, the third baby, the one that the patient identifies as herself, is not really dead. Although the dream content is graphically unpleasant, there is a hopeful quality that is embedded in the final discovery. Essentially, the patient's unconscious dream message is stating that the child (the one that she identified as herself) that she thought was dead is not really dead. She may have wanted to "abort" the memory of what occurred to her, leaving this part of herself "dead," but she cannot. The dream is letting her know that the authentic self has survived in spite of the trauma and betrayal.

After disclosing the last dream to the therapist, we see the struggle that many individuals with trauma histories go through—they want to know and don't want to know what really happened to them. In the case of this patient the integration process has already begun. The excerpt from the same case that follows reflects how that integration process occurs over time. The session you are about to read took place approximately three months after this dream material emerged in the therapy.

In this session excerpt we see the beginnings of a lifting of the dissociative defenses and the struggle toward integration of a reality-based sense of self

Session Excerpt

Laura: Thank you for returning my call after hours. I really appreciated it.

Therapist: Yes, I was sorry I didn't get it until the next morning when I tried to reach you. Why don't you tell me what happened? You sounded very upset.

Laura: It's John. Oh, I don't know what to think anymore. I'm so confused. I know it's not really him. There are so many things that I'm having to look at right now. I hate coming out of the fog and seeing so many things this clearly. What have I done with my life? Where have I been? I've been in a constant mess all of my life. I've refused to face it. What did I think? By not looking at it, did I think my problems would go away? It's so hard to face the reality of all of it—my kids, my unpaid back taxes, the deprivation that has been the story of my entire life from childhood. Why can't I just get on with it? I feel so ashamed!

Therapist: I know this is really painful for you, but maybe we can slow this down a bit. Take your time. We have plenty of time. Take a deep breath. Why don't you start with telling me what happened when you made the phone call to me?

Laura: It was John. I went over to his house to ask him a favor. He knows that my car is on its last legs, and I just wanted him to come with me to the car dealership, to just be there while I talked to the guy, so I didn't feel alone. I don't even know if I can get a car loan. Just having him there would have helped me not feel so ashamed. And I told him that when I asked him to come with me.

Therapist: So what did he say?

Laura: (beginning to cry) It was awful. He was so mean to me. He said he was sick and tired of me using people, and it's time that I woke up and started facing reality. He said that he's known me for four years and I haven't changed my life at all. I'm always broke and scraping by, my business is just limping along, and it's time I stopped "blowing smoke up my ass." He also said, "Your therapist is just blowing smoke up your ass too, coddling you and letting you go on like this. You're in the same place that you were when you started." He's right you know. He's speaking the honest truth from the place of reality. This is what I've been avoiding all my life, waiting for people to "frigging" rescue me.

Therapist: Now wait a minute. It's one thing to speak to someone about reality or to say no to a request because they don't think it would be helpful or they're tired of being helpful. It's another thing to deliver that message in such a horribly shaming way.

Laura: You're right, and a part of me knew that at the time, and I was so angry with him. I told him what I was feeling about going to the dealership and that I was full of feelings of shame, and what did he do? He goes off on me and makes me even feel worse about myself. So, that's why I made the phone call to you.

Therapist: I'm glad you did. He went too far, didn't he? You didn't deserve to be talked to in that way. I'm so sorry. It sounds like he's really angry with you, or that some piece of his own shame is being triggered right now; perhaps, that is because so much is breaking through for you around your childhood trauma.

Laura: That's what my sister (the one who is in therapy) said to me when I called her. She said, "Boy, what's up with him? Does he have issues or what?" That made me feel a little better. But, I knew it anyway even before she said it to me. I'm so mad at him, I'm done. He crossed a line. I'm not calling him or reaching out to him. That's it.

Therapist: He does owe you a big apology. I know that this relationship has been very important to you . . . (pt. interrupts)

Laura: He would never do that. If I tried to talk to him about it, he would just say that I'm making a big deal about it, trying to turn it back to him because I can't take the truth.

Therapist: And you could say, "There's a difference between hearing the truth and how the truth is delivered."

Laura: He doesn't buy any of it. Oh, what made me walk out the door is when I said to him that I would never talk to him in this way, he said that he was just delivering the truth. He also said that he would never ask people for money because he prided himself for always pulling his own weight in this life.

Therapist: Do you hear his attempts to compensate for his own shame in that statement? Do you also hear his anger around you leaning on him when he never lets himself lean on anyone?

Laura: Yes, it's always one-sided. He can be the guru, the one who has the answers. He never self discloses or lets himself lean on me.

Therapist: Then, perhaps all of his feedback isn't exactly neutral; perhaps, in delivering his message of "the truth," he may be overlooking a few things.

Laura: I know. I've been there for his family for years. I was instrumental in bringing him back to be in a relationship with his own kids. I'm the liaison between them, and their relationships are so much better now.

Therapist: And if we put a monetary value on that, it rather levels the playing field, don't you think

Laura: There's more. Here he is telling me that I'm not pulling my own weight, when he's living with his adult daughter because he didn't save enough money for his retirement. But I do know that he's right about me being in a fog. I feel so badly about myself. Why can't I get out of my own way? I don't even know where to go in this session.

Therapist: Do you mind if I share some of my thoughts and observations for a couple of minutes? The first place we can focus is to look at what's happening around your feelings of shame. Don't you find it interesting that just as you're coming out of the fog around your childhood trauma, to the point that you were able to ask questions of your mother and sister about what happened in your childhood, that the fog is also lifting in your present life?

Laura: I actually hadn't put that together, but what does that have to do with anything?

Therapist: One of the things we've been talking about in terms of moving out of a dissociated state around childhood trauma is that there is so much internalized shame that comes out in the process. What we have to be careful about right now is to try to safeguard against you not turning around and imposing those feelings of shame onto the present when your eyes are beginning to open up in all areas of your life. It's actually a tremendous sign of progress. It's a sign of integrating the past with the present and holding it all at once. I must tell you that I am so touched that you are able to look at where you are in your life right now with so much honesty. That in itself takes so much strength. You couldn't do that a year ago.

Laura: I know that. You're right. I'm staying with it in the present and not disappearing so much more of the time. As painful as it is, I know it's better for me to face it. But when John treated me the way he did, I just collapsed and got so confused.

Therapist: I know that this is confusing, but let's not get ahead of ourselves and jump to the relationship. Let's stay focused on you. First, I want to point out that you didn't collapse in quite the same way that you had in the past. Before, you would have shut yourself off and felt completely isolated. Instead, you called me and you called your sister.

Laura: I know. I wouldn't have done that a year ago.

Therapist: So, if we pause for a moment and take an overview of what has been happening around your uncovering your childhood abuse, I want to say that I don't think this would have been possible *unless* we had taken the time to focus on your strengths and talents first. Remember when you started becoming really successful in your business a couple of years ago? You needed to accumulate those positive experiences and begin trusting in your creativity and your talents before you could dip back into the trauma this directly.

Laura: Yes, I see what you're saying. And you know what's funny, now that you mention that, as bad as I was feeling I went to do two presentations in two days for thirty people. I did a great job and got so many emails and comments afterwards, but I feel I went into those meetings in a different way. I didn't worry about whether I had eye make-up on or if I felt too fat. I just went in and showed them myself. I even got angry in front of the group regarding one of the participant's comments. I mean it was appropriate and everything. I didn't embarrass her, but so many people appreciated my candor. I also apologized to them and let them know that I was dealing with some issues of anger in my life right now. I got emails about that too. I wasn't afraid to take some risks rather than try to perform and present a "perfect professional image."

Therapist: So, your authenticity trumped your fear. Is that what you're telling me?

Laura: Yes, (sounds surprised) I guess I am. You know what the funniest part was? A year ago, even six months ago, people's praise and feedback was so important to me. I didn't even care about it that much. I mean it was nice to hear, but I didn't *need* to hear it in the way I had.

Therapist: And what that tells us is that you have internalized this belief in yourself. But more than that, you held that internalization of your authentic self in the face of looking at the more difficult, painful parts of reality. You're able to hold them both at the same time.

Laura: I guess I am. I hadn't seen it that way. I need to hold them both at the same time, don't I? Otherwise, I'll just keep repeating this pattern.

Therapist: That's true, but I think that the pattern is already changing slowly. We just have to make sense out of all the feelings as they're unfolding.

Analysis

In contrast to the dream sequences recorded several months earlier, this session begins with an urgent, off-hour phone call from Laura to her therapist. (It should be noted that this was the first time that the patient used emergency contact during the five years she had been in treatment.) Obviously, we can regard this phone call as a reaching out for help. It also represents a shift in her level of trust in the therapist and her ability to use the therapeutic relationship when she is experiencing feelings of isolation, panic, and confusion.

Laura begins this session filled with intense feelings of shame over the state of her life, as she is now beginning to become aware that the dissociative fog is beginning to lift. The therapist begins by slowing Laura down as she attempts to relate her feelings of shame and the reason for her phone call. The therapist does so, in part to help stop the flooding of Laura's overwhelming feelings of shame in that moment, and in part to begin a phenomenological tracking process, in an attempt to gather information as to what transpired to trigger such a flood of intense emotion.

Apparently, what triggered the feelings of shame was a phone call where Laura tried to reach out to John in an attempt to ask for help in purchasing a new car. She reported that she thought that his presence at the car dealership would help her counteract the feelings of shame she anticipated having around asking whether she would qualify for a car loan. She experienced John's reaction of impatience and further shaming as a hurtful betrayal.

For individuals with trauma histories there are usually deep wounds around trust. Any tentative gesture in the form of reaching out for help can be a devastating disappoint. In this case Laura's disappointed request for help was compounded by the fact that she had very clearly expressed anticipated shame that would be triggered by the car purchase. For Laura, her partner, John, had become the equivalent of a perpetrator when he delivered his feedback in such a shameful manner. To compound her injury further John attacked her therapist (in a very uncharacteristic fashion) telling her that what she needed, instead, was to grow up and face reality.

It is unclear why John responded in this manner. We can only speculate that either the patient had been leaning on him too often, or that John's own shame sensitivity had been triggered. Notice that Laura agrees with John's assessment of her at this point, after his shameful comments of derision. She then labels herself as "bad" and connects her failure to reach her old idealized standards of performance to her underlying wish for rescue. Although Laura's wishes for rescue (Quadrant Three) are now coming to the surface consciously, the therapist does not point this out. Instead, she is quick to make an intervention on behalf of the client's strength and intuition, pointing out the important difference between "speaking the truth" and delivering that information in a shaming way.

Laura's next comment indicates signs of her growing strength as she is able to say, "You're right, and a part of me knew it at the time." Here we see evidence of *knowing and not knowing* as we see Laura making an attempt to revert to her old organizing schema, one in which she perceives herself as defective. However, rather than lapsing into her confusion or victimhood, this time Laura knew enough to call her therapist, someone she could trust. When patient and therapist were able to process her disappointment together, the therapist emphatically states, "He went too far." In an attempt to recover from the disappointment in this relational exchange, the therapist then said that at the very least John owed her an apology.

Notice that Laura interrupts and begins to share more detailed information about John's limitations (Quadrant Two). The therapist then makes a connection to the timing of the patient's coming out of her fog with recent exchanges she had been having with her mother and sister. She wonders if this might account for the recent insights she had been having where she saw contemporary relationships more clearly. At this juncture the therapist is attempting to present a larger perspective, reminding Laura of how far she has come in the last year of treatment.

Laura is able to recover from near fragmentation around her disappointed attempt at reaching out. She is then able to regain access to recently acquired gains she has made in the therapy, demonstrating that she is able to put her feelings of disappointment and shame in perspective. She volunteers that she was not so thrown off by her recent feelings that it interfered with her performance at work. At the end of this session, the therapist is able to frame what Laura just said as a sign of her authenticity triumphing over her fear.

SUMMARY

Trauma is a difficult subject—it is difficult to acknowledge much less treat. Entering into a therapeutic relationship with individuals who suffer from childhood trauma requires patience and courage on both parts. The task of healing trauma requires that we enter deeply into the affective territory of shame and horror that is at times excruciatingly difficult to bear. As such, exposing the reality of trauma has been regarded as somewhat of a taboo subject both for the lay-person and professional alike. Unfortunately, this very human and understandable reaction is what often contributes to the sense of isolation many traumatized individuals feel.

Victims of trauma typically attempt to hide their secrets, either through dissociation, minimization, or creating overdetermined standards around performance, based on their wish to be seen as "good" or normal or competent. Each of these strategies represents an attempt on the part of patients to maintain psychic equilibrium, while keeping their internalized sense of shame and self-loathing from themselves and from the world. After all, traumatized individuals were taught never to share their secrets or were told that what happened to them was their fault, their own doing. Thus, the task of exposing the true costs of trauma, and in turn helping individuals recover their authenticity and personal dignity, is no small feat.

This chapter has dealt with a full range of trauma, from parental misattunement or neglect to the extremes of physical and sexual abuse. We have placed trauma on a continuum because at all levels its contribution to dissociation is profound. We recognize that our position can create problems for forensic analysts who are looking for a clear demarcation between legal victimhood and legal non-victimhood. However our decision is based on the clinical evidence of our therapeutic and supervisory experience of the intimate connection between dissociation and trauma at all levels.

The reader may find the examples of physical and sexual abuse difficult to read and even more difficult to contemplate. Indeed they are, sometimes to the point of being too overwhelming to take in. We have noted earlier that trauma is contagious and the contagion is likely to be insidious. The therapist is no exception to such contagion. We are talking about material that is known and not known, remembered and not remembered, heard and not heard. But working through our own pain and shame allows for the immersion in the patient's often terrorizing experience of trauma and the psychic wounds created by that trauma. This witnessing is understood on a deep level (Danielian, 2010c) and the "traumatized patient can sense the 'oneness' of the intersubjective experience unfolding with the protective other" (p. 246).

It should be noted that this chapter should not be construed as a proto-col for the treatment of traumatized patients who fall on the more extreme end of the continuum. (As stated earlier, combined treatments seem to be the best approach for these individuals.) Rather, this chapter is an invitation to therapists to explore the often complicated link between shame, underlying trauma, and overdetermined attempts to maintain psychic integrity. As such, the material covered in this chapter is meant to be a way of helping therapists familiarize themselves with the complex relationship between dissociation and trauma. The Four Quadrant diagram illustrating how trauma manifests in personality construction is meant to help therapists negotiate the often complex task of healing, one that involves the recovery of trust and the recovery of self. It is our hope that therapists will be sensitized to the diagnostic subtleties of the telltale signs of trauma and the myriad ways in which trauma can announce itself.

NOTES

1. False memory syndrome created a media sensation in the early 1990s. The politicized debate seems to have lost steam in the last decade as the burgeoning field of neuroscience has revealed deeper truths about how the brain actually stores memory. We now know (Siegel, 1999; Solomon and Siegel, 2003) that implicit traumatic memories can persist in the recesses of the brain indefinitely in a form described as a somatosensory experience. These are dissociated memories moored ("encrypted") in short-term memory (the limbic system), unable by virtue of their traumatic nature to complete their journey to long-term memory storage and hence to become available to the conscious mind. An often terrifying recall of the memory can be triggered in treatment or even more likely during a life crisis or a trauma-specific trigger (Herman and Harvey, 1997). It is the intense emotional persistence of these traumatic memories, not necessarily their cognitive accuracy that is of critical importance in psychotherapeutic work with these patients. Readers interested in False Memory Syndrome can consult Lindsay and Read (1995), van der Kolk and Fisler (1995), Loftus and Ketcham, (1994), Feldman-Summers and Pope (1994), Freyd (1996), Herman (1995).

2. Yehuda, Giller, Southwick, Lowy, and Mason (1991) who conducted research on hypothalamic-pituitary-adrenal dysfunction in individuals suffering from the effects of chronic stress and/or trauma stated that chronic exposure to stress permanently alters how individuals are able to deal with their environment on a day-to-day basis and also how adept they are at coping with acute stressors that may occur in the future. Kolb (1987) stated that excessive stimulation of the central nervous system during episodes of trauma is likely to result in permanent neuronal changes that can have a long-term negative impact on learning, habituation, and stimulus discrimination.

3. MRI scans of abused and neglected children showed evidence of cortical atrophy and ventricular enlargement. DeBellis et al. (2002), conducting a study on pediatric patients with reported cases of trauma revealed that the intracranial, cerebral, prefrontal cortex, right temporal lobes, and areas of the corpus callosum all were smaller in development than in normal subjects. This poses problems with right and left hemisphere integration, and the executive functioning skill sets of the prefrontal cortex that are responsible for judgment, impulse control, and our ability to measure and respond to external threats.

CHAPTER 8

Re-Imagining Transference
An Update

> One need . . . not be afraid of the negative [transferential] reactions
> of the patient for they constitute, with iron necessity, a part of every
> analysis.
>
> —SANDOR FERENCZI AND OTTO RANK (1925, P. 40)

> The concept of transference as organizing activity is an alternative
> to the view that transference is the manifestation of a biologically
> rooted compulsion to repeat the past. In addition, transference as
> organizing activity focuses more narrowly on the specific patterning
> of experience within the analytic relationship, to which both patient
> and analyst contribute.
>
> —ROBERT STOLOROW ET AL. (1987, P. 37)

OF ALL the tools of the trade that fall within the rubric of psychotherapy, transference is probably the most misunderstood and
underutilized. For practicing clinicians, transference often evokes a range
of reactions, from avoidance to confusion to feelings of dread. Positive
transference is generally "normalized" and associated with a successful
treatment, while negative transference is often experienced as a sign that
something has gone terribly wrong. If negative transference is framed as
a sign of failure, it is not a far stretch to see how therapists can take those
negative reactions personally, becoming weary, defensive, or assuming that
someone must be at fault. Either patients must be blamed for being resistant
or difficult, or therapists must shoulder the burden of blame for allowing
negative transference to erupt in the first place.

When transference and countertransference are framed in such a polarized fashion, it becomes easy to see why working with transferential dynamics often remains *fuzzy* in the minds of clinicians. It is true that being on the receiving end of negative transference can feel uncomfortable; however, trying to prevent it means that important aspects of the treatment either go underground or remain unexamined. It also means that certain assumptions and/or needs within the therapist remain unattended as well. Although positive transferential responses generally don't produce the same degree of discomfort, if therapists mistakenly interpret these communications as a sign of a healthy working relationship or if they hear such comments as a confirmation of their exceptional talents and abilities, the dynamic of overidealization remains untouched. Unexamined feeling states within the patient *or* the therapist quickly can become a dangerous combination, something that the field has been loath to examine whole-heartedly.

Over the years our supervisees have reported that in the beginning years of practice, it took a bit of time to get *a feel* for what transference really is and how to recognize it. When we asked our more seasoned trainees to give us a simple description of how a beginning therapist might begin to recognize a transferential communication as it unfolds in the treatment, this is the synthesis of what they said.

> Transference is simply a feeling that you have during a dialogic exchange where something doesn't quite hang together. For example, when you're listening to a patient, he may begin to respond to you in a way that doesn't seem to reflect what's happening between you. Either he distorts what you just said or omits key aspects of a communication from the session before. Much of the time you can recognize this not just by the content of what's being said but by the feeling tone, the charge behind the words, or the overgeneralizations that are presented as "simple facts." Often, you can recognize a transferential communication through your own counter-transferential response. Perhaps, you begin to have a reaction when the patient makes assumptions about your intent, or reports back to you something that you said in a way that was not entirely accurate, or the patient may say something that crosses a boundary line of familiarity.

When our beginners-group of trainees were asked the same question, here is what they came up with in terms of their understanding of transference and countertransference.

Transference is when a patient's unfinished business is projected onto the therapist in a way that begins to affect the real therapeutic relationship. If left unattended for too long, it will begin to have a detrimental impact on the treatment. Counter-transference is when your own personal "stuff" starts to cloud your ability to be effective, neutral, and clear. Or as another trainee put it, "Countertransference is when you like the patients too much or you don't like them enough."

Both of our training groups did a conscientious (if not pointed) job in capturing many of the elements of the relational complexity of transference and counter-transference. Clearly, both groups were able to identify a key component to this clinical dynamic, that the very nature of the *subjective relational experience* of psychotherapy makes it more difficult to tease apart transferential responses from countertransferential reactions. Transference *interpersonalizes* the patient's unconscious organizing schemas, schemas which lie at the heart of the patient's characterological structure. As such, transference constitutes an important cutting edge of therapeutic action, *a live here-and-now enactment* of important material not yet in awareness but edging closer to it. Therefore, as we create foundation stones of understanding, working with transference means working in the subjective *present* because, first and foremost, this is where the therapeutic dialogue becomes personal. For example, in the very beginning phases of treatment the patient and the therapist are joined in a process of examining symptoms and problems from the vantage point of information-gathering, largely about the recent or distant past. A patient may begin therapy by telling you about his overcontrolling father and how he feels about that relationship. He may even be able to make the connection that he suspects that this is at the core of his anxiety. But when the patient begins to experience *you* as overcontrolling or judgmental, and that the therapy is beginning to make him feel anxious, this is when the action moves into the transferential present. If we are to use transferential dynamics to their full advantage, attempts to maintain an objective or expert stance offer neither immunity nor help in working effectively with negative transference reactions.

A second foundation stone in our understanding of transference is to emphasize that transference is precisely *how* we gain direct access to the early organizing schemas of childhood. It is through transference enactments that we are able to both *see* and *feel* how compulsively driven overidealizations, in the service of protecting against feelings of shame or fears of annihilation, were created in the first place. Using transferential material as it surfaces creates a clinical opportunity, one that allows us to help the patient shift unconscious, habituated enactments to a conscious level of understanding. In this way the patient can relationally challenge old patterns and assumptions and experience new and safer ways of being in connection through the therapeutic relationship. When therapists are not "seduced" by flattering idealization, do not retaliate as negative transferential statements are revealed, nor take advantage of the patient's vulnerability to meet their own needs, they are able to champion authentic communication. As such, new organizing schemas develop and split-off parts of the psyche can be integrated into a more complex whole.

OVERVIEW OF HISTORICAL BACKGROUND

Because of the emotional charge associated with the manifestation of transference or countertransference, we have found that there is a surprising paucity of detail for therapists throughout their careers to understand and manage this important relational dynamic. We have also found that this is an area in the literature where a polarization of thought is more likely to occur. Some forms of treatment avoid working with the phenomena of transference altogether, while other schools of thought offer little elaboration on how to use the manifestations of positive or negative transference to their full therapeutic advantage. However, for the last quarter of the twentieth century, Arnold Cooper has documented what he calls a "quiet" yet powerful revolution taking place in psychodynamic theory and practice, a revolution that has continued to pass, so to speak, under the radar. Nowhere has this "quiet" revolution been more profound than in our understanding of transference.

As defined by Freud, transference had always meant a "resistance to drive-derived aims that are aroused toward the analyst" (Cooper, 1987, p. 82). But as Cooper has pointed out, current views emphasize that transference is best conceptualized as the patient's *experience of the therapist at any given point in the treatment process.* Furthermore, transference must be understood within the systemic integration of the interpersonal and the intrapsychic, and as such represents an integration of the phenomenological moment with the entire past. The complexities of the patient's subjective experience, certainly including the dissociative splits we have been describing in this manual, continue to illuminate the past experiences of the patient. While there-and-then can illuminate the here-and-now, the there-and-then *does not replicate* the here-and-now. Transference is not an exact replication of the past because the characterological structure or the sense of self-in-relationship is in a continually evolving process of change. More precisely, the here-and-now contains an updated version of the past as a result of the assimilation and accommodation of new information into the organizing schemas of the psyche.

As the field evolves and transference is unmoored from its drive-derived basis, it becomes something that is much more sensitive to the nuances of the evolving therapeutic relationship and the potential ruptures or conflicts which can develop in the treatment. For example, when the patient is in the throes of acute or chronic self-loathing, we can expect the patient to *also* be experiencing transference feelings about the therapist. The patient might imagine that the therapist is joining in on the loathing, perhaps even secretly holding the patient in contempt. Fear and shame can quickly become the driving forces of these psychodynamics. Similarly, when the patient begins to confront the processes of dissociated belief systems involving major idealizations, the patient becomes even more fearful of the therapist's contemptuous judgments, now against the patient's "egocentricity." Again unacknowledged shame, conscious or unconscious, becomes a major impediment to allowing painful dynamics to surface, especially to surface transferentially.

Why has the revolution of our understanding of transference been occurring under the radar? Why did experience-near personhood have to enter *sotto voce* to replace intrapsychic drive derivatives? Freud and his followers saw energy-discharge as a promising new science of psychology, explaining equally both normal and abnormal behavior. Within the original paradigm, making relationships the primary focus of psychodynamics constituted an undoing of hard-won "science" and the undesirable replacement of drives with the unscientific and unbiological relativism of social meanings. But Gill (1983) maintains that the revolution, quiet or not, has been on-going in its insistent replacement of natural science with a meaning-making and experience-near information processing science.

How transference is understood also determines how countertransference is handled. Hence what theory has to say about the *process* of change becomes crucial. Stephen Purcell (2004) has made the deep argument that, beyond the first two sources of countertransference—the therapist's unconscious conflicts and the therapist's meaningful understanding of the patient's experience—*theory* is a third source of countertransference. We might ask, deep in what sense? Purcell maintains that every theory carries within itself its own burdens. Theoretical conceptions cannot help but color what the therapist *hears*. Is it possible to listen without preconception? As inviting as such an ideal might sound to help us fully immerse in the present, ultimately it is impossible. Therapists are human beings and human beings have both conscious and unconscious reasons for individual beliefs and theoretical persuasions. This is particularly true of the metapsychological assumptions underlying one's theory, assumptions which commonly go unexamined along with their countertransferential risks.

All theories are vulnerable because of human limitations, but not all theories are vulnerable to the same degree. Theoretical systems that make a determined effort to explore their metapsychological assumptions are less likely to add to countertransferential reactions although, as we have stressed, no theory can remain immune to the possibilities. For example, we should always ask, do our observations within the dyadic exchange within the treatment match our theoretical assumptions, or are we trying to fit what we hear into existing theories? As we move from a deterministic, natural science metapsychology to a process-oriented, experience-near metapsychology, we reduce the temptation to objectify or dismiss human subjectivity or, expressed differently, to confuse detached knowledge with direct experience.

Since the practice of dynamic psychotherapy cannot eliminate these hazards, we would do well to be as conscientious as possible about how our theories pre-select what we *see*, especially in the typically unconscious realm of the theory's meta-assumptions. For example, Aron (1996), Balint (1968), Gill (1994), Levenson (1991), Mitchell (1988), and Wachtel (2008) highlight the distinction between a "one-person" and a "two-person" approach to understanding and managing transference dynamics. Here, we can clearly see how the metatheoretical assumptions underscore how transference is handled. In a "one-person" approach, based mainly on Freud's assumptions about psychotherapy as an "objective" science, the therapist is seen as neutral, a blank slate where the patient then projects early, unresolved longings and frustrations onto the therapist. The therapist makes "an objective" interpretation in the service of revealing and resolving the transferential dynamics. Negative reactions or objections to the interpretations are seen as a part of the patient's resistance.

In a "two-person" or intersubjective approach (Stolorow, et al., 1987), a relational and therefore subjective understanding is used to manage the transferential communication. Transference is conceptualized as an organizing activity, and the patient's experience of the therapeutic relationship is assumed to be shaped *both* by input from the analyst and how that input is assimilated by the patient (p. 43). Stolorow et al. summarize a metapsychological understanding of the transference dynamic as a "bipolar organization of experience" where "insight through interpretation, affective bonding through empathic attunement, and the facilitation of psychological integration are indissoluble facets of a unitary therapeutic process. Every interpretation derives its mutative power from the intersubjective system in which it takes form" (p. 105). As we can see from this explanation, how therapists conceptualize transference interventions is based on the theoretical meta-assumptions, which in turn color the quality of their therapeutic relationship over time.

In the area of narcissistic disturbances we can hear the refrain, "I know that you are trained but I'm not an object here, something you've read in a textbook." To be sure, this response would likely involve a transferential reaction, but we cannot preclude out-of-hand that our theory has not triumphed over our attunement. As Purcell (2004) has reminded us, "theory . . . is always a component element in the construction of countertransference and is sometimes a major factor in the shaping of analytic events" (p. 646). In an age of objectification, painful narcissistic sensitivity to being "desubjectivized" *cannot* be overstated.

Moving from Linear to Non-Linear Thinking

Lest the reader become pessimistic of progress in developing a deeper but still utterly disciplined understanding of our work, we turn to recent optimistic developments in non-linear theory, or as it has been misleadingly dubbed, "chaos theory" (Galatzer-Levy, 2009). Transcending a mechanistic worldview, Galatzer-Levy insists that we must accustom ourselves to the fact that non-linear dynamics are actually much more common in the world than linear dynamics. It has been said that linear lines do not exist in nature. If the line were extended long enough, curvature would begin to show.

We can add that human nature is also a part of nature. If humans have invented the straight line, then no matter how productive the linear line has been in the understanding of ourselves and of our brains, it is still an invention. Perhaps a judicious statement at this point would be that the linear line has outlived its usefulness and that non-linear dynamics are coming to the fore. This is certainly true in psychodynamic theory and practice. Non-linear sounds "strange" to the ear because it has been ignored for decades if not longer. It has been ignored because there was resistance to a paradigm shift, not because it was any less scientific or valid.

A quote from Galatzer-Levy is instructive, "The term does not entail anything . . . mysterious, vague, or outside of ordinary experience" (p. 1236). We may add that clinical theorists, especially classical analytic theorists, overlooked non-linear dynamics because they seemed to undermine the more familiar line of cause-and-effect thinking so common in early psychoanalytic work. This is another example of how the unexamined metapsychology of a theory can blunt a practitioner of his or her own theory-bound countertransferential enactments. To counter linear thinking, Galatzer-Levy emphasizes *emergence* in the psychodynamic process, "the coming together of elements to form new configurations with new functions" (p. 1234). As a case in point, he advises that we consider the telling description offered by Thelen and Smith (1994) on how children learn to walk, a crucial emergent development in children. Examples of emergence are when children "suddenly" seem to turn a corner on walking, talking, and self-feeding without pre-warning, to the delight of their parents.

As well, Galatzer-Levy strongly stresses that "much of the influence of linear thinking is likely to be implicit [unconscious?] and carried forward without knowledge or appreciation of its underlying sources" (p. 1244). The linear thinking can be buried in the very theory the therapist is employing. Applying this insight around the therapist's unconscious assumptions or theoretical paradigm even further, he provides a delightful but revealing dialogue between a "snowflake" in treatment and the snowflake's "classical" analyst:

> *Analyst:* From what you have told me, you are remarkably like your many siblings. You all have six-fold symmetry and delicate branching structures. Yet each of you is different from the others. This doubtless reflects a wish to be your own individual snowflake.

> *Snowflake:* You are right that we are all different, but try hard as I can, I cannot recall, despite having recollections going all the way back to life inside mother cloud, when or why I became different. It just feels like I was always that way.

> *Analyst:* In the highly conformist culture from which you came, being different must feel absolutely necessary and, at the same time shameful, so you repressed the events that lead to your particular structure.

> *Snowflake:* (as defiantly as it can get) Perhaps your assumption that my mind operates like your conscious mind, by way of coherent narratives, is a function of your unanalyzed narcissism. Perhaps a few more years on the couch would prepare you to analyze a snowflake (pp. 1242–43)!

We note that systemic thinking, embedded in meaning-making orientations, keeps us more consistently focused on the subjective realities of a snowflake and of the realities of a patient's experience. Were our patients as forcefully authentic as this snowflake, perhaps our understanding would have advanced more quickly than it has. Leave it to say, this delightful example illustrates how, viewing the interpersonal and intrapsychic simultaneously, we are thereby able to see how each contributes and becomes part of a larger whole.

In terms of shifting from a linear to a non-linear approach, several important changes in our posture of *listening* are involved. We will cite five:

1. Freud recommended a posture of "evenly-hovering attention" but he did not count on his theory pre-figuring his capacity to listen (Appelbaum, 2011). As much as we try, we cannot purge our schemas from our listening. The best we can do is hold our schemas loosely, keep them in front of our eyes and hope thereby to allow a fuller immersion in the patient's subjectivity.

2. We move from listening in a linear mode to listening in a non-linear mode. The non-linear mode shifts us from attributing what we see in the present exclusively as part of the historical past, to seeing influences from both the past and present as continuing and evolving factors in the characterological make-up in the *present*. This is a paradigm shift. Because the chimera of causal determinism in mental health problems forces us to think in an unproductive straight line, we are better served if we are able to move toward conceptualizing our listening as a series of concentric circles leading to a systemic mode of understanding where each part is simultaneously connecting and affecting every other part. The prime engine of change becomes not single causes but broader and more enhanced circles of meaning.

3. Phenomenological process is elevated over content. The meaning-making connections between part and whole become more available to us the more we immerse ourselves in the moment. In other words, rather than rushing to interpret, and thereby imposing the therapist's meaning prematurely, the moment-to-moment inquiry process in the present allows for greater degrees of contextual detail and the patient's subjective organizing schemas to reveal themselves.

4. Listening for dissociative splits in the here-and-now, through part-whole analysis, heightens our awareness of experience-near emotions, such as shame, denial, disavowal, disconnection, and derealization. This is a more process-oriented focus than listening for classical repression and resistance. If we can understand the moment-to-moment unfolding in the patient's character structure, both the present *and* the past can be better understood. Constructing meaning in the present is not the same as reconstructing the past. The focus on constructiveness flowing out of immersion makes the patient and therapist more fully active participants in the treatment process.

5. A theory of listening without feedback is a theory of listening which cannot correct itself. Drawing on the pioneering work of Norbert Wiener, Galatzer-Levy (2009) states that "Feedback occurs when a system's previous output changes what it does next . . . the results of actions become part of the input to future steps" (pp. 1229–30). Feedback loops are built into information-processing systems and in terms of psychic process allow for important reflexive learning. For example, part-whole process becomes productive when such loops are present in the therapist's mode of listening.

Dan Siegel (2003), neuropsychiatrist and author, agrees with this non-linear view of how parts influence the whole in a recursive feedback loop. Describing the human mind as a complex system, he states:

> The behavior of the component parts of a complex system can be described by assessing their emergent states as they change across time . . . . The *non-linear* dynamics of complex systems describe the ways in which small changes in initial input to the system can lead to large and unpredictable outputs . . . The human mind, and indeed pairs of minds and communities of minds, meet these criteria for complex systems. (pp. 3–4)

Siegel's description of non-linear dynamics of complex systems can be applied to the therapeutic relationship. It allows for a process that has the capacity to introduce small changes in the "initial input to the system" that can have over time the power to create new emergent properties both relationally and intrapsychically. One way to frame our understanding of emergent properties in the clinical arena is through the lens of transference, for it is here that the past intersects with the present through the therapeutic relationship. If the transferential dynamic can be seen as an opportunity to introduce a greater degree of complexity to the patient's projections and expectations of "the other," the emergent property in any given moment may be the unfolding of greater understanding, acceptance, and trust. This in turn may lead to the emergence of greater degrees of authenticity and spontaneity within the personality.

For example, a patient comes into a session and says, "You must think I'm your most difficult patient. All I ever do is complain." Rather than giving reassurance too quickly, the therapist has an opportunity to listen and explore the patient's assumptions in greater detail. By exploring the fears and the underlying shame, the patient has an opportunity to engage in a way that allows him to release the grip of shame and expand his confidence relationally. This in turn may have an accrual affect over time that will lead to the emergence of a more complex understanding of self-in-relationship. In our view the greatest therapeutic leverage to facilitate healing and growth happens most profoundly when we enter into the transference dynamic unfolding before us.

Toward that end, all aspects of our work, certainly the listening posture we adopt around sensitivity to pick up on transferential cues, are especially significant. How we listen has everything to do with understanding and processing transference. Transference is omnipresent in treatment from the first day to the last. Each issue, every mood, and every conflicted emotion in the patient carries its own transference quotient. Most of the time, neither the patient nor the therapist needs to comment on it, any more than transference needs to be vigilantly monitored in personal conversations between friends. Transference needs to be held lightly but mindfully. As such, the timing of our comments is based on the inquiry process of part-whole analysis. For example, we may wonder about the relational impact on the patient when she reveals new information or powerful feelings. In a natural light-handed way, we may wonder with the patient how it feels to be sharing this information with us in the present. This gentle form of inquiry can set the stage for deeper transferential dialogue along the road.

Seen in this context, we have come a long way from the singular "transference neurosis" of drive-derivative schools. Instead, transference is seen to shift with the patient's evolving representations. This makes possible the useful understanding of transference at any point in the therapy, even at times early in the treatment process. Enhanced transferential recognition allows a richer and deeper understanding of the patient's here-and-now experience. It is no longer the "third rail" of classical interpretation fraught with resistance and repression.

Perhaps, a new framework for understanding transference can evolve as we embrace non-linear thinking and complexity theory. We watch for the emergent properties that will inevitably begin to unfold by virtue of the simple fact that the patient is engaging in a dyadic therapeutic relationship. transferential responses can be seen as an opportunity to leverage those exchanges in a way that increases the potential for growth in any given moment. This, in turn, may help us see how even difficult transference responses can lead to positive outcomes in the treatment.

THE ELUSIVE QUALITY OF TRANSFERENCE

When therapists attempt to actively engage in intuitive listening for transferential communication, they report that at first it is often difficult to pin down. One supervisee gave an example where a patient said to her, "You know, you *never* dust under your couch. There are always dust balls under there." The supervisee shared with us that she began to question herself, feel a little embarrassed, and then the next day she found herself vacuuming under her couch. When she caught herself doing this, she realized the transferential communication that had transpired.

Of course, we can reflect upon the old joke about transference— sometimes a cigar is just a cigar—when it comes to the risk of overanalyzing every comment from a patient. (It was true that the supervisee had dust under her couch.) But it is the *tone* in which the comment is made, the *timing* of the comment, and the *context* in which the comment is being said that determines whether a statement is really a transferential communication. By asking ourselves what had occurred just prior to the patient's statement, we can begin to see how part-whole analysis can be used to help us better understand transferential dynamics.

For example, if we were to use part-whole tracking and apply it to this example around dust under the couch, we might ask:

- Was there something that was said in the prior session that possibly had shamed the patient or made her feel uncomfortable?
- Was the comment an attempt to level the playing field and induce similar shame in the therapist?
- Was the comment an attempt to disconnect from material that was too close or too affectively uncomfortable in that moment in time?

By asking ourselves these questions, wondering whether we have just uncovered masked shame, overidealization, or hidden hostility, we can apply part-whole analysis (as discussed in chapters 4 and 5) to transference. The patient's comment about the dust balls is a *part* of something we are yet to understand in more detail. Careful listening and asking further questions in the present will determine whether the statement is a *part* that is connected to a larger whole. Using part-whole analysis is one of the ways that we can determine whether a comment is a transferential clue to hidden material or whether "a cigar is simply a cigar."

When we interviewed our trainees about the level of preparation they received on transference, they reported that there was very little time spent in graduate school and during internships where transference was even taught. They stated that they understood the *concept* of transference but not how to work with it in any constructive way. One trainee stated that when it comes to working with transference, it feels like walking into a dark room and then being handed a hot potato. She was not quite sure *how* to recognize it, or what to do once she was in the middle of it.

Another trainee asked the question, "How can you differentiate a transferential response from a response where a patient is actually bringing up a legitimate concern about the treatment from a place of his or her own authenticity?" This is a very helpful question, one that cuts to the heart of why working with transference can be so difficult. Determining the answer to this question hinges on the therapist's ability to discern the patient's concerns accurately and nondefensively. It also depends on the context in which the statement is made.

For example, let's say that a therapist is on the quiet side and then yawns during a session, and the patient says, "Sometimes I feel that you're not even listening to me. You just yawned. Are you tired; are you bored?" Is this a transferential statement or not? The process we would go through to answer this question is as follows.

First, we look to the patient's background. Let's say that we know that this patient's parents are both very detached. Before we make any interpretation or connection to the patient's history and his comment, we need to pause and ask ourselves, "Am I being a bit detached with this patient? Is there something about his manner that is producing a mild reaction in me? Am I unusually tired today?"

If we are tired, we may wish to reassure the patient that the yawn had nothing to do with him or what he was saying, rather than immediately directing the focus back to the patient. We could follow this by asking for further affective clarification, wondering whether the patient has felt similar feelings about the therapist in the past. The phrasing of the question is important. By staying in the relational present, it is more likely that you will get additional information about how the transferential *parts* connect to other parts and the larger relational whole.

Note that it is not uncommon for therapists to respond to a negatively charged transferential statement with a slightly different question, such as, "Do you often feel that people become bored with you?" This shift *away* from the present exchange may produce an even more intensified negative reaction because the statement suggests a negative interpretation/judgment back to the patient. By staying in the relational present, you are likely to get more information and less reflexive defensiveness.

Staying in the relational present also provides non-verbal reassurance to the patient after he has asked a challenging question. By asking for more information about what you are *not doing*, you are sending a message that you have not taken offense at the comment and that you welcome dialogue about the patient's perceptions about you and the process. Finally, when it comes to transference, the patient will keep repeating comments that reveal hidden fears or longings until the transferential enactment can be addressed more fully.

On the other hand, if the therapist repeatedly yawns during subsequent sessions, the patient has legitimate cause for concern as it appears that ruptures in the attunement seem to be coming from the therapist's side of the subjective relational equation. Negative reactions at this point are less likely to be exclusively transferential. If a therapist deflects away from himself and back to the client again, it will likely result in greater rupture and distrust.

One of the reasons that transference is so hard to define or describe adequately is due to the variability within the context in which any given exchange takes place. It is also because transference dynamics are on *the edge of the action,* so to speak. Patients first become aware of having feelings for or about the therapist as an experience that is just on the edge of conscious. For example, the patient's internal dialogue on a semi-conscious level might be an expression of his or her ambivalence—*of course I trust my therapist, yet how can I really trust anyone?* This ambivalent struggle may often be experienced in the early dialogue, a struggle that is held privately if not fleetingly. However, when the patient utters this concern out loud, a shift in the treatment is beginning to occur. That is why seemingly innocent reactions and "one-liners" often telegraph what is about to come. These utterances are like a canary in a mine shaft. We are beginning to see or sense what has heretofore been invisible to the naked eye.

COMMON BELIEFS, FEARS, AND ASSUMPTIONS: WHY THERAPISTS AVOID WORKING WITH TRANSFERENCE

In our clinical supervision we have found some fairly predictable and universal responses to the discomfort with working with transference:

- There is a fear on the part of therapists that they will make the patient feel uncomfortable if they ask direct questions about the relationship. By asking patients to comment on feelings, thoughts, or assumptions they may have toward the therapy or the therapist, clinicians will often state that they don't want to put the patient on the spot. The rationale is that if therapists directly ask patients to comment on how they feel about the therapist, it would seems to be too bold or "impolite," therefore, running the risk of making the patient feel uncomfortable.
- There is a fear that if the therapist probes into potential negative transference issues the therapy will "blow up." By exploring negative feelings the patient may have over disappointments or failed expectations, therapists often fear that emotions will intensify, doing permanent damage to the treatment. To allay therapist anxiety we should mention that transference CAN be subtly and safely palpated and that this technique

can be taught. (A case example illustrating how negative transference can be used to therapeutic advantage is highlighted at the end of this chapter. Also, see chapter 2 for further elaboration).

- There is a fear that negative transference is a sign that the therapist has failed to manage the treatment successfully. Negative feeling states, anger directed at the therapist, or the expression of unrequited wishes expressed in a demanding way, can actually be a sign of progress or a breakthrough in the therapy. This may indicate that a more direct expression of disappointment may be moving from the unconscious into consciousness. Once exposed, the therapist has a greater opportunity to process both the disappointment and the anger, while simultaneously giving reassurance that the relationship is intact. However, attempts to avoid negative transference inevitably fail to capitalize on opportunities for the therapist to help the patient incorporate this split-off material into the intact psyche.

- There is a misconception that an idealized positive transference means that therapy is going well. The underbelly of the positive transference is the unexpressed, unrequited wish for rescue or salvation. This actually signifies that there are unintegrated parts that are being projected onto the therapist. Without exploration and examination, the therapy remains on the surface, arguably serving the needs of the therapist more than the patient.

- There is a fear that if the therapist uncovers transferential material, it is equivalent to opening Pandora's Box. This fear essentially stems from an incomplete understanding of part-whole. Therapists working in a linear mode believe that if they try to address a problem in one area, it won't have repercussions in another area. When it does, therapists are often surprised or confused and back away from a deeper understanding of how the parts fit into the whole.

- There is a belief that if the therapist stays focused on behavioral strategies and clear goals around current problems, transference won't surface in the treatment. Often transferential material does not surface initially in the therapy, thus it is understandable how short-term treatment models bypass the need to attend to transferential cues. However, there are numerous instances where patients with severe narcissistic or borderline issues enter into short-term therapy contracts, and hidden expectations for cure end up in therapeutic ruptures and crises.

- There is a lack of adequate clarity and attention to standards and practices around maintaining a therapist's mental health throughout the lifespan of a career. It is a frequent practice for therapists to allow supervision to slide to the back burner one or two years after licensure.

Therefore, the checks and balances that would normally help monitor blind spots that could lead to boundary violations, burn-out, or
the misuse of transference remain unexamined because of inadequate
supervision and/or therapist isolation. Practicing in a vacuum runs the
greatest risk of the potential for unmonitored transference reactions.
Catching transferential issues early in the treatment is the best way of
using the transference response to a therapeutic advantage.

- There is a fear of the loss of "the expert role." If the therapist loses his
or her status as the expert, there may be a concomitant fear of loss of
value. If a therapist admits a mistake, faces the patient's transferential
disappointment head on, is there a secret fear that the therapist has lost
the position of authority? One can see how an investment in maintaining an objective stance serves to elevate our status both financially and
narcissistically. If a therapist is unseasoned, holding on to a position of
"expert" may become even more overdetermined.

We have found that the above reactions often stem from therapists'
fears following unsuccessful attempts at managing the transference; thus,
avoidance of transference dynamics is a reflexive response for many unseasoned therapists. On the other hand, if a therapist encounters a highly
charged negative response, there is an equal likelihood that she will overcompensate in an attempt to mollify the patient's feelings. For example, if
a patient makes a strong negative transferential comment, such as, *"I don't
think I can continue to work with you any longer because you're too cold
and withholding,"* the therapist may make an overcorrection in a number
of ways. She may try to bend over backwards giving the patient reassurance
to "prove" that she is not cold and withholding, thereby intensifying overidealized longings and expectations that will eventually spiral into further
negatively charged transferential demands. Or, she may try to defend herself
by overly explaining her good intention or to shift to a more intellectualized
position.

Asking patients for more subjective impressions as to what has led
them to feel the way they are feeling "in the moment" is the way out of this
transferential dilemma. Too often therapists do not probe directly enough
into the details of patient frustration. Although the above example represents a fairly intensified transferential communication, often we will hear
"milder" forms of patient dissatisfaction. Here is an excerpt from a consultation between a colleague and a man who was dissatisfied with his therapy
after being in treatment for six months. We find that the following dialogue
is illuminating and unfortunately fairly typical.

Consulting Therapist: Why don't you start by giving me an overview of what's been going on in your therapy thus far.

Patient: It was helpful at first especially when I was getting over the break-up of my relationship. But now it just seems like we're at a standstill. I come in and I tell him my problems. He offers support and suggestions about what I can do differently. He even challenges my negative assumptions. I leave, don't follow through on his advice, come back the next week, feel like a jerk and a loser for not following through. I can tell he's getting a little frustrated with me.

Consulting Therapist: Do you ever talk about your parents or your past history to explore where your negative assumptions come from? Does he ever ask you why it so difficult to follow through?

Patient: No, not really. We seem to be focused on solving my problems.

Consulting Therapist: Do you ever express your frustration with the process directly to him?

Patient: Well, I did say that I think we're at an impasse.

Consulting Therapist: And what was his response?

Patient: He just encouraged me to stay with the process and went back to talking about things I might do to re-enter the dating scene.

Consulting Therapist: He didn't explore your comment any further? Did he ask you why you felt the therapy was at an impasse?

Patient: No, he just said, "These things take time."

Consulting Therapist: Did you ever suggest to him that he seemed frustrated with you?

Patient: Oh no, that feels too uncomfortable. Maybe I should just find another therapist, but then again I don't want to hurt his feelings.

It is clear from the above exchange that transferential material is right under the surface. When the first therapist failed to explore the patient's comment about the treatment being at an impasse, the patient was left to sit silently with his frustration, which we can speculate is a repetition of a relational dynamic for him. If left unaddressed, what often occurs in these situations is that the frustration will build within the patient (and quite possibly the therapist) to the point that there may be a premature termination.

As a general rule of thumb if dissatisfaction or negative transference is not addressed early, it will build. Also, as you can see from the above example, the opportunity to seize on the emergent property of honest communication between them has been lost. If the therapist had been able to move into deeper inquiry, the patient would have felt heard rather than being asked to do something to solve his own problem. For long-standing, entrenched relational patterns, advise-giving or simple support is typically not enough to effect long-term change. It is through the emergence of the transference that we have the opportunity to use the unfolding relational exchange to make a difference.

TRANSFERENCE AND THE FOUR QUADRANT MODEL

In our Four Quadrant Model we emphasized the importance of suspending our impulse "to do something" until we have understood what was *not* being said, that is, until we understand what aspects of the self are being hidden from the therapeutic interaction. We also addressed the technique of palpating subtle cues of transferential communication and being able to track and monitor part and whole simultaneously. When should we address transferential cues once we have identified them? The question is identical to when we should address the parts of a whole once the parts have been identified. The four quadrant systemic whole can be of significant help in making these clinical decisions.

If we apply the Four Quadrant Model to the examination of positive transference, for example, we might begin by asking how positive transferential feelings may be masking hidden feelings of vulnerability, defectiveness, or overdetermined compensatory behaviors. If a patient with a high degree of grandiosity coupled with a high degree of professional success enters treatment due to symptoms of anxiety, he or she may try to *join* the therapist by creating an alliance of specialness. This may take the form of flattering the therapist's intelligence or making subtle references of inclusion in an elite group that the patient has deemed worthy of his or her trust and respect. If the therapist *does* feel flattered and/or overly impressed with the patient's success, he or she may avoid asking questions that could challenge the patient's grandiosity.

Although the timing of when to inquire into the grandiosity is critical, it is important to respond with gentle but probing questions early in the process. If a patient comments, "I couldn't just work with any therapist. I need someone who is able to keep up with my intellectual pace," the therapist might ask the patient how the pace seems now. Not only is this a way to begin palpating the transferential statement to learn more, it also indirectly sends a message back to the patient that the therapist is aware of the patient's high standards (Quadrant One) and the negative judgment (Quadrant Four) that occurs when people fall short.

On the other hand, if a patient is a self-effacing type, he or she may overly elevate the therapist's status and/or expertise in the service of maintaining a stance of passivity with a secret wish for rescue. As an example, when conscious but dystonic symptoms of anxiety located in Quadrant Two become less split off from the non-conscious but ultimately syntonic posture of loyal waiting in Quadrant Three, we can also expect an intensification of transferential dynamics, possibly through an increase in passivity or lack of initiative. A transferential intervention will be indicated at some point, but the success and ease of that intervention will depend on how well the therapist is able to palpate and track subtle cues. The therapist may say, for example, "I know that you are very appreciative of what you are learning in therapy, but I'm wondering if sometimes when you ask for my opinion, you may also have some ideas of your own." This sends a message back to the patient that hidden, dependent longings are being noticed.

If these opportunities are missed, however, the patient will eventually experience a build-up of frustration that is likely to erupt through some expression of negative transference. Using the above example, let us say that as the treatment progresses, the therapist and patient are able to make connections between events that trigger symptoms of anxiety and the patient is able to see how disappointed expectations of others often triggers increased symptoms. Even though the dystonic aspect of the presenting symptoms begins to be integrated into conscious awareness, the patient continues to present as helpless, seemingly unable to protect against future disappointments that will retrigger anxiety.

Until enough frustration mounts, the therapist may not recognize that the source of the transferential reaction of passivity is stemming from the patient's loyal waiting. Typically, loyalty issues are not expressed directly. They are often recognized when the emergence of communications of frustration from Quadrant Four enters into the dialogue. By listening to the underlying message within this material, the therapist can begin to wonder if the patient's loyal waiting is being taxed by the therapist's lack of rescue. Making a comment that attempts to pair the frustration with a possible underlying wish for rescue is preferable to commenting either on the passivity directly or on the negative comment outside of the context in which it is grounded. As with other aspects of the treatment, the skill in anticipating the relationship between the quadrants will help the therapist speak to the disappointment before it erupts into a full-blown negative transference reaction. Again, we are able to see how palpating the transference depends on how well the therapist is able to resonate with all four quadrants of the model.

MISUSES OF TRANSFERENCE ON THE PART OF THE THERAPIST

One goal of this treatment manual is an attempt to systematically increase skills in reading transferential meanings through deeper therapeutic listening and the part-whole inquiry process, which is clarified through the Four Quadrant Model. Intensive supervision, formal training, and personal therapy of course greatly increase the improvement of such skills. However, it needs to be pointed out that, no matter what the level of training, narcissistic vulnerabilities and blind spots on the part of therapists can exist. For example, prevalent studies (among many sources, see Pope 1990) consistently show a 7–12 percent rate of erotic contact between therapists and their patients. The typical profile of an offender is an older male therapist treating a female patient. Compounding these fundamental boundary violations is the frequent denial of responsibility by the offending therapist. The denial is usually in the form of attributing the charges to dissociated fantasies by the patient, incestuous wishes, or to a wish to retaliate against the therapist.

A case in point is the recent revelation of the psychoanalyst Muriel Dimen (2011). After thirty years of "silent shame," Dimen broke through with a painstaking re-examination of boundary violations by her well-established psychoanalyst whom she saw over the course of a decade or more. Her analyst never accepted responsibility nor thought his actual transgression of physical embracing and passionate kissing needed analytic scrutiny, leaving the patient with no external validation and with extensive self-shame. Dimen further contextualizes her silent shame inside the professional culture of psychoanalysis itself, a culture that "named sexuality the site where pleasure and danger combust, each serving the other's fuel. Yet this is the place where psychoanalysis keeps shaming itself, or being shamed" (p. 68).

Inadequately treated narcissism is a tenacious characterological malformation, whether in patients, therapists, or analysts. What role can training play in reducing the incidence of sexual transgressions in our field? We offer several recommendations:

1. In the preparation of therapists we propose a far more intensive and systematic focus in both theory and practice of the role of dissociative splits. As discussed previously, these are compulsively created self-idealizations in the therapist and the often hidden self-shame associated with them. Nothing less, we believe, will enable the therapist to begin to heal these splits and to develop the capacity to resonate between the quadrants we have defined.

2. Psychodynamic theory as traditionally understood has not been helpful in reducing boundary violations within the treatment. In fact in several

ways it can be seen as harmful. For example, the theory-driven demarcation between positive and negative transferences creates special vulnerabilities in the therapist. He can continue to bask in the positive transference of his patient as confirmation of his own special qualities, and to do so long after the patient has reached the point of being able to give it up. As we have seen, these dissociated splits allow the therapist to "personalize" the positive transference and unconsciously to undermine any effort to get at its roots. As we have also previously suggested, it cannot just be assumed that positive transference promotes patient growth while negative transference retards it. In fact Andrea Celenza (2007), an authority in the field of abuse, notes that the most frequent finding in boundary transgressions is the persistent intolerance of negative transference. We would add that this is likely true with non-victims as well. Although studies have shown that transgressors span a wide variety on DSM diagnoses, our experience has been that their narcissistic character pathology is the one common denominator. In transgressors, there appears to be a severe "allergy" to negative transference. The transferential splits are tenaciously held, and there is difficulty giving up the dissociation between positive and negative or seeing how they are unintegrated parts of a larger whole.

3. With narcissistic splitting, the therapist can easily confuse positive transference with the establishment of a therapeutic alliance. In the case of Muriel Dimen, her analyst would respond to her turmoil with "a sagacious air, that he had sailed these perilous passages before" (p. 43). We take his response to be part of a larger whole of attempted therapeutic reassurance from an objectified distance while in reality he created a block between the patient and her valuable subjectivity. The "map of psychoanalysis" (p. 43), as Dimen put it, was only his to know.

4. Another seriously damaging impact of these unexamined splits within the therapist is the extent to which the therapist's shame is countertransferentially derealized and disowned. The patient is thereby required to "own" all of the humiliating shame to allow untouched and untouchable the therapist's "absolute self-confidence" (p. 43).

5. Finally, training can offer the warning that, like all theory, psychodynamic theory carries its own dangers. Traditionally, the characterological present, including the characterological structure of both the patient and therapist, has been rendered secondary to the patient's instinctual "past." We are reminded again of Stephen Purcell's (2004) point that beyond the therapist's understanding of the patient's subjective experience and the therapist's unconscious conflicts, theory itself can be a third source of countertransference. We can only guess at the theory

guiding Dimen's analyst but clearly it served the function par excellence of protecting his egocentricity and narcissistic fragility. In Katie Gentile's (2011), "Lapsus Linguae, or a Slip of the Tongue," (IARPP online Colloquium Series No. 18, May 9–22) telling question, "to what extent do our theories create the material that we face coming back to us from our patients?"

Aside from specific narcissistically dissociated transgressions, what can be said about how to deal with negative transferential reactions? Negative reactions mean different things coming from different patients and different points in the treatment. For example, patients with an overassertive expansive character structure will early on be likely to test or compete with the therapist with subtle or less than subtle hints at devaluation. This may take the form of devaluation of the treatment or the therapist. Conversely, compliant self-effacing patients will likely be idealizing the therapist for significant periods of time and subtle negative reactions will not occur until later.

Moreover, as we have continued to stress, understanding positive and negative transferences in isolation from each other is insufficient. What needs to be underscored is that each reaction is dissociated from the other within the characterological whole. Thus, both transferences are always present; but when one is consciously active, the other will be conspicuously disavowed. The reader will notice that in our Four Quadrant Model, we are here referring to the transferential split between loyal waiting of Quadrant Three and revenge enactments of Quadrant Four. Positive transferences can be expected when the client is psychologically functioning in Quadrant Three and negative transferences can be anticipated as the client begins to move into the dynamics of Quadrant Four. Negative transference is likely to surface earlier if grandiose self-idealizations from Quadrant One make it imperative that the patient devalue the positional authority of the therapist.

Further delineations are possible. With overattached self-effacing character solutions, an idealized transference to the therapist will likely be easily established. Negative transferences will be delayed until the client can begin to recognize that the magical expectations, conferred on the therapist, are integrally and systemically related to the client's self-denial and self-hate. Both poles of the dissociated split will be obstructing the client's self-development (real self). Expressed otherwise, significant movement from the "idealized self" to the "real self" can be expected to carry with it transferential transformations in the treatment. With overasserting expansive character solutions, the reverse sequence is likely to be seen. The client may continue for some time to devalue the process. The client will not be able to sustain a more realistic appraisal of the therapist until the client begins to experience that the inability to trust or depend on others is (again) integrally and systemically connected to unachievable perfectionistic demands on self and other. And again, both sides of the dissociated split are obstructing the client's self-development. Of course when this shift begins to occur, we can expect accompanying changes in the tenor of the transference as well.

REFRAMING THE THERAPEUTIC POSTURE

From the vantage point of the Four Quadrant Model, transference can be viewed as a barometer of where the patient is situated in the characterological splits with which he or she is wrestling. As such, transference is one of the ways to *operationalize the Four Quadrant Model through the use of the therapeutic relationship.* A willingness to move into the transference involves the therapist listening in a more systemic fashion, that is, listening for parts of an as yet unintegrated whole. Listening in this way moves us to a non-linear mode from the historical past to the experiential present of phenomenological process, and as noted earlier, to heightened awareness of shame, humiliation, denial, and disavowal. This requires the subjective use of the therapist's self by entering into and engaging in the transferential enactment that inevitably will occur within the treatment.

Consistent with this listening approach to understanding, processing, and utilizing transferential material in many phases of treatment, we have maintained that the traditional demarcation between positive and negative transference has been primarily theory-driven. Early on, Ferenczi (1995/1985) criticized Freud (his analyst) for not being more cognizant of the subtleties of negative transference and of its therapeutic possibilities. In our position, all positive transferential material has buried within it negative transferential material, and similarly all negative transferential has buried within it positive transferential aspects.

The transferential posture which promises the best vantage point in treatment is for the therapist to mentally position herself or himself halfway between the positive and negative poles. Remarkably, this is advantageous in working with either positive or negative transferential material. With *positive* transference, the therapist is in touch with the contributions that positive transference can make toward relationship-building and trust. At the same time, the therapist is equally in touch with the growth-potential of de-idealizing the therapist and hence working through perfectionistic pseudo-solutions. With *negative* transference, the therapist is in touch with the patient's willingness to risk all in registering painful, often very shame-inducing, affect toward the therapist and with the encouraging capacity to take risks for the benefit of the therapy. At the same time, the therapist is equally in touch with, again, the patient's de-idealizing of the therapist and hence, again, contributing toward working through the same perfectionistic pseudo-solutions. Positioning ourselves subjectively mid-way between poles of the whole allows us to "see" the whole more easily and therefore to intervene therapeutically without recourse to framing positives or negatives as "good" or "bad."

For didactic reasons, we will concentrate our energies on how positive and negative transferences dynamically evolve in the treatment situation. Certainly, other relational issues can beneficially or adversely affect the outcome of treatment. The real relationship between therapist and client is of course critical to positive treatment outcomes. Conversely, persistent iatrogenic lapses by the therapist and abusive or anti-social behavior by the client prior to any engagement in the treatment process will likely adversely affect outcome. The latter may involve defiance, impulsivity, oppositionality, addiction issues, more severe psychopathology, or other undiagnosed conditions.

STAGES OF WORKING WITH TRANSFERENCE

Our trainees frequently ask whether transferential material unfolds in a sequential manner, and if so, what they should look for in terms of tracking content material and/or encouraging the transferential exchange. They also wondered whether the timing of transferential interpretations makes a difference in how successful the outcome of the dialogue might be. These are important questions; yet, they are somewhat difficult to quantify in any absolute sense because the nuance of transferential communication is not linear or formulaic. The ease or facility in handling the emergence of transference takes time before a therapist gains a sense of mastery. Questions about transferential dilemmas are best handled in on-going supervision on a case by case basis. That being said, the emergence of transferential material often does intensify over time. As such, we have provided a description of the relationship between the deepening of the therapeutic relationship and how both positive and negative transferential material may evolve in the treatment.

Stage One

In the treatment situation, the real relationship has a chance to develop to the extent that the therapist is able to identify, mobilize, and support constructive forces in the client, including buffering acute stages of self-hate. The client begins to trust the therapist and begins to develop patience and curiosity in the treatment process. As a result a constructive therapeutic alliance develops. Of course, idealizations will be looming as part of the picture as well, but there is also a hoped-for realistic basis built into the alliance as a result of the therapeutic work. Although the treatment alliance is not typically considered part of a positive transference in dynamic theories, the interaction between the two is important. For example, idealized beliefs about the therapist could be useful in establishing an early treatment alliance.

But a positive transference alone is insufficient to maintain an alliance because idealizing trends will themselves become the center of attention at some point in the treatment. Again, we refer to the Four Quadrant model for clarification. If the positive transference is centered on loyally waiting for the therapist to provide rescue or a magic cure (Quadrant Three), eventually the frustration (Quadrant Four) will begin to be directed toward the therapist. With no real relationship to fall back on to mutually reflect upon these feelings and wishes, the therapy quickly moves onto very shaky ground. If the treatment begins to feel as if it is on shaky ground, this is one indication that the transference dynamic has shifted into a deeper level of analysis, which we are identifying as Stage Two.

Stage Two

It is fair to say that a therapeutic alliance may be kick-started by idealizations about the therapist, but these idealizations will not sustain the patient long unless actual therapeutic progress is being made. When sufficient progress is made, patients will be able to experience the stranglehold their characterological solutions have imposed on them. Often this stranglehold is initially experienced through an enactment of the transference. The example mentioned in Stage One is one such indicator. On the one hand we have begun to see the idealizations about the therapist (created out of pervasive anxiety, shame, or the wish to be rescued) give way to a de-idealizing process. This is critical in moving the treatment in the direction of health and integration. In one sense the articulation of frustration aimed at the therapist may be viewed as a sign of growing confidence and/or health as the patient is demonstrating enough trust in the therapist to take the risk to reveal material from Quadrant Four. In another sense this is a critical time in the therapy because if the therapist mishandles the transferential communication by becoming defensive or retaliatory, the patient's worst relational expectation and fears are confirmed. In other words, the downside of the transferential enactment has been reenacted by both the patient and the therapist.

The manifestation of negative therapeutic components should not be viewed as problematic. Rather, negative transferential material can have a healthy edge as well. It becomes an opportunity to process and work through the hidden components from Quadrants One, Three, or Four in a way that allows for further conscious integration. These components of the patient's motivations and behaviors typically involve disappointment experienced around hidden longings. It is only when hidden material begins to be expressed relationally in the present that characterological structures or organizing schemas can begin to be modified. These modifications will affect the patient's sense of self-agency and self-worth.

Stage Three

Dynamic therapy creates and maintains its own forward momentum, but the momentum can be interrupted by either the patient or therapist (or both) sitting on a plateau of comfort. Typically this occurs after some desirable changes have taken place. For example, ventilation of feeling and some purposeful environmental changes will often lead to symptom reduction, which can easily be taken for structural change. Positive transference will be in evidence, seemingly confirming the optimism. However unless the de-idealizing process has been engaged, the patient's symptoms can easily re-intensify or be replaced with another set of symptoms. Life experiences can renew or recreate symptoms but a more dynamic reason can be an internal attack against the self for entering the dangerous territory of gaining relief. Am I not shamefully abandoning my family members who are still in distress? Won't people expect even more "degrees of perfection" from me? Am I being set up to fail?

Once any psychic change has taken place, there will likely be evidence of a minor or major degree of backlash. Pre-knowledge of the likelihood of a backlash equips the therapist to be mindfully anticipating, and perhaps palpating, just these seemingly regressive forces during the entire time the patient has been making good strides in being able to verbalize conflict and its accompanying anxieties. This is another way of expressing the therapeutic advantage of situating oneself and maintaining an equidistance between positive and negative poles of a larger whole. Under these circumstances, collusion with the patient's hidden desires to "get better" without substantial investment in self-examination becomes less likely so that therapeutic momentum continues to be maintained and gains constructively consolidated.

As we have stressed, if the negative transferential material has dynamically developed from the treatment process, (not from an egregious error or boundary violation on the part of the therapist) the manifestations of negative transference represent important treatment gains. In addition if positive gains are held in a manner that does not allow for the re-emergence of overidealized wishes of others (Quadrant Three) or a reinvestment in grandiose self-image (Quadrant One), then the consolidation of therapeutic gains becomes more internalized through an investment in authentic self-satisfaction. In a sense they are a sign that the characterological system has begun to be able to connect with itself.

SUMMARY: WORKING WITH TRANSFERENCE

Once transference is moved to a relational, non-linear mode of understanding, the treatment of transference and the monitoring of our own countertransferential reactions becomes less daunting and less shameful. Transference emerges out of the subjective relational stew that is part of the therapeutic process. Its emergence is non-linear; it is partially conscious because it is articulated within the session, but it is also partially dissociated because it is enacted but not consciously *owned*. It is the therapist's job to contain and monitor these enactments in the subjective present, holding a non-defensive posture that is attuned to the opportunities that will allow for the integration of parts into an increasingly complex and integrated whole. We have suggested that working with transference is at the cutting edge of emergence. By seizing the unfolding moment, using it in the service of healing and growth, we are able to help the patient experience the self in relationship in safer and more integrated, spontaneous, and authentic ways.

We want to emphasize that the relational dynamic of transference is a concept that can be taught, a skill set that can continually develop. Even the most seasoned therapists can become more proficient at palpating and managing the transferential exchange. Working with transference is not all that forbidding once we *admit* that it is forbidding. Unfortunately, many beginning therapists are embarrassed to report to supervisors when transferential and countertransferential material begins to surface; yet these are inevitable phenomena within any treatment encounter. When clinicians embrace the subjective stance of the therapeutic relationship, they are freed-up to explore the nuance and subtleties of this dynamic. The experience-near posture permits us to work with transference more productively and constructively. Without that, we would continue to be at a loss as to how the historical past is truly connected to the experiential present.

The rewards of working with transference from an experience-near, subjective position are enormous, as evidenced by a deepening of the therapeutic encounter, greater honesty, and the healing and integration of compulsively driven organizing schemas. One of the most frequent and per-haps valid criticisms of our field from outsiders, as well as patients, is the suspicion and distrust they feel toward the objectifying stance of the "all knowing" therapist. This perception is unfortunate because it short-changes the real understanding of the power of this craft when it is used at its best.

Closing Chapter Comments and Questions from Our Trainees

Question: It seems as though it is important to mention that sometimes patients might react to the therapists' actual discomfort, hesitancy, or frus-tration. When this occurs and they make a comment, is this a transferential response?

Response: When patients observe real discomfort, hesitancy, or frustration on the part of the therapist, the observation itself is not necessarily trans-ferential. This is especially true if the discomfort, hesitancy, or frustration is time-limited and not a recurring phenomenon. However, when the patient is observing a recurring pattern on the part of the therapist, the patient will likely develop transferential concerns in the treatment around issues of safety, trust, and abandonment. Overall we can assume that transferential reactions will originate from an overdetermined amalgamation of the pres-ent and the past, simultaneously encompassing and integrating reactions to the therapist's issues and reactions from the patient's history.

Question: Can you say more of what to do when you're in the middle of a negative transference exchange?

Response: In the heat of a negative transference, even though the patient may be demanding something from a place of disappointment, the question is "What is the patient really demanding of us?" Certainly it isn't necessar-ily that we expose more of ourselves so the patient doesn't feel that we are cold and withholding (see Case Example 2 in the appendix to this chapter). It is an opportunity to explore in more depth what it is about the treatment that makes the patient feel that the therapist is withholding. Generally, it is a feeling of shame that is beginning to emerge. Revealing more about our-selves in that moment may not necessarily address the underlying shame that lies within the patient.

Question: I noticed that in the section of this chapter entitled "Misuses of Transference," the case example that you used with Muriel Dimen and her therapist was quite powerful and disturbing. It really did illustrate an over-looked area of our field. But I must admit that I had a concern that the very good point you were making about misuses of transference might be mini-mized by some therapists. They will see the severity of this action and say,

"Oh, this would never happen to me," or "Other therapists might get into these boundary violations, but this doesn't apply to me" and therefore not concern themselves with more common infractions of misuses of transference. Can you give some examples of less blatant infractions?

Response: You raise a very good point and a question that we should spend time talking about at length. The misuse of transference is something that is best understood if transferential missteps are viewed on a continuum. Certainly, sexual boundary violations are on the extreme end of the continuum. However, less-blatant examples would include chronically being more than five minutes late for a particular patient, not returning phone calls to a difficult patient in a timely manner, giving too little notice for a vacation, or overly disclosing personal information. It is certain that the patient will have some form of reaction to any of these examples. For patients who are a little sturdier it wouldn't necessarily be an egregious error; but for patients with abandonment issues, it can get more complicated. It would certainly become a transferential misstep *if* the therapist responded with irritation to the patient's anger that she was not being given enough notice of the therapist's vacation (see case example 4 in the chapter appendix that follows). In this way the patient would more than likely feel ashamed, confused, and possibly less likely to bring her reactions around abandonment to the therapist.

Perhaps one of the most underestimated transferential missteps that frequently occurs is when therapists attempt to extend themselves and frame it as "just being helpful." One example that a colleague shared with us occurred with a patient who had an intrusive mother who was overly controlling and always trying to give the patient advice. After several months into the treatment the patient began sharing with the therapist (whom she had to travel some distance to see) that she was thinking of moving to the therapist's town because close friends also lived there and it would make it easier to make her appointments. She had a high degree of ambivalence about this, however, as she owned a home and had many friends in her own vicinity. It was at this point that the therapist began to energetically try to convince the patient that it would be a good idea to move. She even offered to help give her contact information about rentals and employment opportunities. The patient's response was one of discomfort and subsequent mistrust. When she brought these feelings up with the therapist in a subsequent session, the therapist became defensive, telling her that she was "just trying to be helpful" and that she thought that the patient was having a transferential overreaction to her mother. Although some part of this may have been true, when a therapist makes an interpretation about a patient's childhood after loosening the boundaries inappropriately, the result will generally be (with good reason) increased distrust of the therapist.

Question: Are you saying that if you sit with transference and try to ask clarifying questions you get a window into their organizing schemas? Is that how it shows up, at the edge of their conscious? It sound as if we're describing transference to be the dynamic "blind spot" in the patient's organizing schema. It's as if it blinds them so that they can't see anything else.

Response: Yes, that essentially is the definition of psychopathology. When the patient's (or sometimes the therapist's) organizing schema is so narrow or overdetermined, it limits the possibility of considering any new outcome or scenario. The goal of the therapy is to widen the patient's lens so that the patient can see more possibilities in the present reality. It will also enable the patient to relinquish fears and feelings of shame that fuel the overcompensation and prevent the patient from being able to live out his or her full potential.

Question: How do I work with overly idealized positive transference? Sometimes I think it's easier to spot negative transference; it might feel more intimidating to work with, but I know I need to say something. I may not know what to say, but I know I need to take some sort of action. But what do I do with a comment like, "Boy, you're really good at what you do." I mean what if the patient keeps saying it or seems overly appreciative for any comment I might make?

Response: If it happens more than once, you are right to begin to question an overdetermined positive transference reaction. It may be a signal of loyal waiting, or passivity in general, or a growing expectation that you will produce more and thus the patient won't have to do much heavy lifting in the therapy. These are our initial speculations, so asking an open-ended question might give you more information, such as, "What is it that gives you that feeling?" If you suspect passivity and a hidden wish for rescue, you might say, "You know, it takes two people for this process to work."

In that way, you are telegraphing to them early on in the therapy that passive rescue is not what the therapy process is about. Later, if negative transference surfaces, you have this firm ground to stand on. It becomes more difficult for the patient to express surprise at his or her need to make some effort. It may sound like a naïve response, but it is well considered. When you start to see that the organizing principles of patients involve a repeated deflection away from themselves in terms of personal agency, we are not too far away from the patient considering you to be "magical" and larger than life.

We can also refer to the Four Quadrant Model with the above example. By making the comment, "You know, it takes two people for this process to work," you are essentially palpating the transference. This comment plants a seed, and this is what we mean by palpating the transference. You anticipate that loyal waiting is under the surface, and if that is the case, disappointments in loyally waiting are not far behind. By making this comment *early* in the treatment, we are communicating in-between the lines that we suspect that reactions from Quadrant Four in the form of negative transference are directly connected to the wishes contained within Quadrant Three.

The comment is also diagnostic. Depending on the response or the intensity of the response, you will have an early indication of how fixed this compulsive organizing structure is.

Trainee: I can see all sorts of connections to the model through the transference. I can also see how loyal waiting and disappointment connects back to Quadrant Two. If the patient doesn't express disappointment directly to the therapist in that moment, he may internalize it in the form of increased depression or anxiety or substance abuse.

Response: Yes, now you are seeing how loyal waiting is not just an organizing structure in the psyche, it is transferential because it involves a relational component to complete the dance. Reinforcing the loyal waiting by taking the compliment too seriously runs the risk of inflating the therapist's sense of self or allowing the patient to inflate the therapist and thereby maintain his or her own deflated, passive position.

Question: Can we talk about "little" transference communications, you know "innocent one-liners" that patients say as if they're just making light conversation? I feel as though I need more basic examples to help me recognize when transference is occurring.

Trainee 1: Oh, I've got one. I just bought a new couch for my office, and it was as if the couch then became a safer blank slate for patients to communicate with me. Here are some of the comments that I thought were transferential communications. It's amazing that people seem to express themselves more freely about my couch than they do about the therapy itself.

Examples:

- "Oh, you got rid of your couch. Where's the old couch?"
- "Why did you get a new couch? I liked the old one."
- "Where did you get this couch? I'd like to get one for my house."
- "I'm glad you got rid of that couch. It didn't help me at all."

- "Oh, it must be *nice* to be able to get a new couch."
- "Oh, you got a new couch. It's really bland, just like the old one."
- "I don't know if I can get used to this new couch. I felt I had just broken the old one in."

Response: You're absolutely right. Patients will often let their reactions to you or the treatment in general come out through less direct lines of communication. What we do clinically with these "innocent" one-liners is really the question. Sometimes it is prudent to simply make a note of the comment and let it go. In other instances these one-liners can be viewed as entry points which we have discussed in previous chapters (Part-whole). In this case the entry point is leading us to gathering more information through a transferential disclosure. The patient is commenting about something in the present that pertains to the therapist directly, her couch. Phenomenological listening and asking follow-up questions will allow us to learn more about our patients' organizing schemas, their fears, their assumptions about relational interactions, or how they have been secretly viewing the therapist. On the other hand, we may find that by asking for further clarification too transparently, patients will become defensive, an indication by patients that the hidden intent behind the one-liner has been noticed by the therapist. Patients may then feel exposed and shamed by the therapist probes for further clarification.

In general, transferential communications will develop and intensify as the treatment unfolds. Over the course of time there will be multiple opportunities to move into a deeper level of transferential dialogue, so the therapist ought not to feel pressure to catch or respond to every transferential communication. However, if a patient continues to make similar comments repeatedly or has the same assumptions around certain therapeutic exchanges, the therapist is on more solid ground, so to speak, to comment on the pattern of the response. This is less likely to produce a feeling in patients that their every word is being microanalyzed. If the patient mentioned above comes in and notices that the therapist purchased a new lamp and makes a similar comment that the lamp is really bland, the therapist can reflect that she remembers that the patient made a similar comment when she bought a new couch. She could then use the word "bland" as an entry point and ask about what this means to the patient, what this triggers in the patient, or what the patient may be trying to communicate to the therapist about how she feels walking into the room.

Chapter Appendix: Case Examples
Illustrating Transferential Interventions

In this section we will provide four transferential case examples with varying levels of difficulty. After each case supervision example, we have provided either a brief analysis or a list of questions for the reader as a way of further integrating the material from this chapter. Each of the cases represents some form of therapeutic challenge in terms of managing transference, either the positive manifestation or the negative. In addition we will highlight how to anticipate and recognize when positive transference may lead to a therapeutic "set-up" for negative transferential reactions. We will also illustrate how to palpate the transference by staying in the "transferential present" in the service of attenuating disappointments and integrating more of a conscious awareness of how expectations and disappointments in relationship are interconnected.

Case Example 1: Working with a Fragile Positive Transferential Alliance

This is a young woman in her mid-twenties who comes into therapy due to feelings of anxiety and difficulty with decision-making around getting started in her career. She initially reported that she felt guilty moving away from home to get a better job because she was afraid her father would be critical and her mother would become very depressed. This patient is the oldest of four children who was charged with responsibility for her younger siblings. Her father held her to high standards at school, and she had little opportunity for friendships or social activities until she left for college. Although she attended a college close to home and lived with her family, she was able to expand her social network to include some friendships and casual dating relationships. The patient began therapy two months ago when she moved into her own apartment for the first time.

Patient: I really like coming here. I feel safer, like if I'm heading for the shoals, you won't let me crash. (smiling) Guess all your patients tell you that. (pause) You know my father is a control-freak. He blew up again last night when I showed up forty-five minutes late for a family dinner party. I told him that a work call ran over, and I couldn't let mom know I was running late until I got in the car. I only live five minutes away, so I got there as fast as I could, but I had to listen to him berate me, telling me that I ruined everyone's dinner. He went storming off, sulking and slamming doors. I'm getting a little tired of his tantrums, but when I have these feelings, I start to feel guilty. I guess I never know what will set him off.

Therapist: Does he treat your mother the same way?

Patient: Sometimes, but he's not as hard on her as he is with his kids.

Therapist: Does anyone complain about being blamed?

Patient: No, he just vents, I guess it's better than having a heart attack. You can't argue with him anyway. He gets furious.

Therapist: Are people afraid of him?

Patient: Yes and no. I was thinking about what you said—that I seem to be pretty hard on myself and take criticism on myself if I think I've let people down.

Therapist: Yes?

Patient: You know I'm the oldest child, and from the age of eight I was expected to look after the others, even though I was a kid myself. Both of my parents worked and were tired and I didn't want to put more pressure on them.

Therapist: Like you were supposed to be a "junior adult" helping your parents raise the family?

Patient: Yeah, something like that, I was supposed to be a model for the others, and not give anyone any problems. It bothers me talking about this. Maybe I'm angry about it. Did I feel I got cheated? I don't know (choking up). It confuses me. I always thought I was just a responsible person anyhow. I thought I was just someone who didn't like making waves.

Therapist: I guess you're asking if you were responsible because that's just the way you were or you were responsible because you were forced to be?

Patient: That's right! You are so right! I never really thought about it, I never really thought about myself. That's just the way it was.

Therapist: How does it feel saying that?

Patient: I don't know. I guess I thought that I was just supposed to give to others.

Therapist: And never take.

Patient: (pained) Like there was never enough to go around. I guess I always thought that if I asked for anything, I'd be more of a burden on my parents, like I'd be taking the food out of someone else's mouth (pause). I don't know how I got to be talking about all this. You know Dr. M. you have an amazing way of drawing me out. I went to this therapist about a year ago when I was in college, and the person was *nothing* like you. You seem to be able to make me really think about things.

Following Session

Patient: I had an awful dream last night. A kid was swimming in the ocean and I suddenly realized he was too far out. I went out to warn him and just then a huge wave swept over him. No one was around to help. I screamed and panicked and woke up really upset. I think I felt that I should have realized sooner that the kid was too deep. No one was near enough and I blamed myself.

Therapist: And there was no lifeguard.

Patient: No, I was all alone.

Therapist: How old were you in the dream?

Patient: Maybe a teenager.

Therapist: You were young yourself. All this responsibility was placed on you, and there was no one to help.

Patient: I can't stand talking about this. I want to run away and be safe.

Therapist: Does it feel safe talking about this?

Patient: I don't know. I know I said I felt safe coming here. I know you'll help me feel safe.

Case Analysis

In these two brief vignettes we see the patient registering the beginning stages of a positive transference which is palpably both wistful and fearful. However, she seems to feel that talking may be a dangerous activity for her (Session 1, Entry 1). We notice that both patient and therapist are keeping a distance about what might be the nature of the danger. When the therapist alludes to family fears of her father (Session 1, Entry 6), the patient responds carefully and ambivalently. Is she afraid that even in absentia her father will retaliate against her? Is she afraid that merely expressing anger about her father is a malevolent act which could hurt or even kill her father? We must assume both fears are involved, plus other fears which have yet to come to light.

This patient is almost beseeching the therapist to keep her safe; but, it appears, she is never quite sure the therapist can pull it off (Session 2, Entry 9). As the therapist, we might begin to wonder what safety would mean to this patient. What it would take? Is the patient indirectly asking that the therapist not ask questions that would allow the patient to be overwhelmed? Does the patient fear that the direct nature of the therapist's questions will become too intrusive, reminding her of her father's intrusiveness? Or is there fear that the therapist isn't as strong as her father and not even be able to keep himself safe? Or is there fear that the therapist will pursue goals beyond what the patient can tolerate, thus exposing the patient to feelings of anxiety, shame, despair? While the patient is in a positive transferential state, it is a fragile state. It can only stay positive if the patient can convince the therapist that the patient needs safety above all else.

Questions for Our Readers

1. As the therapy proceeds, in what ways can the therapist sustain the patient's trust without colluding with her in hiding from the "unknown dangers"?
2. How do we understand the patient's frightening dream following the previous session (Session 2, Entry 1)?
3. What are the issues concerning whether the patient feels the therapist can keep her safe? To what extent is it an unconscious warning from patient to therapist?
4. In Session 2, Entry 8, the therapist returns to the "unsafe safety" of the positive transference. The statement, "Do you feel safe talking about this," seems to run the risk of the patient being exposed to an almost child-like magical protection which she feels she needs to be able to survive.
5. Do you agree with the therapist's decision?

Case Example 2: Challenges in Working with Pervasive/Intensified Negative Transference

Patient: So we really need to address our relationship. Last week I came in to tell you about my weekend away with my sister and my boyfriend. I know that I was telling you about how upset I was that she kept flirting with him, but you just let me talk the whole time and we didn't get to discuss the issues of a few weeks ago. I suppose you don't even remember that I had mentioned that I was upset about the direction of the therapy. Aren't you supposed to remember those sorts of things? But no, you just let me go on and on, like you didn't really care about me or that you can't even remember what I say from week to week. When stuff like this happens, it makes me think you're not really tuned into me.

Therapist: It seems like I'm not listening?

Patient: Yeah. It seems sort of futile to me. You don't get me, I feel invisible, damn it. Asking me another question like you did just now, is that supposed to make me feel better? Why don't you do something other than sit there in that professional pose of passive indifference?

Therapist: (Appealing to her intellect, I indulge her in my thumbnail about the therapeutic value of engaging in this process). I say, "Can we look together at what happens for you when I misunderstand you or hurt you? Sometimes when these sorts of ruptures happen, there is something that is being triggered from the past." (Pt. interrupts): "Now wait just a minute! That's what I mean. You're saying this is all about me? You don't think you become defensive," and then . . . (Therapist interrupts), "I didn't think I was being defensive. I'm sorry if you thought I sounded defensive."

Patient: Don't you think I know that you're not trying to hurt me on purpose? But when I sense your distance, I say to myself, "See, she's just like all the rest of them."

Therapist: Like the rest of them? Are you saying therapy with anyone is a dead end street, that it's hopeless to even keep trying?

Patient: Yeah, because you come very well-recommended and look where we are. Aren't you supposed to know how to deal with me in these situations?

Therapist: Like these situations where you're trying to express your frustration?

Patient: When you become defensive and it creates a bad reaction in me.

Therapist: You keep insisting that I'm becoming defensive. But try to tell me what your reaction is when you feel me being defensive.

Patient: I feel invisible.

Therapist: Invisible?

Patient: I hate to say that this is how I think I felt with my parents, but I think I do feel insignificant.

Therapist: Do you feel insignificant in here?

Patient: When I feel like I have to keep telling you what you're not doing correctly, yes, I don't trust that you will ever get it.

Therapist: Help me understand what it is that I don't get.

Patient: (Silent, looking a little angry, a little like crying) I can't really find the words to describe it (quiet for a while).

Therapist: Hm. Does it feel like it's happening right now?

Patient: Not exactly, but it still sucks.

Therapist: When we get to this place together, I know that it feels as if you can't tolerate me or the process anymore. But it also feels as if this frustration isn't just about me.

Case Consultation with Trainees

Patricia: Oh, my. It must be pretty difficult for you to sit with all of this. I could tell you were doing your best to stay neutral and not get hooked. As a way of beginning, can you tell us a little bit about her background and how long you have been seeing her?

Therapist: She's a thirty-two year old divorced woman, and she has been in treatment with me for about sixteen months. She has had a history of running through multiple therapists throughout her life, starting from the age of sixteen. In terms of her earlier family relationships, I think her parents vacillated between being afraid of her and doting on her every wish. It's as if no one can live up to their standard. In reality, however, I think they were probably fairly ineffective as parents. They approached their own lives, and I suspect their parenting, from a place of anxiety. Her father seemed to over-idealize her, and she says they had a special relationship. He passed away three years ago. Shortly after that she divorced her husband and became involved in her current relationship. According to her report, both of these men have failed her in major ways, including her disappointment regarding the flirtatiousness with her sister that I mentioned earlier. Apparently, now I have fallen into a long line of disappointing therapists category as well.

Jack: Was the interaction between you always like this, or did the transference intensify at some point?

Therapist: It was always this way from the beginning.

Patricia: Maybe what would be helpful is to discuss the excerpt from your process recording and take a look at it in sections, line by line, to see what's happening transferentially and how there might be different responses.

Trainee One: I think she must be carrying a great deal of shame, simply because she has such an intense need for people to be there for her. She must deflect away from that shame by attacking people, trying to put them on the defensive.

Trainee Two: I think her default position is to interact primarily out of Quadrant Four, if we can call that a pattern.

Jack: Yes, both of these dynamics are occurring. The pervasiveness of her comments from Quadrant Four certainly does point to a sense of inadequacy and probably hopelessness that she is trying to defend against.

Patricia: Also, there is an overall tendency to shift the focus to you, how you're feeling, what you're doing or not doing. She is quite good at shifting from feelings of her own inadequacy and hopelessness to what you have done that is ineffective or inadequate. We see it in the first three lines, and in the fourth line when she interrupts you saying, "when *you* become defensive," then again in the sequence where she compares you to the rest of her therapists. However, I think your steadiness paid off because by the end of the session it seemed as though you had a bit of a breakthrough.

But before we get to that, let's start with the very first exchange. She lets you know that you have failed her in the therapeutic relationship by letting her go on and on. What is being conveyed by what is not being said here?

Therapist: She's letting me know that she wants me to direct her somewhere without having to ask. It's as if she's telegraphing through her disappointment that she has almost a magical wish for me to know where she wants me to go without having to say anything.

Jack: Yes, given her extreme responses, this indicates that the wishes in Quadrant Three are highly charged which in turn means that the transferential dynamics are becoming more problematic and more difficult to track. She is throwing so much at you that she does not leave much room to maneuver. And what happens after that?

Therapist: She tells me that this is a sign that I don't care about her and she questions the utility of therapy.

Jack: Right, which again presents a picture of the relationship in all-or-nothing terms. If you have failed her by not caring enough about her to know what she is thinking, then perhaps the therapy is worthless. In other words, it won't fulfill her intense longing in a way that matches her standards perfectly.

Patricia: Yes, so if we move to your next comment, you ask her directly if it doesn't feel as if you're listening to her, encouraging her to stay with the process and talk to you about her disappointment. I can see how you're trying to direct her away from the all-or-nothing thinking that Jack has pointed out. But I'm wondering if that might have sounded too intellectualizing to her. What else might you have said that would have stayed a little closer to the feeling tone in the present? Actually, I'm throwing that question out to the whole group.

Therapist: Well, I guess I could have repeated her statement about this being a sign that I don't care about her. That might be a way to slow her down and help me track her before she jumps to something else. Then I could follow that up with asking her what happens next, once she's convinced herself that I don't care.

Jack: Excellent. In this way you would be learning more about the sequence of what happens when she first experiences disappointment in the session, and then what she tells herself about what that disappointment means. You would be slowing down the interaction in that way, especially slowing it down around the intensity of the negative transference.

Patricia: I agree. Slowing things down with this patient's negativity is very important. When there is this much negative affect being directed at you, slowing things down not only can give you more information, it can help regulate the affect and keep it from escalating into further accusations.

Trainee One: You could ask her what being empathically attuned means to her. Get her to go deeper with her explanation.

Jack: Yes, that would be an equally good suggestion. Slow the dialogue down and invite the conversation to stay in the present while conveying that you are interested in knowing more about what her experience of the therapy currently is. You also demonstrate that you're not frightened by her criticism.

Patricia: Great suggestions. So if we move to your statement about "looking together at what happens when I misunderstand you," you try to appeal to her intellect by extending an invitation for the two of you to look together at what happens when you either misunderstand or "hurt" her. She quickly interrupts to add, "OR when you become defensive." What just happened in that small exchange?

Trainee Two: She felt in a one-down position and she had to quickly level the playing field.

Jack: Yes, and what does this forecast to you?

Trainee One: I think it is a perfect example of how touching on the patient's vulnerability too quickly moves her into a position of shame so that she has to do something to externalize the shame, and the way she sees to do that over and over again is by retaliating.

Patricia: Yes, when a patient needs to level the playing field with a retaliation that puts you in a one-down position, shame is just beneath the surface. She describes the futility of feeling invisible and her anger at being made to *feel* invisible. Yet, invisibility is a painful issue with her, and she doesn't want to go there. One thought I might suggest in this sequence is that you could simply *not* comment on her interruption, and direct her back to your invitation to look at what happens when she experiences a sense of disappointment with you.

Jack: Yes, by doing so you are conveying to her that she can up the ante and you won't be thrown off. This paradoxically can also be very containing to a patient who appears to be escalating a negative transference. In this situation the manifestation of the negative transference that is being directed at you is actually the patient running away from both her affect AND you, her therapist, as fast as she can. The reason is that the patient is humiliated to observe how "weak" she feels because she can't stay with her own wishes and feelings without becoming dysregulated. She finds herself deflecting everywhere else, from detailed descriptions of her trip to criticizing you for being "defensive." Dynamically we can assume that the patient feels weak when she sees herself running away from the therapeutic process. That is when she attacks.

Patricia: I know this is a very taxing situation. Thank you for your openness in presenting this case. It takes strength to remain as neutral as you were, and it seemed to have some pay-off in the end. With your gentle, non-retaliatory persistence, by the end of the hour the patient was able to become tearful and state that she didn't have the words to describe her feelings. This is a sign of a bit of a breakthrough where the patient is able to be more openly vulnerable in your presence.

Case Example 3: Using Negative Transference to Leverage Change

This is a young woman in her late thirties with severe social anxiety, affect dysregulation, chronic feelings of loneliness and worthlessness, and overly high performance standards for herself and others. Her family history includes an intrusively hovering and critical mother and an alcoholic father who was both physically and verbally abusive. A victim of childhood trauma, this patient often witnessed her father severely abuse both her mother and youngest brother. The patient, herself, was sexually fondled by a cousin at the age of ten, and there was some question as to whether her sister was sexually abused as well.

During the course of this long-term treatment there was an initial "honeymoon" period where the patient appeared to be making progress around limit-setting with family members and in her personal relationship. However, after ending a somewhat controlling and abusive relationship with her partner during the second year of treatment, the patient's symptoms began to intensify. Various trials of medication were tried with moderate success. Also, there was a brief hospitalization to help stabilize the patient when she was acutely suicidal. This was followed by a round of EMDR in conjunction with DBT, again with little long-term effect. The framework was also tightened around the patient's use of alcohol, as it appeared that she had been drinking in the evenings as a form of self-soothing. After the hospitalization and conjoint therapies, the patient stopped drinking and the treatment stabilized for almost a year.

An overview of the treatment revealed a patient who initially appeared to be cooperative and hard-working in the therapy. She was verbally compliant, insightful, and followed through on all recommendations. It became obvious over time, however, that there was a repeated pattern of self-destructive acts that resulted in an undoing of the gains in the treatment: stabilization of affect and improved functioning were followed by episodes of hyperarousal and "collapse." These episodes of relapse appeared to manifest in three to six month cycles. It should be noted that during the entire time of treatment the patient continued to function extremely well at work, was able to purchase a home, and reconnect with one sister and her younger brother. The trajectory of the therapeutic relationship moved from initial cooperation mixed with guardedness to an intensification of a forced positive transference as reflected by idealizing statements such as, "You're the only person who really understands me," "I don't know what I would do without you," and "You know how hard I'm working in here, don't you?"

Following a series of what appeared to be minor disappointments at work and in her social network, the patient nervously announced in a therapy session that she had been keeping something a secret. Sheepishly she reported that she had resumed drinking. When asked about the details, the patient stated that at first she had resumed her drinking gradually, being quick to add that she didn't bring this up with the therapist because she thought she had it under control. Then, the drinking began to be more serious, where she drank to get drunk just about every evening. This culminated in a rather dangerous episode where she had a black-out and that scared her. When the therapist asked how long this had been going on, the patient became more defensive and vague in her responses. When the therapist pressed, the patient had admitted that this had been going on for over six months. With each question that the therapist asked, the patient became increasingly defensive, stating, "You should be proud of me for letting you know. Why are you giving me such a hard time?"

With the therapist trying to give reassurance that she was trying to be helpful with safety in mind, she stated that the drinking had to stop and suggested some form of alcohol treatment. The patient refused, stating, "I can do this myself, I've done it in the past." Again the therapist pressed the issue, pointing to the cyclic nature of her gains followed by backslides coupled with feelings of shame. Using alcohol to self-soothe or dull the shame and loneliness was not an adequate coping strategy. As the patient dug her heels in refusing help with the drinking, the therapist wondered with the patient why she was adamantly refusing help and advice. The patient stated, "You know that I listen to everything that you say. Your opinion is the only thing that matters. Why are you being so hard on me?" Meeting the negative transference head on, the therapist said, "Yes, I know that our work is really important to you, but it seems that you have also been picking and choosing what risky behaviors are important to bring up or not bring up in here. In this instance it appears that you decided on your own that you could break an important agreement we had made together as a part of our treatment contract; but the only way you could do that was by keeping it a secret."

Analysis

Here we clearly see negative transference coming to the forefront. The therapist handles the situation by responding in a measured, concerned way, while also setting a firm limit. The patient's negative transference enactment represents a combination of feelings of shame coupled with a fear of retaliation on the part of the therapist (in keeping with typical responses of her parental figures). One positive dimension of this negative transference example is that the patient's angry rebellion is actually a breakthrough in being able to directly speak back to an authority figure. A second positive dimension of the enactment is that the patient trusts the therapist enough to break the secret in spite of her feelings of shame and fears of retaliation. The negative transferential enactment is a test of the durability of the therapeutic relationship in the service of health and growth. It could also be seen as a compulsively driven, repetitive behavior of hiding, one manifestation of resistance to the treatment. If we view the enactment as a communication back to the therapist, the patient is essentially asking:

- Will the therapist shame her like her father had done in the past?
- Will the therapist underreact like her mother or will she contain the dangerous behavior by providing additional support and help?
- Will the therapist respond in a way that conveys to the patient that she is taking the patient's situation seriously and that her painful enactment has been heard?

As we look at the history of this case over the course of treatment, essentially the patient's cyclic nature of improvement and decompensation is a reenactment of core themes about shame-based beliefs about herself and the untrustworthiness and eventual unreliability of others. The patient's learned coping strategies are to prevent shameful feelings from erupting while trying to get her needs met and to maintain some form of alliance to try to master feelings and needs on her own. In a sense the internalized message she held on to was, "If you ask for help or express your feelings, you are weak. If you are weak, it proves you are unworthy and must be punished or shamed." As we can see, this full-blown enactment brought the core theme to the surface through the direct transferential communication. In that regard it represents both a crisis and a breakthrough in the therapy.

Much like "bottoming-out" in AA terminology, this case illustrates the positive opportunity contained within the manifestation of negative transference. The therapist initially had to prove a steady, long-term influence through many ups and downs of the treatment, proving that she would not abandon the patient when the patient failed to "get better" in a timely manner. At this juncture both the patient and the therapist each had a right to say what they needed to say. The client needed to directly rebel against the authority figure, and the authority figure had to set a limit without abandoning her but without being in collusion with her either.

The therapist needed to take a stand. Often with more severely traumatized/dysregulated patients, this stand or breakthrough involves bringing in a third party to help neutralize the transference intensity. With patients who display more of a borderline organization, the transference eventually escalates to a primitive level. Because the positive transference is in such a precarious place to begin with, any therapeutic questioning of the patient's judgment or behavior begins to threaten the positive connection. With borderline dynamics the already shaky boundaries start to get more permeable and then start to collapse. This collapse is experienced by the patient in historically familiar terms where the therapist now potentially begins to feel more and more like the patient's previous abuser. The relationship experienced transferentially has been reduced to all-or-nothing terms. It is, therefore, experienced by the patient as "defeat or be defeated" or even "kill or be killed."

When working with this degree of borderline dynamics, we are eventually confronted with the all-or-nothing organizing schemas through the transferential enactment. In this case example the therapist handled the all-or-nothing split in a way that her father could seemingly never do. It is as if the therapist is saying "I'm also as strong as your father, but in a very different way. And, I'm not going to let you harm yourself. If that includes confronting your negative transference, I'll do whatever I need to do, but I'm not giving up on you."

This transferential communication registers on a basic level to the patient. It is as if she begins to experience the realization, "This person is challenging me, but she doesn't want me to die. She's on my side." However, the full integration of this trust (or breakthrough) often doesn't occur until a third party intervention is added in order to break the intensity of the transference dynamic. It is at this juncture that hospitalization or the introduction of a second form of treatment is useful. In this case the patient was willing to try a second treatment of DBT with a very seasoned therapist who worked in close conjunction with the primary therapist. Adding a third party to the equation at this point of treatment has an effect of bringing the therapeutic relationship into the real world and into the light of day. Timing is everything. If the therapist had introduced a third party intervention prior to the negative transference eruption, it would have been less likely to have a long-term positive effect.

In this case example the third party intervention around transference stabilization and affect regulation was effectively utilized and internalized by the patient. In addition a core shift on a relational level also helped to heal many of the traumatic parental messages and failures of relational attunement. In instances where there is childhood trauma, the patient often cannot get better until he or she faces the terror of the situation of the abuser. A third party "proves" that the therapist is not like the abuser because by bringing a third party in, the therapist is saying that there is no need for secrets. What we are doing in our therapy can be shared with the other therapist, and vice versa.

In borderline mechanisms the idealized poles of the vertical splits are heavily protected in the unconscious or dissociative reactions. This is because they occupy so much of the psychic space that the splits are dangerous to uncover or, put otherwise, boundaries are still too porous to contain any uncovered split. For a lengthy period of time in treatment (probably years), the patient will be concerned with alleviating disturbing symptoms of hyperarousal, fugue-like states, and chaotic relationships. However throughout this period of time in therapy, the patient's transference feelings will be gradually intensifying. This is important progress but it also means that reenactments of abuse will progressively enter into the transference, putting the patient in unconscious fear of abuse from the therapist or, alternatively, abandonment. It is as if the patient were locked in the therapist's attic only to be brought out for secret "exchanges" which no one is ever to know about. As this dissociated cycle of abuse occupies more and more of the transference and the transference thereby occupies more and more of the patient's psychic space, worrisome symptoms of suicidality as well as other self-destructive impulses can re-intensify.

Negative transference organically emerges and intensifies as the treatment of borderline and severely narcissistic conditions progresses. We are of the opinion that such transferential negativity is the most powerful instrument of characterological change available for these conditions. As the negative transference matures and intensifies, it manifestly carries more and more of the traumatic affect directly into the consulting room, which is to say, into the therapeutic alliance. This can be a chaotic period but also, undeniably, a high-gain phase of treatment. Properly seen and therapeutically handled, negative transference becomes an intense dynamic force for personality integration.

As overdetermined as this sounds, it is the natural and necessary evolution of the long-term treatment of the borderline condition. But at this critical juncture, an intervention from the outside may be imperative. It needs to be timed to the height of the enactment now vested in the transference. There can be many different forms of intervention. The therapist may direct the patient to an outside consultation, or to concurrent DBT, or to a concurrent twelve-step program, or, if indicated, to appropriate hospitalization (since this acute stage is likely to be disruptive to the therapist as well, the therapist can also profit from consultation). All outside interventions have the same goal: opening up the abuse reenactment to a third party, thereby ending the tyranny of secrecy and demonstrating to the patient that she (or he) no longer needs to fear leaving the therapist's attic. If this process can be implemented, both patient and therapist will have arrived at a safer, more trusting, and less shameful phase of therapy, a phase which can productively move forward with solid gains.

Case Example 4: Palpating Negative Transference to Leverage the Integration and Consolidation of Gains

Negative therapeutic reactions can occur in therapy in any phase of treatment. Consider the following in the fourth year of therapy, and notice how the transformational charge around overdependence is mitigated over time as the patient is able to consolidate gains from the treatment.

Patient: How come you only told me a month ago that you were going on a three week vacation two months from now? People have told me their therapists tell them six months or even a year ahead of time. I feel as if you are taking me for granted. I'm not the pushover type any more like I used to be. I have rights here too. And I don't want to be called Ms. anymore!

The patient has reacted strongly to the therapist giving her "insufficient" notice that the therapist is going on vacation in two months. She takes this as evidence that the therapist does not grant her the same elementary rights that the therapist possesses as a participant in the relationship. If we assume that the patient has had difficulty asserting her needs in the world, we can appreciate the progress she has made in registering a need and forcefully taking a position criticizing her therapist.

Of course, we can also assume that issues of abandonment are painfully coming to the fore for this patient, as well as humiliation for feeling so much vulnerability. But like every other evolving or unfolding manifestations in treatment (including symptoms, defenses, dreams, or character structure), transference phenomena in our understanding can fruitfully be seen as the product of conflicting forces of health and illness (Horney, 1950; Danielian, 1988). Overdetermined condensations of health and illness exist in all phases of treatment but grasping the balance of these forces of emerging authenticity (real self) and compulsivity (idealized self) during periods of heightened transference is especially helpful. In the above example of the patient's reaction to the therapist's announcement concerning vacation time, the therapist will optimistically be able to acknowledge the patient's gains, acknowledge the patient's ability to find her voice, and decide whether the therapeutic investment in formality by the therapist ("don't call me Ms. anymore") is experienced by the patient as painful distancing in stressful moments.

In another brief exchange with a patient, we can see further transference phenomena representing the culmination of therapeutic gains:

Patient: (forcefully) I seem to be going through a change in how I see you. I've always thought of you as someone who is famous and must be revered in your field. Maybe you are all that but also I'm feeling more that you are a human being just like me and everyone else. This doesn't change how grateful I am about what we have gone through together. It's just that I'm not idealizing you any more in the way I used to. There is a difference between idealizing someone and feeling gratitude for what that person has offered you, isn't there?

Therapist (with a bit of a smile): I think you know there is a difference. You can feel it. Can you describe the feeling?

Patient: It feels like I'm growing up.

The patient has negotiated a movement from idealizing the therapist (and we can assume others in her life) to seeing through the defensive nature of her idealizations and how they have held her back in her life. This is an example of transferential de-idealization of the therapist that is recognized by the patient as a major gain in her treatment. We can say that the gain is seen as emerging out of an intersubjective matrix and is therefore shared by both patient and therapist.

In a final example, the patient brings in transferential material, this time coming near the end of a successful long-term treatment, an ending agreed upon by both therapist and patient for the past year of treatment.

Patient: When we are finished here, I can't imagine never seeing you again. You feel like a dear friend to me. I mean are a therapist and a patient forever prohibited from ever even having a cup of coffee together? How does it work?

Contrary to many patients, this patient does not anticipate seeing the therapist professionally again. It is an anticipation of closure after a lengthy treatment with the same therapist combined with, we assume, some longing and uncertainty about what the therapist is feeling at this important juncture.

Follow-Up Clinical Application Questions for Reflection

1. How would you respond to the above patient's questions on termination?
2. What are the underlying expectations that are being conveyed within this patient's comments?
3. How could you begin to apply the Four Quadrant Model to understanding how you might begin to palpate the transference?

CHAPTER 9

Loyal Waiting Unpacked
How to Use Phenomenological Tracking to Enhance Our Understanding of Quadrant Three

> What can we gain by sailing to the moon if we cannot cross the abyss that separates us from ourselves?
>
> —THOMAS MERTON (THE WISDOM OF THE DESSERT, P. 11)

A FREQUENT REQUEST we hear from our trainees is to provide them with case analyses that illustrate the progression of treatment over the course of several months. Specifically, they wished to learn more about tracking the pace of the therapeutic inquiry process, the timing of interpretations, when to direct and when not to direct a patient toward deeper disclosure, and how to measure subtle shifts or signs of progress over time.

In response to their request, this chapter is devoted to the application of the Four Quadrant Model following a single case study over the course of six months of treatment. We selected a case that features the theme of loyalty, and we will observe how struggles around loyalty have played out in one man's life over the course of three decades. Loyalty issues begin to surface within the treatment, first through revelations about family secrets and then dynamically between the patient and the therapist. With the patient's permission we have included direct excerpts from his sessions to illustrate what we believe is often the least understood of the quadrants, Quadrant Three, Loyal Waiting.

There are a total of six excerpts included in this chapter as well as background information that provides a synopsis of the patient's family history and current relational/work history. After each excerpt there is a brief analysis provided by the therapist as well as discussion points that create a pause in order to ask questions of the reader as the case progresses. The excerpts that were selected specifically highlight how one session consciously or unconsciously builds on exchanges from preceding sessions, often in a nonlinear fashion.

BACKGROUND INFORMATION

Colin (not his real name) is a fifty-three year old, divorced male who had been in therapy for approximately eight months at the time of the first recording of the sessions you are about to read. Colin initially entered treatment due to symptoms of acute depression after the break-up of a short-term relationship with a woman we will call Mary. Although he was not particularly attached to Mary, he admitted that he was struggling with the fact that she was the one who had ended the affair rather than his finding the courage to end the dissatisfying relationship on his own. Colin admitted to a repeated pattern in relationships, where he seemed to become either the caretaker or the object of criticism to the point that he felt that he lost the sense of his independent identity.

Colin's early family history was one of deprivation and physical abuse at the hand of an alcoholic father. Colin reported that his mother was quite passive, almost childlike. The extent of the abuse on the part of the father was so great, that two of his siblings suffered terrible fates; one committed suicide at the age of twenty-eight, and the other made a serious, though unsuccessful suicide attempt at the age of twenty-one. The motivation behind the suicide and the unsuccessful attempt is unclear, but Colin suspects that it was his brothers' way of either getting back at their father, or it was a cry for help to get him to stop the abuse.

Colin admits that his brothers suffered enormously both physically and mentally, as they seemed to be the primary target of the father's rage and attacks. In turn Colin felt guilty about not being able to help either of his brothers more effectively. He described his own relationship with his father as ambivalent; he both hated him and felt sorry for him. Each of the other three siblings struggled with their father's drinking and abuse, but no one with the exception of Colin left the small town in Wales where they were raised.

What likely saved Colin from a fate similar to his siblings was that he was very gifted intellectually. He had been selected at an early age to attend a school with a reputation of high academic achievement. While at this school, he sought out a teacher, who encouraged him to move away from home and attend a private boarding school at the age of ten. The boarding school was in close proximity to his grandmother's home, and he often spent weekday evenings and overnights with her. Colin saw his grandmother as someone who loved him unconditionally and attributed his salvation to his grandmother's loving presence as well as his teacher's kindness. However, he also experienced the decision to leave the family unit to go to boarding school as an act of disloyalty, as he never again felt as though he fit in with the rest of his family members. They treated him with a combination of envy, suspicion, and contempt. As a result he always felt like "the odd man out."

Colin's adult relationship history was subsequently conflictual, full of ambivalence, often as a result of making bad choices in partners. His latest break-up ended after a six month affair that he had entered on the rebound after the ending of a ten year relationship with a very dependent/critical woman. Colin described all of his relationships, including one marriage that ended in divorce after twelve years, in terms of *giving himself up in order to remain in the relationship.* Upon further inquiry the patient was able to identify a sequence to his pattern with women. First, he would become aware of a problem with the partner, a character flaw, as he described it, something that bothered him quite early on in the relationship. He would fail to speak up, however, either in hopes that he could change his partner or because of a fear that if he voiced his concern or his needs, it would anger her and she would end the relationship.

This silencing of his own voice made him somewhat passive and dependent, and at the same time withholding and avoidant. After a period of months, sometimes years, his partners would invariably begin to complain that he was commitment phobic. Again, rather than speaking up, he would continue to accept the criticism in silence. When he entered therapy, Colin was convinced that he was "defective and incapable of love." It appeared that he had wholeheartedly embraced his partners' assessment of his shortcomings, and he announced that his goal upon entering into therapy was to try to understand why he was incapable of love.

In reality Colin was very warm, engaging, and quick-witted. He possessed numerous strengths that boded well for productively utilizing a long-term therapy. He was bright, humorous, generous, and he possessed a highly developed capacity for self-reflection. In addition Colin had a close circle of male friends, long-term relationships that he highly valued and nurtured. He also was well-respected in his community and held a responsible, highly technical job. However, the disconnect between his romantic relationships and the other sectors of his life was quite remarkable. It is here that we find the dynamic of loyalty playing itself out through an unrequited "repetition compulsion" between his loyalty to his family of origin and his desire to break free. In order to survive in his family, Colin had essentially to remain silent and not challenge his father for fear of being shamed or beaten. As a reward for his "obedience" he could remain the protected son, the drinking buddy with his father in the local tavern. Clearly, the patient repeated this pattern of subservience and self-protection through silence in his marriage and in each of his subsequent romantic encounters.

First Session Excerpt

We begin this sequence of therapeutic exchanges with a dream that the patient shares at the beginning of a session:

> I had a dream last night. It was really strange. When I woke up, I didn't know if it was real or just a dream. I was in this dark building and there were other people wandering about. They were in different corridors and different rooms, but I could hear them talking and whispering. It seemed like they were all up to something, something dangerous and illegal, but I don't know why I thought that. I also felt as though I knew them, but I don't know how I knew that either. I couldn't see them or recognize any of their voices. Anyway, then it was as if I was transported to a different place. I was in the woods somewhere. I was disoriented, lost. Then, someone came up to me out of the darkness and said, "I know who you are. I saw what you did in that house." It was at that moment that I realized what I had done. I had killed someone in the house. I became terrified in the dream. I didn't remember doing anything, like I had amnesia; but the minute the person spoke to me in the woods, I knew that what he had said was true. It was as if a part of me did something that another part of me couldn't acknowledge. I woke up in a cold sweat. It took me awhile to realize where I was and that nothing had happened.

Analysis

This dream occurred shortly after a session where Colin had confessed more detailed information about his father's abuse of his brothers. He also had disclosed that in his early adolescence Colin had difficulty controlling his anger, often challenging his father, until he had a revelation in adolescence that he could "win" by not letting his father see that he could get to him. The last time he could remember expressing his rage was when his father broke his mother's wrist in a fight they had had over something meaningless. He remembers screaming at his father as he watched him storm out of the house to calm his rage by going to the local pub. Colin connected the turning point in his adolescence, when he stopped letting his father get to him, to a Christmas morning two years later. He shared that his father had locked him out of the house on that cold Christmas morning, and rather than pounding on the door to get back in, he walked the quiet streets for hours, giving his father time to calm down.

Upon retelling the dream, Colin volunteered his own interpretation. He felt that his unconscious was trying to tell him that there was a part of him that was capable of committing unthinkable acts, that it was possible for him to block his feelings to the point that they were likely to erupt in unexpected ways. The dream had left him feeling that he couldn't trust himself. Although this is one possible interpretation of the dream (and given this man's early family history repressed rage is a likely possibility), another equally plausible interpretation to the dream is that Colin's disclosures about his family of origin from the session before had triggered deep-seated feelings around loyalty and betrayal. The symbolic significance of his killing someone in the dark house may have represented the breaking of a long-standing taboo of silence. Clearly, his ambivalence, fear, and struggle around finding his voice in a way that wouldn't result in unintended violence is part of the dream communication back to the therapy.

If the therapist had gone with an obvious or strict interpretation of the dream, focusing exclusively on Colin's unresolved aggression, it could run the risk of missing the dynamic relationship between therapeutic disclosure and the struggle to keep old loyalty ties to family. In this session the therapist began her interpretation by wondering about the timing of the dream and whether this might have any connection to his disclosures in the previous session. She connected the image of the dark house to his family house, that in the dream as in his life, he felt like an outsider, being left a bit "in the dark." She also wondered if what he had shared about his father was, in a sense, killing some idealized or protective image he continued to hold around his feelings about his father. In this way the therapist began to subtly palpate the dream content connecting it to the issue of loyalty, an issue that was beginning to surface in the treatment.

Discussion Points for Therapists

1. What do you think would have happened if the therapist had agreed with the patient's dream interpretation?
2. What assumptions might the patient make if the therapist had joined in his interpretation?
3. How might you continue to track the loyalty theme in future sessions?

Second Session Excerpt (Several Weeks Later)

Colin: I'm going home to Wales next week, and I was thinking that the deepest part of myself is still connected there, connected to the land. I love the land, walking on the heath, through the villages. Then my mind jumped to what we were talking about last week. I want to get back to that notion of loyalty or loyalty misplaced because I don't completely understand it. I started connecting the idea of loyalty to people's loyalty to a sense of place. Maybe that explains why I could never really feel at home in America, because my heart and soul are so deeply connected to the land in southern Wales. Then that got me to wondering whether I was doomed from the start. Maybe there is something that I don't understand about this loyalty business.

Therapist: What is it that you don't understand?

Colin: Well, the concept is elusive to me. I know it's important and that all of this connects to my feelings about my father somehow. We've been talking about the impact of my father's abuse on my family. I now appreciate and understand how his rages and his own self-destructiveness left a deep impression on me, in more ways than I ever realized. I can see how this gets in my way and that I repeat some of those behaviors in my own life, but I don't completely understand what this has to do with loyalty. When I think about my father, I see him as a tragic figure. I also have come to believe that he was invested in that image of himself somehow, and that part doesn't make complete sense to me.

Then I got to thinking about whether or not I'm really more invested in ache and loss in my life than anything else. I wonder if I'm a bit of a tragic figure myself. I wonder if that's what keeps me in a perpetual state of ambivalence. So, then that gets me back to thinking about moving back to Wales. There's some part of me that knows that I wouldn't really be happy living there, but I persist in keeping the fantasy alive. I know I love to visit, but if I did move back, I'm sure I'd start missing the parts of my life in America that have afforded me a better life than I ever would have had in my old village in Wales. There's no work for someone like me over there, not at the rate of pay I'm making in the States.

But, then I get confused again because *I really do love* walking along the Welsh countryside. My love of the land is legitimate; I feel at peace and connected to a part of myself that's lost to me over here. I wonder if what all of this really means is that I value things more when I can't have them. Of course, if that were the case, then it would mean that the reverse is also true—that I can't really appreciate what I've got when I've got it.

So much of my life is tied up in loss. I have an investment in loss, my brother, David's loss of speech after his suicide attempt, my mother being stuck in her misery, and my father's abusiveness. All of us, my whole family—look at us, all of us are miserable in some way. We're all invested in misery and loss. Tragic figures the lot of us.

Therapist: Tell me more about what feels tragic to you.

Colin. Well, it's my parents, isn't it? They really didn't know what they were doing, and it had an effect on all of my siblings. No one escaped without deep scars. I don't really blame them though. I tell myself, maybe it was because they were too young or there were too many of us. But, I did have an instinct that they weren't really there for me. So you see. There was a loss, an early loss for me.

Therapist: You were aware of that at an early age?

Colin: Yes, looking back I can see me as a young boy getting hit, my brothers getting hit, beaten by my father. Not my sister though. She was spared. But, even when I was very, very young, I had an older emotional self that knew this was wrong. I'm not sure Johnny or David ever really knew. I think that's why they kept trying to please my father. Now, I can see the loyalty there. But I rebelled, fought back, and finally left altogether. Yes, from an early age I knew this was wrong, and I also knew that I was smarter than my parents.

Therapist: How did you know you were smarter than your parents?

Colin: Well, my father was smart, actually. He was really smart and creative. But he dulled it. I suspect it was the only option he had. It's what everybody did working in the factory, that and drinking to get drunk. That was the norm. My mom, well she's not smart, but she has emotional intelligence. The problem was she had nothing to anchor it in. My father wasn't there. She's actually the seat of my loyalty to poverty.

Therapist: What do you mean?

Colin: She had common sense. You know, that's what's wrong with our culture. We don't value common sense. We value the intellect, logic, being book smart. But my mother, she is a survivor, and she's in touch with her feelings. She would tell it as it is. She goes deeply into her feelings, like with my brother's suicide. She would tell someone about it, people she barely knew, and she would sob inconsolably, almost as if it happened yesterday not twenty years ago.

Therapist: It seems as if you're saying that you admire your mother's ability to be a survivor and show her feelings, but it's as if she's remained stuck in her emotions as if no time has passed. By having access to her emotions, it doesn't seem to help her move beyond her initial grief in any way.

Colin: Yes, there is a stuckness, as if she's never grown up. There is a general naiveté about her. She's still a young girl in many ways, a bit lost, but she's refreshing and real. There's no bullshit with her. Remember when I told you about going home for a visit a couple of years ago; she confided in me that my father had had an affair when we were young kids. Well, she sent a very clear message to him, she did. Either he left the other woman, or she was taking us kids and leaving him. Now that's an adult decision, isn't it? And that's when we moved to the next town. I never knew why until a few years ago. And after that, my father straightened up a bit. I don't think he dared have any other affairs after that.

Therapist: When you talk about your parents, I am always struck by how you are able to capture the elements of their sweetness, their goodness, the potential that you saw in them even if they weren't able to ever realize that full potential. You know, that part of yourself that you were describing to me, that older emotional self that was able to clearly see how their parenting was so limited, that part of yourself that was wise self beyond your years? Well, that part of yourself was also able to see and preserve your parents' sweetness, their goodness. I wonder if that is what keeps you connected to them. I'm wondering if that's how we might understand where your loyalty lies.

Colin: I think what you're talking about is compassion. But, when I read the Dali Lama and he speaks about compassion, he's not stuck. I'm stuck in compassion. I'm deeply attached to loss. That's the Thomas Hardy piece of me, stuck in the mire of anguish, retreating into my loss. Sometimes I just want to say, "Fuck You, Thomas Hardy. Don't you ever just want to smile?"

Therapist: Don't you think there's a difference between compassion and loyalty? But if you see them as synonymous, I can appreciate your confusion and frustration.

Colin: Yes, it is confusing. I never really thought about them being different. Maybe if I could figure that out, I could stop feeling so stuck in my compassion.

Therapist: Do you think that there is any connection to your feeling stuck in your compassion and your mother feeling stuck in her misery?

Colin: Oh, my God. I never thought about it like that.

Therapist: That's the tricky thing about loyalty. Consciously, we think that we're identifying with something that's positive, in your case, the positive parts of your parents. But under the surface of consciousness, we often repeat some of the negative or unresolved aspects of our parents as well.

Colin: So you think I do that with my mother?

Therapist: I think you do a bit of that with both of your parents. You identify with your father's intelligence and creativity and have used both of these talents within yourself to succeed professionally. And yet, you get a letter in your file because you storm out of a meeting as a way of expressing your frustration. With your mother, you value her ability to wear her heart on her sleeve, and yet you have just told me that you're both stuck in your loss and anguish as well as your compassion. So, you remain stuck, just like your mother.

Colin: Well then, I haven't gotten very far, now have I?

Therapist: Actually, I think you've come very far. The fact that we're having this conversation at this level of depth is a sign of that. You are making all sorts of connections and insights. Also, I want to get back to Thomas Hardy for a minute. I heard what you said about your identification with Thomas Hardy. It seems to mirror your loyalty to your anguish and suffering. But, I also heard you get angry; you're fed up with remaining stuck in that bleak world of angst. In fact, saying, "Fuck you, Thomas Hardy" was one of the most refreshingly honest expressions of your own anger that you've said in here. Maybe you're trying to let me know that you're getting fed up with staying stuck in this form of loyalty to your parents as well.

Colin: (No response. Silence.)

Therapist: I can appreciate your dilemma. You identify loyalty to your parents as what is responsible for making you a compassionate, forthright person. But now we can also see that there is a growing part of you that is beginning to get frustrated with this position because it feels like a dead end. Yet, you do not want to give up seeing yourself as a compassionate person either.

Colin: You hit the nail on the head; that's my dilemma. I just never thought about it in these terms before.

Therapist: You know, I think that this is the biggest challenge when it comes to our attachment to others. We feel a deep connection to those we love; yet, if those people are limited and we love them nevertheless, it becomes very complicated to sort this all out emotionally.

In your case you see what is precious and valuable about your parents as an important piece of life's puzzle, and you fear it might get lost if you question any aspect of your loyalty to them. You also have a keen sense of how many people in this country seem to be drifting off track into superficiality and inauthenticity. You don't want to give up on those pieces of what you love about your parents because they are a reminder, a beacon back to common sense and decency.

Colin: Yes, it's the part of myself that I take pride in. I hate all of the airs people put on trying to be more important than everyone else.

Therapist: Yes, but I wonder if that pride clouds the picture in a way.

Colin: What do you mean?

Therapist: Well, I wonder if part of what makes it more complicated for you is that those pieces of goodness that you hold onto around your parents are a small fraction when we compare it to the sum total of all of the abuse you had to endure. I wonder if it is because of the weight of the deprivation and abuse, perhaps, that's precisely why you remain loyal to the good parts of them; they are the parts that you cannot afford to lose. Perhaps, this explains your own stuckness around compassion and also why you keep shooting yourself in the foot.

Colin: Yes, I have never been able to understand that part of my behavior. It does go against my vow never to be like my father. So, are you suggesting that by doing stupid things to shoot myself in the foot I'm actually proving my loyalty to my father?

Therapist: You know loyalty is a complicated thing. You are loyal to their goodness, but you seem to *prove* your loyalty by making choices in your own life that exemplify some of the less desirable aspects of who they were. It's as if you're saying, "See, I haven't really left you. I'll express my anger in self-destructive ways just like you dad, and I'll carry my compassion and emotional depth in a way that you do mom, stuck as a prisoner of compassion."

Colin: Well, I think we've reached the nub of it, haven't we?

Therapist: Yes, and it's going to take some time to sort out all of the pieces that we've talked about today.

Analysis of Session

At the beginning of this session Colin brings up the topic of loyalty, connecting it to his ambivalence around where to live. On the one hand he expresses his authentic love of the Welsh countryside; on the other hand he knows that his longing to return is based on something that may never ultimately satisfy him. He concludes rather pejoratively that he values things more when he can't have them. Although the statement may express elements of truth, it also functions as a means of foreclosing his own curiosity about the nature of his struggle. He further concludes that he may have adopted a loyalty similar to that of his father, seeing them both as tragic figures.

When the therapist asks him to say more about what was tragic, Colin names the parents' shortcomings but is careful not to blame them in any way. Instead, he explains that their abuse and neglect was a product of either being too young or having had too many children. Besides, he knew from an early age that it was wrong, and he used his intelligence (being smarter than his parents) as a form of self-protection and self-reliance. Rather than connecting with Colin's protective stance toward his parents, the therapist refers back to what the patient knew even at an early age about his parents not being there for him. In this way she subtly reinforces the authentic self.

Immediately thereafter, we see a resurgence of the loyalty to his father, where Colin says that his father was smart too. He explains that his father had no real options in life other than to dull his creativity with drinking. He follows his explanations of loyalty to his father by supporting mother as well, stating that although she was not smart in terms of traditional measures of intelligence, she was emotionally intelligent and had common sense. Here, he makes a further revelation around the power of his loyalty connection—the loyalty to poverty, being a survivor and being able to survive with one's emotions intact. Rather than choose the option his father took to numb his intelligence and creativity with alcohol, his mother did not sacrifice her emotional life. However, this left her stuck in her feelings of misery and loss.

At this point the therapist points out that mother's having access to her emotions offered her little help in moving her beyond her initial grief. By focusing on this part of Colin's disclosure, she hoped that her comment would act as a probe, encouraging Colin to disclose more about how loyalty to his mother's posture works in the face of her continually suffering. In response the patient calls his mother both naïve and refreshing, then further defends her by sharing that she can step up to the plate when necessary.

The therapist then makes a key observation, connecting his "older emotional self" to seeing his parents' goodness, wondering if this is at the heart of his loyalty struggle. She then moves to help Colin begin to make a distinction between compassion and loyalty and wonders if he can see any connection to being stuck in his "compassion" to his mother being stuck in her misery. Colin chastises himself for not getting very far in the therapy, but the therapist holds her steady position, neutrally affirming the patient's positive momentum. She offers as an example Colin's expression of anger when he expressed frustration with Thomas Hardy and shared that she saw this as a refreshing and honest expression of his authenticity. She follows this with appreciating his dilemma—his loyalty is partially responsible for his ability to preserve his compassion and honesty. Yet, she reflects that he is also beginning to get frustrated because it feels like a dead end. With this statement the therapist is attempting to model for Colin how it is possible to hold both parts of the loyalty dilemma simultaneously.

It is here that Colin is able to put the parts together for himself, by say-ing "You hit the nail on the head; that's my dilemma." The therapist contin-ues to move further, to connect the parts into an even more complex whole by talking about Colin's fear of losing the parts of his parents that are pre-cious to him if he dared to modify his position of loyalty in any way. Colin agrees and reveals that it is here that the core of his pride is located. Again, the therapist wonders at what cost—how might this form of pride get in his way or cloud the picture? Here, she connects the sum total of his life with his parents, where Colin sought to minimize the deprivation and abuse, in an effort to preserve the parents' goodness. She wondered if this was also at the root of his feelings of his self-destructive actions. It is then that Colin is able to connect another part to the whole, now being able to see how by behaving in similar ways his self-destructive actions might act as proof of his loyalty to his father.

Discussion

This session is a useful illustration of how a therapist can use phenomeno-logical tracking in a way that takes us deeper into the loyalty dynamic. The therapist is able to penetrate Colin's ambivalence that acted as an organizing schema to keep the old homeostatic balance of family loyalty. It is through phenomenological tracking that we are able to more clearly see how the Four Quadrant Model functions to comprise a cohesive, though compulsively driven self-structure. The patient reveals how his sense of self (Quadrant One) is connected to both father and mother (Quadrant Three) though his loyalty to each of them is embodied in somewhat different ways. We also see elements of Quadrant Four begin to manifest within this session. Rather than only reporting on his anger as it is expressed in the outside world, Colin brings his anger into the session through the Thomas Hardy exchange.

When a patient reveals this much new material in one session, particu-larly around issues of family loyalty, it is likely that a re-entrenchment in the old homeostasis will follow.

1. What might you anticipate will happen in future sessions around a pos-sible unconscious re-entrenchment?

2. What would you do as the therapist if you noticed a bit of a backslide?
3. How might you use the backslide to gain further information into part-whole analysis?

Third Session Excerpt

The session begins with Colin reporting on an incident with a co-worker whom he felt was judging him, making gender stereotypes about all men, including him. He stated that this woman's general attitude is that all men avoid commitment, that they care about one thing only, sex, and he's sick and tired of his co-worker adopting a smug and superior attitude over him. We begin by listening to what he would say to her . . .

Colin: I'd tell her, "You don't really know me at all. You don't know the depth of my feelings, the way that I reflect long and hard about commitment, that I want a committed relationship. You don't see the other side of things, (turns to the therapist and says as an aside—I'm just learning that now in here, in fact). So, I'd tell her, "You don't see how Marsha participated in what went wrong in our relationship, how she wasn't honest, how she could never confront anything. I'm tired of taking all of this onto myself, and I'm sick and tired of your judgments, so fuck you!"

Therapist: (pause) Do you want to tell me about the "fuck you"?

Colin: I have a right to be pissed off, don't I?

Therapist: Yes, of course you have a right to be angry when people pass unfair judgments on you, but what would be accomplished by saying that out loud to her? We've been talking about finding ways to express your anger without resorting to your father's tactics. If you end the statement in that way, how would anything be resolved or worked through between you?

Colin: Yes, of course she would get defensive and that would be the end of that.

Therapist: Is that what you want? Is it important that you strike back when you've been misunderstood, or do you want to keep a door open, to invite her to see you more completely, so that the relationship might have a chance of moving forward in a better way?

Colin: Well, that's the problem isn't it? I was never taught to talk about feelings in a way that teaches people how to work things through. That's what builds real bonds between people, isn't it? That's what deepens real bonds of loyalty between people. We never did that in my family. We had a loyalty with each other that didn't mean anything really. It was based on blood, all being in the same bloody mess together. It's like my brother, Johnny, he was so loyal to my father, even though my father abused him unmercifully. It's like Johnny is loyal to the *idea* of family. It's all based on blood, but it's a shallow loyalty really. You can see it in how he treats his wife and his kids. He doesn't do anything to work toward something deeper. None of us in our family do; we never talk anything through.

Most of my relationships have been the type of never talking things through. My relationship with Marsha was like that, so it never really went anywhere. So many things were avoided, and then over time the relationship just fell apart. And finally near the end of our relationship, when she did want to talk, it was all about blaming me, blaming me for avoiding commitment. But we never talked about the real issues. Eventually, I learned to anticipate what was coming when she said, "We need to talk." I was just waiting for the shoe to drop. When she started in with the blame, I just shut down and took it. Eventually, I began to believe it about myself.

Therapist: Yes, and if you never were taught to talk something through as a child, of course, it makes sense that your automatic response would be to shut down when someone is criticizing or blaming you.

Colin: Yes, I didn't have the tools to talk about the metaprocess—to analyze how we were speaking to each other, you know, to talk about where we went wrong in how we were talking about things as they were unfolding. (*Side bar: This patient actually used the term "metaprocess" *without* it being introduced as a concept by the therapist.)

Therapist: That's right. If you can pause and reflect on the process, you have a chance to change it.

Colin: Nobody in my family ever came close to doing that. Everybody either reacted or tried to hide.

Therapist: So, let's get back to the loyalty piece about your family, about what you said about your brother Johnny, about loyalty being about blood. Can you say more about that?

Colin. It's a knee jerk kind of loyalty, what you fall back on when nothing else is there. You know, it's like what you Americans have with all this patriotism bullshit. It's not real. It's based on the idea of something, people wanting to know what tribe you belong to. If you're not in their tribe, they can't trust you. It doesn't have anything to do with real relationships. If we based things on real relationships, getting to know one another, it wouldn't be so easy to fight with one another, to start wars. All wars are about blood. We have to ignore the reality that we're all people in order to start a war with them. We have to block out the reality that we're all suffering, we all want to put food on our tables. That's what my brother did with my father. His loyalty wasn't based on any real relationship with him. There's no reason that's based in reality anyway, to be loyal to my father, a guy who beat Johnny and the rest of us up all the time, who came home drunk all the time and all hell would break loose. Johnny's loyalty to my father isn't based on real interactions of tenderness or caring. It's based on an idea.

Therapist: What do you think all of this has to do with *your* loyalty to your father?

Colin: Immediately what I thought of when you asked that question was class loyalty. My knee jerk prejudices are to romanticize the class loyalty card. So, I guess I'm doing the same thing as my brother in a way. I'm glossing over the real experience of growing up in a blue collar family. In reality I know that many parts of growing up blue collar weren't so great. But, I insist on maintaining my position of romanticizing it—my kind of loyalty—because I saw how the middle class and upper class rendered us invisible. The working class is poorly understood. We're easily written off, but there's an enormous amount of depth and richness to be learned from the working class poor. So, I guess my loyalty is a way of speaking up, wearing it as a badge of honor, because I don't want to lose the parts that I'm grateful for.

Therapist: So, the way the loyalty lives out in you is a wish to be seen, to not be treated as if you don't count, as if you're invisible?

Colin: Yes, and I'm not the only one who feels this way. Where I come from there's a distrust of people who rise above their class. There was this barrister who lived in our town, grew up just like the rest of us. But he went away to school, got an education and made a better life for himself. Nobody trusted him. I didn't trust him.

Therapist: Why do you think you didn't trust him?

Colin: Because he was a phony. I could see it. I was onto him.

Therapist: But you're not a phony, and you've made a better life for yourself.

Colin: Yes, but I never really gave up my blue collar identity. I still go around with a chip on my shoulder. That's what gets me into trouble at work sometimes. I say exactly what I see, calling a spade a spade, exposing when people are being phony or taking the easy way out.

Therapist: Yes, and sometimes your response is to swear or insult the other person, just as you were tempted to do with your co-worker when we started the session.

Colin: Well, I think it's self-defeating, really. It doesn't make sense. I grew up being beaten up, but I find some way to put a positive spin on it. I tell myself, "See, you've learned how not to let it get to you. It toughened you up. It's made you stronger. Not like those weaklings who come from the middle class. They've never learned to tough it out; and look at them at work, a bunch of whining, complaining prima donnas." (Turning to the therapist, he says) Look how crazy that sounds. See what I've done. I've managed to turn violence into a good thing.

Therapist: Maybe that's the only choice you had growing up. Maybe, that's the way you learned to survive at home, long enough until you eventually used that toughness to give you the strength to leave. You know, sometimes violence teaches us some important lessons—how to be tough, how to defend oneself in extreme circumstances, and how to see through the violence.

Colin: Now, a better way would be to look at it a bit more objectively with compassion to see where it's failed me.

Therapist: Yes, and how has it failed you?

Colin: The whole thing is about belonging, not really knowing where I—the real me—all of me—not knowing where I belong, that's the real failure. So, I can look at my father, now, not with rage or the superficial loyalty of my brother, but I could ask myself, "How did he end up this way? Wasn't he suffering too? He couldn't find any place to belong either. But, he had no way out, poor bugger." It's taken me a long time to see this with compassion. Now I can see that behind everything he did was a great emptiness. He was a product of WWII. He was only fifteen when the war ended, but everyone in Wales told stories about the war for years, talking about the Germans and Hitler and his oppression and annihilation of the Jews. The irony was that I thought of my father as a little Hitler, and living at home was like living in a prisoner of war camp.

Therapist: So, is that how he failed you, through his inconsistency and cruelty? Do you think that you can bring yourself to feel some compassion for yourself, the part of yourself that had to endure that oppression?

Colin: I never said anything about compassion toward myself. I was talking about my father.

Therapist: That's interesting. You were pretty quick with that clarification.

Colin: (smiling) Oh, you noticed that did you?

Therapist: So, what do you make of that?

Colin: I guess it means that I haven't gotten to the point of feeling that same compassion for myself that I've come to feel for my father.

Therapist: Hmm. So, I'm wondering if that's how the old rules around loyalty still play themselves out. You can cut your father a break. You *must* cut your father a break because no one ever dared challenge him in your family, and that's what you were taught about blood loyalty to family, right? But the other part of that old loyalty contract was that the same rules never could apply to anyone else in the family. Just to your father. Everybody else had to keep their place in a one-down position.

Colin: Until my brother, Johnny got big enough, so that one day he got so fed up he punched my father so hard he threw him across the room. That put an end to that. At least he didn't try beating us up anymore. It's a good thing Johnny did it first, because if I tried to punch him, it wouldn't have worked out so well. I'm too small, and he would have beaten me up even worse.

Therapist: But, don't you see? You still allow him to beat you up by remaining harsh with yourself inside, not treating your own self with more compassion.

Colin: (Very quiet) I let him do that to me because I always knew I was stronger than he was. I knew I wasn't empty inside. I always knew I could escape someday.

Therapist: Yes, I see that your compassion for your father is so strong. But the loyalty demanded that you couldn't outshine him either, couldn't leave him altogether. Otherwise, you'd be just like the barrister, right? Nobody would trust you.

Colin: (dejected) Yeah, I'd be completely alone, no more family, no more sense of place. No place else to go because in Wales at the time there were class barriers from the middle class that were impermeable. They would never, ever let a blue collar guy like me into their ranks. Now, I see why I came to America.

Therapist: So, maybe we can pick up next time taking a closer look at why it's still so hard for you to turn some of that compassion toward yourself.

Analysis

As this session begins we hear Colin reporting what he would say to a co-worker who makes superficial judgments about him. On the one hand Colin is able to stay with his anger and we can view this as a partial gain, a movement toward health. On the other hand we see him revert to expressing anger in the style reminiscent of his father. When the therapist asks him to tell her more about the "fuck you," Colin defends himself by saying he has a right to be angry, which of course he does. At this juncture the therapist tries to palpate the all/nothing expression of rights and freedoms in an attempt to indirectly challenge Colin's old loyalty configuration. She does so by wondering if there might be other ways to communicate his points. Colin then reveals more about what is behind the comment. He was never taught how to talk about feelings or differences in a way that addressed issues directly *and* worked things through in a way that actually could build *real* bonds between people.

In this session Colin is able to discern the difference between superficial (blood) loyalty and loyalty that is based on constructive interactions. Although Colin can *see* the difference, he distrusts his capacity to develop such skills, referring to past relationships where he (and his partners) fell short. When the therapist directs him back to asking how this might connect to his loyalty to his father, his immediate association is to his romanticized prejudices about class loyalty. This form of loyalty is overdetermined, romantically driven by very real class discrimination; however, Colin is now able to see that his *real* experiences growing up in a blue collar family weren't great. Yet, he continues the idealization because he was rendered invisible by the upper classes. Thus, the maintenance of loyalty to class is worn as a badge of honor, serving the function of avoidance of the real pain associated with his family rendering him invisible as well.

Colin's underlying pain, stemming from his family rendering him invisible, initially presents as a focus on class loyalty. (It wasn't just me; it was all of us who were rendered invisible). It is unclear whether the therapist missed the opportunity to make a connection between class invisibility and Colin being rendered invisible by his family, or if she chose to allow the dialogue to continue because the timing of this interpretation did not feel quite right. In his next statement Colin appears to be further bolstered by his romanticized charge around class discrimination, and he mentions that he is not the only one who feels this way. He is joined by many others of the working class. At this point we might speculate that Colin has given us a glimpse of transferential material (contained within Quadrant Four). By making a comparison between classes, he may be indirectly telegraphing to the therapist that this is something she couldn't possibly understand assuming she came from a different class background. Rather than speaking to the potential transferential association, the therapist makes a mental note and chooses to hold off, waiting for more material to emerge.

Colin then shifts to an example about a barrister in his village who was shunned for making a better life for himself. At this point the therapist does offer a comment in an attempt to shift away from a more entrenched position of all-or-nothing thinking. She does so by noting that he had made a better life for himself and she does not regard him as a phony. Thus, she reinforces his authenticity and uniqueness. Colin is quick to remind her that he never gave up his loyalty position to class, using it to unmask the people who are phony at work. Now, the therapist moves to comment on material from Quadrant Four, reflecting that he uses insults or swearing to make his point. By waiting until Colin reveals more directly his strategy of devaluing, the therapist is now on firmer ground when she makes her interpretation, hopefully allowing for a shift of Quadrant Four material into consciousness. As we can then see, Colin now must face the down side of his strategy, and he is able to admit that his behavior is self-defeating in terms of truly being seen and/or appreciated. This insight is then followed by other connections. Colin is now able to see how he had framed his father's beatings as a way of toughening him up and making him stronger, which doesn't make any real sense to him.

At this juncture we note a shift in the dialogue. Colin is able to rejoin in a positive alliance with the therapist and admit to her that he thinks it's crazy to turn violence into a good thing. He then suggests that a better way of thinking about it *objectively* and *compassionately* would be to examine where this strategy failed him. This alliance on his own behalf is short-lived, however, as we observe what again happens when he begins talking about his father. His compassion shifts away from himself and back to his father. When the therapist attempts to direct this compassion back to Colin, the old allegiance to father comes forward with considerable force as Colin says, "I never said anything about compassion toward myself." Here, the therapist makes an observation, noting the quickness of his reflexive response, thus exposing the loyalty position of Quadrant Three.

This exchange offers us an excellent example of how many patients can voice rebellion to the constraints of invisibility through Quadrant Four without giving up their position of loyal waiting. The therapist is unwavering, however, using this patient's reflexive response to point out the apparent rules of the old blood loyalty contract—no one could be cut any slack around compassion other than father. Everyone else had to remain in a one-down position. Old loyalty bonds remain fixed in the present as evidenced by Colin's continued harshness with himself. Despite having the knowledge that he was stronger, he has yet to allow himself to completely outshine his father.

In this session we see Colin's old loyalty stance reassert itself through his elaboration on class loyalty. Presenting it as a pure positive, he justifies his actions as a means of exposing the superficiality of the upper class. Not only does this preserve his loyalty to blood, it offers a distraction from facing what his own family members did to render him invisible. The therapist's steady tracking allowed her to gain further clarification as to the intricate balance between Quadrants One, Three, and Four. Eventually, this pays off as we see how the complexity of the loyalty contract with the father is further exposed. It is interesting to note that at the end of this session Colin connects back to his early ambivalence around living at home or in America. His final statement marks a shift out of the romanticized, ambivalent position toward a statement that is anchored in the reality of breaking the very real social class barrier.

Discussion

1. How does the patient's ability to reveal greater degrees of emotion in the session relate to his growing tolerance of releasing the old loyalty connection to his father?
2. What further work needs to be done in this area?
3. How might you pursue the class loyalty piece even further?

As an aside, class loyalty is an interesting sub-text when we consider how loyal waiting might manifest in Quadrant Three. It is definitely a universal dynamic that cuts across ethnicity and geography, as we can see from this patient's disclosures. The real opportunities that underlie these discussions with regard to class loyalty are at the heart of many people's authenticity. Once the scars of prejudice and discrimination (around race, gender, or class) are brought to the surface and validated, individuals are then free to take the best parts of their background and experience, the lessons learned, and use them in a way that can heal personal wounds and speak out against the further subjugation of others. In Colin's case he was exposed to a number of class experiences, from blue collar working class to the rarified air of the academic upper class. Through the exploration of his personal loyalty dilemma, he may have the opportunity to combine the richness from both worlds into a forceful, intelligent presence, one that could offer a great deal of wisdom to many.

Fourth Session Excerpt (Very Next Session)

Colin: So we were going to begin with looking at why it is so hard to feel compassion for myself.

Therapist: Yes, so what have you thought about this week? I see that you brought in a piece of paper with some notes.

Colin: Well, first off, I thought about my brother, Mickey. I imagine that if he was exposed to an upper middle class environment like I was, he'd come to some easy judgments about all of that.

Therapist: What do you mean?

Colin: He'd be briskly dismissive of the lifestyle, where I am ambivalent. I can see that it's not all bad, just a different way of doing things. This parses into my next point—it just goes to show my poorly developed sense of self. I'm much better when I'm challenged directly by authority.

Therapist: I'm not sure I'm following you, better in what way?

Colin: I usually have a better sense of self when I'm being challenged. It helps me crystallize a sense of my own identity. It's not so amorphous.

Therapist: How so?

Colin: I remember going to a Saturday detention, when I was caught smoking in the boy's room, and I had to write an essay against smoking. They thought they were giving me a punishment, but I really got into it. I was writing reams and reams, even went up to the proctor and asked for more paper. Hardly a punishment. He was surprised. You know, you can take up a stance and then build on it. You can argue any point, whether it's authentic or not. But, at least I was arguing for it clearly, and I felt stronger.

Therapist: So, if you don't know if it's authentic or not, how does it make you feel stronger?

Colin: That's what I mean by authority giving you something to push against. It clarifies things. It cranks up the rhetoric, and then you know where you are.

Therapist: You know where you are?

Colin: It's a sense of self that is created by circumstances, not from within. I don't have a very strong sense of self from within. Maybe because I was taken out of my hometown grammar school and sent to the private school with those other middle class kids. I was only ten. I didn't know who I was. I had a confused sense of loyalty. It was good because I was given options, but I never really knew where I belonged. Not knowing where I belong, I don't know who I am. My mom asked me, "Do you ever think about being posh, you know, having lots of money?" When I asked her that same question, Mom says, "No, I'd never want that. That's not who I am. That's not for me." I've always had a bit of a problem with that.

Therapist: Is that where you experience your ambivalence?

Colin: No, that's very clear, but it's a kind of clarity that closes things off. It closes off a lot of possible experiences.

Therapist: Are you saying that this makes things clear for you or is it clear for your mother?

Colin: I don't know what you mean.

Therapist: A bit earlier I thought that you said that being exposed to private schooling at the age of ten was good because you were given options. But, then you said that you never really knew where you belonged, and in not knowing where you belonged, you didn't know who you were. How is that clear? Your mother seems to be clear about her position of where she belongs. It sounds like you're expressing a struggle with that. Is this part of your confusion over loyalty and belonging?

Colin: If you go and you live in a big house, but everyone around you is saying "No, I would never do that. That's not for me." But let's say, you don't feel that way. You like it. But they're saying something else, it's confusing.

Therapist: So, you weren't supposed to like it.

Colin: No one said I wasn't supposed to like it, but they said that I came back from school with pretentions.

Therapist: What pretentions?

Colin: Well, I'd come home from school on holidays and in the summer, and I'd find a bunch of money in with the knives and forks, and I'd say, "Why don't you put the bills in one place, so you won't lose them?"

Therapist: How is that pretentious?

Colin: Well, it's middle class. Working class people are more chaotic.

Therapist: So, you make a statement to try to help alleviate some of the chaos, and it's called pretentious?

Colin: Yeah, and my mom eventually ended up calling me a snob. I even tried to take over paying the bills. I said to myself, I can do this better than they can. But, it wasn't appreciated. I was called a snob, trying to be better than they were.

Therapist: You tried to make things better, to alleviate the chaos, and you were called a snob. Did you believe this about yourself?

Colin: A part of me did, but a part of me started looking elsewhere.

Therapist: Looking elsewhere?

Colin: Looking to leave the country, leave the family, to create as much distance as I could.

Therapist: So, if we move this conversation back into the present, what do you make of their logic, having just shared all of this with me?

Colin: Well, I see their defensiveness in it, but I don't get angry. (long pause) I think this is what you meant by wondering where the compassion for myself went, isn't it? (pause) Because I was mishandled, wasn't I. For my mother, it was selfish, really. It was a way that she tried to prevent losing her son.

Therapist: So, in a sense you are telling me that your mother was being selfish?

Colin: Yes, well, no, not really. She just didn't have the imagination.

Therapist: You think this is a problem of imagination?

Colin: Yes, she didn't have the capacity.

Therapist: She didn't have the capacity to imagine a better life for her son?

Colin: Well, I suppose that's a good way of putting it. I never thought about it like that.

Therapist: So, if you think about it as not having the capacity to imagine a better life for you than for herself, what feelings start to come up? Where do you go with that?

Colin: When you said it just now?

Therapist: Yes.

Colin: I guess I'd have to admit that she was selfish.

Therapist: If you admit that she is selfish, would that be being disloyal to her?

Colin: Yes, but then, I would have to make a choice. But I didn't. I couldn't physically leave them, so later I guess I just did things to be aggravating until I got kicked out. I lived with another family for six months. Then, I came back, and I was greeted as the prodigal son by my mother. She didn't mean the things she said. Mark (brother) left emotionally—he vacated emotionally, just decided that they were all crazy and got out as soon as he could. Funny thing is, I thought he was being so selfish.

Therapist: What did your mother say to you when she kicked you out?

Colin: She said, "If you don't like the way we are and you think you're so much better, then leave. Go on, get out!" I left, and then I came back six months later. She didn't really mean get out.

Therapist: What did she really mean?

Colin: Probably, why do you have to be so ornery?

Therapist: Ornery?

Colin: No, she was probably really saying, "Why can't you be like us? If it's so bloody good out there, why don't you just go?"

Therapist: That sounds pretty mean.

Colin: Well, it's defensive. It's weak. It's coming from fear. (pause) Boy, what we're talking about is that my loyalties are more deeply divided than I thought. It's deep. It's emotional. It's not just an intellectual exercise that I go through in my head.

Therapist: I think you're right.

Colin: I'm not like Mickey, who just got up and moved to the other side of town. He's not as sensitive as I am.

Therapist: And what were you feeling when you just told me "it's deep, it's emotional?"

Colin: Loyalty to my mother, to leave the family is to leave my mother. I'm acutely aware of how that will affect her. That's my curse. I can imagine putting myself in the other person's shoes, actually becoming the other person. Then I feel the impact that my words or my actions would have on them. My acute awareness of how my actions will affect others to my own detriment. It's paralyzing.

Therapist: It seems as though this experience of what it means to be loyal presents you with an untenable choice.

Colin: No wonder I stay ambivalent. No wonder I have trouble making a commitment or really planting myself somewhere.

Therapist: Okay. We've uncovered quite a bit today. Why don't we pick up on this next time.

Analysis

Colin begins this session by announcing that he can see how old loyalties to family are connected to his poorly developed sense of self. He links his inability to initiate action on his own behalf to not having a crystallized sense of self, other than when he is pushing against an aggressor. His sense of self becomes mobilized and clarified through the experience of an external threat. This session then moves into Colin being able to talk more openly about his *confusion* as to how to sort through his loyalty tangle. He admits to having an appreciation of private schooling, the opportunities it gave him to dream of a better life. But then he was put in a double bind by being accused by his mother of being pretentious.

This session marks a shift from a discussion of loyalty that was primarily centered on father to the deeper complexities of his feelings about his mother. Shortly into the session the therapist connects Colin's confusion around loyalty to his mother's selfishness and her inability to let her son go. Colin, maintaining his refusal to feel any anger toward his mother, explains that his mother's inability to hope for more for her son's life was due to a lack of imagination on her part, not selfishness. The therapist questions this and asks Colin to explain how this is a lack of imagination. At this point Colin reluctantly admits that he is aware of her selfishness. Noting his hesitation, the therapist asks if admitting this out loud feels like an act of disloyalty. Colin then reveals something most interesting. He states that if he admitted this consciously, it would mean that he would have to make a choice about his mother (and his family). Instead, he lets the therapist know that he would prefer to act out his anger and his disappointment indirectly, thereby getting "kicked out" rather than having to choose to leave. Here we see an example of knowing and not knowing simultaneously.

In this way we see how Colin maintains his position of loyal waiting for the other to commit the first act of aggression (separation). Another part of the puzzle falls into place. This is an unsettling resolution, however, as Colin cannot rest easy in this form of "permission." His sense of isolation and disconnection eventually pulls him back to home, where his mother greets him as the prodigal son. Feeling relief at the reconnection, he excuses his mother's retaliation by explaining that she really didn't mean it. He and his mother are connected emotionally, unlike his brother Mark, who could just leave home, unhampered by the emotional bonds of connection. It is his brother, the patient reveals, who is the selfish one because he is able to think only of his own well-being.

The therapist continues to track Colin's logic, asking what he thought his mother really meant when she said, "Get out." The patient translates his mother's communication to mean, "Why can't you be like us. If you think you can find something better, just leave." The therapist voices her own reframe in an attempt to articulate elements of Quadrant Four by stating, "That sounds pretty mean." It is an intentional comment, timing-wise, because she believes that Colin is ready to handle the growing awareness of his mother's retaliatory capacities. (Apparently, the father isn't the only one who has the capacity to punish.) Again, Colin takes a protective, joining stance with his mother. However, at the end of this session, we see Colin having an easier time being able to understand how deep the loyalty theme runs, how paralyzing the loyalty attachment with his mother really is. Furthermore, he is able to connect this to the source of his ambivalence and his difficulty breaking free to make a new commitment and plant himself elsewhere. This is building up to a realization of how much this loyalty contract is really costing him.

Discussion

Notice how Colin's awareness of the complexities of his loyalty to family has now allowed him to identify the major source of his ambivalence—an inability to separate fully from his mother. He is able to admit to his mother's dependence on him and can see, at least in part, how this is an act of her selfishness and limitation as a mother. His inability to break free has more to do with his emotional resonance to his mother, equating a break from her as the equivalent of cutting off his emotions or hardening himself, becoming like his brother.

1. How would you describe the shifts in the patient's organizing schema around loyalty? (a) Where do you see a modification in the all-or-nothing organization? (b) Where is the sense of absolute loyalty still present?
2. Do you notice the patient's increased ability to make connections without having to quickly resist the therapist's reflections and comments? Can you see this as a sign of shifting loyalties toward mother?
3. Where/how might negative transferential responses to the therapist emerge at this point in the therapy?

Fifth Session Excerpt (Several Weeks Later)

Colin: I keep thinking about loyalty. It's fascinating. You see, I didn't have much other than my native talents to set up against my family loyalty to blood, except for my teacher Kevin, but we've already talked a great deal about him.

Therapist: Last week you started to tell me about relationships that are more current.

Colin: Yes, with Marsha I was first attracted to her physically, and then the bond was based strictly on loyalty after that. My true feelings about her, as I think back on that relationship, weren't really permitted. Everything had to stay unexamined. The dynamics that remained unspoken, like her need to prove her competence when she really felt completely incompetent, never got addressed. What she demanded of me was unconditional approval around *everything* she did. The least little challenge or question from me put such a strain on the relationship. Eventually, I just stopped.

What that woman really needs is therapy. So, now that we've been talking about loyalty, I can see it so much more clearly after all these years. I couldn't see it then because of a sense of loyalty to what I had chosen. So, what it means is that I deflect away from my own judgments and trust other people's world view. That's what I mean about losing myself. It never even occurs to me that something might be wrong with the other person's judgments of me.

Therapist: But you do know on some level because you are able to report what happened *and* your reactions to what happened just now. I understand how you learned to bury the reactions and not express them to the women you were involved with. But, is that the same as losing yourself?

Colin: Yeah, that's what I was talking about last week. I was seeing it and not seeing it. Five years ago I couldn't see it that clearly. I needed to step away from the relationship before I could admit things to myself. That's what you have helped me with—that my perceptions were valid. (pause) I'm still afraid that that could happen again if I ever got into a relationship.

Therapist: How so?

Colin: Well, that's my fear, that the closeness will confuse me. I need that space in order to protect myself. Then, that leaves people feeling a lack of connection from me.

Therapist: So, you have a fear that the closeness will make your own perceptions, your own sense of who you are disappear? And, are you saying that you keep a little distance from people in order to maintain your identity?

Colin: Well, that would depend on the partner I chose, now wouldn't it?

Therapist: Yes, so are you saying that today you might be able to be a bit more discerning about the partner you pick? Wouldn't picking a better partner mean that you could pick someone who would honor your perceptions as well as your needs?

Colin: Well, they would have to do more than that. They'd have to encourage me . . . because I've spent so much time burying my own perceptions, distracting the person away from myself, that they would have to bring me back to my own admissions and opinions. You do that in here with me—when I go on and on about the world and other people—you bring me back to myself. That's what I need in a partner. So, I'd be expecting a partner to be a therapist. That's not a great role. I have such a great capacity for deflecting. It's so automatic, I'm appalled by it.

Therapist: And yet, here we are talking about it in a very different way. The fact that you are able to reflect upon your patterns, and your frustration with yourself is actually a very good sign. Your frustration is letting both of us know that your strategy of loyal waiting isn't working out so well anymore. It was the only choice you had as a child, but perhaps now, you are seeing other options. Maybe there are new choices before you.

Colin: Like what?

Therapist: Well, you could talk with me about someone you might be interested in as well as what might confuse you, and we could process it in the moment. If you continued to pursue the relationship, you could practice making your voice heard in a way to achieve greater clarity and understanding between you.

Colin: You're making me think about all those times when Marsha would ask to take a break because we had a misunderstanding, and she would say she wanted to think about it. Then when we would come back together, there was no talk or no resolution at all. To me, it felt like taking a break was a way of punishing me. "If I withhold myself from you, you will miss me and appreciate what you had." That's what I like about being single. It's not so damn complicated.

Therapist: Now, I just want to point out that we were talking about your frustration as actually being a sign that your old loyalty position wasn't working for you anymore and maybe there are other options for yourself. Are you telling me that the only other option is to remain single? Do you think that every relationship with a woman needs to be so compromised?

Colin: (pause) I suppose this all goes back to my mother.

Therapist: What makes you say that?

Colin: Oh, my God! She was very complicated. Well, she's not complicated, but I have very complicated feelings about her (pause) protective feelings, sentimental feelings. It disarms me.

Therapist: It disarms you?

Colin: Well, I romanticize that relationship in ways that aren't real.

Therapist: So, tell me how that works.

Colin: (long pause) I don't know if it answers it, but are you familiar with Jane Austin's novel, *Emma*? These characters don't seem to get mired in the complicated aspects of nurturing. They are protective and make right decisions. In other words, their judgment doesn't get clouded. The adults, Mr. Knightley to be exact, had authority in the world, so he could see the potential in Emma. So feelings get attached to the right person, so she can grow into her own potential. So, what happens to me is I don't live up to that model because my protective feelings confuse things.

Therapist: Are you talking about your protective feelings about your mother?

Colin: Yes, I don't live up to the role model of Mr. Knightley.

Therapist: But your mother was the adult in your relationship. Isn't that what we're talking about, that it was your mother who didn't live up to protecting you? It's as if you have flipped the role of who is the parent and who is the child in need of protection.

Colin: Yeah, I need to stay as Mr. Knightley in a relationship.

Therapist: Doesn't that put you right back in a caretaker role? Isn't that how you told me you lose your sense of self? What if you could imagine that you could stay in the role of Emma in a relationship, the person with potential who needs to be encouraged by someone as fair-minded and adult-like as Mr. Knightley?

Colin: Yeah, that's what Kevin, my teacher, did for me. He was like a mentor. He saw my potential but challenged me as well when I started to slack off. It was like in the book. It wasn't just about being applauded. Emma was called up short when she wasn't nice to people. Mr. Knightley told Emma to apologize for treating someone badly. That's it—preparing you for the world, to do right in the world.

Analysis

At the beginning of this session we see Colin reflecting on his prior relationship of ten years. When Colin began therapy, he was still highly protective of this relationship, holding his former partner in a somewhat elevated position. He continued to remain in periodic contact with her for years and would often drop everything to help her out when she called. Colin explained that he was still quite attached to her adolescent son, whom he saw on occasion. He confessed that Marsha used to get him to do favors for her. In this session, however, we see what the product of time spent in conversation about loyal waiting has done to help Colin put this relationship into a more realistic perspective. He no longer regrets his "mistakes" and has also been successful at setting limits with her when she calls.

Having a clearer perspective on this relationship, Colin now reflects on his fears around beginning a new relationship, not wanting to lose himself again. Although he is expressing his fears, it should be noted that this marks an important internal shift, where Colin is able to freely express a desire to preserve his authentic sense of self. The therapist tries to reinforce this shift by offering encouragement, pointing to the fact that by voicing his concern, he is able to recognize potential vulnerabilities within himself. Colin agrees and refers to a discussion from the prior session where his conscious awareness of *process dynamics* is deepening. He can articulate both "seeing and not seeing," thereby recognizing dissociative splits as they are occurring. He attributes these gains in insight to the therapist validating his perceptions and intuitions.

We also see Colin being able to express more of what he would need if he were to enter a healthier relationship, "They would have to encourage me," because he is now able to see how easy it is for him to bury his perceptions.

The therapist provides reassurance around his fears and invites him more actively to process his confusion in the present. After he discloses that he would need a present-day relationship to include some of the attributes of a therapist, perhaps Colin unconsciously needed to create more distance between himself and the therapist in the session at that point. Again we see a swing back to vestiges of all-or-nothing organization. Colin suggests that one solution to his dilemma would be to remain single to avoid the complication. The therapist elects to move away from the potential transferential discomfort, instead repeating her reassurance, observing Colin's gains and offering support to help him work through his confusion. The therapist does not let the reactive solution to stay single remain, however. Instead, she asks if every relationship with a woman needs to be so compromised. Interestingly, it is Colin who now directs the focus back to his mother, without any prompting by the therapist. He then offers his thoughts about why he believes his relationship with his mother is so complicated. He admits that she "disarms" him, and as a result he romanticizes the relationship in ways that aren't real. (Notice the shift in Colin's ability to talk about the real and the idealized version of his hoped-for relationship simultaneously. Here, we see a movement toward further integration.)

Colin uses the Jane Austin novel to illustrate his recognition of the necessary ingredients that would constitute a healthy parent/child relationship. What is *most* interesting here is that in the retelling of the story about Mr. Knightley and Emma, Colin reverses the roles and puts himself in the adult (Mr. Knightley) position and his mother in the child (Emma) position. He concludes that he doesn't live up to the model in this book because his protective feelings for his mother confuse things. What is missed (and here is where the confusion lies) is that his automatic default position is to believe that he must assume the adult role when he imagines being parented by his real mother. She is incapable of assuming the Mr. Knightley role for him.

The therapist is quick to point out this discrepancy and wonders if he could imagine being in any role other than caretaker. Could he imagine being in the Emma role? The session ends with Colin going back to the one adult figure in his life who did demonstrate these qualities, his teacher Kevin.

Discussion

1. What is your sense about how much the patient was able to receive the therapist's offer of help to resolve his fears around not losing his identity in future relationships?

2. How would you explain what occurred at the end of this session?
3. What is your sense about how much the patient was able to internalize the therapist's suggestion of imagining being in any role other than caretaker with a woman in his life? (a) What would the patient have to give up in order to do so? (b) What feelings might need to surface in order for this to happen?
4. How would you describe the shifts around loyalty and loyal waiting that have occurred thus far?

Sixth Session Excerpt (Three Months Later)

Colin: Two phrases came to my mind while I was sleeping. I was thinking about where we left off last week, and I think that's why these two phrases came to mind in a dream. The first one was hearing a voice speaking to me saying, "You know, your psychic make-up is more female than male." The second phrase was my own voice saying, "Think of me as someone who isn't here." My guess is that this has something to do with invisibility or holding in my own feelings.

Therapist: These two phrases came to you in a dream?

Colin: Yes, just last night or early this morning. I think I was semi-conscious. I was imagining myself as a four year old kid. I don't have many memories as a kid, so I'm imagining how I must have been feeling. I do actually remember a memory of being four and standing in the doorway, and adults were saying, "Wow, we need to pay attention to what we say around him. He has an acute memory."

Therapist: Do you think that you had that image in the dream based on that memory and those phrases that came to you?

Colin: I was thinking that I was trying not to be noticed. I was the first born and got a lot of attention, but I'm uncomfortable with it. I remember trying to be like an Indian, breathe shallowly, not to be caught, not to be noticed. I had this sense internally that I was pretty odd—pretty lonely. I didn't go to school with my friends because I was sent to private school. So I was on my own a lot.

Therapist: You described yourself as odd, but when you talked about trying to be an Indian, it sounded like you were describing feeling unsafe at home.

Colin: Yes, there were too many fights, too much violence in the air. It was a feeling thing. Too much shrapnel in the air.

Therapist: Odd, lonely, unsafe. Which do you think came first?

Colin: The oddness came later. One of the first things you picked up on when I started coming here was that I take on all the blame for doing poorly in relationships, that I'm somehow the odd one, the inept one in relationships.

Therapist: Yes, back then I was talking about noticing that you take on all of the responsibility for your relationships going sour. Is that what you mean by feeling odd and lonely?

Colin: I just didn't fit in the same way. I think my home life is what made me feel that way.

Therapist: How so?

Colin: Because it was so chaotic. When I was older, I was ashamed of it. Did I tell you, when I was fourteen the leader of our gang—it wasn't really a gang, it was a group of guys that hung around together—anyway, the leader of the gang said, "If you were a girl, you would be my girlfriend." I knew what he was talking about. I have the ability to be intimate. People confide in me.

Therapist: It strikes me that you are describing positive capacities, the ability for people to confide in you, the capacity for intimacy.

Colin: Well, yes. This is the same point that we were talking about last week. You know, I was sensitive, but these qualities were called selfish; they were detrimental.

Therapist: Detrimental to whom?

Colin: Myself. Maybe everyone else around me was only concerned about self-protection—the gang I hung out with and my family. That's what I mean by odd. I wasn't macho enough. I thought about trying to be, but that would just be playing by other people's rules. I wouldn't be being me.

Therapist: That sounds like you realized it would have put you in a double bind. You had to become tough like them just to fit in, but it really wasn't a part of who you were. That's a pretty tough place to be in as a child. But, I'm a bit confused. How is that related to selfishness?

Colin: Well it isn't, but I wanted to get back to what we were talking about last week.

Therapist: Do you mean when we were talking about how your mother used that term, when she called you selfish when you challenged the status quo in any way?

Colin: Yes. You know, when I left last week I was thinking about various times I've been called selfish. But you know, maybe I wasn't really selfish.

Maybe everyone else was being selfish by calling me selfish. Maybe I was taking care of myself. (pause) Like my mother, maybe *she* was selfish.

Therapist: Go on.

Colin: I know where you're trying to go with this. You're trying to get me to feel. I don't want to feel it. It's a way of protecting myself.

Therapist: And, it's protecting you how?

Colin: I think it keeps me from remembering what happened because it's too painful—so I had to change it, which means distorting reality, and that's probably what led me to feel odd. It's probably not odd at all. We're all odd when you think about it. I think it was different when my grandmother was alive. I would go there, and it was safe. I felt special then. That all changed when she died. I was only eleven or twelve. It reminds me of my mother almost dying in child birth with my youngest sister. I bet I picked up on that and was afraid, especially after I experienced losing my grandmother.

Therapist: Is that why you feel protective of your mother?

Colin: Yes, and no. She trusts me.

Therapist: Is that why it's difficult for you to feel any of your feelings when you think about her calling you selfish?

Colin: (pause) Well, then (pause). Okay, I'll tell you something I don't think I've shared with you. About three years ago, when I was visiting my mom in Wales, I got really, really sick. She didn't take care of me. She let me stay in the other room and die. That's what it felt like. I would have taken care of her if she were that sick. I was really sick.

Therapist: Didn't she even check in on you?

Colin: You would have thought so. A normal person would have checked in at least once a day. But, she didn't. Not even once in three days.

Therapist: As you tell me about this, do any feelings come up right now?

Colin: No. I understand she's just through with mothering. I don't blame her. I could see that she might be done after having raised six kids with no help.

Therapist: Yes, I understand that you are trying to be fair, to keep your compassion present in our conversation right now. I'm not trying to get you to give that up, to become macho/not yourself. But you were really sick, even worried about dying. (long pause) Even under these urgent circumstances, you seem to protect her, explaining that what she did had a logical explanation.

Colin: She's my mother, after all.

Therapist: Yes, and you were in need of real care. Does all caring for a child stop at a certain age? Even if that adult child is so sick that he thinks he might be dying?

Colin: Well, that's her way of being odd.

Therapist: So, your way of being odd is to be sensitive, a caretaker of others, and her way of being odd is to neglect her children when they're sick?

Colin: She's done with that now. She says, "You're grown now, take care of yourself."

Therapist: Even when you're sick and you can't get out of bed for three days?

Colin: No, it's just her way of being odd. (long pause) Is she so wrapped up in herself? I can't imagine it.

Therapist: (pause, then quietly and gently) But, isn't that the reality of what you just disclosed to me?

Colin: No, that's just the way she is odd, like me. We're all odd in my family in our own ways.

Therapist: It's interesting that you're using the same word to describe members of your family, even though the behaviors are very different. What do you make of that?

Colin: Well, what do you make of it (laughs)? My oddness had to do with my sense that I wasn't like others, that I didn't belong because I wasn't a man's man.

Therapist: Again, you're describing a strength you have as being problematic, not fitting in.

Colin: Well, I didn't say it was a good thing. But, sometimes you just want to be one of the gang.

Therapist: Sounds pretty lonely.

Colin: You have no idea.

Therapist: Why don't we pause for a few seconds and take a moment to reflect on what's happened in here today.

Colin: Well, I put out more about who she really is. I suppose it's different when you put together all the facts at once.

Therapist: How so?

Colin: Cumulative facts are more forceful. I guess I can see that more of me is disappointed in her.

Therapist: So, *there* is a feeling you have on your own behalf. And when you said that just now, do you feel that you have been disloyal?

Colin: No. (In a quiet, subdued voice) No, not so much anymore. I feel a bit of relief, if you want to know the truth. I finally let myself say what must have been in there for so many years. Oh, my God. (Begins to cry for the first time)

Analysis

In this our final excerpt of this series, we see Colin able to access further memories from childhood (his early childhood memories had been virtually absent to this point). Two phrases came to him in a dream, both revealing a struggle he had with assuming his true identity. He also remembers being uncomfortable with the attention he received as the first born, trying not to be noticed, trying to breathe like an Indian. He describes an internalized sense of who he was as being odd, lonely, and on his own.

The therapist comments on the self-description of being odd and isolated and reframes these words as conditions that describe a lack of safety. Colin agrees and gives more detailed information. When the therapist repeats the words, odd, lonely, unsafe and asks which came first, she is trying to help the patient make a connection to his negative self-description, pointing out that it is an attempt to attenuate feelings around his childhood deprivation and lack of safety. Colin picks up on this immediately saying, "The oddness came later." He then remembers that the therapist had pointed this out early on in the treatment. He is now able to see that his pattern of taking all of the responsibility for things going wrong in relationships stems from what he had to compensate for in his family of origin.

This is the first time that Colin is able to admit feelings of shame directly—for being born into his family, for being ashamed of his capacity to feel intimacy, and for people confiding in him. From where he came these feelings were called "odd"—more female than male. Working with Colin's disclosure of shame, the therapist reframes this as evidence of his health and the strength. Colin is able to see this, even agree, but reflects that nevertheless, where he comes from, he was viewed as odd and selfish. He had to play by other people's rules, be macho and insensitive. However, this also puts him in a double bind because he realizes he would be forsaking his true self if he did so. As the therapist affirms the double bind, she also directs him back to his primary relationship with his mother. Apparently, Colin had been doing quite a bit of reflection over the past several months and was finally able to state that maybe he wasn't the selfish one; he was just being real and it was other people who were being selfish when they tried to quiet his voice. He then admits with more conscious conviction that maybe his mother *was* selfish after all.

This is a profound admission, one that shifts the loyalty contract in the direction of self-preservation and toward a new version of loyalty that includes both the positives and the down-side of his early home environment. When the therapist asks him to go on, Colin backs away from the feelings behind what he had just revealed. Very clearly, he tells her, "I don't want to feel it. It's a way of protecting myself." As we examine the dialogue at this juncture, perhaps, it would have been better if the therapist paused and noticed Colin's admission—that he realized that his mother was indeed selfish. In doing so she could have underscored the break in the absolute tie of the old loyalty contract, allowing more time for Colin to metabolize the present moment.

All is not lost, however. The therapist's next move is to direct Colin back to his feelings of protectiveness of his mother and wonders if this is why he has trouble getting in touch with his own feelings. It is then that Colin reveals a piece of information about his mother that he has kept from the treatment for over a year. He tells of an incident where his mother failed to offer any care for him when he was very ill. After this admission Colin tries to recover his protective stance of his mother and a portion of his loyalty, telling the therapist that he doesn't blame his mother; he could see that she was done with mothering.

In the next series of exchanges the therapist presses more directly, challenging Colin's defense. But first she links his response to his concern around not losing his compassion, that part of his authenticity. She tells Colin that by talking about this she is not asking him to become macho or anything other than himself. (She is essentially saying, "I won't do to you what others have done"). Then, she directs Colin back to his need to protect his mother, even in these extreme circumstances of neglect. Colin's loyalty statement, "She's my mother, after all," is countered by the therapist's response, which attempts to anchor them both in the reality of what true compassion should look like—taking care of someone when they were so sick that they fear dying. The dialogue continues with a bit of a struggle between them around the old loyalty and Colin's right to have his legitimate needs and expectations of others met.

Sensing this struggle, the therapist asks that they both pause and reflect on what has just occurred. This pause breaks the struggle, and Colin is able to admit that he shared more of the complete picture. Having said this he is able to see the force behind connecting the parts into a reality-based whole. It is at this point that the patient is able to feel his disappointment in a pure form, without the need to move back into a position of loyal protection of his mother. It is also at this point that he is able to feel the relief and begins to cry.

Discussion

The culmination of this session results in Colin revealing that the old loyalty contract has worn thin. By sharing the recent story of his illness back in Wales, he is offering proof positive that there is no way that his mother will ever be able to meet his needs, even on his death bed. If his needs exist and he claims a right to them, he will have to feel the disappointment he has been trying to protect himself from admitting all of these years. The unfolding details of this case hopefully have given the reader a better sense of the complexity of rich relational detail that can be harvested when we enter the territory of loyal waiting.

Case Review Questions

1. What function did loyal waiting serve in terms of actually preserving the patient's sense of authenticity?
2. Discuss the relationship between loyal waiting and the rigid construction of black and white thinking that we find in dissociative or vertical splitting.
3. How do you think the construction of the protective stance of loyal waiting protects any number of patients from feelings of shame?

SUMMARY

As with all configurations of loyal waiting, Quadrant Three takes on a more entrenched position when feelings of shame and an underlying sense of betrayal are being defended against. Here the idealized other is paired or fused with an overidealized self-image (Quadrant One). In this case Colin only allowed himself the "right" to use his insights and his capacities in the service of exposing the superficiality of the upper class, while maintaining his sense of loyalty to his blue collar identity. In this way he can use his intelligence without feeling caught in an act of his own betrayal to old family loyalties. This is the underlying dilemma of a child of a narcissistic parent—no amount of care-giving will ever be enough because the parent is hell bent to switch positions with the child—to make the child the parent and the parent the child.

No child can withstand that amount of deprivation and come out unscathed. In the earlier parts of this therapy, the idealizations that manifested from Quadrant One took the form of a belief that he should have been able to raise himself. Not only that, he also believes that he should have been able to meet his mother's needs at the same time. Thus, the loyalty contract could remain intact. Anything that fell short of this idealized construction would be considered a failure to the idealized self. Colin tried very hard to succeed in his efforts, but the task is undoable. A child cannot raise himself, let alone raise his mother.

Every loyalty dilemma is a dilemma of a double bind. If the patient really ever changes and identifies outside of his family or changes his position and becomes inclusive of others outside of his class (breaking the absolute standards around loyalty), he is essentially dead to them. In Colin's case he would get written out of the family, ostracized, which would be the ultimate form of punishment. In absolute bonds of blood loyalty, the punishment is always severe. When you combine this with a home environment that is filled with deprivation, isolation, and loneliness, breaking the old loyalty bonds becomes even more difficult.

As we think about the conditions of Colin's upbringing, he has shown an enormous amount of courage and internal fortitude throughout his life as well as within the therapy. In spite of the odds, he was able to hold onto what was most precious to him (his emotional tenderness), to claim a degree of his gifts and talents, and to move to America, an act of separation, where he perhaps unconsciously was lying in wait until the opportunity presented itself to begin the process of recovering his full potential. More is yet to be done before Colin fully consolidates the gains made in treatment thus far, but he is on his way to recovering his authentic self.

CHAPTER 10

Consolidation of Gains

You need not, and in fact cannot, teach an acorn to grow into an oak tree, but when given a chance, its intrinsic potentialities will develop.

—KAREN HORNEY (1950, P. 17)

CONSOLIDATION of a client's therapeutic gains is an integral part of the treatment process. However, since compulsive systems are internally well-integrated and tightly wound, they do not release their grip easily. A compulsive system is quite able to "swallow-up" a therapeutic gain by re-interpreting the breakthrough as a harbinger of all that the compulsive overidealization was designed to ward off.

Each of the pseudo-solutions we have described in this manual has, as we have said, its own witch's brew. The *detached resigned solution* has a horror of "involvement" because the patient unconsciously considers it an invitation to intrusiveness and coercion. The *overattached self-effacing solution* equates healthy self-assertion with willful selfishness. *The self-inflating expansive solution* dreads being made into "a patsy." Each of these characterological solutions is a systemic whole which fights gains as if they were a threat to their existence.

Indeed they are. But once the therapist recognizes the explicit terms of the internal war being waged, the therapist can strive to protect each gain by highlighting and reinforcing the constructive moves as parts of precious "growing pains." The notion of an internal war is central to being able to work successfully in consolidating structural gains. When treatment oscillations occur, the therapist's trust and confidence in the therapeutic process (which means faith in the client's ability to negotiate the process) becomes critical to protecting gains. The therapist marks the gain as one more example of the client's inherent constructive forces being liberated. While neither symptom relief nor recovery of childhood memories qualify as structural characterological gains, symptoms are likely to abate and memories return as the patient begins to relinquish overidealized illusions which are draining the client's inherent inner resources supporting growth.

The reader will note that we have made a sharp distinction between health and illness. For consolidating gains, it is an especially important distinction. The distinction is always important, but self-realizing is an entirely different process from self-idealizing (Horney, 1950). We are born with the capacity for the former. We only develop the coping strategy of self-idealization in an attempt to ward off fears and anxieties born out of interpersonal misalignments in our formative years. One could say that psychotherapy picks up at the point where our self-development became stunted due to insufficient parental attunement to our growth needs.

Terms such as "good" narcissism vs. "bad" narcissism betray a misunderstanding of character structure as well as a misunderstanding of compulsivity, and are misleading to the practicing therapist. With such facile terms, the basic struggle in psychotherapy for systemic self-change can become obscured or even undermined in the therapist's mind, allowing understanding of health to become prone to varying prevailing cultural fads and fashions. Narcissism cannot be narcissism unless it is compulsively driven, perfectionistic, and overidealized which means that it is at war with the client's autonomous needs to grow. Unless negotiating the conflict between realizing and idealizing can be seen as the fundamental goal of dynamic psychotherapy, the movement toward health, including each individual client gain, can get disengaged from the struggle.

Consolidation of gains, therefore, requires a somewhat different posture from the therapist. Instead of listening just for part-whole completions of a characterological whole, we focus "listening energy" on identifying and supporting often nascent constructive signs in the intersubjective space, in growing intrapsychic capacities, in evolving interpersonal relations, and in dream representations of health. The following is a case example where the patient begins to sense some changes in the way she is processing memories and feelings. Notice how she unconsciously or reflexively turns a sign of progress into a negative judgment about herself. Notice also, how the therapist handles this exchange.

Early Signs of Emerging Authenticity

Caroline: I went back to the Big Book Step Study and am redoing my "resentments." It's funny but as I read what I wrote the first time, I realized that I skimmed over the surface of things.

Therapist: What do you mean?

Caroline: I didn't name anything specific. In the first iteration I wrote down all of my resentments of my sister and husband, Peter. With my sister, I wrote that I resented that she was my father's favorite. But I neglected to add that she was competitive with me and undermined me in front of Dad. I know that she did it to paint herself in a favorable light. And when it comes to Peter, he didn't pay enough attention to me, or he seemed to care more about his own interests than mine, not to mention that I didn't think he always told me the truth. Now, when I went back and filled in more of the specific details, I am writing that I resent Peter because he didn't care enough about me to even show up for my poetry award at the national conference. My parents came, my kids came, but he had a board meeting to go to that he said was more important. When I connected my resentment of not being cared for to his specific behavior, it really made a difference. Or when I filled in the details about suspecting that my husband wasn't always truthful, I now let the reality sink in that my husband kept a lot of things hidden from me. Looking back, I caught him in several white lies. I knew that down deep I never felt I could trust him. It's amazing how much more powerful these statements are when you fill in the specifics.

Therapist: So you are saying that something has shifted in you.

Caroline: Well, I'm feeling my resentments now, rather than treating all of this as an intellectual exercise. It's so much more intense. You know, I don't think I could have handled looking at the whole truth this directly a couple of years ago. I think that my feelings would have overwhelmed me. That's been my problem, hasn't it? I avoided things and just pretended to believe what I wanted to believe, that we had a happy marriage because my husband was so charming and everyone loved him. He was charming alright, but he kept a big part of himself hidden, like he had a secret life almost. And I played right into it. I never questioned him, and he was a master at avoiding getting caught.

Therapist: So, how are you feeling about all of that now?

Caroline: I feel like a stupid jerk.

Therapist: You just made some connections on a feeling level. This is important, something new for you. Then, I see how you very quickly use the insights you've gained in therapy to look back over your life and beat yourself up? How is that fair to yourself and all of your effort? Don't you think that this might be just another way of avoiding looking at the truth about what you are seeing about your husband?

Caroline: Yes, I know, and I do have a tendency to err on the side of giving other people the benefit of the doubt to the point that I block out anything unpleasant or uncomfortable that I don't want to confront. The problem is that I'm terribly afraid of offending anyone. I want everyone to like me; I never want to hurt anybody's feelings.

Therapist: So you think that if you speak the truth and that truth shines an unfavorable light on people, they will become angry?

Caroline: Yes. I'm afraid if I do, then people would leave me. The thought of it makes me panicky, and I start to shut down.

Therapist: I'm remembering something right now, something that you told me several months ago. Didn't you say that you had never lived alone in your adult life? You went straight from your parents' home into a marriage, and shortly after that you had three children. Maybe, you've never really had a chance to get to know who you are as a real person.

Caroline: Oh, I'm terrified of that. I always need a circle of people around me to tell me who I am, to give me definition.

Therapist: What happens when you imagine not getting that feedback from others?

Caroline: I feel like I'd come unglued. I would become a jelly fish, some sort of undifferentiated mass.

Therapist: You would lose your sense of self?

Caroline: Yes, that feeling of becoming like a jellyfish has happened to me a couple of times in my life. It was terrifying, and I didn't know how to make sense of it. That's why I always need a circle of influence around me. That's why I'm afraid to leave this job even though I hate it. I need the feedback and structure to give me a sense of purpose. That's why I work so hard to please everybody and to get them to like me. (pause, and then in a very quiet voice) And yet, at the core I know that there is something else that is there that is me. At least, I'm coming to recognize that there is something solid at the core of me.

Therapist: Yes. Do you think you could tell me in words what is at the core of the real you?

Caroline: I'm not sure I can. Nobody's ever asked me to do that.

Therapist: Go ahead, give it a try.

Caroline: Well, I think that at the core, I am decent and kind. Even though I work hard to please other people, I also think that these words describe something about who I really am at the core, whether I had to please other people or not.

Therapist: I think so too. Do you want to know what I see? I have noticed that you have a way of seeing and remembering an incredible amount of the details of a situation, and then you are able to synthesize all of that information and describe it in a very articulate way. That's a pretty great skill set to have. This is a part of what I see as your core strength.

Caroline: Yes, I've been told that by other people before. I guess it is true. I got that feedback in grad school a lot.

Therapist: So, you can recognize that and believe that about yourself. Is there more that you can tell me about the core of who you are?

Caroline: I think that I am acutely aware of the pain and suffering of the world. I think that I feel it more than most people do. It's more difficult for me to shut the awareness of suffering down. It's overwhelming sometimes. But then, if I'm so aware, why don't I do something to help the suffering people of the world. Okay, it's overwhelming, so what do I do? I do nothing. I freeze up, and then I crawl back into my comfortable secure world.

Therapist: Now, I heard the first part of what you said as a description of what's at your core. But the second part of what you were describing sounded more like you were remembering a strategy that you used, something from the distant past. It reminded me of something that a child might have been told by a parent. Sometimes parents who are depressed or self-absorbed put pressure on children to fix them or fill their adult void or take care of their needs. Because you were so sensitive, maybe this felt like pressure. We know that your mother needed you to take care of her needs, and your father was absent all too frequently.

Caroline: But, I still could be doing more today, and I'm not.

Therapist: That's a pretty big weight you're putting on your shoulders. Where do you think the weight of that expectation comes from?

Caroline: I don't know. I guess I'm too hard on myself.

Therapist: Do you think it might be possible that a long time ago you were given a set of expectations that was too great for a child to bear? Do you secretly still harbor a belief that you should be able to do the impossible?

Caroline: Of course I do, but I'm getting so tired of it. It makes me angry. I'm tired of having to be so careful. It's my turn to live my life now.

Therapist: And one of the ways that can happen is by staying focused on what's at the core of who you are. You don't have to jump into doing something or critique yourself for not taking action immediately. We have time to talk about all of this, let it unfold. If you slow the process down just a little bit, it might help you to become more curious and reflective. And as you just demonstrated, you easily began to identify core pieces of yourself. Maybe that's how you learn how not to turn into a jellyfish.

Caroline: (smiling)

Therapist: What's the smile about?

Caroline: I'm not sure. Perhaps we've just turned a corner. I feel as if I've just opened a new door, a way of being in conversation with someone where I can take the time to just talk about who I am without feeling pressured to do something.

This case example occurred fairly early in the treatment process, and clearly there is more work to be done. Even at this early stage, however, we are able to see how the patient is beginning to make connections on a feeling level. By including more detail about the reality of what occurred to her in her marriage, she is momentarily able to burst the bubble of overidealization. However, her anxiety around the fear of the loss of connection reflexively throws her back into her old way of organizing her sense of self-in-relationship. She must be the one at fault; she must take back full responsibility for any failures in the relationship. In this case she experienced the insights around her husband's lying as something that was shameful—she should have confronted him earlier. She shouldn't have let herself get "duped." When the therapist stops her for calling herself a jerk, she is attempting to soften the overdetermined standards in Quadrant One.

By slowing the process down the therapist is able to point out that this self-blame can be a distraction, one that might lead her away from the very insights she had had about her husband in the session. There is a readiness within the patient to hear the therapist's caution. The patient is then able to admit that she has a tendency to give others more of a break than she gives herself. This allows the therapist to connect various pieces of information from her past in the service of consolidating potential gains. The therapist remembers that she never had a chance to separate from her family of origin and consolidate a firm sense of self on her own. Instead, she moved from her parents into a marriage at the age of twenty. Again, we see the underlying fear around being alone or abandoned without a firm foundation of a sense of self. And yet, we also see that the patient is able to admit that she is becoming aware of a solid core within her, an awareness that was buried prior to entering therapy. Here the therapist works with helping the patient express some of those core aspects of herself, thus encouraging the strengthening and consolidation of the patient's growing sense of authenticity.

The reader can see that the principles that guide the consolidation of gains are the same principles that have guided us in identifying compulsively driven character trends. What is compulsive and what is not compulsive? What is health and what is not health? As the treatment progresses, the focus of the therapist gradually shifts from assiduously undoing non-health to assiduously supporting emerging health.

The remainder of this chapter will be dedicated to helping the reader identify entry points that actually lead to opportunities for consolidation of new ways of thinking and behaving. In the following case examples, note that an experience-near immersion in the patient's struggle allows the patient to feel the growing wholehearted alliance between the therapist and the patient's endangered self. The patient grasps more deeply that this is a fundamental alliance fueling the therapeutic acceptance that "each time the patient understands the meaning of a relapse, he comes out of it stronger than before" (Cantor, 1967, p. 199).

CASE EXAMPLE ONE

Case Example One is a vignette that will be presented in two parts. In the first vignette Dr. Kate, one of our trainees, presents to the group a case which she believes has come to a stand-still. Dr. Kate expressed concern that her patient would leave treatment, just as she had done with two previous therapists. The case presentation begins with a brief overview of identifying information and presenting patterns thus far in the treatment. This is followed by actual dialogue between the two of us and Dr. Kate. An analysis of the supervisory exchange will follow at the end of "Part One" and "Part Two" of the case vignette.

Part One

Presenting Patterns

Hannah is a single forty-seven year old woman whose presenting problems are "low self-esteem" and relationship difficulties. The specific precipitant that brought her into therapy with Dr. Kate five years ago was difficulties at work. At that time the patient explained that she had begun to feel underappreciated in a position that she had been in for five years. Apparently, due to changes in management, the patient was assigned to a new boss, and her work-related discomfort began shortly thereafter. Hannah had a good working relationship with her old boss and wasn't pleased about her reassignment. Dr. Kate made attempts at encouraging her to try to work through her feelings around this transition, but Hannah abruptly decided it was time for her to leave her job. She later admitted to Dr. Kate that she rarely stayed in any job position for more than five years as she either lost interest or she got bored because the position was no longer challenging.

Now, five years later, Hannah is employed at a major high tech firm, where she single-handedly walked the staff through a major reorganization. The consultant who had worked with the firm told the CEO that if it weren't for Hannah's persistence and vision, this organizational transformation would not have been able to happen. Hannah's own reaction to this positive feedback, according to Dr. Kate, was that neither the feedback she had received nor her own sense of accomplishment carried any weight in terms of altering Hannah's sense of her job satisfaction.

Instead, Hannah declared that she was at another turning point in terms of her work and had been thinking of leaving this job as well. When pressed as to why, she responded that she didn't trust that the newly hired staff were really on board or supported her efforts. Given this pattern of relational disappointment at work over two job rotations, we can surmise that Hannah evidences a marked split between her actual level of professional achievement and her "sense" of her own accomplishments.

Historical Information

Hannah's family history includes a brother who is a year younger, and three step-siblings. She is very close to her brother but quite detached from her siblings in the new step-family. Her parents divorced when she was four years old, and the patient's mother became quite controlling, critical, and overly enmeshed. Mother blamed the patient for father leaving and also told the daughter that it was up to her to get the father back. For years Hannah made every effort to get her father to come back, and was actually successful for a brief period of time. However, after a brief reconciliation, father left the mother permanently.

After leaving for the second time, Hannah's father eventually started a new family and did not remain in touch with Hannah for nearly two decades. It was only by happenstance that the patient later met up with him in a grocery store only to discover that she has three half-siblings all ten to fifteen years younger than she. At present she is in contact with her father and his family, but describes it as an unfulfilling relationship, stating that he is cold and distant. She has little in common with her half-siblings, although her step-mother makes overtures to try to get closer to the patient. The step-mother appears to be overly needy, according to the patient, and tries to confide in her.

Hannah's relationship with her own mother is described as "unloving and quite critical," both in childhood and in the present. Although her mother pushed Hannah to succeed academically and socially, she was never satisfied with her daughter's accomplishments, despite Hannah's history of academic and professional success. Mother's critical and demeaning/demoralizing voice around Hannah's many accomplishments over the years has had quite a debilitating effect on her sense of self-worth. Dr. Kate notes, however, that when the mother talks to others, she boasts about her daughter's accomplishments, as if she were claiming them as her own.

Hannah's present and past relationship history has been remarkably unfulfilling. She has very few close female friends and regarded herself as a loner in high school and college. In terms of intimate relationships, this patient has never been married but does use Internet dating services with quite a bit of success. She is an attractive woman and gets a number of dating opportunities through this means. However, no relationship seems to last for more than a few months. The patient seems somewhat frustrated with this, complains of being lonely, but rarely wishes to spend much time in therapy talking about her present relationship challenges and disappointments. Instead, the primary focus of the therapy is on work and family of origin issues.

Group Consultation

Dr. Kate begins this consultation session by informing us that Hannah had just announced that she "felt stuck" in the therapy. Although she had talked about many important issues over the course of her treatment, essentially she felt that her life was still the same. She wasn't happy with work, and she did not feel close to any member of her family other than her brother. Dr. Kate confessed to us that she was feeling stuck in the treatment as well.

When we asked about recent events that may have triggered this comment to her therapist, Dr. Kate reported that her mother had just left from a recent visit, leaving the patient frustrated because the mother had overstayed her welcome. We asked Dr. Kate if she had been able to talk with the patient about why she had let the mother stay for two weeks when she had initially tried to set a limit of staying for only three days. Dr. Kate reported that the patient essentially states that it does no good trying to talk to her mother. The mother always inserts herself and somehow gets her own way.

We begin this consultation with our questions to Dr. Kate.

Jack: Have you ever tried role playing the conversation with this patient between the mother and daughter? What do you think about the idea of role playing possible dialogue scenarios? Have you ever done anything like that?

Dr. Kate: No, I haven't. What were you thinking of?

Jack: Well, what do you think about the idea of having her role play herself and you become the mother, to get a clearer sense of how she actually responds to the communication exchange, where she gets overwhelmed. It might be important to understand better what puts an end to the conversation?

Dr. Kate: I would be afraid of overwhelming her in a role play situation. I'm afraid that I would risk having her identify me too much with her mother.

Patricia: One of the things that I sometimes do to mitigate the risk of too much intensity is to ask the patient to go through as much of the actual dialogue between (in this case) your patient and her mother as it actually happened in the present. But I ask the person to try to replay what she *remembers* about the incident in the past tense.

Then, I ask the patient to imagine that we would be able to go back and replay the conversation. In this instance I might invite the patient to role play the mother, and I would role play the patient. In my part of the role play, I would intentionally add new dialogue that is a bit more assertive or self-advocating. During these exchanges I essentially try to push the envelope by giving a voice to what it might sound like to challenge the mother more directly. This is a way of giving the patient indirect permission as well as modeling other choices (and potential outcomes) around the habituated interaction between them. Sometimes this type of role play interaction can help to penetrate the patient's hopelessness or despair by demonstrating that the mother isn't quite as powerful as the daughter assumes.

Jack: Yes, that might be a good way to start, perhaps a way that the patient could tolerate the potential breakthrough of affect a bit better. Eventually, you could assume the role of the mother, or parenthetically say out loud what the mother might be thinking or trying to convey through tone—giving voice to the unspoken dynamic of parental control. For example, you could say out loud, "You need to listen to me and remain subservient to me." Or you could articulate something about the relational dynamics of competition and the taboo of the daughter ever being allowed to surpass mother. You could articulate what has remained unspoken between them as a means of talking about the covert rules within this family system.

Patricia: Yes, this would mitigate any fear you might have about the daughter confusing you with her mother. In a sense you are saying it's okay to speak the unspeakable, and also to challenge the old rules of engagement.

Jack: What we're saying, Dr. Kate, is that we need to find a way of penetrating the emerging surface of the negative transference. Giving language to the frustrations that the patient is feeling toward the mother is a way to do that. Otherwise, the mother remains protected and you become the target of the frustration through the negative transferential feelings.

Patricia: The phrase that keeps coming to my mind is *suffering in silence*. Could you find a way to introduce that into the session as a way of giving her permission to begin speaking about negative feelings and frustrations in general?

Jack: Yes, that's good. It creates an opening to bring something into consciousness that is central to the unspoken dynamic between them. It also gives language to something that heretofore has remained invisible.

Dr. Kate: I see what you're saying. I *could* give language to the unspoken. I like what the term *suffering in silence* telegraphs. It conveys my empathy and my awareness that there might be material under the surface that she's afraid to bring up in the office. Maybe, I'll use it as an entry point—to imagine with her what she might say, or at the very least what she might be thinking but is editing out.

Patricia: Another angle from which to approach this material is to focus on how the patient feels when she receives positive feedback from someone. You said that when she reports her positive accomplishments, it has had no impact on her. Could you wonder with her if she has to remain silent about this as well?

Dr. Kate: Yes, she does seem to minimize herself by saying that what she recently did at work was something anyone could do.

Jack: This is where you could use phenomenological tracking to get her to focus on what was said, how she felt about what was said in the moment.

Dr. Kate: What should I ask her?

Jack: You could ask her questions such as, "Did you believe what people were saying about you to be true? Did you think they were exaggerating? Could you trust what they were saying? Did you think they had a hidden agenda?" Questions like that can act as prompts, to get her to increase her conscious awareness of what she is thinking or feeling in the moment about other people's feedback. I suspect she tunes much of it out. You could also ask questions that are directed more toward her internal feeling state—such as, "Did the praise make you feel uncomfortable?"

Dr. Kate: She does say that she feels guilty when she receives too much positive feedback.

Patricia: And that's how we can direct it back to the mother again—the dynamic between them around competition and accomplishment. As a follow-up you could ask her what happens if she feels that she stands out too much.

Jack: You could also direct the dialogue toward a transferential question. For example, you might ask "Have you ever felt uncomfortable with me when I have given you praise?" Or "Have you ever felt uncomfortable relying on me in any way?"

Dr. Kate: I don't think she's at a point of feeling like she's relying on me. She's telling me that she feels stuck, and I'm afraid she's about ready to drop out of treatment.

Patricia: Well yes, she's right on target. She's been seeing you for five years.

Dr. Kate: Laughing, "Oh my. I can't believe I didn't see that connection."

Jack: Does it ever feel to you that your patient is registering frustration with her therapy or with you during an actual session?

Dr. Kate: Not directly, but indirectly. I guess I feel I should be able to do more.

Jack: You know, negative transference rumblings aren't necessarily a bad thing. It can actually be seen as a breakthrough. She trusts you enough to begin to have the courage to complain. In other words doing more in this case might mean that you are able to finesse a gain by working *with* the negative transference feelings as they present themselves within the session. It's an opening for the two of you to talk about what it feels like to be stuck. For the patient, more than likely she only sees her own failure, but she is unable to show these "shameful" feelings to you. It moves the two of you into a conversation about what constitutes trust between two people.

Dr. Kate: Right, it helps to see the positive in the negative.

Jack: Yes, and in this instance how do you think it could help?

Dr. Kate: Well for starters, it might open up the topic of shame, and Hannah has huge amounts of shame. If she began talking about her own sense of failure and how her perceptions around failure make her feel, maybe it would take some of the pressure off of her need to perform.

Jack: And having that conversation was something she could never do with her mother.

Dr. Kate: Yes, I can see how that would open up a big avenue for conversation. (smiling) Suddenly I don't feel quite so stuck with her.

Patricia: If you think about it, there are many entry points for dialogue in terms of her performance expectations. For instance, this could lead to the two of you talking about: what would happen if she didn't have to be upbeat all the time, challenging her mother's assumption around "people don't like it if you are depressed."

Or you could ask her what she might devote her energy toward if she weren't worried about how she came across to others. In other words, it gives you an opportunity to change gears in terms of how you talk about what she is reporting. It frees both of you up to not remain fixated on her hopelessness and the paralyzing shame she feels about ever breaking free of her performance standards.

Jack: This in turn would allow you to support her around challenging some of mother's expectations in all sorts of areas. Just out of curiosity, does she ever tell you that she shuts down or becomes frightened about confronting her mother?

Patricia: Or, does she ever talk with you about *wishing* that she could speak to her mother directly about her feelings of anger or shame?

Dr. Kate: No, she doesn't speak up. She either acquiesces or she acts out in ways that are more avoidant.

Patricia: What do you mean?

Dr. Kate: Well, last Christmas, her brother invited her to come to spend time with his family and her nieces. But, her mother also wanted her to spend Christmas with her. Rather than choose to see her brother (and his family) which she loves to do, she chose her own solution that both avoided a direct challenge of her mother and allowed some distance. Instead of spending time with any of her family members, she spent Christmas by herself at a ski resort.

Jack: Has she ever told her mother why she stays away?

Dr. Kate: No.

Jack: Has she ever been able to relate it to her mother's toxic expectations of her?

Dr. Kate: She stays away from her mother because she knows it always makes her feel badly about herself.

Jack: Ah-ha! There you have it. You have another entry point to talk about disappointment and how she protects her mother by swallowing her own negative feelings. The result is that she feels badly about herself, but it temporarily resolves the loyalty bind with her mother.

Dr. Kate: Yes, but she's also thumbing her nose at her mother because she didn't spend the time with her either, don't you think?

Patricia: Yes, here is how we see the loyalty conflict play itself out in terms of the dual expression of maintaining Quadrants Three and Four. She remains loyal to mother by not choosing a different family member (brother), but she can express her anger at her mother through a more passive form of revenge: going to the ski resort. She can do this all without any direct verbal confrontation of her mother at all. So, she is able to maintain the old homeostatic balance of her loyalty to mother and her own feelings of rage simultaneously. The resourcefulness of the psyche is amazing. Here we see how the old organizing schemas allow her to avoid challenging her mother directly, but she does manage to get even.

Jack: Yes, this is how we can recognize the enactment of the loyalty conflict between the quadrants. Our next move is to try to give language to this dynamic struggle within the therapy. Once we begin to inquire about the dilemma about how she makes choices, we begin to uncover the patient's struggle around loyalty, fear of losing mother, and being annihilated by mother all at the same time.

Analysis of This Session

In this session Jack primarily focused on the emerging negative transferential material as an important turning point of the therapy. The patient has allowed herself to express to the therapist that she is dissatisfied with the progress she is making in the therapy and in her life. Patricia then highlighted what happens when the patient's expectations for change don't get met, and she reverts to her old pattern of distancing every five years. However, in this case example, rather than acting out her disappointment, there is an opportunity to explore her negative feelings verbally and more directly. She does not need to "suffer in silence," and then leave.

Understanding the emergence of negative transference as a sign of therapeutic progress is often confusing as well as counter-intuitive. At best, the affective resonance in the room creates a bit of cognitive dissonance for most therapists. Unconsciously or perhaps subtly, we may inadvertently work to avoid (or at least mitigate) the disappointment and discomfort that is beginning to emerge. When negative transference is viewed as opportunity, however, it allows us to tolerate our own social discomfort. In turn this offers us more direct access to the patient's feelings of shame, disappointment, or expectations around performance.

In doing so, we are able to expand the conversation to learn more about buried feelings and memories. We are also sending a non-verbal signal to the client that it is okay to express feelings that were once taboo or not tolerated by parental figures. This is one way that we can begin to work with old patterns of loyalty. By breaking the rule of *suffering in silence,* we thus allow for the consolidation of gains around the patient's very real accomplishments. And by working with the loyalty dilemma on a transferential level, we are able to help the patient take ownership of her authenticity and mastery.

As noted, it may feel counter-intuitive to think that episodes of negative transference can lead to the consolidation of gains. However, in this case, by focusing directly on Hannah's worst transferential fears about the effectiveness of treatment, Hannah and her therapist have the opportunity to further consolidate the treatment alliance. If the therapist fails to acknowledge the negative transference reactions and does not invite the patient to explore her feelings more fully, she runs the risk that these feelings will remain under the surface. This in turn can lead to further enactments of the patient's negatively charged testing of the therapist, eventually leading to further distancing and possible termination of treatment.

In this session Hannah's old pattern of her loyalty dilemma is expressed through her discouragement about ever feeling better, including a loss of hope that "understanding" can change anything. Although this is a breakthrough of sorts, the patient's articulation of her frustration is not enough to turn the negative transference into an opportunity for joint curiosity and exploration. Without slowing down the dialogue, asking for more details around the disappointment, reflecting back what we hear and understand about the patient's frustration, the therapeutic opportunity could be lost. In other words, it is up to the therapist to frame the disappointment in a way that invites the patient to speak further, both as a way of assuaging anxiety for speaking up in the first place, and to lessen the risk of further entrenchment of negative affective reenactments.

If this opportunity is lost or if the therapist becomes confused, defensive, or overly accommodating, the potential negative transference breakthrough can deteriorate into an eventual therapeutic rupture resulting in the client leaving therapy and acting out once again her old pattern of distancing. The real therapeutic leverage occurs when we find ways to explore the patient's expectations and wishes more consciously and verbally. This in turn can gradually open the door to exploring what she does when those unspoken wishes remain unfulfilled.

With reference to the Four Quadrant Model the first part of this clinical example focuses on the interplay between the dynamic tension played out between Quadrant Three (unconscious/syntonic) and Quadrant Four (unconscious/dystonic). Addressing the homeostatic balance between these two quadrants must occur before a consolidation of the patient's authentic talents and accomplishments can unfold. Up to this point in the treatment the patient has been patiently and loyally waiting for the therapist to "do something" to change her life, and when that doesn't happen, her loyal waiting begins to wear thin. The dynamic tension would be resolved by playing out her disappointment through an act of revenge, expressed through ending the therapy. Palpating the negative transference is a way of giving permission to voice impermissible feelings and wishes around disappointment, thus, creating an alternative avenue for expressing her feelings of frustration.

This is a two-fold endeavor. The therapist first invites curiosity and encouragement by asking the patient to talk about what she expected to happen or hoped would happen. Second, the therapist can invite the patient to explore what thoughts or feelings come up when hopes are dashed. In addition the therapist can work with the patient to help her distinguish between her disappointment about herself and "performance" in therapy and her disappointment with the therapist.

With this differentiation, the therapeutic dialogue is allowed to shift in the direction of transferential experience and communication. By raising the idea with Hannah of articulating her disappointment aloud, the therapist is telegraphing to the patient her permission about where the therapy is allowed to go. This is a necessary step in preparation for the patient to become ready to articulate how her own performance standards are directly connected to her mother's criticisms. By opening the door to exploring how the patient's high expectations are connected to her inability to please or satisfy her mother, the pressure that has been building around negative transference has a high likelihood of diminishing. In cases where there is a history of a client failing to meet performance standards, the pressure to *do something* is subliminally contagious. As we see Dr. Kate had begun to feel badly that she had not been able to make the patient feel better. However, by learning to palpate the emerging negative transferential material, Dr. Kate can turn these comments into a therapeutic advantage.

In preparation for reading the second half of this case scenario, we have provided a list of potential areas that would move the case toward further degrees of integration of the various parts with the whole. Some anticipated areas for exploration in the following weeks and months are likely to be as follows:

1. The therapist can work with the patient toward being able to see how the relationship between her drive for success is connected to both her harsh standards and her oversensitivity to slights. Building on this connection, the therapist can then direct the patient to the similarity between her own harshness and the mother's devaluing of her accomplishments. Ideally, the patient's distancing and core defensive structure can be discussed in light of this early relationship.

2. This could then lead to the uncovering of the mother's fear of her own inadequacy. We can assume on some level (consciously or unconsciously), that Hannah's mother lives in mortal fear of exposure of her own inadequacy; therefore, she has a wish to subjugate others at any price. We can also assume that Hannah must be aware of her mother's fragility on some level. Making a connection between loyally assuming a one-down position as a means of keeping her mother alive and intact is the price that the patient pays for *suffering in silence*.

3. Although we would hope that Hannah would begin to see the cost of suffering in silence, the therapist must also be prepared to uncover and explore some of the pay-offs of this sacrifice: "keeping mother alive" by remaining silenced. This form of sacrifice is an aspect of the patient's own grandiosity (Quadrant One) that is being fed by the wish/belief that she is being asked to do something that only she can do. This connection to grandiosity is yet another way we can understand how the underlying wish (originally infantile) for mother to change and do something to take care of her also plays itself out in the transference. Thus, the sacrifice of loyal waiting of Quadrant Three is connected to her own overdetermined efforts around performance and suffering in silence, as well as connected to the expectation that she places on her therapist to adopt a similar strategy with her. Until this connection is made the patient is likely to hold onto her old pattern of relating. Furthermore, it is because of the unwillingness to give up on these wishes and longing that the patient can justify her distancing and devaluing as a way of expressing her "justifiable" reasons for retaliation (Quadrant Four).

4. An alternative route to accessing the material contained within the split between loyal waiting and revenge enactments is to shift away from a focus on Quadrants Three and Four and move to focusing more directly on Quadrant One. Patricia suggested to Dr. Kate to reflect to the patient why she didn't appear to be able either to believe the positive feedback about her performance, or allow herself to take in the positive comments of other people who noticed her efforts.

By focusing on the patient's reactions to positive feedback from others, we shift the focus back to Quadrant One where we can then invite the patient to become more curious about *how* she processes feedback from the outside world. This invitation is a beginning step in the therapist's attempts to crack through both the overdetermined standards from Quadrant One as well as the enmeshed loyalty system between mother and daughter. The therapist can open the dialogue further by asking a series of questions.

- Can the patient take in any feedback from anyone other than her mother or can she believe any feedback about herself that goes against her mother's view?
- What would happen if the patient dared to consider that what others think about her accomplishments might be true? Could she alter her perceptions about herself and increase her sense of self-worth?
- Would that be a safe or unsafe situation?

By asking a question about safety we begin to "forecast" that we suspect that surpassing or out-shining someone else creates an unsafe environment. Again we are working with the loyalty system of Quadrant Three, but in this instance less directly. The derivative focus on "others" and how they handle competition is, perhaps, a safer way to enter into the material. It is one step removed and can allow us to approach her fears around retaliation without focusing on the mother directly just yet.

Part Two

Six to Eight Months Later

Dr. Kate: I just wanted to give you an update on that woman I presented several months ago. She's been doing very well, but I'm a little confused about what just happened over the past couple of weeks.

Jack: Can you give us a little background on how she had been progressing up to that point?

Dr. Kate: If you remember, I was feeling stuck with this woman six/eight months ago. I think that she was feeling stuck in the therapy as well. I was afraid that she would eventually just terminate and not let me know until the last minute, saying it was a good effort but nothing could really change much for her.

Jack/Patricia: Yes, we remember.

Dr. Kate: Well, she's made some great progress since then both in the therapy and in her life. I would summarize it as saying that it seems as though she has found her anger, and consequently she has found her voice. She's actively setting much better limits with her mother and not feeling guilty about it, and she has been able to talk about her mother's envy and attempts to undermine the patient's work in therapy. Also, as you recall she had over-idealized her father as he was the less malignant parent of the two. However, now she is able to see that his behavior was similarly self-centered in abandoning her to her mother. She has also been able to see that his reconnecting with her in adolescence was more about impressing his new wife than any real concern for her. So, she's been able to voice anger toward both of her parents in her sessions with me. She also feels lighter and less depressed, and, I might add that she's starting to feel more empowered at work.

Patricia: What has she begun to do differently at work?

Dr. Kate: She has begun to trust the relationship she has with the new CEO, and I think she's finally begun to trust and value her own unique abilities. She has also said that at least the CEO sees and values her abilities as well. My patient truly does have a gift of seeing the big picture, thinking systemically, and also anticipating trends in the market place.

But, here's what throwing me right now. Several months ago the treasurer of this organization was told that he and his people needed to get figures ready so that she (my patient) could present these figures to the board. When she asked for the figures, the treasurer, who she says is an "incompetent politico," told her that he never remembered receiving any memos to that effect, and that he simply was not going to be able to meet her demands. She then reported getting so angry that she blew up at him.

Jack: Was that the case? Did you ask her what she said?

Dr. Kate: Yes, she told him, "That isn't good enough. You did have enough notice about this and you lied to me about not receiving notification. Your incompetence really pisses me off."

After they ended the phone conversation, she began to doubt herself, beating herself up for "losing it" and for behaving in such an unprofessional manner. She worried that he would retaliate, so she told the president what she did immediately. The president made light of it and told her that she would speak to him to make sure that he didn't pull a stunt like that again. Even with this reassurance, she was very rattled. We spent quite a bit of time in my office with her ruminating over her worries about repercussions and her failure to act professionally.

I think that there are other things that compound the situation. There is a female co-worker who is quite lazy and wants to grab all of the limelight, taking credit for or trying to sabotage other people's accomplishments as a way of making herself look good. Unfortunately, this person is quite well known in political circles in the community. My patient is convinced that people are afraid to stand up to her. A couple of days ago, she had a meeting with the company's external consultants who were looking at the marketing department which my client is directly responsible for. They told her that they did not want to hire internally within her department because people didn't have the right credentials. They wanted to hire outside the system and place the person she doesn't trust in an elevated place in that department. This threw my client into a tail spin. And that's why I'm so confused.

Jack: Can you articulate your confusion?

Dr. Kate: The amount of despair she is feeling right now seems disproportionate to the gains we have made. She is actually immobilized and had to take a couple of days off from work. She scheduled an emergency session with me and was sobbing hysterically in my office. She kept saying, "Nothing ever works out, nothing ever works out." Despite my trying to reassure her, she seemed inconsolable.

Patricia: Can you tell us what you tried to do to console her?

Dr. Kate: I told her that she doesn't know if this is a done deal, and I suggested that she go to her president with her concerns. I also tried to remind her that her department had just come off two major successes in terms of marketing efforts. So, she went to the president, who did reassure her that the consultants did not have the last word, and she wasn't going to accept their recommendation. That settled her down somewhat, but only after the president reassured her that no amount of corporate political influence would sway her into rewarding someone who hadn't earned it.

Jack: Okay. She's up, down, and up again. Let's try to conceptualize her disappointment in a less direct way. Perhaps you're trying to measure gains too quickly in a linear fashion.

Dr. Kate: I think she's in touch with her anger and because of that she sees reality more clearly, both historically with her family and at work. But, I'm afraid that unless she gets constant reassurances, all of that will slip away so rapidly. I also think that this co-worker is reminding her too much of her mother and she doesn't feel safe.

Patricia: Yes, I think you're right that safety issues are being stimulated by various people within this organization. So, one of the ways we might start thinking about what has been activated is to wonder if a certain amount of success has stimulated her wish that she won't have to confront untrustworthy people like her mother ever again. I'm wondering if this new wrinkle might be re-stimulating her fear that her gains won't last, that someone might take them away from her just like mother did. Consequently, I wonder if this might be throwing her back into an overidealized wish for rescue.

Jack: Yes, rescue, once and for all, or being able to see reality clearly enough so that people like this won't bother her ever again. Let me follow up on Patricia's point. You know when a patient is finally able to express bottled up anger, we see a bit of healthy spontaneous self-expression along with overidealized expansiveness simultaneously. She may feel that she has a right to tell people off for being incompetent, then she feels ashamed at discovering her wishes around retaliation. Beating herself up, self-doubt, and a disbelief that others won't punish her occur as her anger comes rushing to the fore. But that doesn't minimize the gains that have been made.

Patricia: I agree with Jack. Kate, let's back up and take a look at how much progress you have made with this woman. We're talking about going from both of you feeling stuck in the treatment to her being able to confront the painful reality about both of her parents, feel and express anger toward them, and feel empowered in her position at work. Six months ago she was ready to quit her job because the old CEO had left, and she didn't know if she could work with this new individual. Good work, Dr. Kate!

Dr. Kate: Well, thank you. Yes, I think it is pretty remarkable how far she has advanced. It's easy to forget that when you're in the middle of it with a patient. I guess I'm concerned that she's using her anger partly as a way of turning against herself, punishing herself for becoming too powerful.

Jack: Well, there may be a bit of truth to that, but we also can look at it from the vantage point of flexing her muscle a little bit. There is an opportunity to consolidate some of the gains she has recently made. We need to be careful not to jump down too hard or too quickly on this sort of interpretation. It runs a greater risk of her hearing you as joining in with her wishes and standards that she must do everything "perfectly" the first time. She thinks there is no room for practice.

Patricia: Yes, give her a little time to find her way, and give her reassurance that you have confidence in her. That will have a consolidating and integrating effect in and of itself. You can reframe her beating herself up as her attempts at self-reflection, trying to make sure that she doesn't express her anger in the punishing way her mother did toward her. Also, her expression of deeper emotion in your office over the consultants' recommendation could be viewed as her grief over past disappointments coming to the surface. She has to be carrying an enormous amount of grief over the deprivation and retaliation that were directed toward her in childhood by both of her parents. I'm wondering if these latest two incidents at work threw her into at least a partial awareness of her grief. If you can frame it in that way, you can further reinforce the forward momentum and progress in the therapy.

Dr. Kate: Oh, that's interesting. Of course, that makes sense, but how could I work with her to maximize the impact of that connection with her?

Jack: Before going there, let's hesitate a bit, letting her "luxuriate" in her gains. She needs to rest on her accomplishments for a while, because they are significant. She's a person who learned to push herself all of her life. Let her luxuriate, and your reassurance can take the form of reminding her of how far she has come.

Patricia: You could also frame her self-doubt not as a backslide, but as her attempt to find a new measuring stick for what an appropriate response of anger would look like. You can give her permission to not have to do it perfectly at first; talk with her about finding her way, practicing until she gets her own voice just right. You can tell her that this takes time and that you will help her sort it out. This is another form of reassurance. So, she's getting environmental reassurance from her boss, that her boss has her back, and she's getting therapeutic reassurance from you that she doesn't always have to push herself so hard.

Dr. Kate: And eventually, she'll find her way back to her grief?

Jack: Yes, without us pushing. The process is taking care of itself.

Case Analysis

In this case update we see the impressive gains that have been made in a few short months. It is clear that the patient has settled down in the therapy and has no plans of terminating. For a therapist to expect that there would be no back-steps or faltering of confidence is unrealistic. Yet, when we see someone making consistent gains over several months and then seem to backslide to an earlier dysregulated state, it can be confusing and/or misleading for any therapist. The double-edged sword of a real therapeutic gain is that it often can re-stimulate the expansiveness of grandiose wishes. Success can be used in the service of integrating a sense of authenticity, but it can equally amplify an expansive sense of the overidealized self or wishes of invulnerability (Quadrant One). The wish to be impenetrable continues to be part of the expansive character solution through much of the therapeutic process. In working with these compulsively habituated tendencies, it is important not to lose sight of the equally powerful gains that are being made around authenticity. Realizing this double-edged sword is precisely the way in which we hold the dynamic tension simultaneously.

We have used this second case example to illustrate how we can intentionally develop a therapeutic strategy around working toward the consolidation of gains. Our strategy in working with Dr. Kate was to begin with a more comprehensive understanding around the power of the expansive wishes. Hannah wishes that she could say whatever she feels without recrimination or retaliation. When she communicates to her co-worker in a less than professional manner, her old fears around retaliation set her into a tail spin. When she tells Dr. Kate about the co-worker who is untrustworthy, the underlying wish is the hope that she wouldn't have to encounter distrustful people ever again. Our first suggestion in this consultation session was to point out that this is a normal, predictable pattern for individuals with a narcissistically punishing parent. The wish for protection, to feel safe in an absolute sense, is a normal response once initial gains in treatment begin to manifest.

The second component of our strategy in helping Dr. Kate understand how she can use this therapeutic moment in the service of consolidation of gains was to help her *reframe* the patient's apparent faltering into a sign of progress or growth. In order for any positive reframe to be effective, it has to speak to elements of truth. In this case the patient's fears around "losing her cool" with the treasurer were partially valid. She had a right to be frustrated and angry with his incompetence, but she could have expressed her anger in a way that was different from her mother. Here the therapist can lead with a reframe around her increased ability to be self-reflective; then, she can try to give reassurance and mitigate her catastrophic fears.

Finally, the suggestion to give her time to luxuriate in her gains is an important one. Patients need time to let new behaviors and beliefs consolidate. The tendency to go back to old organizing schemas is strong when initial gains are not firmly integrated. Here is where the therapist's reassurance is quite valuable. It conveys confidence and trust in the patient's developing authenticity. It also makes way for the patient to be able to move into deeper, underlying feelings of grief. If she cannot have the "magical" wish for absolute protection granted as she moves forward in life, then she will have to grieve the loss of the wish for an ideal mother. Grieving this loss is the important next step in this therapy. Here we see how the consolidation of gains around self-esteem and the permission to express her anger can actually lead to yet deeper areas of work and recovery. This is how the parts connect to the whole in ever increasing concentric circles of growth.

Case Example Two

In this last case example we will come back to a client with a trauma history that we presented in chapter 7. We have selected this case vignette to close this manual because it illustrates the healing process and consolidation of gains that can occur with patients with moderately severe trauma histories. This case recording occurred approximately six months after the session that was described in chapter 7. Although her work is not finished, you can see the progress that has been made around consolidation in just a few short months.

Laura: It's been a pretty amazing week.

Therapist: How so? Good amazing or not so good?

Laura: (laughs) A little bit of both. Actually, I've been feeling an incredible amount of joy. It's so hard to talk about it. I have so much to talk about with you today, but the words just won't come. I'm afraid that I'm not making sense or that there's so much there I'm not sure how to capture it accurately.

Therapist: Why don't you give it a try? You said the same thing last week, and you were very clear then.

Laura: Okay. Well first of all, things have finally come to a head with Helen (friend). I'm not sure I handled it correctly. I think I reached out too much, but I was honest and that's a good thing. I also got into it with Charlie (boyfriend). I got so angry, I just let it rip. I also got angry with Helen, but I'm not sure that ended as well.

Therapist: Are you trying to critique how well you did in terms of speaking up and being truthful? Do you think you have to do this perfectly?

Laura: Right. There I go again with that perfection thing. But, what I'm trying to say is that I think that all of my feelings, the intensity of my feelings, didn't exactly belong to either of them. I'm projecting feelings about my mother onto both of them. I see how I've spent my entire life trying to please others. I bend over backwards, and I take the blame for things that aren't entirely mine. However, I must say that I caught myself this time. When I began to be aware of doing that, I stopped and didn't work so hard to make things better between us. I actually started to intentionally distance myself from Helen, and my mother and my sister for that matter, too. So, I can see where they all might feel hurt and confused right now by my changed behavior. But it was the only thing I could do at the time to protect myself, until I felt a little stronger. I know I need to feel a little sturdier with all of this.

Therapist: You have every right to do that, you know.

Laura: (begins crying softly) I think for the first time I'm really feeling all of my feelings. I'm finally feeling sad for me as a little girl. I've just been sobbing all week. I can't seem to stop.

Therapist: What do you think happened that allowed you to access those feelings?

Laura: You know, I told you that Helen said she wanted to talk with me, that she was disappointed in our friendship. I tried reaching out to her a number of times this week to talk things through, but she kept jerking me around, telling me today wasn't a good day, that she didn't have time to come over for dinner the next day. Anyway, I knew she was trying to punish me because she was hurt that I've become more distant. And there's a part of that that's true. I have been avoiding her because I'm afraid to tell her that I'm angry that the whole friendship always needs to center around her. It's always about her, her daily dramas, her hissy fits storming out of the room, and then everyone rushing to her to make her feel better. Anyway, when she kept putting me off, I started to get real scared. Then, I realized that this is exactly what my mother used to do to me. Exactly! And then I thought, if I'm this scared as an adult, how scared must I have been as a little girl. I felt so sorry for myself as that little girl. (Begins sobbing deeply, long period of silence).

Therapist: It's taken a long time to get to this place. I can see that there is deep sadness, but I can also see that you are beginning to have enormous compassion for that little girl who was so scared.

Laura: (crying) I know, I know. It feels good too, like something is opening up in my heart.

Therapist: Do you think that this is partly why you were also able to feel so much joy this week?

Laura: Yes, yes. I can see how this is all connected. And the great thing is that I've been able to share this joy with Charlie. It's like I'm a little kid. Every new thought I have, every insight that pops into my head, I have to rush to share it with him.

Therapist: What has his response been to you?

Laura: Oh, he's joyful with me too. He's so excited for me that I'm finally discovering all of this. But, let me tell you about what happened with Helen first. Finally, at the end of the week, I stopped chasing her and didn't call her again. Then I got an email the next day, ripping me up one side and down the other. She took absolutely no responsibility for her part, and I could see that what she was saying was exaggerated and a distortion. But, it still hurt. And there was an element of truth in all of it.

Therapist: So, what did you do?

Laura: I emailed her back, but in the email I think I took on too much responsibility. So, I went over and we talked. When I saw her I could also honestly see how hurting she was too, so I tried to reach out and apologize for hurting her. That part was genuine; I felt it in my heart. But it was also a mistake because it gave her an opportunity to begin analyzing me from a superior position, just like my mother does. And that's where I think I lost it and started projecting all of my feelings onto her that I have for my mother.

Therapist: Wait a minute. Do you think *all* of it was projection? Don't you think you have a right in the present, in that moment to be angry with how she was treating you?

Laura: Well, yes. But my mother is exactly the same, and I don't want to project my feelings onto Helen. It's not fair.

Therapist: I think you're being a little hard on yourself. So, your delivery is a little choppy at first. So some of it is blurred with the feelings and connections you're making about your mother. Aside from all of that, you've been feeling this way about Helen for some time. Isn't that legitimate in its own right?

Laura: Yes, I guess so.

Therapist: Don't you think that over time as you begin expressing your feelings more freely, you might get more comfortable, that you might get better with practice? It's just like any other new skill you learn. It feels awkward at first, then, you become more refined.

Laura: I like that image. So, maybe I didn't do such a bad job after all. I did get angry, but I didn't lose my sense of self. I didn't take back any of my feelings for what I felt I had a right to be angry about.

Therapist: Great. So how did things end?

Laura: That's the scary part. She got me to admit that I can be bitchy sometimes just like her, and I distance myself, so that means that we're exactly the same.

Therapist: She ended the conversation by needing to make you exactly the same?

Laura: Yes, and it felt really creepy. We're not the same, but she needed to make us the same to feel better about herself. But, I think I do that too. I used to think that Helen and I were so similar, and I try to make Charlie and me the same too. I guess I wanted her to catch up with me. I was angry that I was changing and she wasn't. So maybe she's right.

Therapist: Why do you think you couldn't bring yourself to say, "No, we're not the same."

Laura: I just couldn't. That's where I became confused.

Therapist: Okay, so let's look at that . . . (Pt. interrupts)

Laura; No, let me tell you what happened with Charlie first.

Therapist: Okay, go ahead.

Laura: Well, remember I was telling you that he was joyful for me, really happy for me. But, I also noticed that whenever I'd tell him some new idea I had, or how excited I was about reading something, he'd have to shoot it down a little bit.

Therapist: What would he say?

Laura: He's say something like, "Well that's how you're feeling now. But, pretty soon this excitement will wear off, and you'll see that the ideas of that author in the book you're currently reading aren't all that special." Or he'd say, "I'm happy for your joy, but it seems a little naïve."

Therapist: Yes, I see where that is taking a bit away from you, almost like he needs to keep the upper hand. Is that what it felt like?

Laura: Exactly! And that's when I made a mistake. I told him his comments felt undermining, and I accused him of guarding his heart, not doing any of his own work on himself. And he got so angry with me. He started screaming at me to not make pronouncements about what he was doing or not doing to take care of himself. You see, that's what I mean by my trying to make everybody the same. Because I was changing I wanted him to be changing with me. Why couldn't I just let him be where he was?

Therapist: Perhaps, your comment hit a little too close to the mark. Perhaps, what you saw was his own defensiveness.

Laura: Maybe, you're right. Maybe he's afraid that I'll grow beyond him. Maybe I'm afraid that I will too.

Therapist: That's the same dilemma you had in your family, especially with your mother and sister.

Laura: Oh, I have to tell you about this amazing dream I had last night. There were two white boards in the dream, and on the first one was a list of all of the qualities about Helen that were clearly spelled out.

Therapist: Do you remember the list?

Laura: Yes, things like, she is selfish and vindictive. She punishes people when they don't meet her every need. She is angry all of the time but never expresses it directly. She has no joy. She does things for others but in a begrudging way.

You owe her big time when she thinks she has done you a favor. And then I realized these were the exact qualities that described my mother. The dream made it all so crystal clear. And on the other white board was a list of names of all of the people in my life who needed me to be exactly the same as them—my ex-husband, my sister, my friend from college. On some level they all made a demand on me to be exactly like them . . . well, to be exactly like they were when it came to being stuck in their own pain. Then I saw all of their faces, and I realized that I don't even know who these people are really. It's as if each of them is an empty shell, and only when they attach themselves onto me, they become real. How strange. See, I told you none of this was making any sense.

Therapist: Oh, it's making sense alright. I think that what your dream is telling you is that you are seeing your most intimate relationships, more clearly. This must be quite unsettling.

Laura: It is; that's what I mean that none of this is making any sense.

Therapist: But, your dream is letting you know that each of the people on that list is an empty shell. That makes a lot of sense to me. It reflects what you've been voicing about them for some time now.

Laura: Yes, but it's hard to take that in. Maybe it's not that it doesn't make sense. Maybe it's that it's too hard to look at.

Therapist: Yes. (pause) Do you think it's interesting that Charlie wasn't one of the people who showed up on the second white board? You were talking about some disappointment with him in our session today. Do you think that your dream is also trying to highlight that even though you become disappointed in him from time to time, that he possesses very different qualities from the other people on the second white board?

Laura: I'm not sure. Maybe so. Maybe my dream is letting me see that there is something different, more substantial about Charlie than the people who were listed on the white board. (pause; pt. begins to cry). I just realized how much of my life I've wasted, wasted on these relationships, relationships with people who wanted me to disappear. They needed me to disappear or be the one who exposed my pain so they could feel better. But, I'm not going to do it anymore! I'm tired of being nice to everybody, tired of being everybody's sacrificial lamb. I need to speak my own mind, speak the truth. I've wasted enough of my life, and it's too beautiful to waste anymore. (continues to cry; long pause, then the patient looks up, making eye contact with the therapist)

Therapist: (pause, and then a smile) Laura, I just want you to know that everything that you've said in here today is making perfect sense. Painful as some of these realizations are, you are definitely beginning to see things more clearly. Bravo!

Analysis

The session begins with the patient saying that she had a pretty amazing week. This is followed by a statement that she is struggling with how she can put her feelings and insights into words. It should be noted that patients will frequently voice some confusion around trying to integrate new information or ways of being in the world into their old organizing schemas. The therapist offers encouragement, reminding her that she had said the same thing last week, and she had been quite articulate. In this way the therapist is telegraphing to the patient that she is able to listen, track, and make sense out of the changes that are unfolding, changes that often feel overwhelming to the patient.

Laura then begins by reporting how she handled a relationship with a female friend, a relationship that had been fairly one-sided in the past. Laura demonstrated an increase in strength by standing up for herself. However, she then regretted the manner in which she had expressed her angry feelings. The therapist stopped her stating, "You have a right to do that, you know." Notice that the words, *you have a right*, are a direct communication in support of the patient's authenticity. At the same time they are also a subliminal challenge to the patient's overdetermined standards of perfection. When the therapist asked if Laura felt she had to express herself perfectly, Laura was then able to go deeper into her feelings of grief and disappointment. By asking this question, the therapist is trying to help the patient slow down enough to create room for a shift in the overdetermined standards of Quadrant One. In doing so she is hoping that Laura is able to move toward the consolidation of gains around authenticity, demonstrated by a less critical view of herself and her behavior.

Notice that when the therapist gives this permission to slow down and take the time that she needs to feel sturdier, Laura starts to cry in relief. She then begins to articulate her thoughts and feelings toward herself in a much gentler, more protective manner. Laura is then able to express sorrow and sadness for the little girl who had to work so hard to please others. She feels sadness over the realization that all of her efforts were in the service of people who did not value her well-being as much as their own.

The therapist then reinforces Laura's efforts and insights, reminding her of how long it has taken to get to this place, that much important work and effort has been done on both of their parts. Again, the therapist notices the positive gains that are emerging from the patient's ability to feel her grief. At this moment we see the disintegration of overidealized longing for rescue, where Laura is able to make a choice for self-compassion over loyal waiting for the other. This shift in attitude toward self-compassion is critical for the healing process that stems from ruptured attunement at the hands of narcissistic parents.

For the first time Laura is able to equate her sadness about feeling good to what she describes as "something is opening up in my heart." This is a pure form of the expression of authenticity. At this juncture the therapist seizes on the opportunity to link this insight to her earlier disclosure of feeling joy this week. The authentic emergence of the self *does* produce a sense of joy, as it symbolizes a well-spring of relief after so many years of remaining in hiding. We will notice, however, that a few minutes later Laura again reverts to a negative self-analysis around how she handled her disappointment with her friend, Helen. She felt that she had given her an opportunity to project a position of superiority over her just like her mother did. Consequently, Laura again became harsh with herself, fearing that her reaction was a projection of her negative feelings about mother being displaced on her friend.

Although there may be some truth in this analysis, the therapist chooses to move toward a position that reinforces the patient's growth by challenging Laura and wondering if her reaction was entirely based on projection. Didn't she have a right to her legitimate feelings in the present? This is followed by offering reassurance, encouraging Laura that with practice she will learn to become more refined in the authentic expression of her feelings, including her negative, angry feelings. This is an example of how the therapist is able to use a reframe to assist in maintaining a forward momentum toward the emergence and consolidation of gains.

The session ends with Laura reporting a dream. It appears to be an integration of the insights that had been gained around the previous encounter with Helen. Her dream consisted of seeing two white boards, one that summarized a picture of Helen's real qualities. It is noteworthy that the use of words in the dream, presented through the visual image of a white board, had a quality of consolidation—seeing the reality of her friend's limitations being presented to her in a way that she couldn't avoid. She had to take in the information provided on the white board.

On the second white board the dream offered another form of consolidation by providing a generalizing effect of the gains made through her breakthrough interaction with Helen. The most intimate relationships in her life, the board revealed, were enmeshed and pulling her toward self-sacrifice and unhealthy merger. Laura's breakthrough revelation in the dream was the realization that these people in her life were all empty shells. When the therapist observed that Charlie wasn't on the second white board, Laura was able to make a further consolidation around differentiation. It was at this point of differentiation that Laura was able to grieve over how much time had been wasted on relationships with people who wanted her to disappear.

This case example offers multiple repetitions of gains followed by insights followed by attempts to revert to the old homeostatic balance.

The therapist's perseverance in seeing the growth within each moment of self-doubt and the encouragement that followed helped the patient integrate further insights as well as allowing her to feel some hope that future relationships (although not perfect) could offer more substantial possibilities.

Summary

Although consolidation of gains is a concept that is typically associated with the ending phase of therapy, it is somewhat short-sighted to reserve the application of this skill set to the termination phase of treatment. It is true that the termination process does create unique opportunities for integration and consolidation, but the task of a therapist is to listen for burgeoning signs of growth at every phase of treatment. Listening for subtle signs, noticing shifts in attitudes or behaviors, are some of the ways that therapists can facilitate (and maximize) forward momentum and growth. If the consolidation of gains is simply understood as a part of termination, therapy is then essentially reduced to a linear process.

In our view the construction of defensively based character solutions are composed of complex, dynamic, and intricately bound systems. The dismantling of old patterns that maintain a compulsively driven homeostatic balance requires a non-linear approach, one that listens for opportunities to connect split-off parts to other parts and also to the whole. Adopting this metapsychological position requires that the therapist assume a posture of listening where she or he can spot emergent properties as they tentatively unfold in the subjectively held present.

As with every forward movement, there is generally a short-term recoil effect to the old homeostasis until changes can be metabolized into deeper psychic integration. This is to be expected, and the consolidation of gains requires repeated efforts, a revisiting of material over and over again. The "ah hah" moment that Freud spoke about is not generally an insight that springs out of nowhere from the unconscious. It is the product and the culmination of months and years of work, where the "ah hah" moment is essentially the consolidation of gains. Piaget spoke about this process from a cognitive, developmental perspective decades ago when he identified the dual process of *assimilation and accommodation*. In order to change our organizing schemas about reality and how the world works, we must assimilate a great deal of information that challenges our existing paradigms and assumptions *before* we can change those very same paradigms and assumptions and incorporate the old information with the new into an expanded view of reality. As Piaget reminds us, it takes time before the accrual of information can be assimilated and reincorporated into an expanded, more complex organizing schema.

In many respects this is precisely how the unfolding process of dynamic psychotherapy works. We create a therapeutic alliance then enter into a discovery process where old assumptions and defenses are challenged. If we demonstrate a trusting presence and a facility around deep listening, we are able to process new discoveries, coupled with bumps and challenges along the way. Out of this process, the therapeutic bond is strengthened, and our patients begin to reveal their most hidden and shameful feelings to us. Out of this new holding environment, one that is in the service of the emergence of the authentic self, the client is able to then experience new ways of being in relationship. These relationships are no longer built on overidealized wishes for rescue but are based on the prototype of a trusting therapeutic relationship, a relationship that has stood the test of time.

We have offered many tools and concepts throughout this book. The consolidation of gains is one of many ways of conceptualizing and utilizing a non-linear metapsychological approach to the process of psychotherapy. Placing consolidation of gains at the end of this book is in no way meant to reflect a linear approach to organizing this manual. As we have stated, consolidation of gains is a concept that can be used at any phase of treatment. However, the greatest opportunities for consolidation do not occur until sufficient time has transpired. The therapeutic relationship has to have a chance to develop, where negative transference can be transformed into a deeper understanding of how to handle and recover from disappointments, where the patient has developed greater degrees of curiosity and greater capacity for self-reflection, and where disavowed affect has had a chance to come to the surface. The growing integration of dissociated aspects of the self is the result of these efforts.

The consolidation of gains also builds upon an understanding of the tools and techniques mentioned in earlier chapters, concepts such as listening in the present, learning how to utilize language in a way that allows the therapist a clear entry into deeper dialogue, learning how to use negative transference to a positive advantage, and reframing our patients' assumptions in a way that allows them to expand their curiosity rather than foreclose the growth process. We hope that the concept of consolidation, as well as the many other concepts provided in this manual, will provide additional skills toward the mastery of this long learning curve of the art and science of psychotherapy.

References

Appelbaum, D. (2010). On Learning to Enquire: Revisiting the Detailed Inquiry. *American Journal of Psychoanalysis* 70:78–85.

Arlow, J. A., and Brenner, C. (1964). *Psychoanalytic Concepts and the Structural Theory.* New York: International Universities Press.

Aron, L. (1996). *A Meeting of Minds: Mutuality in Psychoanalysis.* Hillsdale, NJ: The Analytic Press.

Balint, M. (1968). *The Basic Fault.* London: Tavistock.

Beebe, B., and Lachmann, F. (2005). *Infant Research and Adult Treatment: Co-Constructing Interactions.* New York: The Analytic Press.

Benjamin, J. (1991). Father and Daughter: Identification with Difference—A Contribution to Gender Heterodoxy. *Psychoanalytic Dialogues* 1:277–299.

Bromberg, P. M. (2001). *Standing in the Spaces.* New York: Psychology Press.

Broucek, F. J. (1991). *Shame and the Self.* New York: Guilford Press.

Cantor, M. B. (1967). Mobilizing Forces toward Self-Realization. *American Journal of Psychoanalysis* 27:188–199.

Celenza, A. (2007). *Sexual Boundary Violations.* New York: Jason Aronson.

Chodorow, N. (1989). *Feminism and Psychoanalytic Theory.* New Haven, CT: Yale University Press.

Cook, A., Spinazzola, J., Ford, J. D., Lanktree, C., Blaustein, M. Cloitre, M., et al. (2005). Complex Trauma in Children and Adolescents. *Psychiatric Annals* 35:390–398.

Cooper, A. M. (1987). Changes in Psychoanalytic Ideas: Transference Interpretation. *Journal of the American Psychoanalytic Association* 35:77–98.

Courtois, C. A., and Ford, J. D., eds. (2009). *Treating Complex Traumatic Stress Disorders: An Evidence-Based Guide.* New York: Guilford Press.

Danielian, J. (1985). The Negative Therapeutic Reaction: Crisis of Practice or Crisis of Theory? *The American Journal of Psychoanalysis* 45:109–118.

———. (1988). Karen Horney and Heinz Kohut: Theory and the Repeat of History. *The American Journal of Psychoanalysis* 48:6–24.

———. (2010a). Meta-Realization in Horney and the Teaching of Psychoanalysis. *The American Journal of Psychoanalysis* 70:10–22.

———. (2010b). Review of A. Tershakovec, *The Mind: The Power that Changed the Planet* (2007). *The American Journal of Psychoanalysis* 70:100–104.

———. (2010c). A Century of Silence. *The American Journal of Psychoanalysis* 70:245–264.

DeBellis, M. D., Keshavan, M. S., Frustaci, K., Shifflett, H., Iyengar, S., Beers, S. R., and Hall, J. (2002). Superior Temporal Gyrus Volumes in Maltreated Children and Adolescents with PTSD. *Biological Psychiatry* 51:544–552.

DeRosis, L. (1974). The Invented Self: Karen Horney's Theory Applied to Psychoanalysis in Groups. *The American Journal of Psychoanalysis* 34:109–121.

Dimen, M. (2011). Lapsus Linguae, or A Slip of the Tongue? *Contemporary Psychoanalysis* 47:35–79.

Fairley, B. (1947). *A Study of Goethe.* Oxford: Clarendon Press.

Feldman-Summers, S., and Pope, K. S. (1994). The Experience of "Forgetting" Childhood Abuse: A National Survey of Psychologists. *Journal of Consulting and Clinical Psychology* 62:636–639.

Ferenczi, S., and Rank, O. (1925). *The Development of Psychoanalysis.* New York: Nervous and Mental Disease Publishing Company.

Freyd, J. J. (1996). *The Logic of Forgetting Childhood Abuse.* Cambridge, MA: Harvard University Press.

Galatzer-Levy, R. M. (2009). Finding Your Way through Chaos, Fractals, and Other Exotic Mathematical Objects: A Guide for the Perplexed. *Journal of the American Psychoanalytic Association* 57:1227–1249.

Gentile, K. (2011). Lapsus Linguae, or A Slip of the Tongue? Discussant: *International Association of Relational Psychoanalysis and Psychotherapy.* Colloquium Series, No. 18, May 9–22. Office@IARPP.net.

Gill, M. (1983). The Point of View of Psychoanalysis: Energy Discharge or Person? *Psychoanalysis and Contemporary Thought* 6:523–551.

———. (1994). *Psychoanalysis in Transition: A Personal View.* Hillsdale, NJ: The Analytic Press.

Goethe, J. W. (1785). Philosophical Studies quoted in B. Fairley (1947). *A Study of Goethe.* Oxford: Clarendon Press.

Goffman, E. (1959). *The Presentation of Self in Everyday Life.* New York: Anchor.

———. (1963). *Stigma.* Edgewood Cliffs, NJ: Prentice Hall.

———. (1967). *Interaction Ritual.* New York: Anchor.

Herman, J. L. (1995). Crime and Memory. *Bulletin of the American Academy of Psychiatry and Law* 23:5–17.

———. (1997). *Trauma and Recovery.* New York: Basic Books.

Herman, J. L., and Harvey, M. R. (1997). Adult Memories of Childhood Trauma: A Naturalistic Clinical Study. *Journal of Traumatic Stress* 10:557–571.

Horney, K. (1939). *New Ways in Psychoanalysis.* New York: Norton.

———. (1945). *Our Inner Conflicts: A Constructive Theory of Neurosis.* New York: Norton.

———. (1950). *Neurosis and Human Growth: The Struggle towards Self-Realization.* New York: Norton.

Horowitz, M. J. (1978). *Stress Response Syndromes.* New York: Jason Aronson.

Howell, E. F. (2005). *The Dissociative Mind.* New York: Routledge.

Johnson, S. M. (2004*). The Practice of Emotionally Focused Couple Therapy.* New York: Brunner-Routledge Publishers.

———. (2008). *Hold Me Tight: Seven Conversations for a Lifetime of Love.* New York: Little Brown and Company.

Kardiner, A. (1941). *The Traumatic Neuroses of War.* New York: Hoeber.

Karen, R. (1992). Shame. *The Atlantic Monthly.* February.

Kaufman, G. (1985). *Shame: The Power of Caring.* Cambridge, MA: Schenkman.

———. (1989). *The Psychology of Shame. New* York: Springer.

Kelman, H. (1971). *Helping People: Karen Horney's Psychoanalytic Approach.* New York: Science House.

Kernberg, O. (1970). Factors in the Psychoanalytic Treatment of Narcissistic Personalities. *Journal of the American Psychoanalytic Association* 18:51–85.

———. (1974). Further Contributions to the Treatment of Narcissistic Personalities. *International Journal of Psychoanalysis* 55:215–240.

———. (1975). *Borderline Conditions and Pathological Narcissism.* New York: Jason Aronson.

Kohut, H. (1966). Forms and Transformations of Narcissism. *Journal of the American Psychoanalytic Association* 14:243-272.

———. (1971). *The Analysis of Self.* New York: International Universities Press.

———. (1977). *The Restoration of the Self. New York:* International Universities Press.

———. (1984). *How Does Analysis Cure?* Chicago: University of Chicago Press.

Kolb, L. C. (1987). Neurophysiological Hypothesis Explaining Posttraumatic Stress Disorder. *American Journal of Psychiatry* 144:989–995.

Levenson, E. A. (1991). *The Purloined Self: Interpersonal Perspectives in Psychoanalysis.* New York: Contemporary Psychoanalysis Books.

Lewis, H. B. (1971). *Shame and Guilt in Neurosis.* New York: International Universities Press.

———. (1988). The Role of Shame in Symptom Formation. In M. Clynes and J. Pankseep, eds., *Emotions and Psychopathology.* New York: Plenum Press.

Lewis, H. B. quoted in R. Karen (1992). Shame. *The Atlantic Monthly,* February.

Lewis, M. (1995). *Shame: The Exposed Self.* New York: Free Press.

Lindemann, E. (1944). Symptomatology and Management of Acute Grief. *American Journal of Psychiatry* 101:141–148.

Linehan, M. (1993). *Cognitive-Behavioral Treatment of Borderline Personality Disorder.* New York: The Guilford Press.

Lindsay, D. S., and Reed, J. D. (1995). "Memory Work" and Recovered Memories of Childhood Sexual Abuse. *Psychology, Public Policy, & the Law* 1:846–907.

Loftus, E., and Ketcham, K. (1994). *The Myth of Repressed Memory*. New York: St. Martin's Press.

Lynd, H. M. (1958). *On Shame and the Search for Identity*. New York: Harcourt, Brace.

Mitchell, S. (1988). *Relational Concepts in Psychoanalysis*. Cambridge, MA: Harvard University Press.

———. (2000). *Relationality: From Attachment to Intersubjectivity*. Hillsdale, NJ: The Analytic Press.

Mitchell, S., and Aron, L., eds. (1999). *Relational Psychoanalysis: The Emergence of a Tradition*. Hillsdale, NJ: The Analytic Press.

Morrison, A. P., ed. (1986). *Essential Papers on Narcissism*. New York: New York University Press.

———. (1997). *Shame: The Underside of Narcissism*. New York: Routledge.

———. (1998). *The Culture of Shame*. Northvale, NJ: Jason Aronson.

Nathanson, D. L. (1987). *The Many Faces of Shame*. New York: Guilford Press.

———. (1992). *Shame and Pride: Affect, Sex, and the Birth of the Self*. New York: Norton.

Oremland, J. D., and Windholz, E. (1971). Some Specific Transference, Counter-transference and Supervisory Problems in the Analysis of a Narcissistic Personality. *International Journal of Psychoanalysis* 52:267–275.

Paris, B. (1999). Introduction to *Karen Horney: The Therapeutic Process*. New Haven, CT: Yale University Press.

Phillips, A. (2002). Introduction to *Wild Analysis* (Sigmund Freud). London: Penguin.

Pope, K. S. (1990). Therapist–Client Sexual Involvement: A Review of the Research. *Clinical Psychology Review* 10:477–490.

Purcell, S. D. (2004). The Analyst's Theory: A Third Source of Countertransference. *International Journal of Psychoanalysis* 85:635–652.

Renn, P. (2010). Psychoanalysis and the Trauma(s) of History. Discussant: *International Association of Relational Psychoanalysis and Psychotherapy*. Colloquium Series No. 17, December 6–19. Office @IARPP.net.

Scheff, T. J. (1997). *Emotions, Social Bond, and Human Reality*. Cambridge, UK: Cambridge University Press.

Scheff, T. J., and Retzinger, S. M. (2002). *Emotions and Violence: Shame and Rage in Destructive Conflicts*. Lincoln, NE: iUniverse, Inc.

Schneider, C. (1977). *Shame, Exposure, and Privacy*. Boston: Beacon.

Schwaber, E. (1983). Construction, Reconstruction, and the Mode of Clinical Attunement. In A. Goldberg, ed., *The Future of Psychoanalysis*. New York: International Universities Press.

Senge, P., Scharmer, C. O., Jaworski, J., and Flowers, B. S. (2004). *Presence: Human Purpose and the Field of the Future*. Cambridge, MA: SoL.

Siegel, D. J. (1999). *The Developing Mind: Toward a Neurobiology of Interpersonal Experience*. New York: Guilford.

Solomon, M. F., and Siegel, D. J., eds. (2003). *Healing Trauma: Attachment, Mind, Body, and Brain.* New York, London: Norton.

Starr, K. E., and Aron, L. (2011). Women on the Couch: Genital Stimulation and the Birth of Psychoanalysis. *Psychoanalytic Dialogues* 21:373–392.

Stern, D. N. (2004). *The Present Moment: In Psychotherapy and Everyday Life.* New York: Norton.

Stolorow, R. D. (1986). Toward a Functional Definition of Narcissism (197–209). In Andrew P. Morrison, ed., *Essential Papers on Narcissism.* New York: New York University Press.

Stolorow, R. D., Brandchaft, B., and Atwood, G. (1987). *Psychoanalytic Treatment: An Intersubjective Approach.* Hillsdale, NJ: The Analytic Press.

Suttie, I. D. (1935). *The Origins of Love and Hate.* London: Kegan Paul, Trench, Trabner & Co.

Thelen, E., and Smith, L. (1994). *A Dynamic Systems Approach to the Development of Cognition and Action.* Cambridge, MA: MIT Press.

Thrane, G. (1979). Shame and the Construction of the Self. *The Annual of Psychoanalysis* 7:321–341.

Tomkins, S. S. (1963). *Affect/Imagery/Consciousness: II. The Negative Affects.* New York: Springer.

van der Kolk, B. A. (1987). *Psychological Trauma.* Arlington, VA: American Psychiatric Publishing, Inc.

———. (1994). The Body Keeps the Score: Memory and the Evolving Psychobiology of Posttraumatic Stress. *Harvard Review of Psychiatry* 1 (5): 253–265.

———. (2005). Developmental Trauma Disorder. *Psychiatric Annals* 35:401–408.

van der Kolk, B. A., and Fisler, R. (1995). Dissociation and the Fragmentary Nature of Traumatic Memories: Overview and Exploratory Study. *Journal of Traumatic Stress* 8:505–525.

van der Kolk, B. A., McFarlane, A. C., and van der Hart, O. (1996). A General Approach to Treatment of Posttraumatic Stress Disorder. In van der Kolk, B. A., McFarlane, A. C., and Weisaeth, L., eds., *Traumatic Stress: The Effects of Overwhelming Experience on Mind, Body, and Society.* New York: Guilford.

van der Kolk, B. A., McFarlane, A. C., and Weisaeth, L., eds., (1996). *Traumatic Stress: The Effects of Overwhelming Experience on Mind, Body, and Society.* New York: Guilford.

van der Kolk, B. A., van der Hart, O., and Burbridge, J. (1995). *Approaches to the Treatment of PTSD, Extreme Stress and Communities: Impact and Intervention.* NATO ASI Series, Series D, Behavioral and Social Sciences, Norwell, MA: Kluwer Academic.

Wachtel, P. L. (2008). *Relational Theory in the Practice of Psychotherapy.* New York: Guilford.

Watkins, C. E., Jr. (2011). Is Psychoanalytic Education Effective? *The American Journal of Psychoanalysis* 71: 290–292.

Westkott, M. (1986). *The Feminist Legacy of Karen Horney.* New Haven, CT: Yale University Press.

Winnicott, D. W. (1952). Psychosis and Child Care. In *Collected Papers* (1958). London: Tavistock.

———. (1960). Ego Distortion in Terms of True and False Self. In *The Maturational Processes and the Facilitating Environment* (1965). New York: International Universities Press.

Yehuda, R., Giller, E. L., Southwick, S. M., Lowy, M. T., and Mason, J. W. (1991). Hypothalamic-Pituitary-Adrenal Dysfunction in Posttraumatic Stress Disorder. *Biological Psychiatry* 30:1031–1048.

Index

abandonment (*see also* annihilation), 83, 101, 174-177, 190-191, 248-249; and alienation from self, 174; and shame, 174-177; childhood safety 101, 190; negative transference, 263-266; trans- ferential, 248- 249

alienation, 83; from self, 22, 29, 81, 174; all-or-nothing thinking, 123, 264, 286, 298; black and white thinking, 123, 305

amygdala, 200

annihilation, 189, 196; fears of, 67, 189, 196

Appelbaum, D., 229

Aron, L., *x*, 11, 12, 226

attunement, 14, 21, 24, 157, 169, 177, 204; and empathy, 83, 159, 181, 226; and shame, 172, 177; and trauma, 162, 193; and trauma to children, 80-84; misattunement, 162, 182, 218, 308; relationship, failures of, 13, 21, 169, 177, 182, 204, 265; ruptures of, 24, 169, 177, 188, 234

Atwood, G.E., 11

authentic self (*see* real self), 13, 21-24, 44, 48, 63, 72, 99, 159; consolidation of gains, 5, 336-338; *vs* idealized self, 22,

70, 72, 73, 80, 93, 242; *vs* self-hating self, 5, 11, 15, 23, 48, 51, 70, 130, 160-162, 171, 242, 244

Beebe, B., 114

belief systems, 5, 44, 46, 225

Benjamin, J., 11, 13

Block, P. 110

borderline dynamics, 174, 179, 264-266

bottoming-out, 264

boundaries, 94, 100, 133, 169, 192

boundary violations, 236, 240, 249

Braithwaite, J., 164

Brandchaft, B., 11

Bromberg, P.M., 156

Broucek, F. J., 157, 185

bullying, 166, 191

burn-out (*see* trauma/compassion fatigue), *x*, 184, 236

Cantor, M. B., 313

Celenza, A., 241

centeredness, 29

chaos theory, 227

character solutions, 5, 21-24, 71-72, 112, 116; and alienation from the self, 22, 27-30; and four-quadrant model,

About the Authors

Jack Danielian, Ph.D., is a licensed psychologist, supervisor, and Dean of the American Institute of Psychoanalysis of the Karen Horney Center. He is a training and supervising analyst and is on the faculty of the Institute. Dr. Danielian has lectured internationally and nationally on psychoanalytic issues, intercultural communication, and intergenerational effects of genocide. He is the author of numerous professional publications and is a contributing author to several books. He and his wife live in Exeter, New Hampshire.

Patricia Gianotti, Psy.D., is a licensed psychologist, clinical supervisor, and managing partner with Woodland Professional Associates, a group private practice in North Hampton, NH. Dr. Gianotti is a seasoned lecturer and facilitator and has taught at Washington University and the University of New Hampshire. She has presented at various professional conferences, including Division 39 of the APA. Her most recent publication appeared in *The American Journal of Psychoanalysis*. She lives in North Hampton, New Hampshire, with her husband, Stephen.

Jack Danielian and Patricia Gianotti can be contacted at www.Listening withPurpose.com. Information about on-line webinars, conferences, and seminars, as well as inquiries about individual and group Skype case consultations, can be obtained through this website.